OXFORD EC LAW LIBRARY

General Editor: F. G. Jacobs
Advocate General, The Court of Justice
of the European Communities

EC SEX EQUALITY LAW

OXFORD EC LAW LIBRARY

The aim of this series is to publish important and original studies of the various branches of European Community Law. Each work will provide a clear, concise, and critical exposition of the law in its social, economic, and political context, at a level which will interest the advanced student, the practitioner, the academic, and government and Community officials.

Other Titles in the Library

European Community Law of State Aid
Andrew Evans

External Relations of the European Communities
I. MacLeod, I. D. Hendry and Stephen Hyett

Directives in European Community Law
Sacha Prechal

EC Tax Law
Paul Farmer and Richard Lyal

The European Internal Market and International Trade
Piet Eeckhout

The Law of Money and Financial Services in the European Community
J. A. Usher

Legal Aspects of Agriculture in the European Community
J. A. Usher

Trade and Environmental Law in the European Community
Andreas R. Ziegler

EC Competition Law
third edition (forthcoming)
Daniel G. Goyder

EC Sex Equality Law

EVELYN ELLIS

CLARENDON PRESS · OXFORD
1998

Oxford University Press, Great Clarendon Street, Oxford OX2 6DP
www.oup.co.uk

Oxford New York

Athens Auckland Bangkok Bogota Bombay Buenos Aires
Calcutta Cape Town Dar es Salaam Delhi Florence Hong Kong Istanbul
Karachi Kuala Lumpur Madras Madrid Melbourne Mexico City
Nairobi Paris Singapore Taipei Tokyo Toronto Warsaw

and associated companies in
Berlin Ibadan

Oxford is a trade mark of Oxford University Press

Published in the United States
by Oxford University Press Inc., New York

British Library Cataloguing in Publication Data
Ellis, Evelyn, 1948–
European Community sex equality law / Evelyn Ellis.—2nd ed.
p. cm.—(Oxford European Community law series)
Includes bibliographical references and index.
1. Sex discrimination—Law and legislation—European Union
countries. 2. Sex discrimiation in employment—Law and
legislation—European Union countries. 3. Equal pay for equal work—
Law and legislation—European Union countries. I. Title.
II. Series.
KJE5142.E44 1998 98–4467
ISBN 0–19–826224–8

1 3 5 7 9 10 8 6 4 2

Typeset by Vera A. Keep, Cheltenham
Printed in Great Britain
on acid-free paper by
Bookcraft Ltd., Midsomer Norton, Somerset

Table of Contents

General Editor's Foreword
to the Second Edition

The subject of this book, the principle of equality for men and women in European Community law, is a subject of intrinsic importance in a variety of ways. It brings together questions of fundamental human rights, issues of great social importance, and policy matters of very considerable economic significance. Community law in this field has had, and is continuing to have, a substantial and immediate impact on such matters as pay, on access to and conditions of employment, on pensions, on social security benefits, etc.

However, many of the issues discussed in this book are of even wider significance. This is because the principles developed in the field of sex equality, and the lessons to be learnt, are often relevant across the whole field of Community law. It is remarkable to recall that the notion of equality for men and women figures only once in the Community Treaties, and that the provision in question, Article 119 of the EC Treaty, appears to be little more than a statement of principle, and is confined to the field of equal pay for equal work. Nor do the Treaties confer any specific legislative competence for the implementation of the principle of equal pay or of equal treatment generally. In these areas, perhaps more than anywhere else, the Court of Justice, and to some extent the Community legislature, have put flesh on the bones of the Treaty.

The role of the Court was strikingly apparent in its decision in 1976 in the second *Defrenne* case which applied to Article 119 the principle of direct effect, requiring the courts of the Member States to enforce its provisions directly. The article has continued to take on new life in the recent case-law, most notably in relation to the position of part-time workers and in relation to occupational pension schemes. On the legislative front, a series of major measures on the implementation of the principle of equal treatment in various sectors has in turn given rise to a substantial volume of case-law, extending most recently to such sensitive issues as the rights of transsexuals and the subject of affirmative action. The issues are so sensitive that some critics of the Court might accuse it of occasionally sacrificing legal correctness on the altar of political correctness.

There can however be no doubt that many principles of fundamental importance to the Community legal system are to be found in the Court's case-law on sex equality, including the use as an exceptional judicial technique of the prospective ruling, the spelling out of the conditions in which directives may produce direct effect, the elaboration of the duty of national courts to interpret and apply national legislation in accordance with relevant directives, and the developing principle of the duty of national courts to provide all remedies necessary for the full enforcement of Community rights.

The new edition of this book will therefore be welcomed not only as an analysis of a subject of inherent importance but as illuminating the Community legal system, since the subject is one which is indispensable for all students of the workings of Community law.

Francis G. Jacobs
April 1998

Preface

The period since the publication of the first edition of this book in 1991 has witnessed some crucial developments in the European Community law regulating equality of opportunity between the sexes. Some of these developments are the result of judicial decisions, others the product of new legislation. Some will be generally welcomed by those supportive of the law in this area, others not. The Amsterdam Treaty of 1997, though not yet in operation, presages a significantly enhanced emphasis on sex equality law in the future and its provisions in this field have therefore necessitated detailed examination. As regards equal pay, perhaps the most important developments have been the judicial decisions on access and entitlement to pensions and related payments. There have also been significant steps—some forward and some backward—in the European Court of Justice's thinking about the concept of discrimination and its constituent elements. Both the Court and the Community legislature have, in addition, begun to try to tackle the issues posed by pregnancy and parenthood and the law on equal treatment has also extended itself beyond the relatively straightforward confines of the male/female distinction to take on board the complex difficulties presented by transsexualism. The problems posed in relation to the availability and appropriateness of remedies for discrimination have re-surfaced and the Court has had to confront the highly charged question of positive action on a couple of occasions. There has been an avalanche of cases concerning the principle of equal treatment in social security, although their outcome on the whole demonstrates the inability of the existing law to redress the underlying social and economic problems in this area. In addition, there have been a number of developments in the basic principles of Community law, in particular in relation to the legal effects of directives, to state liability to individuals for breaches of Community law and to the procedural autonomy of the Member States; in so far as these matters have repercussions for people asserting their rights in relation to sex equality, they have also required examination in this second edition.

As its title indicates, the subject matter of this book is the European Community law on sex equality. Although easy in theory, it is often difficult in practice to draw a strict line of demarcation between Community and national provisions; in particular, it is tempting to trespass into the realms of speculation about the consequences of Community law for the domestic rules on equal pay and equal treatment. The author has tried to resist this temptation as far as possible and to discuss domestic law only when it is relevant to understanding Community law. However, for ease of terminology and in deference to an English-speaking readership, UK courts are referred to in the text simply by the names by which they are usually known in the UK and without reference to their nationality; the nationality of domestic courts in other jurisdictions is specifically indicated.

The author would like to express her thanks to Professor Nick Wikeley for his scrutiny of and helpful comments on Chapter 4, to Chris Docksey for explaining the current state of play in relation to a number of legislative initiatives, to Laurence Bebbington for his patience in helping with the electronic retrieval of important information, and to her family for their cheerful and robust support. For the opinions expressed in this book, as well as for any errors, the author is of course solely responsible.

Evelyn Ellis
December 1997

Table of Cases

1

Introduction

Anybody who writes a book about sex equality, it would seem reasonable to suppose, believes that the subject is of great importance. The present writer is no exception. The right to equality of opportunity irrespective of sex is as fundamental to a civilized society as freedom of speech, freedom of religion or of political creed, or the right to equality notwithstanding race. Without the right to equality irrespective of sex, the individual remains unable to exploit his or her talents to the full and cannot make the most of what life has to offer: inequality is simply unfair. The community at large suffers too since valuable resources go untapped and potential gifts remain unrealized. The law and the apparatus by which it is administered, of course, play a vital part in sustaining the notion of equality as between the sexes; the law cannot do the whole job, since peoples' attitudes and cultural and other influences will always overlay it, but it can prove highly instrumental in shaping behaviour and expectations.[1]

For a number of reasons which will be discussed in the present chapter, European Community (EC) law provides an ideal vehicle for upholding the principle of sex equality; it has embraced the notion of non-discrimination between the sexes, as least as regards pay, ever since the Economic Community first came into existence. One reason why this is of the utmost significance to the citizens of the Member States of the Community is because of its undoubted potential for growth. It is well known that when the European Coal and Steel Community (ECSC) Treaty was concluded in 1951, and the Treaties establishing the European Economic Community (EEC) and the European Atomic Energy Community (Euratom) were concluded in 1957, their chief instigators intended their immediate end to be economic welfare but their long-term

---

[1] See also Byre, 'Applying Community Standards on Equality', in *Women, Equality and Europe*, eds. Buckley and Anderson (Macmillan, London, 1988). For an expression of the view that EC law is not at present committed to the principle of real sex equality, see Fenwick and Hervey, 'Sex Equality in the Single Market: New Directions for the European Court of Justice' (1995) 32 CMLRev. 443. Similarly, see Fredman, 'European Community Discrimination Law: A Critique' (1992) 21 ILJ 119 where powerful arguments are marshalled to demonstrate that EC law currently fails to address the underlying structural obstacles to progress for women.

goal to be political integration amongst the states of Europe.[2] The architects of the three European Communities had personally witnessed the destructive forces of nationalism; many had seen their countries overwhelmed and occupied during the Second World War. They were increasingly aware of the rise of the superpowers and of the threat of Communism in the East. The Schuman Declaration of 9 May 1950, which preceded the formation of the ECSC, made very clear its author's ultimate political aspirations. Robert Schuman, the French Minister for Foreign Affairs, proposed that the whole of the French and German coal and steel production industries be placed under a common 'high authority', within the framework of an organization open to participation by the other countries of Europe. He went on to explain:

The pooling of coal and steel production will immediately provide for the setting up of common bases for economic development as a first step in the federation of Europe, and will change the destinies of those regions which have long been devoted to the manufacture of munitions of war, of which they have been the most constant victims. The solidarity in production thus established will make it plain that any war between France and Germany becomes, not merely unthinkable, but materially impossible.

His overall plan was to build a united Europe 'through concrete achievements, which first create a "de facto" solidarity'. The Coal and Steel Community was to be just a first step in an ever-tightening web of economic, and thus political, integration. It was believed that the integration of the coal and steel industries would create common spheres of interest as between the French and the West Germans, which would encourage greater political friendship between those nations; further common economic and social issues would then begin to present themselves and a political framework would have to be established to deal with them. Gradually, the process would gather momentum. This scheme for what might today be termed 'rolling interdependence' between the states of Europe is now and has from the start been clearly echoed in the founding Treaties. It was taken a stage further when the Member States pledged themselves in the Single European Act of 1986[3] to make greatly increased use of majority voting in the Council, thereby relinquishing a significant portion of their national sovereignty in favour of the Community. Furthermore, despite the antagonism of many, in particular the British government, to the use of the word 'federal' in the Treaty on European Union of 1993,[4] it is clear that that Treaty nevertheless

---

[2] See in particular Ionescu, *The New Politics of European Integration* (Macmillan, London, 1972), and Kitzinger, *The Politics and Economics of European Integration* (Greenwood Press, Westport, Conn., 1963).

[3] Henceforth the SEA.

[4] Henceforth the TEU. This Treaty is also known colloquially as the Maastricht Treaty.

continued the progress towards tightening the web; its Preamble proclaims the Member States:

Resolved to mark a new stage in the process of European integration undertaken with the establishment of the European Communities,

. . . [And] Resolved to continue the process of creating an ever closer union among the peoples of Europe . . .

It also transformed the nature of the enterprise so as to create the 'European Union', founded upon the European Community but also directing its attention to the wider issues of a common foreign and security policy and justice and home affairs.[5] The Amsterdam Treaty of 1997, concluded after the holding of the Inter-Governmental Conference mandated by the TEU,[6] made numerous technical changes intended to reinforce the economic, social, political and other links between the Member States.[7] To what extent, and at what speed, Europe will make further practical and theoretical progress towards political union of course remains to be seen.

However, the federalist concept which underpins the European Communities is vital to an understanding of the real significance of EC sex equality law. The Treaties and their present provisions were in no sense intended to be an end in themselves. They are no more than a staging post in the ultimate design. The social provisions, in common with the rest of the Treaties, were expected to grow and develop as the linkage between the Member States became closer. Indeed the means for their development was specifically provided in the Treaties. The Treaties also, of course, provide for the accession of new Member States[8] and, since the original Schuman Declaration, the Communities have more than doubled in size from the original six Member States to the present fifteen.[9] Other States, including some in Central and Eastern Europe, will undoubtedly gain membership in the foreseeable future. What this means in practical terms is that a continuously developing body of sex equality laws is now able to reach a very large, and potentially expandable, group of people.

---

[5] Note also that the original title 'European Economic Community' was abbreviated to the 'European Community' by the TEU. The new title will be used in the present work, except where quotations are taken from pre-TEU literature.

[6] See TEU, Art. N(2).

[7] Art. 12 and the Annex to the Treaty of Amsterdam renumbered the articles of both the TEU and the EC Treaty. For ease of exposition, however, the discussion in the main text will follow the original lettering and numbering. The new numbering will where appropriate be referred to in footnotes by means of braces, thus: {Art. X}.

[8] Treaty on European Union, Article O {Art. 49}; ECSC Treaty, Art. 98; Euratom Treaty, Art. 205.

[9] The UK, Ireland and Denmark became members of the Communities from 1 Jan. 1973; Greece acceded as of 1 Jan. 1981, Spain and Portugal as of 1 Jan. 1986, and Austria, Finland and Sweden as of 1 Jan. 1995.

An element of dynamism is contained within this formula which is almost always lacking in any wholly domestic context.

Crucial to the concept of federation is the existence of a distinct legal system, belonging exclusively to the federation itself. This means that the federation must be able both to create its own laws and to enforce them effectively through its own system of courts or tribunals. The drafters of the European Community Treaties, eager as they were to create the seed from which a federation would grow, were aware of these needs and therefore provided for a system of Community law, together with appropriate lawmaking powers, enforceable through the medium of the European Court of Justice (ECJ) and the local courts. Essentially, they made provision for both primary and secondary tiers of Community law. Interestingly, the Treaties stop short of the use of the actual word 'legislation' in describing the legal system which they create, presumably for the political and psychological reason that this might have proved unacceptable to national parliaments at the time of accession to the European Communities.

The main primary source of Community law, and the only type which is relevant in the field of sex equality, is the founding Treaties, together with the amendments which have been made to them over the years. Of the three founding Treaties, the only one to make specific reference to sex equality is the EC Treaty and it is with that Treaty that this book is therefore mainly concerned.[10]

The EC Treaty contains a number of provisions which are relevant in this field. First, there is Article 119[11] itself which enunciates the principle of equal pay for equal work irrespective of sex. As the Treaty was originally drafted, this was the only explicit mention anywhere in it of the principle of sex equality[12] and so it provided the inspirational springboard for the subsequent developments in this area. Secondly, there are those Articles which provide the legal authorization for further, secondary legislation. The Treaty makes absolutely clear the need for specific authorization for particular measures of secondary legislation in Article 189,[13] which enables

---

[10] Henceforth, unless otherwise stated, all Treaty references in the present work will be to the EC Treaty.

[11] {Art. 141}.

[12] A number of references to sex equality were added by the Amsterdam Treaty, as will be discussed.

[13] {Art. 249}.

the European Parliament, the Council and the Commission[14] to make secondary EC legislation 'in order to carry out their task', but only 'in accordance with the provisions of this Treaty'. In other words, the institutions may only create fresh secondary legislation where a particular provision of the Treaty authorizes this. They possess no inherent or implied lawmaking capacity.

Article 119 itself conferred no secondary lawmaking power until its amendment by the Amsterdam Treaty. A new paragraph (3) was, however, inserted by that Treaty, providing:

The Council, acting in accordance with the procedure referred to in Article 189b,[15] and after consulting the Economic and Social Committee,[16] shall adopt measures to ensure the application of the principle of equal opportunities and equal treatment of men and women in matters of employment and occupation, including the principle of equal pay for equal work or work of equal value.

The breadth of this enabling provision is noteworthy; it permits measures in general and is not limited to any one form of legislative instrument.[17] It is expressed to extend to measures ensuring equality of opportunity and is not restricted to those simply outlawing discrimination.[18] Furthermore, it encompasses not merely pay equality but also other aspects of equal treatment. The important issue of how far it will be permitted to extend to equal treatment outside the traditional world of paid work will depend on the policy adopted by the ECJ in relation to the interpretation of the word 'occupation'.

The Amsterdam Treaty also created a new Article 6a:[19]

Without prejudice to the other provisions of this Treaty and within the limits of the powers conferred by it upon the Community, the Council, acting unani-

---

[14] For general discussion of the powers and functions of the main institutions of the Communities, in particular the European Parliament, the Council, Commission, and ECJ, see Hartley, *The Foundations of European Community Law* (Clarendon Press, Oxford, 3rd ed. 1994); Wyatt and Dashwood, *European Community Law* (Sweet and Maxwell, London, 3rd ed. 1993); and Weatherill and Beaumont, *EC Law* (Penguin, London, 2nd ed. 1995). For the changes made by the Amsterdam Treaty, see *The Treaty of Amsterdam: Text and Commentary*, ed. Duff (Federal Trust/Sweet & Maxwell, London, 1997).

[15] {Art. 251}. Art. 189b, which was also amended by the Amsterdam Treaty, creates a complex decision-making process which begins with the submission of a proposal by the Commission to the European Parliament and the Council; these latter two institutions must subsequently both agree to the making of the new instrument, in conformity with a procedure and time-scale set out in the Article, if it is to be adopted.

[16] This Committee consists of 'representatives of the various categories of economic and social activity, in particular, representatives of producers, farmers, carriers, dealers, craftsmen, professional occupations and representatives of the general public': Art. 193 {Art. 257}.

[17] See discussion below of the different legislative instruments available in EC law.

[18] For discussion of the differences between the concepts of non-discrimination and equality of opportunity, see Chap. 5.

[19] {Art. 13}.

mously on a proposal from the Commission and after consulting the European Parliament, may take appropriate action to combat discrimination based on sex, racial or ethnic origin, religion or belief, disability, age or sexual orientation.

The opening phrase of this Article indicates that Article 119(3) will usually be the appropriate provision for legislation dealing exclusively with sex discrimination; however, Article 6a would be useful for the enactment of a composite measure which addressed discrimination based on a number of different classifications. Like Article 119(3), Article 6a authorises all types of legislative or other instrument but it should be noted that its ambit is restricted to the prohibition of discrimination and that it does not extend to measures to promote equality of opportunity on the wider scale.

Before the creation by the Amsterdam Treaty of enabling provisions dealing expressly with sex equality, more general enabling provisions had to be utilized for the enactment of secondary legislation in this area. The most obvious candidates were Articles 100 and 235.[20] Article 100 permits the Council, acting unanimously on a Commission proposal and after consulting the European Parliament and the Economic and Social Committee, to make directives[21] 'for the approximation of such laws, regulations or administrative provisions of the Member States as directly affect the establishment or functioning of the common market'. This is often called 'harmonization' legislation. Article 235 is generally a little wider in its scope and provides:

If action by the Community should prove necessary to attain, in the course of the operation of the common market, one of the objectives of the Community and this Treaty has not provided the necessary powers, the Council shall, acting unanimously on a proposal from the Commission and after consulting the European Parliament, take the appropriate measures.

Some further bases for harmonization legislation were provided by the Single European Act of 1986. In particular, a new Article 100a[22] was thereby added to the original EC Treaty. Article 100a is expressed to be by way of derogation from Article 100 and was inserted specifically in order to further the aim of achieving the complete internal market, in which there are no internal frontiers. Its usefulness in the context of sex equality is, however, somewhat limited by the fact that it does not authorize legislation relating to the rights and interests of employed persons. Article 118a was also added by the Single European Act; it used merely to mandate Council directives for improving the health and safety of workers.[23] However, the

---

[20] {Arts. 94 and 308} respectively.

[21] For the definition and characteristics of a directive, see below.

[22] {Art. 95}.

[23] In this form it provided the authorization for the Pregnancy Directive (Directive 92/85, OJ [1992] L348/1), discussed in Chap. 3.

Amsterdam Treaty generalized the provision[24] and today its successor, Article 118,[25] provides that the Community will support and complement the activities of the Member States in the following fields:

—Improvement in particular of the working environment to protect workers' health and safety;
—Working conditions;
—The information and consultation of workers;
—The integration of persons excluded from the labour market . . .;
—Equality between men and women with regard to labour market opportunities and treatment at work.

To these ends, the Council is authorized to adopt directives setting 'minimum requirements for gradual implementation, having regard to the conditions and technical rules obtaining in each of the Member States'.[26] Such directives must not, however, impose administrative, financial and legal constraints in a way which would hold back the creation and development of small and medium-sized undertakings. The Council is also permitted to adopt measures 'designed to encourage co-operation between Member States through initiatives aimed at improving knowledge, developing exchanges of information and best practices, promoting innovative approaches and evaluating experiences in order to combat social exclusion'.[27] Such action is to be in accordance with Article 189b,[28] after the Council has consulted the Economic and Social Committee and the Committee of the Regions.[29] Exceptionally, however, in order to take action *inter alia* in the fields of social security and social protection, the Council has to act unanimously on a proposal from the Commission, after consulting the European Parliament, the Economic and Social Committee and the Committee of the Regions.[30]

Until its repeal by the Amsterdam Treaty, the Protocol on Social Policy annexed at Maastricht to the EC Treaty provided a vehicle for a special kind of secondary legislation in the field of sex equality.[31] The Protocol contained an Agreement on Social Policy, acquiesced in by all the Member States apart from the UK which refused, whilst under Conservative administration, to be involved in any further extension of the powers of

---

[24] It absorbed into the body of the EC Treaty the provisions which had formerly been contained in the Agreement on Social Policy, discussed below.
[25] {Art. 137}.
[26] Art. 118(2).
[27] Ibid.
[28] {Art. 251}.
[29] Established by Arts. 198a-c {Arts. 263–5}.
[30] Art. 118(3).
[31] Art. 239 {Art. 311} provides that Protocols annexed to the EC Treaty are to form 'an integral part thereof'.

the Community in the field of social policy.[32] Legislative action[33] pursuant
to the Agreement took place according to the usual EC institutional
procedures but without the participation of the UK in the relevant Council
meetings since such legislation did not bind the UK.[34] It could supplement
but not detract from the pre-existing body of EC law, the so-called 'acquis
communautaire'.[35] Curtin questioned the legal status of such 'legislation',
pointing out that the wording adopted by the Protocol authorized the
participating states to adopt acts 'among themselves' and arguing that the
products of such agreements could not constitute EC law with the qualities
set out in Article 189.[36]

Several instruments were nevertheless concluded under the aegis of the
Protocol and Agreement, the first being the Directive on Works Councils.[37]
This was followed by a European-level collective agreement on Parental
Leave signed on 14 December 1995. The agreement was subsequently
enacted in the form of a directive in June 1996.[38] A directive on parental
leave had been proposed as long ago as 1984, but was consistently opposed

[32] It was suggested by some writers that the UK's social policy opt-out could be contrary
to a 'higher principle' of Community law (i.e. superior in legal force to the written rules of
the Treaty), such as that of the uniform application of EC law or the principle of legal
certainty, and that it was therefore invalid. See Hartley, 'The European Court, Judicial
Objectivity and the Constitution of the European Union' (1996) 112 LQR 95, Whiteford,
'Social Policy After Maastricht' (1993) 18 ELRev. 202, and Curtin, 'The Constitutional
Structure of the European Union: a Europe of Bits and Pieces' (1993) 30 CMLRev. 17.

[33] Art. 2(2) permitted the Council to adopt directives in accordance with the procedure
referred to in Art. 189c {Art. 252}, after consulting the Economic and Social Committee.
Art. 2(3) permitted unspecified action to be taken by the Council unanimously on a
proposal of the Commission, after consulting the European Parliament and the Economic
and Social Committee, in areas which included social security and the protection of
workers. Art. 4 envisaged Community level collective agreements which could, in certain
circumstances, be implemented by a Council decision on a proposal from the Commission.
See further Fitzpatrick, 'Community Social Law After Maastricht' (1992) 21 ILJ 199 and
Watson, 'Social Policy After Maastricht' (1993) 30 CMLRev. 481.

[34] Thus creating for the first time the potential for a 'two- speed Europe'. For the view
that the Protocol created a real danger of 'social dumping', in other words, 'investment by
companies in the United Kingdom where labour costs are lower than in other Member
States, which will result in workers in those other Member States being forced to accept
lower standards in order to avoid unemployment', see Watson, op. cit., n. 33.

[35] See the opening recital to the Protocol.

[36] Curtin, op. cit., n. 32. The Commission, however, asserted that 'the Community nature
of measures taken under the Agreement is beyond doubt, which means that the Court of
Justice will be empowered to rule on the legality of directives adopted by the Eleven and to
interpret them' (Communication concerning the application of the agreement on social
policy presented by the Commission to the Council and to the European Parliament
COM(93) 600 final). To the same effect, see also Bercusson, 'The Dynamic of European
Labour Law After Maastricht' (1994) 23 ILJ 1.

[37] Directive 94/45, OJ [1994] L254/64, as to which see also Burrows and Mair, *European
Social Law* (Wiley, Chichester, 1996), Chap. 14. At a lecture in the University of Birmingham
in 1995, Prof. Giorgio Gaja pointed out that the adoption of the usual EC system for the
numbering of such directives was deceptive because it implied that they were ordinary
instruments of EC law; furthermore, he asserted that this confused the legislative system.

[38] Directive 96/34, OJ [1996] L145/4, discussed in Chap. 3.

by the UK government on financial grounds. The proposal was resurrected after the Social Policy Agreement came into force. Another measure which had remained stalled for a long time because of the intransigence of the UK government of the day was a proposed directive on the burden of proof in sex discrimination cases and on the definition of indirect discrimination; the social partners decided that they did not wish to negotiate an agreement on this matter, but progress was made towards the enactment of legislation when unanimous political agreement[39] was reached on a common position at a Council meeting in the summer of 1997;[40] the directive was eventually enacted in December 1997.[41]In addition, an agreement between the social partners was reached in June 1997 on discrimination against part-time workers.[42] This was transposed into law by another directive adopted in December 1997.[43] After its election in May 1997, the new Labour government of the UK announced its intention to commit itself to all the instruments agreed by the other Member States under the Social Policy Agreement.[44]

Secondary EC law is of three types: regulations, directives, and decisions.[45] Article 189[46] defines the basic attributes of each. Regulations are stated to have 'general application', which means that they create binding legal obligations for every person within the EC. This is not to say that they necessarily in fact impinge on the legal situation of each and every legal person within the Community, since they are frequently of a highly specialized nature and regulate only specific activities or industries. They do, however, create general law and thus have the potential actually to affect the legal position of any legal person within the Community. Their nearest equivalent in domestic legal terms is parliamentary legislation. Article 189 goes on to provide that regulations are binding in their entirety and 'directly applicable in all Member States'. The meaning of this latter phrase is not at once self-evident, but it is clear from comparison with what Article 189 goes on to say about the effects of

[39] Including that of the UK.

[40] COM(96) 340 final.

[41] The provisions of the draft directive dealing with the definition of indirect discrimination are discussed in Chap. 2 and those dealing with the burden of proof are discussed in Chap. 3.

[42] See CREW Reports (1997) Vol. 17, No. 5/6, p. 37 and (1997) 74 EOR 37.

[43] Directive 97/81, OJ [1998] L14/9. At the time of writing, consultations were also taking place between the Commission and the social partners on a Community instrument on sexual harassment; see further in Chap. 3.

[44] The existing instruments are to be re-enacted with the agreement of the UK under Art. 100 {Art. 94}; as Usher has observed in *EC Institutions and Legislation* (Longmans, London, 1998), this suggests that the matters covered by the Agreement on Social Policy fell within the mainstream of EC law all along.

[45] The nomenclature adopted for secondary legislation in the ECSC is somewhat different; see ECSC Treaty, Art. 14. The Euratom Treaty adopts the same formulation as the EC Treaty; see its Art. 161.

[46] {Art. 249}.

directives that it is intended to indicate that regulations have automatic legal force and require no implementing measures to be taken by the legislative or other authorities in the Member States. The ECJ has also confirmed this interpretation.[47] It follows that regulations are the appropriate instrument for achieving uniformity or identity of legal provision throughout the Community.

Directives, unlike regulations, are expressed by Article 189 to be addressed to states rather than being of 'general application'. A directive is binding 'as to the result to be achieved' on each Member State to which it is addressed, but it leaves to the national authorities 'the choice of form and methods'. Directives thus do not take effect within the legal systems of the Member States as they stand. Rather they require the Member States to legislate to achieve a particular end product. They require translation into national law and always contain a time-limit by which such translation must have been carried out. They are chiefly of use when mutually compatible, or harmonized, laws are needed amongst all the Member States, as distinct from where identical provisions are required. In practice, all the secondary legislation to date in the field of sex equality has taken the form of directives, so their nature and effects are particularly significant in the present context.

A decision, according to Article 189, is addressed to a particular legal person or group of such persons. Such persons can include individual people, corporations, and States. The decision is 'binding in its entirety upon those to whom it is addressed'. It does not therefore appear capable of creating any kind of generalized legal obligations.[48]

All three instruments of secondary legislation are required to state the reasons on which they are based and must refer to any proposals or opinions which the Treaty required to be obtained.[49] Because of the breadth of their legal consequences, all regulations and most directives are today required to be published in the Official Journal of the Communities.[50]

[47] In Case 93/71 *Leonesio* v. *Italian Ministry of Agriculture and Fisheries* [1972] ECR 287 the ECJ said at 293: 'Therefore, because of its nature and its purpose within the system of sources of Community law it has direct effect and is, as such, capable of creating individual rights which national courts must protect. Since they are pecuniary rights against the State these rights arise when the conditions set out in the regulation are complied with and it is not possible at a national level to render the exercise of them subject to implementing provisions other than those which might be required by the regulation itself'.

[48] See Greaves, 'The Nature and Binding Effect of Decisions Under Article 189 EC' (1996) 21 ELRev. 3.

[49] Art. 190 {Art. 253}.

[50] Art. 191 {Art. 254}, which was amended by the TEU, provides that regulations, directives and decisions adopted in accordance with the procedure referred to in Art. 189b, together with regulations of the Council and the Commission and directives of those institutions which are addressed to all Member States, must be published in the Official Journal. They enter into force on the date specified in them or, in default of such

The relevant enabling article in the EC Treaty has to be examined in order to discover what type of secondary EC law is permitted in any given instance.

THE NATURE AND EFFECTS OF EC LAW

Because of the power,[51] and indeed sometimes the duty,[52] of national courts in EC countries to seek preliminary rulings from the ECJ[53] in cases pending before them, it has been up to the ECJ on numerous occasions to define the nature and effects of EC law. In so defining these characteristics, the ECJ has clearly been strongly influenced by the federalist ideal underlying the conception of the Communities. It has been able to distil certain specific and vital qualities of EC law, which differentiate it clearly both from the national laws of the Member States and also from traditional international law. In practice, as events have turned out, there has probably been no other field of substantive law in which these principles developed by the ECJ have proved to be more important than sex discrimination.

The case in which the ECJ first began to express the particular characteristics of EC law was *Van Gend en Loos v. Nederlandse Tariefcommissie*.[54] This case concerned the legal effect within the Netherlands of the prohibition contained in Article 12 of the EC Treaty on any increase in customs duties in trade between Member States of the Community. The ECJ made a now-famous statement of principle:

The objective of the EEC Treaty which is to establish a Common Market, the functioning of which is of direct concern to interested parties in the Community implies that this Treaty is more than an agreement creating only mutual obligations between the contracting parties. This view is confirmed by the Preamble to the Treaty which refers not only to governments but to peoples. It is also confirmed more specifically by the establishment of institutions endowed with sovereign rights, the exercise of which affects Member States and also their citizens. Furthermore, it must be noted that the nationals of the States brought together

specification, on the twentieth day following that of their publication. Other directives and decisions must merely be notified to those to whom they are addressed and take effect on such notification.

[51] See Art. 177(2) {Art. 234(2)}, which gives a discretion to national courts and tribunals to request a preliminary ruling where a question of EC law has to be decided before that court or tribunal can arrive at a judgment.

[52] In the case of courts and tribunals against whose decisions there is no judicial remedy under national law; see Art. 177(3) {Art. 234(3)}.

[53] Art. 168a {Art. 225} provides that this jurisdiction remains exclusive to the ECJ, notwithstanding the creation pursuant to the Single European Act 1986 of the Court of First Instance (CFI).

[54] Case 26/62 [1963] ECR 1.

in the Community are called upon to cooperate in the functioning of this Community, through the intermediary of the European Parliament and the Economic and Social Committee. In addition the task assigned to the Court of Justice under Article 177, the object of which is to secure uniform interpretation of the Treaty by the national courts and tribunals, confirms that the States have acknowledged that Community law has an authority which can be invoked by their nationals before those courts and tribunals. The conclusion to be drawn from this is that the Community constitutes a new legal order in international law for the benefit of which the States have limited their sovereign rights, albeit within limited fields, and the subjects of which comprise not only the Member States but also their nationals. Independently of the legislation of Member States, community law therefore not only imposes obligations on individuals but is also intended to confer upon them rights which become part of their legal heritage. These rights arise not only where they are expressly granted by the Treaty, but also by reason of obligations which the treaty imposes in a clearly defined way upon individuals as well as upon the Member States and upon the institutions of the community . . . Article 12 must be interpreted as producing direct effects and creating individual rights which national courts must protect.[55]

It follows from these remarks of the ECJ that EC law possesses two special characteristics in particular: it is 'supreme' over conflicting national law in the Member States, in other words, prevails over such law; and it is, on occasion at least, enforceable by individuals bringing proceedings in the courts of the Member States.[56] In later litigation, the ECJ has taken the opportunity to develop and refine these vital principles.[57]

The Supremacy of EC Law

In *Van Gend en Loos*, the supremacy of EC law was an implication to be made from the ECJ's statements: an individual legal person was held entitled to have Article 12 of the Treaty enforced in preference to the conflicting domestic law of the Netherlands. Having surmounted this tricky political hurdle—in effect, telling a Member State that its own law

[55] Ibid at 12–13. See also Case 28/67 *Molkerei-Zentrale Westfalen/Lippe GmbH* v. *Hauptzollamt Paderborn* [1968] ECR 143, at 152–3.

[56] Reference should be made to more general works on EC law for a full discussion of these concepts, in particular Weatherill and Beaumont, *EC Law* (Penguin, London, 2nd ed. 1995), Chaps. 11 and 12; Hartley, *The Foundations of European Community Law* (Clarendon, Oxford, 3rd ed. 1994), Chaps. 7 and 8; Kapteyn and Verloren Van Themaat, *Introduction to the Law of the European Communities* (Kluwer, Deventer, 2nd ed. 1990), Chap. 2; and Wyatt and Dashwood, *European Community Law* (Sweet & Maxwell, London, 3rd ed. 1993), Chap.4. The discussion which follows in the present text is confined, so far as possible, to those aspects of the concepts which have special significance in the context of sex equality law.

[57] See further Van Gerven, 'Bridging the Gap Between Community and National Laws: Towards a Principle of Homogeneity in the Field of Legal Remedies?' (1995) 32 CMLRev. 679.

was to be ignored—the ECJ gathered courage and became bolder in its formulation of the concept of supremacy of EC law.

Its successor, *Costa* v. *ENEL*,[58] was a strong case in which to test the doctrine of supremacy of EC law because the potential conflict arose in the situation where the impugned domestic law post-dated the contrary EC law, in other words the situation where, in a purely domestic context, a court would normally hold that the later law in time prevailed.

The ECJ held:

The Italian Government submits that the request of the giudice conciliatore is 'absolutely inadmissible', inasmuch as a national court which is obliged to apply a national law cannot avail itself of Article 177. By contrast with ordinary international treaties, the EEC Treaty has created its own legal system which, on the entry into force of the treaty, became an integral part of the legal systems of the Member States and which their courts are bound to apply. By creating a Community of unlimited duration, having its own institutions, its own personality and its own legal capacity and capacity of representation on the international plane, and, more particularly, real powers stemming from a limitation of sovereignty or a transfer of powers from the States to the Community, the Member States have limited their sovereign rights, and, albeit within limited fields, have thus created a body of law which binds both their nationals and themselves. The integration into the laws of each Member State of provisions which derive from the Community, and more generally the terms and the spirit of the Treaty, make it impossible for the Member State, as a corollary, to accord precedence to a unilateral and subsequent measure over a legal system accepted by them on a basis of reciprocity . . . The transfer by the States from their domestic legal system to the Community legal system of the rights and obligations arising under the Treaty carries with it a permanent limitation of their sovereign rights against which a subsequent unilateral act incompatible with the concept of the Community cannot prevail. Consequently, Article 177 is to be applied regardless of any domestic law, whenever questions relating to the interpretation of the Treaty arise.[59]

In subsequent cases, the ECJ has extended its formulation of supremacy so as to encompass not merely the law created directly by the EC Treaty but also secondary legislation made by the institutions.[60] So, for example, a

---

[58] Case 6/64 [1964] 3 ECR 585.
[59] Ibid. at 593–4.
[60] See e.g. Case 43/71 *Politi Sas* v. *Minister of Finance* [1971] ECR 1039; and Case 38/77 *Enka BV* v. *Inspecteur der Invoerrechten en Accijnzen* [1977] ECR 2203, discussed below. But note the exception contained in Art. 234 {Art. 307}: the provisions of the EC Treaty have no effect on rights and obligations resulting from treaties concluded before the entry into force of the EC Treaty between a Member State and a third country. This provision was relied upon in Case C-158/91 *Levy* [1993] ECR I-4287 to justify a ban on night work by women in France which had earlier been held by the ECJ in Case C-345/89 *Stoeckel* [1991] ECR I-4047 (discussed in Chap.3) to contravene the Equal Treatment Directive (Dir. 76/207, OJ [1976] L39/40, also discussed in Chap. 3); the ban was pursuant to a pre-existing commitment to an ILO Convention, which France had not at the relevant time denounced. *Levy* was followed in Case C-13/93 *Office National de l'Emploi* v. *Minne* [1994] ECR I-371.

provision contained in a regulation must prevail over conflicting national law.

In support of its conclusions, the ECJ has put forward several reasons. The one most frequently referred to is the essentially federalist notion of a limitation of sovereignty on the part of the Member States when they acceded to the Communities. The Member States are taken to have transferred a portion of their legislative powers to the new organization, and in the areas where that transfer has taken place the States are consequently now incapable of making their own national legislation.[61] Another, similar line of argument which is discernible in *Costa* v. *ENEL* is that it follows from the whole nature and spirit of EC law that it must be of a kind different from, and higher than, national law. The whole set-up of the Communities is such that Community laws must be intended to be supreme; Member States only undertake to carry out certain actions and to suffer particular restrictions provided that all the other Member States are placed in exactly the same position.[62] Of course, if the Member States possessed general powers to contradict EC law by means of their own national legislation, then all Member States would not be placed in the same position. The notion of reciprocity is central to the Communities, and reciprocity would not exist without the doctrine of supremacy of Community law.

A related rationale which the Court has also sometimes relied on is usually known as the doctrine of 'useful effect'.[63] The useful effect of the Treaty would be undermined if the Member States could contradict its provisions. If, by national legislation, the Member States were able to contradict EC law, there would be absolutely no means of ensuring that EC law functioned uniformly and therefore efficiently throughout the EC.[64]

It is important that the national courts of the Member States also accept the principle of supremacy of EC law; if, as the ECJ holds, the Community so much resembles a developed federation as to confer legal rights directly on individual legal persons, then it follows as a matter of practicality that

[61] This reasoning is evident in the early cases of *Van Gend en Loos* and *Costa* v. *ENEL* and, in more recent times, in Case 63/83 *R.* v. *Kent Kirk* [1984] ECR 2689. See also Usher, *European Community Law and National Law: The Irreversible Transfer?* (George Allen & Unwin, London, 1981).

[62] This reasoning has become somewhat compromised in recent years, with the recognition by the Maastricht and Amsterdam Treaties of the concept of 'flexibility' viz. the principle that certain Member States may opt out of specific aspects of EC law.

[63] See Case 14/68 *Walt Wilhelm* v. *Bundeskartellamt* [1969] ECR 1.

[64] The ECJ has also, on occasion, given other ancillary reasons for holding that EC law is supreme. In particular, it pointed out in *Costa* v. *ENEL* that wherever the Treaty does allow the Member States a unilateral right to legislate, it does so in special provisions. However, these provisions are clearly by way of exception and they would, of course, be quite unnecessary if the Member States anyway had power to pass conflicting national legislation. See [1964] ECR 585, esp. at 593–4.

those rights must be enforceable in national courts. If the national courts were, at this stage, unprepared to enforce EC law in preference to conflicting national law, then much of the value of direct enforcement would be lost. The courts of the original six Member States took a little while to accept what must to them have seemed the very radical notion of supremacy of EC law;[65] however, in the main today it appears that in all the Member States of the Community the idea of supremacy of EC law has gained general acceptance,[66] albeit that the logical route which judges have followed to lead them to this conclusion has not always been the ECJ's theory of the limitation of national legislative sovereignty.

In the UK, the supremacy of EC law has faced a particular difficulty: that of the rival doctrine of the supremacy of the UK Parliament. If, as British judges have traditionally held, the UK Parliament can always do whatever it pleases, how could it ever be constrained by the limitation that it is not to contradict EC law? In particular, if EC law is rendered effective in the UK by an Act of Parliament, as constitutional theory dictates, what is to prevent the repeal of the implementing Act by a later piece of UK legislation which contradicts EC law? Is not the latest Act of Parliament the indication that the judges must unerringly follow if democracy is not to be undermined?

This problem has, in practice, been neatly side-stepped by the European Communities Act 1972, and in particular by the artful wording of s. 2(4) thereof.[67] This provides that 'any enactment passed or to be passed, other than one contained in this Part of this Act, shall be construed and have effect subject to the foregoing provisions of this section . . .'. The 'foregoing' s. 2(1) has already provided that all Community rights are to be available in law in the UK. The ECJ has explained, as has already been seen for example in *Van Gend en Loos*, that the right to have EC law treated

[65] Difficulties were encountered in particular in Italy, France and West Germany. See e.g. the decision of the Italian Constitutional Court in *Costa* v. *ENEL* [1964] 3 CMLR 425, that of the French Conseil d'Etat in *Cohn-Bendit* v. *Ministre de l'Intérieure* [1980] 1 CMLR 543 and that of the Federal German Constitutional Court in *Internationale Handelsgesellschaft GmbH* v. *Einfuhr-und Vorratsstelle für Getreide und Futtermittel* [1974] 2 CMLR 540.

[66] See in particular *Frontini* v. *Minister of Finance* [1974] 2 CMLR 372; *SpA Granital* v. *Amministrazione delle Finanze* Decision No. 170 of 8 June 1984 [1984] 21 CMLRev. 756; *Re the Application of Wunsche Handelsgesellschaft* [1987] 3 CMLR 225; *Administration des Douanes* v. *Société Jacques Vabre* [1975] 2 CMLR 336 and *Nicolo* [1990] 1 CMLR 173. Cf. *Brunner* v. *European Union Treaty* [1994] CMLR 57. See also Steiner, 'The Application of European Community Law in National Courts—Problems, Pitfalls and Precepts' (1980) 96 LQR 126; Pettricione, 'Supremacy of Community Law over National Law (1986) 11 ELRev. 320; and Gaja, 'New Developments in a Continuing Story: The Relationship between EEC Law and Italian Law' (1990) 27 CMLRev. 83.

[67] Cf. Wade, 'Sovereignty—Revolution or Evolution?' (1996) 112 LQR 568. For criticism of Wade's view that a constitutional revolution has occurred through the fettering of Parliament's legislative powers by s. 2(4), see Allan, 'Parliamentary Sovereignty: Law, Politics and Revolution' (1997) 113 LQR 443.

as supreme is a Community right which can be claimed by a litigant. Thus, the effect of s. 2(4) is that, at least until such time as the European Communities Act is repealed, all Acts of the UK Parliament must 'be construed and have effect' subject to the principle that EC law is always supreme over them in the event of conflict. The device relied upon by the European Communities Act is therefore the delegation to the EC institutions of those lawmaking functions which fall within the purview of the EC Treaty; the legal system has not gone to the full lengths which the ECJ says EC law demands and there has, in reality, been no out-and-out transfer of lawmaking powers from the UK Parliament to the EC institutions.[68]

In practice, UK judges have tried wherever possible to utilize what might be called the first limb of s. 2(4) of the European Communities Act and to hold that the relevant domestic legislation is susceptible of a variety of meanings, but that, in the light of s. 2(4), they will adopt the construction which most clearly accords with the demands of EC law. The first statement and application of this approach in the House of Lords came in *Garland* v. *British Rail*.[69] Confronted here with an apparent conflict between s. 6(4) of the Sex Discrimination Act 1975, which at the time of the litigation permitted sex discrimination in relation to retirement, and Article 119 of the EC Treaty which requires equal pay for men and women, the House chose to construe the UK statute in such a way as to make it accord with Article 119. Lord Diplock, delivering the only speech made by their Lordships, said:

[E]ven if the obligation to observe the provisions of Article 119 were an obliga-tion assumed by the UK under an ordinary international treaty or convention and there were no questions of the treaty obligation being directly applicable as part of the law to be applied by the courts in this country without need for any further enactment, it is a principle of construction of UK statutes, now too well established to call for citation of authority, that the words of a statute passed after the Treaty has been signed and dealing with the subject matter of the interna-tional obligation of the UK, are to be construed, if they are reasonably capable of bearing such a meaning, as intended to carry out the obligation and not to be

[68] See Jaconelli, 'Constitutional Review and S. 2 (4) of the European Communities Act 1972' (1979) 28 ICLQ 65.
[69] [1982] 2 WLR 918. See also *Pickstone* v. *Freemans plc* [1988] 2 All ER 803 and *Litster* v. *Forth Dry Dock and Engineering Co. Ltd.* [1989] ICR 341 in the latter of which Lord Oliver commented at 354: 'The approach to the construction of primary and subordinate legislation enacted to give effect to the UK's obligations under the EEC Treaty . . . is not in doubt. If the legislation can reasonably be construed so as to conform with those obligations—obligations which are to be ascertained not only from the wording of the relevant Directive but from the interpretation placed upon it by the ECJ at Luxembourg—such a purposive construction will be applied even though, perhaps, it may involve some departure from the strict and literal application of the words which the legislature has elected to use.'

inconsistent with it. 'A fortiori' is this the case where the Treaty obligation arises under one of the Community treaties to which s. 2 of the European Communities Act 1972 applies.[70]

Where, however, the 'construction' approach is impossible, the UK courts have also been prepared to rely on the other limb of s. 2(4) of the European Communities Act and to hold that UK law which conflicts with EC law does not take effect.[71] This was most dramatically demonstrated in *Macarthys Ltd.* v. *Smith.* This case concerned a demand for equal pay by a woman who had been employed on the same work as a man but in succession to him. In the Court of Appeal, Lord Denning MR had been prepared to adopt the 'construction' approach and this led him to the conclusion that the British Equal Pay Act of 1970 was ambiguous as to whether or not it covered situations of successive, as distinct from contemporaneous, employment of a man and a woman doing the same job; Article 119 of the EC Treaty, on the other hand, he felt clearly governed situations of successive employment. On this basis, he would have been prepared to construe the Equal Pay Act so as to cover successive employment.[72] The other members of the Court of Appeal disagreed with this approach, however, holding that the Equal Pay Act was unambiguous and was clearly confined to situations of contemporaneous employment. The case was then referred to the ECJ for a preliminary ruling as to the meaning and scope of Article 119 and the ECJ held that Article 119 did indeed govern successive employment cases. A head-on conflict was thus produced between Article 119 of the EC Treaty and the later-enacted[73] Equal Pay Act. In these circumstances it was conceivable that the judges might hold that the latest expression of Parliament's will should prevail and that they should therefore enforce the national legislation. On the contrary, however, the Court of Appeal was unanimous in upholding the applicability of Article 119 in this situation.[74] It expressly approved of the doctrine of supremacy of EC law and explained that it was made effective

---

[70] [1982] 2 WLR 934–5. Cf. *Duke* v. *GEC Reliance Ltd.* ([1988] 2 WLR 359 and *Finnegan* v. *Clowney Youth Training Ltd.* [1990] 2 WLR 1305.

[71] An alternative view is that there are not two limbs of s. 2(4) at all because the word 'and' in the subsection is truly conjunctive. If this were the correct analysis of the subsection, the supremacy of EC law would be denied where domestic law could not be construed so as to accord with it which, as is discussed in the text, is not in practice found to be the case.

[72] [1979] 3 CMLR 44. See also Guy and Leigh, 'Article 119 EEC: Discrimination on Grounds of Sex' (1979) 4 ELRev. 415.

[73] The Equal Pay Act 1970 was amended and then brought into operation by the Sex Discrimination Act 1975.

[74] [1980] IRLR 209. On the same principle, see also *Pickstone* v. *Freemans plc* [1987] 3 WLR 811 and [1988] 2 All ER 803; *Parsons* v. *East Surrey Health Authority* [1986] ICR 837, and *R.* v. *Secretary of State for Education, Ex p. Schaffter* [1987] IRLR 53.

by the European Communities Act 1972, at least until such time as that Act was repealed and the EC Treaty repudiated by the UK.[75] The same principle was reiterated obiter by the House of Lords in *R. v. Secretary of State for Transport, Ex p. Factortame Ltd.*[76] The issue there was a potential conflict between Part II of the Merchant Shipping Act 1988 governing the registration of British fishing vessels and EC law. Lord Bridge commented:

By virtue of s. 2(4) of the 1972 Act, Part II of the Act of 1988 is to be construed and take effect subject to directly enforceable Community rights, and those rights are, by s. 2(1) of the Act of 1972, to be 'recognized and available in law, and . . . enforced, allowed and followed accordingly . . .' This has precisely the same effect as if a section were incorporated in Part II of the Act of 1988 which in terms enacted that the provisions with respect to registration of British fishing vessels were to be without prejudice to the directly enforceable Community rights of nationals of any Member State of the EEC. Thus, it is common ground that, in so far as the applicants succeed before the ECJ in obtaining a ruling in support of the Community rights which they claim, those rights will *prevail* over the restrictions imposed on registration of British fishing vessels by Part II of the Act of 1988 . . .[77]

---

[75] See Ellis, 'Supremacy of Parliament and European Law' (1980) 96 LQR 511 and Allan, 'Parliamentary Sovereignty: Lord Denning's Dexterous Revolution' (1983) 3 OJLS 22.

[76] [1989] 2 WLR 997, discussed in greater detail below.

[77] [1989] 2 WLR 1011 (emphasis supplied). See also his remarks when the case returned to the House of Lords after a preliminary ruling by the ECJ: [1990] 3 WLR 818 esp. at 857–8. In the Court of Appeal, Lord Donaldson MR elaborated on the way in which conflicts between UK and EC Law commonly arise, saying: 'underlying the whole of this problem is the unusual (to a British lawyer) nature of Community law, which is long on principle and short on specifics . . . the result is often that the British courts are faced with an undoubted right or duty under British law and a *claim* that an inconsistent right or duty exists under Community law. If the British court can ascertain the nature and extent of this competing right or duty, there is little difficulty in resolving any inconsistency on the basis that Community law is paramount. That is the "acte clair" situation, but it is a comparative rarity. Much more commonly the British court cannot ascertain the nature and extent of the competing right or duty and it is to meet this problem that the right to seek a ruling by the European Court is provided under Article 177 of the Treaty of Rome. But it would be a mistake to think of that court merely as having a greater expertise in Community law than a British court, although this is undoubtedly true. Whatever the formal position, its true function in appropriate cases is actually to make new law by the applications of principle to specific factual situations. A challenge to national law based upon Community law may, when properly analysed, amount to a submission not that the national law is inconsistent with Community law as it then exists, but that upon a reference being made to the European Court, that court will give a ruling creating new and inconsistent rights and duties arising out of settled principles albeit with retroactive effect. In other words, national law is effective at present, but its life-span is predictably short' (1989) 139 NLJ Pt 1, 540, at 540–1.

Direct Enforcement of EC Law by Individuals

(i) Origins of the Principle

The other twin pillar of EC constitutional law which was first described by the ECJ in *Van Gend en Loos*[78] is the right of individual legal persons to have certain of its provisions enforced in the national courts of the Member States.[79] Such a notion is essentially federalist in its basis. Classic international law is concerned primarily with regulating the relations of states *inter se*, rather than with creating rights directly for their subjects. EC law, however, as the legal system for an embryo federation, is concerned at the levels of both states and individuals because a major part of its *raison d'être* is the improvement of the position and quality of life of individuals.

Apart from this somewhat philanthropic rationale, the ECJ is, however, aware of another good reason for giving individuals rights directly under EC law. Many aspects of EC law require implementing action on the part of the Member States, or at least require the Member States to refrain from taking any action which would inhibit their operation. If the Member States act in breach of these duties, Articles 169[80] and 170[81] provide for their prosecution before the ECJ by the Commission and other Member States. Such proceedings are, however, cumbersome and consuming of the Commission's time. In practice, it would be quite impossible for all such breaches to be dealt with through these channels. If individuals, therefore, can enforce their rights directly in their national courts, the procedure is short-circuited. The national court in effect rules that the Member State's action is in breach of EC law and will often grant the individual a specific remedy in respect of it. So, for example, as in *Van Gend en Loos* itself, a demand for an increased customs duty made by a Member State in breach of Article 12[82] of the Treaty cannot be enforced in a national court and an individual charged is not liable to pay the sum involved.[83] As the ECJ

---

[78] Case 26/62 [1963] ECR 1.

[79] See generally Pescatore, 'The Doctrine of "Direct Effect": An Infant Disease of Community Law' (1983) 8 ELRev. 155 and Dashwood, 'The Principle of Direct Effect in European Community Law' (1977) 16 JCMS 229. For a powerful critique of the doctrine of direct effect, see Sebba, 'The Doctrine of "Direct Effect": A Malignant Disease of Community Law' [1995] LIEI 35.

[80] {Art. 226}.

[81] {Art. 227}.

[82] {Art. 25}.

[83] An example from the field of sex discrimination law is provided by Case C-317/93 *Nolte* v. *Landesversicherungsanstalt Hannover* [1995] ECR I-4625, discussed in Chap. 4. The Commission was considering whether to proceed against Germany under Art. 169 in respect of the exclusion of certain categories of workers from its social security system when Ms Nolte, a victim of such exclusion, brought an action seeking the direct enforcement of the equal treatment principle. Had her action been successful, the national legislation would have proved ineffective in the face of the contradictory EC law.

expressed the principle in *Van Gend en Loos*, 'the vigilance of individuals interested in protecting their rights creates an effective control additional to that entrusted by Articles 169 and 170 to the diligence of the Commission and the Member States'.[84]

A provision of EC law which, like Article 12 of the Treaty, is capable of being enforced directly by individuals is referred to in various ways. The ECJ sometimes uses the phrase 'directly applicable' in this context, and at other times uses the expression 'directly effective'. International lawyers also sometimes use a third term, 'self-executing'. Several terms to describe the same concept are at the best of times confusing. In this particular context, however, confusion is even more readily created because the EC Treaty itself, as has already been seen, also refers to 'directly applicable' provisions: Article 189 provides that regulations are 'directly applicable in all member States'. By 'directly applicable' here, it appears to mean 'automatically the law in the Member States'.[85] Whilst this matter is obviously related to the question of whether an individual can enforce the provision in question in a national court, it is not logically identical. Since the EC Treaty is the most authoritative source available here, the present writer therefore prefers to reserve the expression 'directly applicable' to describe the automatic legal force attributed to regulations by Article 189. The phrase 'direct effect' will be taken to refer to those provisions which are capable of enforcement by individuals.[86]

In the early years of its operation, the ECJ dealt with a number of cases in which the major issue was the possible direct effect of a provision of the EC Treaty. It gradually articulated the characteristics required of such a provision to render it 'legally complete' and thus directly effective. That there are four such characteristics was originally made clear in *Van Gend en Loos* and was later explained further through the case law of the ECJ. The provision in question must be clear[87] (since judges in a great variety of national courts will have to apply it and should be able to do so without an

---

[84] [1963] ECR 1, at 13. See also Lecourt, *L'Europe des juges* (Bruylant, Brussels, 1976). Another procedure available in the UK where it is alleged that national legislation infringes the Community's sex discrimination legislation is an action for judicial review at the suit of the Equal Opportunities Commission: *R. v. Secretary of State for Employment, Ex p. EOC* [1994] 2 WLR 409, also discussed in Chaps. 2 and 3. See also Moore, 'Sex Discrimination and Judicial Review' (1994) 19 ELRev. 425, Deakin, 'Part-Time Employment, Qualifying Thresholds and Economic Justification' (1994) 23 ILJ 151, Gordon, 'Judicial Review and Equal Opportunities' [1994] Public Law 217 and Morris, 'Rights and Remedies: Part-Time Workers and the EOC' (1995) 17 JSWFL 1.

[85] See discussion above.

[86] See also Winter, 'Direct Application and Direct Effect: Two Distinct and Different Concepts in Community Law' (1972) 9 CMLRev. 425. Cf. Steiner, 'Direct Applicability in EEC Law—A Chameleon Concept' (1982) 98 LQR 229.

[87] Case 18/71 *Eunomia di Porro v. Italian Ministry of Education* [1971] ECR 811. See also the remarks of Warner AG in Case 131/79 *R. v. Secretary of State for Home Affairs, Ex p. Santillo* [1980] ECR 1585, at 1604.

unacceptable element of variation), unconditional, non-discretionary,[88] and final, in the sense of not requiring any legislative intervention by either the Member States or the Community institutions to make it effective. The fact that a particular Treaty provision is expressly addressed to the Member States does not mean that it necessarily confers any element of discretion on them, and is therefore not enough on its own to preclude direct effect.[89]

(ii) Direct Enforcement of Secondary EC Legislation

Having established the conditions under which Treaty provisions are enforceable directly by individuals, the ECJ then turned to the question of whether, and if so when, the secondary legislation of the EC might also be held to be directly effective. The problems in this area were very much simpler to resolve in the case of regulations than in the case of directives and of decisions. Since regulations are, by Article 189,[90] 'directly applicable' and thus automatically the law in all the Member States without the need for any implementation on the parts of national legislatures, there can be no objection in principle to regulations being, on occasion at least, directly enforceable at the suit of individuals. There is a clear parallel with national parliamentary legislation, some of which is aimed at regulating the position of individual legal persons and so is enforceable by them in the courts, and other aspects of which are not. It thus seemed likely that the ECJ would hold regulations to be capable of producing direct effects, provided that they fulfilled the same four requirements as were applied to Treaty provisions. In practice, because of their very nature as immediately operative legislation, regulations are less likely than Treaty provisions to be too vague or general for direct effect and so the Court has devoted little or no detailed attention to this aspect of their enforcement by individuals. It has, however, held on a number of occasions that regulations are 'capable of creating individual rights which the national court must uphold'.[91]

---

[88] The precise nature of this element has evolved over the years. See in particular Case 28/67 *Molkerei-Zentrale Westfalen/Lippe GmbH* v. *Hauptzollamt Paderborn* [1968] ECR 143, at 152–3, Case 27/67 *Fink-Frucht GmbH* v. *Hauptzollamt Munchen* [1968] ECR 223, Case 57/65 *Luttickev. Hauptzollamt Saarlouis* [1966] ECR 205, Case 13/68 *Salgoil SpA* v. *Italian Ministry of Foreign Trade* [1968] ECR 453, Case 41/74 *Van Duyn* v. *Home Office* [1974] ECR 1337, Case C-271/91 *Marshall* v. *Southampton and South-West Hants Area Health Authority (No. 2)* [1993] ECR I-4367 (discussed in detail in Chap.3), Joined Cases C-6 & 9/90 *Francovich and Bonifaci* v. *Italy* [1991] ECR I-5357 (discussed below) and Case C-91/92 *Faccini Dori* v. *Recreb Srl* [1994] ECR I-3325 (also discussed below).

[89] See e.g. Case 28/67 *Molkerei-Zentrale Westfalen/Lippe GmbH* v. *Hauptzollamt Paderborn* [1968] ECR 143; also Case 43/75 *Defrenne* v. *Sabena* [1976] ECR 455, discussed in detail in Chap. 2.

[90] {Art. 249}.

[91] Case 93/71 *Leonesio* v. *Italian Ministry of Agriculture and Forestry* [1972] ECR 287, at 293. See also Case 43/71 *Politi Sas* v. *Minister of Finance* [1971] ECR 1039, esp. at 1048–9, and Case 41/74 *Van Duyn* v. *Home Office* [1974] ECR 1337, esp. at 1347.

In the cases of directives and decisions, however, the problems were acute. Not being 'directly applicable' under the terms of Article 189, these instruments clearly require legislation by the national authorities of the Member States before they can penetrate into the national legal orders. The intentions of the drafters of the Treaty, it is clear from Article 189, were to make directives and decisions binding legal instruments, but the spheres of obligation which they create were undoubtedly intended to be limited. If directives and decisions are not therefore the law in the Member States until implemented, how could it ever be said that such instruments, taken on their own and in isolation from national implementing legislation, create rights which individuals may enforce in their national courts? It will be recalled that this issue is of special significance in the field of sex discrimination law, where enabling authority for secondary legislation has until recently been sparse and where all the secondary legislation which has been passed to date has taken the form of directives.

Notwithstanding the basic logical obstacle, there is an obvious reason of policy for seeking to hold directives and decisions capable of direct effect. Member States are notoriously slow in legislating to give effect to their EC obligations. The remedy of imposing a penalty on them for non-compliance with a decision of the ECJ was not available until its introduction by the TEU.[92] Thus, at least until recently, the main inducements on States in practice to comply with rulings of the ECJ have been the political embarrassment and corresponding diminution in their negotiating power *vis-à-vis* their partners which would result if they disobeyed them, together with the fear that other Member States might retaliate. This being so, it is understandable that the Court should have been eager to extend the notion of direct effect to directives and decisions: by doing so, it was enabled to rule that that which ought to have been done had in effect been done, even where a Member State was in default and had not in fact passed the required legislation. The argument discussed earlier in the context of the direct effect of Treaty provisions, that the vigilance of individuals provides an important additional means of ensuring that the Member States carry out their EC obligations, is a particularly compelling one where directives and decisions are concerned.

The ECJ, in the early 1970s, seems to have been carried away by the utility of the notion of direct effect as applied to directives and decisions. This led it to pronounce such instruments capable of direct effect without giving sufficient attention to the underlying difficulties of principle. The process began with *Grad* v. *Finanzampt Traunstein*,[93] where it held that a combination of a decision, a Treaty provision, and two directives was directly effective; and *SACE* v. *Italian Ministry of Finance*,[94] in which it held a

---

[92] See Art. 171 {Art. 228}.   [93] Case 9/70 [1970] ECR 825.

[94] Case 33/70 [1970] ECR 1213.

Treaty provision together with a directive to be directly effective. In neither case was there detailed discussion by the Court of the critical question as to how an instrument which was not the law in the Member States could be enforced in the courts of those Member States. For example, in *Grad* the Court held:

However, although it is true that by virtue of Article 189, regulations are directly applicable and therefore by virtue of their nature capable of producing direct effects, it does not follow from this that other categories of legal measures mentioned in that Article can never produce similar effects. In particular, the provision according to which decisions are binding in their entirety on those to whom they are addressed enables the question to be put whether the obligation created by the decision can only be invoked by the Community institutions against the addressee or whether such a right may possibly be exercised by all those who have an interest in the fulfilment of this obligation. It would be incompatible with the binding effect attributed to decisions by Article 189 to exclude in principle the possibility that persons affected may invoke the obligation imposed by a decision. Particularly in cases where, for example, the Community authorities by means of a decision have imposed an obligation on a Member State or all the Member States to act in a certain way, the effectiveness (*l'effet utile*) of such a measure would be weakened if the nationals of that state could not invoke it in the courts and the national courts could not take it into consideration as part of Community law. Although the effects of a decision may not be identical with those of a provision contained in a regulation, this difference does not exclude the possibility that the end result, namely the right of the individual to invoke the measure in the courts, may be the same as that of a directly applicable provision of a regulation.

Article 177, whereby the national courts are empowered to refer to the Court all questions regarding the validity and interpretation of all acts of the institutions without distinction, also implies that individuals may invoke such acts before the national courts. Therefore, in each particular case, one must examine whether the nature, background and wording of the provision in question are capable of producing direct effects in the legal relationships between the addressee of the act and third parties.[95]

Such a statement amounts to little more in reality than a vindication of the principle that directives and decisions *ought* to be capable of direct effect. However, these cases marked the beginning of a series of decisions in which the ECJ upheld the direct effect in particular of the provisions of certain directives. Perhaps the most important case in the series was *Van Duyn* v. *Home Office*,[96] in which the Court upheld the direct effect of Article 3 of Directive 64/221[97] on the exceptions to the principle of the free movement of workers (which is guaranteed by Article 48[98] of the Treaty). The UK government argued that, since Article 189 distinguishes between

---

[95] [1970] ECR 825, at 837.
[96] Case 41/74 [1974] ECR 1337.
[97] OJ Sp. Ed. [1963–4] 117.
[98] {Art. 39}.

the effects of regulations, directives, and decisions, it was to be presumed that the Council, in issuing a directive here rather than a regulation, must have intended that the directive should have an effect other than that of a regulation and accordingly that the former should not be 'directly applicable'.[99] The ECJ nevertheless repeated its remarks in *Grad* almost verbatim and held that the necessity for direct effect in this situation justified the Court in reaching its conclusion.[100]

A significant development as regards the doctrine of direct effect of directives occurred in 1977 in the *Verbond* case.[101] The ECJ was asked about the possible direct effect of a provision of a directive harmonizing turnover taxes. The Court upheld the direct effect of the provision, notwithstanding that the directive had been made under the authority of Article 100[102] of the Treaty. Although the express reasoning of the Court in this case adds nothing to that of its predecessors, the substance of the decision does. In the earlier cases, the enabling Article of the Treaty on which the directive was based had itself always been directly effective; the direct effect of the directive could thus be seen as, in a sense, merely an extension of the Treaty. There can be no question, however, of Article 100 being directly effective: it is exclusively an enabling provision and certainly does not produce any 'final' or complete legal right for individuals. The directive itself therefore, in such a situation, is the source of the whole of the individual's rights. This is, of course, vital in the field of sex discrimination where the existing secondary legislation is based on general and non-directly effective enabling provisions. This fact alone does not present a barrier to the enforcement by an individual of such a directive.

A further important principle which seemed to have been implicitly assumed hitherto was articulated in the *Enka* case.[103] The ECJ held here

[99] This argument was somewhat undermined by the fact that the relevant enabling article in the Treaty, Art. 56(2) {Art. 46(2)}, only permits action here by directive and not by regulation.

[100] Mayras AG tried to be a little more analytical than the Court itself. He pointed out that the Court had said in Case 33/70, the *SACE* case ([1970] ECR 1213, at 1223) that a directive is directly effective 'whenever by its nature the provision establishing (the) obligations is directly applicable'. Mayras AG concluded that: 'when faced with a directive, it is therefore necessary to examine in each case whether the wording, nature and the general scheme of the provisions in question are capable of producing direct effects between the Member States to which the directive is addressed and their subjects' ([1974] ECR 1337, at 1355). For decisions as to the direct effect of provisions of Directive 64/221, see Case 67/74 *Bonsignore* v. *City of Cologne* [1975] ECR 297; Case 48/75 *State* v. *Royer* [1976] ECR 497; Case 30/77 *R* v. *Bouchereau* [1977] 2 CMLR 800; and Case 36/75 *Roland Rutili* v. *Minister of the Interior* [1975] ECR 1219. See also Easson, 'The "Direct Effect" of EEC Directives' (1979) 28 ICLQ 319, and Green, 'Directives, Equity and the Protection of Individual Rights' (1984) 9 ELRev. 295.

[101] Case 51/76 *Verbond* v. *Inspecteur der Invoerrechten en Accijnzen* [1977] ECR 113.

[102] {Art. 94}.

[103] Case 38/77 *Enka BV* v. *Inspecteur der Invoerrechten en Accijnzen* [1977] ECR 2203.

that the provisions of a directly effective directive must take precedence over any national measures which prove to be incompatible with its terms. In particular, an individual can rely on a directive before a national court in order to ask that court to check whether, in the exercise of any discretion left to it by the directive, the Member State has kept within the permissible bounds of that discretion. The directive therefore can act either as a 'sword', giving the individual legal rights where national law does not do so, or as a 'shield', protecting that individual from having national law enforced against him or her where it conflicts with the terms of the directive. Again, this principle is of great potential significance in the field of sex discrimination, where the Member States have a corpus of national laws on the subject, which may on occasion conflict with the EC directives.

Given the policy-driven way in which the ECJ's doctrine of direct effect of directives developed, it hardly seems surprising—at least in retrospect—that serious criticism came to be levelled at it. The clearest and most persuasive criticism came from the French Conseil d'Etat in *Cohn-Bendit* v. *Ministre de l'Intérieure*.[104] Cohn-Bendit, a West German citizen and a leader of the Paris student revolts in 1968, had been deported from France in that same year. In 1975, the Minister of the Interior refused Cohn-Bendit's request to cancel the deportation order without giving any reasons. Cohn-Bendit argued that this action breached Article 6 of Directive 64/221, which required a 'worker' such as himself to be given an explanation for a refusal to allow him to enter another Member State on the ground of public policy.[105] He claimed the right to enforce Article 6 of the directive before the French courts, following the ECJ's decision on the direct effect of this provision in *Rutili*.[106] The case came before the Conseil d'Etat (the highest court in the hierarchy of French administrative courts) when the Minister of the Interior appealed from a decision of the Paris Administrative Tribunal, which had decided to ask for a preliminary ruling from the ECJ. The Commissaire du Gouvernement, M. Genevois, lucidly summed up the logical arguments against the direct effect of directives. The validity of the ECJ's case law in this area did not, he considered, 'spring forcefully to the eye'.[107] In particular, he pointed out that the ECJ had never explained how an unimplemented directive could have an internal legal effect in the Member States. As to the argument so often

---

[104] [1980] 1 CMLR 543.

[105] Art. 6 provides: 'The person concerned shall be informed of the grounds of public policy, public security, or public health upon which the decision taken in his case is based, unless this is contrary to the interests of the security of the State involved.'

[106] Case 36/75 [1975] ECR 1219.

[107] [1980] 1 CMLR 543, at 550.

referred to by the ECJ that the direct effect of directives greatly helps the
enforcement of EC law, he commented:

[According to the third paragraph of Article 189] a directive should limit itself to
formulating an obligation as to the aim to be achieved while leaving to the
Member States the task of laying down the form and the means which will allow it
to be achieved. And one cannot refrain from thinking that it is not only the
effectiveness of the directive that has to be promoted; the effectiveness of the
third paragraph of Article 189 deserves as much and even more to be protected
by reason of the primacy of primary Community law over secondary Community
law.[108]

He also made the point that to permit directives to take direct effect is to
blur the Treaty-made distinction between regulations and directives and
this makes nonsense of the Treaty's stipulation in many instances that the
institutions may act by directive, but not by regulation. The Commissaire's
preferred solution would have been to refer the case to the ECJ and ask it
to reconsider its jurisprudence on the direct effect of directives; to reach a
decision without taking this course and to ignore the existing decisions of
the ECJ, M. Genevois thought 'would be singularly lacking in respect for
the Community Court'.[109] Notwithstanding this advice, the Conseil d'Etat
nevertheless declined to seek a preliminary ruling. Instead, it reversed the
ruling of the Administrative Tribunal. After pointing out that Directive
64/221 is based on Article 56(2) of the Treaty, which authorizes the issue
of directives only and not of regulations, it held:

It follows clearly from Article 189 . . . that while . . . directives bind the Member
States 'as to the result to be achieved' and while, to attain the aims set out in
them, the national authorities are required to adapt the statute law and subordinate legislation and administrative practice of the Member States to the directives
which are addressed to them, those authorities alone retain the power to decide
on the form to be given to the implementation of the directives and to fix
themselves, under the control of the national courts, the means appropriate to
cause them to produce effect in national law. Thus, whatever the detail that they
contain for the eyes of the member States, directives may not be invoked by the
nationals of such states in support of an action brought against an individual
administrative act. It follows that M. Cohn-Bendit could not effectively maintain .
. . that [the deportation] decision infringed the provisions of the directive . . .[110]

The gauntlet was thus thrown down to the ECJ to go back to first
principles and surmount the logical hurdle which it had hitherto avoided.
This it finally did in *Pubblico Ministero* v. *Ratti*,[111] where it held that a

---

[108] Ibid. at 554.
[109] Ibid. at 559.
[110] Ibid. at 562–3. See Simon and Dowrick, 'Effect of EEC Directives in France: The Views
of the Conseil d'Etat' (1979) 95 LQR 376.
[111] Case 148/78 [1979] ECR 1629.

'Member State which has not adopted the implementing measures required by the directive in the prescribed periods may not rely, as against individuals, on its own failure to perform the obligations which the directive entails'.[112] Reischl AG explained the mechanism, which is essentially a procedural one, rather more fully:

It is certainly inappropriate to speak of the direct applicability of a directive. That term is used in Article 189 of the Treaty only for regulations, that is to say, for directly applicable Community legislation, which may also create legal relations between individuals. However, it is clear from the Treaty and has also been emphasized again and again in the case law that a clear distinction must be drawn between regulations and directives, the latter creating obligations only for the Member States. So under no circumstances can one say . . . that directives may also have the contents and effects of a regulation; at most directives may produce similar effects . . . The essence of such effects is that in certain cases, which however constitute the exception to the rule, Member States which do not comply with their obligations under the directive are unable to rely on provisions of the internal legal order which are illegal from the point of view of Community law, so that individuals become entitled to rely on the directive as against the defaulting state and acquire rights thereunder which the national courts must protect. So in such cases one should more properly speak—and that has always happened in the case law—only of the direct effect of directives.[113]

This method of explaining how an unimplemented directive may take direct effect in internal law expressly requires the Member State to be in the wrong; this will not be the case until the time stipulated in the directive for compliance with its terms has run out. It follows that there is an additional requirement to be satisfied before a directive can take direct effect. In the words again of Reischl AG:

[A]s far as directives are concerned, direct effect is hardly an automatic consequence, but merely a reflex effect: it occurs when a Member State does not comply with its obligations and consists in the fact that the state is deprived of the possibility of relying as against individuals and undertakings on its failure to comply with Community law. Accordingly the fact that a directive becomes

---

[112] Ibid. at 1642.

[113] Ibid. at 1650. These remarks were foreshadowed by Warner AG in Case 38/77 *Enka BV* v. *Inspecteur der Invoerrechten en Accijnzen* [1977] ECR 2203, at 2226, when he said: 'Article 189 of the Treaty, although it leaves to each Member State the choice of the "form and methods" whereby it is to give effect to a directive, does not allow it the choice of not giving effect to the directive at all, or of giving effect to it only in pArt. On the contrary, Article 189 says in terms that a directive "shall be binding, as to the result to be achieved, upon each Member State to which it is addressed." A Member State that fails fully to give effect to a directive is in breach of the Treaty, so that to allow it (through its executive or administrative authorities) to rely upon that fact as against a private person in proceedings in its own courts would be to allow it to plead its own wrong.' See also Warner, 'The Relationship between European Community Law and the National Laws of Member States' (1977) 93 LQR 349.

binding on its notification is not sufficient to produce that legal consequence, rather is it the expiry of the period laid down in the directive for the adaptation of national law which is material.[114]

As to the other requirements for direct effect of a directive, he said:

The decisive test is whether it may be said from the nature, general scheme and wording of a directive that it imposes clear, complete and precise obligations on the Member States, does not lay down any conditions other than precisely defined ones and does not leave the Member States any margin of discretion in the performance of the obligations.[115]

In its later decision in *Becker* v. *Finanzampt Munster-Innenstadt*,[116] the ECJ confirmed this approach, saying:

[W]herever the provisions of a directive appear, as far as their subject matter is concerned, to be unconditional and sufficiently precise, those provisions may, in the absence of implementing measures adopted within the prescribed period, be relied upon as against any national provision which is incompatible with the directive or in so far as the provisions define rights which individuals are able to assert against the state.[117]

(iii) Directives and Horizontal Effect

At least one highly significant consequence follows from the ECJ's chosen method of explaining how a directive may take direct effect: it does not provide any mechanism for the enforcement of a provision contained in a directive by an individual *against another individual*. The capacity of EC law to be enforced against an individual, in other words the creation of obligations as well as rights for individuals by EC law, is usually termed 'horizontal direct effect'.[118] It has long been clear that a Treaty provision may create obligations not just for Member States but also for individuals.[119] It was sometimes argued that there was little real difference between a Treaty provision addressed to the Member States, such as Article 119[120] which was held to create obligations for individuals in *Defrenne* v. *Sabena*,[121] and a directive. Furthermore, it was pointed out that anomalies would arise in practice if directives could not be enforced against

---

[114] [1979] ECR 1629, at 1653.

[115] Ibid. at 1650. Cf. the remarks of Warner AG in Case 131/79 *R.* v. *Secretary of State for Home Affairs, Ex p. Santillo* [1980] ECR 1585, at 1609. See also Usher, 'Direct Effect of Directives: Dotting the i's . . .' (1980) 5 ELRev. 470.

[116] Case 8/81 [1982] ECR 53.   [117] Ibid. at 71.

[118] The term 'vertical direct effect' refers to the situation where EC law is enforced against the State or one of its organs.

[119] See e.g. Case 36/74 *Walrave and Koch* v. *Association Union Cycliste Internationale* [1974] ECR 1405.

[120] {Art. 141}.

[121] Case 43/75 [1976] ECR 455, discussed in detail in Chap. 2.

individuals, whilst Treaty provisions could.[122] However, the estoppel-type reasoning adopted in the *Ratti* case is inapposite where a directive is sought to be enforced against an individual: the individual is not at fault in consequence of the non-implementation of the directive by the Member State and thus there can be no question of the individual relying on his or her own wrongdoing before the court.[123] The ECJ perhaps believed that it had made this matter clear in the *Ratti* case and in its later jurisprudence on the direct effect of directives.[124] However, its history of policy-led decisions in this area created a slim possibility that it would find a way around this difficulty and that it would eventually rule in favour of the horizontal direct effect of directives.[125]

That this was not to be was demonstrated by *Marshall* v. *Southampton and South-West Hants Area Health Authority*,[126] where the ECJ held: '[A] directive may not of itself impose obligations on an individual and . . . a provision of a directive may not be relied upon as against such a person . . .'[127] This conclusion was reiterated by the full Court in *Faccini Dori* v. *Recreb Srl*,[128] a stronger case in this respect than *Marshall*[129] since the application of the principle here actually resulted in the plaintiff losing her action. Whilst waiting on Milan station, Ms Faccini Dori had entered into a contract with a private commercial undertaking to take an English language correspondence course. She later sought to cancel this contract and relied

---

[122] Szyszczak has also argued that the legal definition of 'Citizenship of the Union' embraces the imposition of duties on individuals since Article 8(2) {Art. 17} of the Treaty, as amended by the TEU, provides: 'Citizens of the Union shall enjoy the rights conferred by this Treaty and shall be subject to the duties imposed thereby': see 'Future Directions in European Union Social Policy Law' (1995) 24 ILJ 19.

[123] In addition, before the amendment of Art. 191 {Art. 254} by the TEU (as to which see n. 50), directives were not required to be published in the Official Journal and it was argued that grave injustice would result if an individual could be placed under an obligation by an instrument whose terms he or she had no means of discovering.

[124] See e.g. its remarks in *Becker* v. *Finanzampt Munster-Innenstadt* Case 8/81 [1982] ECR 53, quoted above.

[125] For discussion, see Wyatt and Dashwood, *European Community Law* (Sweet & Maxwell, London, 3rd ed. 1993), at 73–6; Arnull, 'Sanctioning Discrimination' (1984) 9 ELRev. 267; Green, 'Directives, Equity and the Protection of Individual Rights' (1984) 9 ELRev. 295; Easson, 'Can Directives Impose Obligations on Individuals?' (1979) 4 ELRev. 67; id., 'The Direct Effect of EEC Directives' (1979) 28 ICLQ 319; and Wyatt, 'The Direct Effect of Community Social Law—Not Forgetting Directives' (1983) 8 ELRev. 241.

[126] Case 152/84 [1986] ECR 723, discussed in detail in Chap. 3. See Foster, 'Equal Treatment and Retirement Ages' (1986) 11 ELRev. 222, and Arnull, 'The Direct Effect of Directives: Grasping the Nettle' (1986) 35 ICLQ 939.

[127] Case 152/84 at 749.

[128] Case C-91/92 [1994] ECR I-3325, noted by Bernard in 'The Direct Effect of Directives: Retreating from *Marshall (No.1)*?' (1995) 24 ILJ 97 and by Robinson in (1995) 32 CMLRev. 629. See also Case 14/86 *Pretore di Salo* v. *Persons Unknown* [1987] ECR 2545, Case C-168/95 *Arcaro* [1996] ECR I-4705 and Case C-192/94 *El Corte Inglés SA* v. *Rivero* [1996] ECR I-1281.

[129] In *Marshall*, the defendants were found to be an organ of the State and the directive could therefore be enforced vertically.

for her right to do so on Directive 85/577 concerning the protection of the consumer in respect of contracts negotiated away from business premises.[130] At the material time, Italy had not taken any steps to implement this directive, even though the time for doing so had expired. Notwithstanding that the relevant provisions of the directive were held to take direct effect, the Court ruled that they could not be relied upon against a private person.[131]

Despite the apparent force of the Court's determination not to accord directives horizontal direct effect, there have nevertheless been some recent decisions which have cast renewed doubt on the scope of the doctrine. A significant characteristic shared by these cases is the involvement in them of two private parties, in addition to the State.[132] Foremost amongst these recent decisions is *CIA Security* v. *Signalson*.[133] CIA marketed an alarm system in Belgium, which had not received type approval under the relevant Belgian legislation. In a commercial dispute with a rival organisation in which it was also argued that CIA was criminally liable, CIA argued that the national legislation enacted during the 1990s was invalid because it had not been communicated to the Commission as required by Directive 83/189.[134] An important issue for the Court was whether CIA could rely on the directly effective notification requirement in its dispute with another individual; if it were allowed to do so, this would be seriously detrimental to that other individual's case. Elmer AG distinguished this situation from that in *Faccini Dori* because, in his view, it was the intention of the present Directive only to impose obligations on the Member States; it did not seek to impose obligations on individuals. He submitted that it was clear that if the State had tried to bring criminal proceedings against CIA for non-compliance with the national legislation, it would have been precluded from so doing by the direct effect of the Directive. He continued:

The fact that the question in this case has been raised in the context of a private action, however, in my view can make no difference whatsoever. It is the State which lays down rules on penalties, prohibitions on marketing etc., and it is the

[130] OJ [1985] L372/31.

[131] The denial by the ECJ of horizontal direct effect to directives has been the subject of considerable criticism. See in particular the submissions of Van Gerven AG in Case C-271/91 *Marshall* v. *Southampton and South-West Hants Area Health Authority (No. 2)* [1993] ECR I-4367, those of Jacobs AG in Case C-316/93 *Vaneetveld* v. *SA Le Foyer* [1994] ECR I-763, at 770–6, and those of Lenz AG in *Faccini Dori* v. *Recreb Srl* op. cit., n. 128. See also Tridimas, 'Horizontal Effect of Directives: a Missed Opportunity?' (1994) 19 ELRev. 621 and Coppel, 'Rights, Duties and the End of *Marshall*' (1994) 57 MLR 859.

[132] So-called 'multi-angular relationships': see Prechal, *Directives in European Community Law* (Oxford University Press, Oxford, 1995), esp. 65–9.

[133] Case C-194/94 [1996] ECR I-2201. See Coppel, 'Horizontal Effect of Directives' (1997) 26 ILJ 69.

[134] OJ [1983] L109/8.

courts who must impose such sanctions regardless of who, under the national rules on procedure, might have brought the case.[135]

The full Court, without referring to *Faccini Dori*, agreed that individuals could rely on the notification requirement contained in the Directive, with the result that the national court must decline to apply a national technical regulation which had not been notified in accordance with the Directive.

Bernáldez[136] concerned civil liability in respect of a road accident caused by a drunk driver. The driver had been held liable, and his insurers absolved from liability, under Spanish legislation. However, the Public Prosecutor appealed against this decision, seeking joint liability for the insurers on the basis of the requirements of two directives. Without making any mention of *Faccini Dori* and basing its reasoning entirely on the policy underlying the directives, namely, the harmonization of insurance and the protection of victims of accidents throughout the Community, the Court held that the directives precluded national legislation from relieving insurers of the obligation to compensate the victims of drunk drivers, although national legislation might provide that in such cases the insurer had a right of recovery against the insured. The net effect of this ruling was thus that, irrespective of the provisions of national law, the directives placed an obligation on a body which was not part of the state (an insurance company) and this obligation could be invoked by another private party (the victim)

In the same vein was *Panagis Pafitis* v. *Trapeza Kentrikis Ellados AE*,[137] concerning an inconsistency between a company law directive[138] and a provision of Greek law which permitted an increase in a company's capital without the consent of the general meeting of its shareholders. Again without making any reference to *Faccini Dori*, the Court held that this national law was precluded by the directive, thereby implying that the directive created rights enforceable against the temporary administrator of the company concerned. Tesauro AG, however, regarded the situation as one of vertical effect, saying that the administrator's appointment and duties were subject to legislative ratification.[139]

Several explanations have been advanced for these, apparently aberrant,

---

[135] [1996] ECR I-2201, at 2226. See also the view of Lord Hoffmann, delivering the judgment of the House of Lords in *R.* v. *Secretary of State for Employment, Ex p. Seymour-Smith* [1997] 1 WLR 473, at 478.

[136] Case C-129/94 [1996] ECR I-1829.

[137] Case C-441/93 [1996] ECR I-1347.

[138] Directive 77/91, OJ [1977] L26/1.

[139] [1996] ECR I-1347, at 1358. For the view that Case C-180/95 *Draehmpaehl* v. *Urania Immobilienservice ohG* [1997] ECR I-2195, discussed in Chap. 3, also constitutes an exception to the principle that directives do not take horizontal effect, see Ward's comments on the case in (1998) 23 ELRev. 65.

decisions. Stuyck maintains[140] that everything depends on the nature of the proceedings pending in the national court; where proceedings are brought by an individual with the aim of enforcing a right against state interference, he concludes that the ECJ allows a directive to confer obligations on individuals. Slot,[141] in commenting on *CIA Security*, has pointed out that the parties in that case did not base their claims directly on the directive and their situation could therefore be distinguished from that of the plaintiffs in *Marshall* and *Faccini Dori*. He reasons that private parties can *indirectly* invoke a directive in order to prevent the application of contradictory national legislation, concluding that '[j]ust as the public authorities cannot enforce national legislation that is contrary to provisions of directives . . ., so individuals cannot achieve such a result'.[142]

It is submitted that these latter views have much to commend them and that further supporting and explanatory dicta are to be found in the ECJ's decisions. It is important to note the Court's formulation that a directive may not 'of itself' impose obligations on an individual.[143] This appears to imply that obligations may nevertheless result for the individual as a more circuitous consequence of a directive. Elucidation may be found in the Court's case law on the supremacy of Community law which emphasises, as has been seen above, the limitation of national sovereignty and legislative power which the ECJ considers to flow from adherence to the EC Treaty. At the very least, this means that national legislation which contradicts EC law in the shape of the Treaty or a regulation is inapplicable; some might go further and argue that it is invalid or *ultra vires*. The effect of this reasoning in the sphere of directives was examined by Mancini AG in *Teuling* v. *Bedrijfsvereniging voor de Chemische Industrie*:[144]

The Commission takes up and develops a view which has received authoritative support in academic circles according to which even where the directive does not contain an express standstill clause, its notification generates a 'blocking effect' inasmuch as it prohibits Member States from adopting measures contrary to its provisions . . . [T]he particular objective of the directive [here] . . . is to harmonize the laws of the Member States by removing existing legislative and administrative differences. Clearly, therefore, the very fact of its adoption places an obligation on the Member States to refrain from introducing new measures which may increase those differences.

---

[140] (1996) 33 CMLRev. 1261.
[141] (1996) 33 CMLRev. 1035.   [142] Ibid. at 1049–50.
[143] Case 152/84 *Marshall* v. *Southampton and South-West Hants Area Health Authority* [1986] ECR 723, at 749. See also Case C-192/94 *El Corte Inglés* v. *Rivero* [1996] ECR I-1281, at 1303, and Joined Cases C-74 & 129/95 *Criminal Proceedings Against X* [1996] ECR I-6609, where the ECJ said that it had consistently held 'that a directive may not of itself create obligations for an individual and that a provision of a directive may not therefore, as such, be relied upon against such a person' (at 6636).
[144] Case 30/85 [1987] ECR 2497, also discussed in Chap. 4.

It may be suggested that such a proposition conflicts with . . . *Ratti* . . . In paragraph 44 of the decision in that case the Court held that until the expiry of the period prescribed for the implementation of the directive 'the Member States remain free in that field'. As with all freedoms, however, that freedom too is subject to limits, and primarily to limits dictated by common sense. Thus there is no doubt that it entails the power to retain in force rules or practices which do not comply with the directive. However, as I have just stated, it is equally certain that such freedom does not include the power to aggravate the defect which the directive is intended to remedy. Indeed it may be that measures adopted during the prescribed period must of necessity be measures intended to transpose the Community provisions. Such measures must at least not conflict with the requirements laid down in those provisions.

That is not, however, sufficient. Further support for the solution which I propose is to be found in the Treaty. The second paragraph of Article 5 requires Member States to abstain from adopting measures liable to 'jeopardize the attainment of the objectives' of the Treaty. The failure to fulfil that general obligation, the lack of co-operation and solidarity which form the substance of that obligation, is in fact the first ground on which the Commission should rely as against Member States which it charges under Article 169 of the EEC Treaty with having disregarded the 'blocking effect', and thus the prohibition of the adoption of retrograde measures, which follows the notification of the directive. Moreover, the Court has often referred to the second paragraph of Article 5 and clarified the limits of Member States' powers in connection with Community measures which are not directives, but which, like them, generate rights and obligations at the end of a prescribed period . . .[145]

These remarks effectively equate the contravention by a Member State of a directive with its contravention of a Treaty provision or regulation. In other words, they suggest that a lightly modified version of the doctrine of supremacy applies to directives: whilst the implementation period for a directive is running, although contradictory domestic law remains applicable, no new contradictory domestic legislation may be enacted and, once the implementation period has elapsed, existing contradictory domestic legislation becomes inapplicable.[146] If this is correct, it means

---

[145] Ibid. at 2513–4. See alsoCase C-262/88 *Barber* v. *Guardian Royal Exchange Assurance Group* [1990] ECR I-1889, in which Van Gerven AG submitted that a directive has, 'as from the time of its adoption and *a fortiori* as from the expiry of the period prescribed for its transposition into national law, become part of Community law and as such takes precedence over *all* provisions of national law' (at 1937; quoted more extensively below). For a limited exception to the 'blocking effect' principle, see Case C-420/92 *Bramhill* v. *Chief Adjudication Officer* [1994] ECR I-3191, discussed in Chap. 4.

[146] See also Case 21/78 *Delkvist* v. *Public Prosecutor* [1978] ECR 2327, where the ECJ held: 'Article 2(2) of the directive provides that pending co-ordination at a later date, each Member State shall determine the provisions relating to good repute which must be satisfied by the applicant. That provision leaves the Member States a wide margin of discretion as to the requirements relating to good repute imposed on applicants . . . A provision of national law whereby an applicant who has a criminal conviction may be regarded as not being of good repute . . . cannot be regarded as exceeding the margin of

that a distinction is rightly to be made between those cases where a directive is the only relevant legal provision and those cases where there is contradictory national law. Where a directive stands alone, *Faccini Dori* makes it clear that a claim cannot succeed where the defendant is a private party. However, where there is contradictory national law, once the period allowed for implementing it has passed, the directive renders that national law unenforceable; this may produce the indirect consequence that a legal obligation flowing from the directive is thereby placed on a private party, as occurred in *CIA Security*, *Bernáldez* and *Pafitis*.

If this reasoning is correct, it means that, even disregarding the principles recently developed by the ECJ to mitigate the lack of horizontal direct effect of directives (discussed below), the scope of the rule that directives cannot take horizontal effect is narrower than was initially appreciated. Once again, because of the important role played by directives in sex equality law, this is especially significant in the present context.

(iv) Meaning of the 'State'

The case law limiting the enforceability of directives against defendants who are private parties has focused attention on the meaning to be attached to the term 'State'. In *Marshall v. Southampton and South-West Hants Area Health Authority*[147] the ECJ indicated the broad stance which it was to take on this matter, saying:

[W]here a person involved in legal proceedings is able to rely on a directive as against the state he may do so regardless of the capacity in which the latter is acting, whether employer or public authority. In either case it is necessary to prevent the state from taking advantage of its own failure to comply with Community law.[148]

Slynn AG explained:

What constitutes 'the state' in a particular national legal system must be a matter for the national court to decide. However (even if contrary to the trend of decisions in cases involving sovereign immunity where the exercise of *imperium* is distinguished from commercial and similar activities), as a matter of Community

---

discretion left to a Member State. Therefore the answer to Questions 3 and 4(a) should be that a statutory provision such as Article 78 of the Danish Penal Code is to be regarded as a provision *validly* enacted by the state within the limits of the directive' (at 2339. Emphasis supplied). See also Prechal, *Directives in European Community Law* (Oxford University Press, Oxford, 1995), esp. 25–6, and the literature further cited therein.

[147] Case 152/84 [1986] ECR 723, discussed in detail in Chap. 3.

[148] Ibid. at 749. See also the submissions of Jacobs AG in Case C-2/94 *Denkavit Internationaal BV v. Kamer* [1996] ECR I-2827, where he said: 'the principle according to which an unimplemented directive can impose obligations only on the state is a principle which has to be understood broadly, if it is not to have arbitrary consequences' (at 2840).

law, where the question of an individual relying upon the provisions of a directive as against the state arises, I consider that the 'state' must be taken broadly, as including all the organs of the state. In matters of employment . . . this means all the employees of such organs and not just the central civil service. I would, thus, reject the argument put to the court that a distinction should be drawn between the state as employer and the state in some other capacity. For present purposes the state is to be treated as indivisible, whichever of its activities is envisaged. It was argued that, where the state is acting as an employer, it should be treated in the same way as a private employer, and that it would be unfair to draw a distinction. I reject that argument. The state can legislate but a private employer cannot. It is precisely because the state can legislate that it can remedy its failure to implement the directive concerned. This consideration puts it at the outset in a fundamentally different position from a private employer, and justifies its being treated differently as regards the right of a person to rely upon the provisions of a directive.[149]

In its decision in *Johnston* v. *Chief Constable of the RUC*[150] the ECJ gave a generous interpretation of the 'State' for the purpose of determining who derives obligations from directives. It held that the Chief Constable of the RUC was part of the apparatus of the 'State', despite the UK government's argument that he was constitutionally independent of the executive. The ECJ ruled:

[I]ndividuals may rely on the directive as against an organ of the state whether it acts *qua* employer or *qua* public authority. As regards an authority like the Chief Constable, it must be observed that . . . the Chief Constable is an official responsible for the direction of the police service. Whatever its relations may be with other organs of the state, such a public authority, charged by the state with the maintenance of public order and safety, does not act as a private individual. It may not take advantage of the failure of the state, of which it is an emanation, to comply with Community law.[151]

The trend continued in *Foster* v. *British Gas plc*.[152] Six female employees of the British Gas Corporation were dismissed in 1985 and 1986 when they reached British Gas's compulsory retirement age of 60 for women. They complained of unlawful sex discrimination, since male employees would not have been required to retire until they reached the age of 65. They could not rely on UK domestic law since, at the date in question, it did not extend to this situation. They argued therefore that EC law governed their case. At the relevant time, British Gas had not yet been privatized.[153] The industrial tribunal dismissed their applications on the ground that Article 5 of the Equal Treatment Directive,[154] which otherwise appeared to govern

---

149 Case 152/84 at 735.   150 Case 222/84 [1986] ECR 1651.
151 Ibid. at 1691.   152 Case 188/89 [1990] ECR I-3313.
153 This occurred in August 1986.
154 Directive 76/207, OJ [1976] L39/40, discussed in detail in Chap 3.

this situation, could only be relied on as against bodies which were 'organs of the State' and that British Gas was not such an 'organ of the State'. The Employment Appeal Tribunal dismissed the applicants' appeal, as did the Court of Appeal[155] which held that the Directive gave rise to legal rights for employees of the State itself and of any organ or emanation of the State, an emanation of the State meaning an independent public authority 'charged by the state with the performance of any of the classic duties of the state, such as the defence of the realm or the maintenance of law and order within the realm'.[156] As a matter of English law the Court of Appeal found that British Gas, a nationalized industry, did not fall within this definition since its powers were not within the province of government. The House of Lords sought a preliminary ruling from the ECJ, asking whether the Directive was enforceable against British Gas. The ECJ delved into the facts in unusual detail for a preliminary ruling and pointed out that, by virtue of the Gas Act 1972, which governed British Gas at the relevant time, British Gas was a statutory corporation responsible for developing and maintaining a system of gas supply in Great Britain, over which it possessed a monopoly. The members of the British Gas Corporation were appointed by the Secretary of State, who also had the power to give the British Gas Corporation directions of a general character in relation to matters affecting the national interest and instructions concerning management. The British Gas Corporation was obliged to submit to the Secretary of State periodic reports (which were laid before Parliament) on the exercise of its functions, its management, and its programmes, and it had the right to submit proposed legislation to Parliament. It was required to run a balanced budget over two successive financial years and the Secretary of State could order it to pay certain funds to the Department of State or to allocate funds to specified purposes. This emphasis on the factual background lent force to the ECJ's ultimate conclusion on the principle of EC law at stake and left no doubt at the end of the day as to how the relevant EC principle was to be applied to the facts of the case. It pointed out that it had:

[H]eld in a series of cases that unconditional and sufficiently precise provisions of a Directive could be relied on against organizations or bodies which were subject to the authority or control of the state or had special powers beyond those which result from the normal rules applicable to relations between individuals. The Court has accordingly held that provisions of a Directive could be relied on against tax authorities (the judgments of 19 January 1982 in Case 8/81 *Becker* . . . and of 22 February 1990 in Case C-221/88 *ECSC* v. *Acciaierie e Ferriere Busseni (in liquidation)* [1990] ECR, local or regional authorities (judgment of 22 June 1989 in Case 103/88 *Fratelli Costanzo* v. *Commune di Milano* [1989] ECR), constitution-

---

[155] [1988] 2 CMLR 697.   [156] Ibid. at 701, *per* Lord Donaldson MR.

ally independent authorities responsible for the maintenance of public order and safety (judgment of 15 May 1986 in Case 222/84 *Johnston* v. *Chief Constable of the RUC* [1986] 3 WLR 1038), and public authorities providing public health services (judgment of 26 February 1986 in Case 152/84 *Marshall* . . .)[157]

From all this, the Court concluded that:

[A] body, whatever its legal form, which has been made responsible, pursuant to a measure adopted by the state, for providing a public service under the control of the state and has for that purpose special powers beyond those which result from the normal rules applicable in relations between individuals is included[158] in any event among the bodies against which the provisions of a Directive capable of having direct effect may be relied upon.[159]

The EC concept of the 'State', for the purposes of the doctrine of horizontal direct effect, is thus characterized by the presence of four factors, namely: (i) the body in question must have been given its powers by the State; (ii) it must have been made responsible for providing a public service; (iii) its powers must be exercisable under the control of the State: and (iv) its powers must be special ones, distinguishable from those possessed by individuals. It is clear therefore that the 'State' in this context has the potential to cover a wide range of organizations and bodies, including for example educational establishments such as schools[160] and

---

[157] [1990] ECR I-3313, at 3348. See also Case 31/87 *Beentjes BV* v. *Holland* [1988] ECR 4635.

[158] In *NUT* v. *Governing Body of St Mary's School* [1997] ICR 334, Schiemann LJ pointed out that it is clear from the use in this passage of the words 'is included' that this was not intended to be an exclusive formula.

[159] [1990] ECR I-3313, at 3348–9, Cf. the Court's statement earlier in its judgment and quoted above in the text, that 'unconditional and sufficiently precise provisions of a directive [can] be relied on against organisations or bodies . . . subject to the authority or control of the state *or* [which have] special powers beyond those which result from the normal rules applicable to relations between individuals' (at 3348. Emphasis supplied).

[160] In *NUT* v. *Governing Body of St Mary's School* [1997] ICR 334, the Court of Appeal held that once a voluntary aided school had decided to enter the State system and had been granted voluntary aided status, its governing body was to be regarded as an emanation of the State. The Court of Appeal considered that it was incorrect to treat the *Foster* criteria in the same way as a statutory definition, and that the main underlying issue was whether the State would benefit from its own wrongdoing in not implementing the relevant directive if the governors were not treated as an emanation of the State. On the facts of this case, if the governors had not been treated as part of the State, the State would have directly benefited financially from its failure properly to transpose the directive. This led the Court to its conclusion despite the fact that not all of the *Foster* criteria were satisfied viz.: (1) the governors had been made responsible pursuant to a statutory instrument; (2) they provided a public service, namely, the provision of education; (3) that service was under the control of the State because of the statutory powers and duties possessed by the Secretary of State and local education authorities; but (4) the governors did not have special powers beyond those applying between individuals because their one distinctive power, that of being able to spend public money, was not the sort of power which the ECJ had had in mind in *Foster*.

universities, local government,[161] the central civil service and nationalized industries.[162] The editors of the *Equal Opportunities Review* have made the point that, even after its privatization, British Gas would still seem to fall within the ECJ's definition of an organ of the State since it continues to have responsibility for providing a public service for which it has special powers and it is under the control of the State at least to some extent since it is a creature of statute.[163] It is perhaps not an exaggeration to comment that this issue remains a minefield, despite the efforts of the ECJ in *Foster* to articulate its concept of the State. Its formulation requires further elaboration, in particular as regards the meaning of 'public service', 'control of the State' and 'special powers'. The matter of course is of critical importance in sex discrimination cases where, if an equality directive has not been properly implemented by a Member State, the success or failure of the claim may depend on whether the employer is or is not to be regarded as an organ of the State.[164]

The policy of the ECJ in this area has clearly been to try to compensate for the fact that directives may not be enforced, on their own, against anybody except for an organ of the State by giving the State as generous as possible a definition. However, this has in turn led to a certain dilution of the logic behind the doctrine of direct effect. As has been seen, the mechanism permitting the enforcement of a directive against the State is the estoppel principle, whereby the State is denied the chance to assert that it has not legislated in circumstances in which it should have legislated. The further that the concept of 'organ of the State' moves from the central, legislation-controlling limbs of government, the more fictitious becomes this estoppel mechanism.[165] Nevertheless, in purely pragmatic terms, it is undeniable that any such development is in the interests of potential sex discrimination claimants.

---

[161] Case 103/88 *Fratelli Costanzo* v. *Commune di Milano* [1989] ECR 1839. In *NUT* v. *Governing Body of St Mary's School* [1997] ICR 334, Schiemann LJ confirmed that, in his judgment, local authorities were certainly emanations of the State.

[162] Cf. *Doughty* v. *Rolls-Royce plc* [1992] ICR 538.

[163] (1990) 33 EOR 40.

[164] For discussion of the approach of the UK courts in sex discrimination cases to the public/private employer dichotomy, see Arnull, 'The Incoming Tide: Responding to *Marshall*' (1987) Public Law 383. See also Curtin, 'The Province of Government: Delimiting the Direct Effect of Directives in the Common Law Context' (1990) 15 ELRev. 195.

[165] See the comments of Van Gerven AG in this context in both Case C-262/88 *Foster* and *Barber* v. *Guardian Royal Exchange Assurance Group* [1990] ECR I-1889. In the latter case, he said: 'individuals . . . are . . . allowed to rely on [a Member State's] default vis-à-vis independent public authorities of the Member State which are not themselves responsible for failure of the latter to transpose a directive into national law. The *nemo auditor* principle has thus acquired a far-reaching ambit (not connected with personal default), with the result that the directive has to a degree been endowed with effect with regard to third parties, in particular to the detriment of the aforesaid public authorities' (at 1938).

(v) Mitigating the Lack of Horizontal Enforceability of Directives

The ECJ has developed two extremely significant lines of jurisprudence whose ostensible policy is to mitigate the failure of directives to take horizontal direct effect. The first is the so-called doctrine of 'indirect effect'. This is the principle that, even where the defendant to an action is not part of the State, so that the directive itself cannot be enforced directly against that person, the terms of the directive may nevertheless be of assistance to the claimant. This is because the wording of the directive must be taken into account by the national court when it is interpreting any national law dealing with the same subject matter; if the national court finds an ambiguity in that national law, then that must be resolved so as to make the national law conform to the directive wherever possible. As the ECJ explained in *Von Colson and Kamann* v. *Land Nordrhein Westfalen*:[166]

The Member States' obligation arising from a directive to achieve the result envisaged by the directive and their duty under Article 5 of the Treaty to take all appropriate measures, whether general or particular, to ensure the fulfilment of that obligation, is binding on all the authorities of Member States including, for matters within their jurisdiction, the courts. It follows that, in applying the national law and in particular the provisions of a national law specifically introduced in order to implement Directive 76/207, national courts are required to interpret their national law in the light of the wording and the purpose of the directive in order to achieve the result referred to in Article 189(3).[167]

A claimant may thus indirectly benefit from the terms of a directive, in particular where national law has been enacted in order to implement it and that national law is susceptible of interpretation in accordance with it.[168] This principle applies even where the time given to the States for compliance with the directive has not yet run out.[169]

Controversy, however, arose where national law dealing with the subject-matter of the directive pre-dated that directive, so that it could not properly be said to have been enacted in response to the directive. The wording adopted by the ECJ in the *Von Colson* case in the passage quoted above is broad enough to encompass this situation, since the Court refers to applying 'national law' generally so as to conform with a directive.[170] However, this aspect of the judgment was technically *obiter* since the legislation in question in that case had in fact been adopted in response to

[166] Case 14/83 [1984] ECR 1891.
[167] Ibid. at 1909.
[168] See also Case 262/84 *Beets-Proper* v. *Van Lanschot Bankiers NV* [1986] ECR 773; Case 80/86 *Public Prosecutor* v. *Kolpinghuis Nijmegen BV* [1987] ECR 3969; *Litster* v. *Forth Dry Dock and Engineering Co. Ltd.* [1989] ICR 341; and Arnull, 'Some More Equal than Others?' (1986) 11 ELRev. 229.
[169] Case 80/86 *Public Prosecutor* v. *Kolpinghuis Nijmegen BV* [1987] ECR 3969.
[170] See also the Court's remarks in Case 80/86, op. cit., n. 169.

the directive. In *Marshall* v. *Southampton and South-West Hants Area Health Authority*, Slynn AG commented:

[W]here legislation is adopted to implement a directive, or consequent upon a Treaty obligation, national courts should seek so far as possible to construe the former in such a way as to comply with the latter. To construe a pre-existing statute . . . in order to comply with a subsequent directive, which the legislature or executive has not implemented, in breach of its obligation, when it has a discretion as to the form and method to be adopted, is, in my view, wholly different. I am not satisfied that it is a rule of Community law that national courts have a duty to do so—unless it is clear that the legislation was adopted specifically with a proposed directive in mind.[171]

Mischo AG agreed with these remarks in *Public Prosecutor* v. *Kolpinghuis Nijmegen BV*[172] and also addressed himself to the question whether Community law in fact even *permits* pre-existing national legislation to be interpreted in the light of a directive. He concluded:

There is no principle of Community law obliging a national court to be guided by the provisions of a directive which is applicable but which has not yet been implemented by the Member State in question in order to interpret a rule of national law which is insufficiently precise. The question whether it may do so in order to confirm the interpretation obtained from purely national elements of appraisal must be resolved on the basis of the national rules of interpretation. On the other hand, a court cannot rely on such a directive to alter, to the detriment of the individual, the interpretation obtained from national elements of appraisal.[173]

This reasoning was based on the inability of directives to produce obligations for individuals, whether directly or indirectly, and it is arguably incorrect. Since newly passed national legislation could create obligations for individuals, it is unclear why pre-existing national legislation should not be capable of being similarly construed. Van Gerven AG took a very different view of the matter in *Barber* v. *Guardian Royal Exchange Assurance Group*,[174] where he said:

[A]n interpretation [of national law] in conformity with [a] directive may not be restricted to the interpretation of national legislation subsequent to the adoption of the directive concerned or national legislation specifically enacted for transposing the directive into national law . . . Frequently, national implementing legislation will be involved as in *Von Colson* but that need not be the case. It is difficult to justify a restriction of the requirement of interpretation in conformity with the directive to the implementing legislation itself (quite apart from the difficulty of determining whether or not a given national provision has been

---

[171] Case 152/84 [1986] ECR 723, at 733.
[172] Case 80/86 [1987] ECR 3969.   [173] Ibid. at 3980.
[174] Case C-262/88 [1990] ECR I-1889, discussed in detail in Chaps. 2 and 3.

enacted for the purpose of transposing a directive into national law) since the directive has, as from the time of its adoption and *a fortiori* as from the expiry of the period prescribed for its transposition into national law, become part of Community law and as such takes precedence over *all* provisions of national law.[175]

The matter was resolved by the decision of a chamber of the ECJ in *Marleasing SA* v. *La Comercial Internacional de Alimentacion SA*[176] in which it was held that, in applying national law, whether prior to or subsequent to a relevant directive, a national court is obliged to interpret the national law so far as possible[177] in the light of the wording and purpose of the directive.[178] Such a conclusion is not lacking in logic to the extent that some have hitherto assumed: a Member State might deliberately draft national legislation in broad terms specifically in order that its meaning should be developed by later EC legislation. Alternatively, a Member State might leave an old Act on the statute book even after the passage of an EC directive because it believed that statute to be capable of being construed in accordance with the directive and therefore to constitute compliance by the State with its EC obligations.[179] The ECJ added in *Wagner Miret* v. *Fondo de Garantia Salarial*[180] that, when interpreting and applying national law, 'every national court must presume that the state had the intention of fulfilling entirely the obligations arising' from a directive.[181]

Exceptionally, however, the ECJ has held that a directive 'cannot, of itself and independently of a national law adopted by a Member State for

---

[175] CasemC-262/88 at 1936–7. Differing views on this question were voiced by the House of Lords at this time. In *Garland* v. *British Rail* [1982] 2 WLR 918, Lord Diplock (delivering the opinion of the House) envisaged the possibility of the meaning of the Sex Discrimination Act 1975 being influenced by the Equal Treatment Directive of 1976. However, in *Duke* v. *GEC Reliance Ltd* [1988] 2 WLR 359, the House refused to take this course. See also *Finnegan* v. *Clowney Youth Training Ltd* [1990] 2 WLR 1305, where the Northern Ireland Court of Appeal and the House of Lords refused to refer effectively the same issue to the ECJ.

[176] Case C-106/89 [1990] ECR I-4135, noted by Stuyck and Wytinck in (1991) 28 CMLRev. 205 and by Maltby in '*Marleasing*: What is All the Fuss About?' (1993) 109 LQR 301.

[177] But note that much play has been made in the literature of the fact that the Court was inconsistent in its use of the phrase 'as far as possible'; contrast paragraphs 8 and 13 of the judgment.

[178] This principle was accepted and applied by the House of Lords in *Webb* v. *EMO (Air Cargo) Ltd* [1995] 4 All ER 577, commented on by Szyszczak in 'Pregnancy and Sex Discrimination' (1996) 21 ELRev. 79 and *id* in 'Pregnancy Discrimination' (1996) 59 MLR 589 and also by Deards in 'Indirect Effect After *Webb* v. *EMO (Air Cargo) Ltd*: How Must National Law be Interpreted to Comply with a Directive?' (1996) 2 EPL 71. See also *Chessington World of Adventures Ltd* v. *Reed* [1997] IRLR 556.

[179] See Ellis, 'EEC Law and the Interpretation of Statutes' (1988) 104 LQR 379, Arnull, 'The *Duke* Case: An Unreliable Precedent' (1988) Public Law 313 and id 'When is Pregnancy Like an Artificial Hip?' (1992) 17 ELRev. 265.

[180] Case C-334/92 [1993] ECR I-6911.

[181] Ibid. at 6932.

its implementation, have the effect of determining or aggravating the liability in criminal law of persons who act in contravention of the provisions of that directive'.[182] In *Public Prosecutor* v. *Kolpinghuis Nijmegen BV*,[183] the Court held that the: 'obligation on the national court to refer to the content of the directive when interpreting the relevant rules of its national law is limited by the general principles of law which form part of Community law and in particular the principles of legal certainty and non-retroactivity . . .'[184] In *Criminal Proceedings Against X*,[185] it added:

> More specifically, in a case such as that in the main proceedings, which concerns the extent of liability in criminal law arising under legislation adopted for the specific purpose of implementing a directive, the principle that a provision of the criminal law may not be applied extensively to the detriment of the defendant, which is the corollary of the principle of legality in relation to crime and punishment and more generally of the principle of legal certainty, precludes bringing criminal proceedings in respect of conduct not clearly defined as culpable by law. That principle, which is one of the general legal principles underlying the constitutional traditions common to the Member States, has also been enshrined in various international treaties . . .[186]

The principle of interpretation of domestic law so as, so far as possible, to make it coincide with the requirements of a directive has been extended by the ECJ to a recommendation. This is of particular significance in the light of the fact that, according to Article 189[187] of the EC Treaty, a recommendation has no binding legal force. In *Grimaldi* v. *Fonds des Maladies Professionelles*,[188] the Court held that, even though the recommendation there in question produced no direct rights on which individuals could rely in their national courts, it did not follow that a recommendation had no legal effect whatsoever. It ruled that:

> [N]ational courts are bound to take . . . [r]ecommendations into consideration in order to decide disputes submitted to them, in particular where they clarify the interpretation of national provisions adopted in order to implement them or where they are designed to supplement binding Community provisions.[189]

The expression 'soft law' has been coined by some writers to describe those EC instruments which are not themselves binding but which act as aids to construction for national courts.[190] Wellens and Borchardt have

---

[182] Case 14/86 *Pretore di Salo* v. *Persons Unknown* [1987] ECR III-2545, at 2570. See also Case C-168/95 *Arcaro* [1996] ECR I-4705.

[183] Case 80/86 [1987] ECR 3969.   [184] Ibid. at 3986.

[185] Joined Cases C-74 & 129/95 [1996] ECR I-6609.

[186] Ibid. at 6637.   [187] {Art. 249}.

[188] Case 322/88 [1989] ECR 4407.

[189] Ibid. at 4421.

[190] See e.g. 'EEC Sexual Harassment Resolution' (1990) 32 EOR 28. See further Klabbers 'Informal Instruments Before the European Court of Justice' (1994) 31 CMLRev. 997.

defined soft law as rules which, although not formally binding, have as their aim and outcome an influence on the behaviour of the Community institutions, the Member States and on individuals and undertakings.[191]

The second major milestone in the ECJ's efforts to mitigate the lack of horizontal direct effect of directives was its decision in *Francovich and Bonifaci* v. *Italy*.[192] This proclaimed the liability in damages as a matter of Community law of a Member State where loss is caused to an individual by the State's non-implementation of a directive provided that the directive prescribes the grant of rights to individuals, the content of those rights is identifiable on the basis of the provisions of the directive itself, and there is a causal link between the breach of the State's obligation and the loss suffered by the individual.[193] The directive in this instance was held not to take direct effect for want of precision,[194] but it would appear that the consequences for the individual claimants and the Member State would have been identical even had it done so, since the defendants to the action were not organs of the state and no action could therefore have succeeded on the basis of direct enforcement of the instrument.[195] The principle was formulated in terms of the liability of a Member State for loss resulting from breach of *any* of its Community obligations and was not restricted to the situation of non-implementation of a directive;[196] such a principle was held to be 'inherent in the system of the Treaty'.[197] In *Francovich*, the Member State's non-implementation of the relevant directive was patently

---

[191] Wellens and Borchardt, 'Soft Law in the European Community' (1989) 14 ELRev. 267.

[192] Cases C-6 and 9/90 [1991] ECR I-5357, noted by Bebr in (1992) 29 CMLRev. 557, by Curtin in 'State Liability under Community Law: A New Remedy for Private Parties' (1992) 21 ILJ 74, by Szyszczak in (1992) 55 MLR 690, and by Parker in 'State Liability in Damages for Breach of Community Law' (1992) 108 LQR 181. See also Craig, '*Francovich*, Remedies and the Scope of Damages Liability' (1993) 109 LQR 595, Steiner, 'From Direct Effects to *Francovich*: Shifting Means of Enforcement of Community Law' (1993) 18 ELRev. 3, and Ross, 'Beyond *Francovich*' (1993) 56 MLR 55.

[193] As Tesauro AG commented in his submissions in Joined Cases C-46 and 48/93 *Brasserie du Pêcheur* v. *Germany* and *R* v. *Secretary of State for Transport, Ex p. Factortame* [1996] ECR I-1029 (discussed further below), this principle has its origins, as has the doctrine of direct effect, in the ECJ's desire to ensure the effective implementation of Community law.

[194] Thus giving rise to speculation as to the precise meaning of the requirement set out by the Court in *Francovich* that the directive must envisage the grant of rights to individuals. See further Joined Cases C-178, 179, 188, 189 & 190/94 *Dillenkofer* v. *Germany* [1996] ECR I-4845, discussed below.

[195] *Francovich* has now, however, entered the ranks of ground-breaking decisions whose own protagonists proved unable to take advantage of the new principle expressed: the directive in question was found not to include within its terms Mr Francovich's employer. See Case C-479/93 *Francovich* v. *Italy* [1995] ECR I-3843.

[196] See also *Garden Cottage Foods Ltd* v. *Milk Marketing Board* [1984] 1 AC 130, *Bourgoin* v. *Ministry of Agriculture and Fisheries* [1985] 3 All ER 585, (especially the dissenting judgment of Oliver LJ) and *Kirklees Metropolitan Borough Council* v. *Wickes Building Supplies Ltd* [1992] 3 WLR 170.

[197] [1991] ECR I-5357, at 5414.

culpable since the period for implementation had expired many years before the action and the State had been successfully prosecuted before the ECJ by the Commission in respect of its inaction. The unanswered question posed was thus whether any, and if so what, lesser level of 'fault' on the part of the Member State would be sufficient to trigger such liability. The ECJ addressed this matter in *Brasserie du Pêcheur* v. *Germany* and *R.* v. *Secretary of State for Transport, Ex p. Factortame*.[198] In both cases, the Court had already held that the relevant Member State's actions breached the Treaty. The Court explained that the conditions under which a Member State incurs liability for damage caused to individuals by a breach of Community law cannot, in the absence of particular justification, differ from those governing the liability of the Community in similar circumstances, since the legal position of the individual should not depend on who is the author of the breach.[199] It went on to draw a distinction between cases where the Member State enjoys little or no discretion, such as where it is required to implement a directive, and those in which it has a wide discretion. Where there is a wide discretion, the parallel with Community liability for normative injustice requires that three conditions must be met in order for there to be state liability to an individual: the rule of law infringed must be intended to confer rights on individuals; the breach must be sufficiently serious; and there must be a direct causal link between the State's breach and the individual's damage. As to the requirement that the breach be sufficiently serious, the decisive test is said to be whether the State has manifestly and gravely disregarded the limits on its discretion. The Court went on to spell out that:

The factors which the competent court may take into consideration include the clarity and precision of the rule breached, the measure of discretion left by that rule to the national . . . authorities, whether the infringement and the damage caused was intentional or involuntary, whether any error of law was excusable or inexcusable, the fact that the position taken by a Community institution may have

---

[198] Joined Cases C-46 and 48/93 [1996] ECR I-1029, noted by Oliver in (1997) 34 CMLRev. 635. See also Craig, 'Once More Into the Breach: The Community, the State and Damages Liability' (1997) 113 LQR 67.

[199] A related, but still unresolved, issue is whether an individual is similarly liable in damages where he or she has caused loss to another by infringing a directly effective Treaty provision. In Case C-128/92 *Banks Ltd* v. *British Coal Corporation* [1994] ECR I-1209, Van Gerven AG submitted: '[T]he right to obtain reparation in respect of loss and damage sustained as a result of an undertaking's infringement of Community competition rules which have direct effect is based on the Community legal order itself. Consequently, as a result of its obligation to ensure that Community law is fully effective and to protect the rights thereby conferred on individuals, the national court is under an obligation to award damages for loss sustained by an undertaking as a result of the breach by another undertaking of a directly effective provision of Community competition law' (at p. 1251). See also Van Gerven, 'Bridging the Unbridgable: Community and National Tort Laws After *Francovich* and *Brasserie*' (1996) 45 ICLQ 507.

contributed towards the omission, and the adoption or retention of national measures or practices contrary to Community law.

On any view, a breach of Community law will clearly be sufficiently serious if it has persisted despite a judgment finding the infringement in question to be established, or a preliminary ruling or settled case-law of the Court on the matter from which it is clear that the conduct in question constituted an infringement.[200]

The Court added that such liability on the part of a Member State can be incurred through the actions of its legislature and that it makes no difference of principle whether or not the Community provisions breached take direct effect. The amount of reparation payable must be commensurate with the loss suffered by the individual;[201] it appears that, although the individual must mitigate the damage, damages are obtainable for loss of profit. Further, where exemplary damages would be obtainable in a similar claim under domestic law, they must be obtainable in a claim against the State for a breach of Community law.[202]

R. v. HM Treasury, Ex p. British Telecommunications plc[203] provided an illustration of a situation in which a Member State's breach of Community law was insufficiently grave to found a *Francovich* claim. After reiterating that it is normally for the national courts to determine this matter, the ECJ held that in this instance it was in possession of all the necessary information to enable it to assess the gravity of the State's conduct itself. The allegation was that the UK had incorrectly implemented a directive and had caused consequential loss to BT. The Court held, however, that the relevant directive was imprecisely worded and reasonably capable of bearing the meaning which the UK had in good faith given to it,[204] albeit that this interpretation later turned out to be erroneous. It was specifically noted that other Member States had shared the UK's interpretation of the directive, which was not manifestly contrary to its wording or objective, and that there was no case law of the Court to provide guidance as to its correct meaning.

This decision is to be contrasted with those in *R. v. Ministry of Agriculture, Fisheries and Food, Ex p. Hedley Lomas (Ireland) Ltd*[205] and *Dillenkofer* v.

---

[200] [1996] ECR I-1029, at 1150.

[201] Tesauro AG explained that the compensation awarded must be 'real and effective'; furthermore, it must be quantified so as to restore the situation to that which would have obtained had the infringement not taken place, at least in financial terms (at 1123). Such a test, of course, accords with the usual measure of tortious damages in English law.

[202] But see *R. v. Secretary of State for Transport, Ex p. Factortame (No.5)*, The Times, 11 Sept. 1997.

[203] Case C-392/93 [1996] ECR I-1631, noted by Oliver in (1997) 34 CMLRev. 658.

[204] The concept of good faith as applied to a State and its legislative machinery might be said to be somewhat elusive.

[205] Case C-5/94 [1996] ECR I-2553, noted by Oliver in (1997) 34 CMLRev. 666. For further discussion of the *Brasserie, Factortame, BT*, and *Hedley Lomas* cases, see Emiliou, 'State Liability Under Community Law: Shedding More Light on the *Francovich* Principle' (1996) 21 ELRev. 399.

Germany.[206] In the former, the UK had refused a licence for the export of live sheep for slaughter in a specified Spanish slaughterhouse because it suspected that the slaughterhouse in question was in breach of a directive on animal welfare. This was held to be a breach of Article 34[207] on the free movement of goods and could not be justified by reference to Article 36,[208] which allows exceptions 'for the protection of health and life of . . . animals', because one Member State is not permitted to adopt unilateral measures designed to obviate a breach of Community law by another Member State. In relation to the issue of whether this conduct was sufficiently serious to provide the basis for a claim in damages against the UK, the Court held:

[W]here, at the time when it committed the infringement, the Member State in question was not called upon to make any legislative choices and had only considerably reduced, or even no, discretion, the mere infringement of Community law may be sufficient to establish the existence of a sufficiently serious breach. In that respect, in this particular case, the UK was not even in a position to produce any proof of non-compliance with the directive by the slaughter-house . . .[209]

In *Dillenkofer*, the main issue was the liability of Germany to would-be holidaymakers who had lost money when certain tour operators became insolvent; had Germany implemented a 1990 directive on package travel by the date stipulated, national law would have been in place guaranteeing the reimbursement of the plaintiffs. Germany argued that, since in its view the period provided for transposition of the directive was inadequate, it was not liable because its breach of Community law had not been manifest and grave; late transposition in itself, Germany maintained, was not enough to render a State liable in damages. The ECJ rejected these submissions, explaining that there was no inconsistency as between its decisions in *Francovich* and the later cases:

[T]he condition that there should be a sufficiently serious breach, although not expressly mentioned in *Francovich*, was nevertheless evident from the circumstances of that case. When the Court held that the conditions under which state liability gives rise to a right to reparation depended on the nature of the breach of Community law causing the damage, that meant that those conditions are to be applied according to each type of situation. On the one hand, a breach of Community law is sufficiently serious if a Community institution or a Member State, in the exercise of its rule-making powers, manifestly and gravely disregards

---

[206] Joined Cases C-178, 179, 188, 189 and 190/94 [1996] ECR I-4845, noted by Oliver in (1997) 34 CMLRev. 675.
[207] {Art. 29}.
[208] {Art. 30}.
[209] [1996] ECR I-2553, at 2613–4.

the limits on those powers . . . On the other hand, if, at the time when it committed the infringement, the Member State in question was not called upon to make any legislative choices and had only considerably reduced, or even no, discretion, the mere infringement of Community law may be sufficient to establish the existence of a sufficiently serious breach . . .

So where, as in *Francovich*, a Member State fails, in breach of the third paragraph of Article 189 of the Treaty, to take any of the measures necessary to achieve the result prescribed by a directive within the period it lays down, that Member State manifestly and gravely disregards the limits on its discretion.

Consequently, such a breach gives rise to a right to reparation on the part of individuals if the result prescribed by the directive entails the grant of rights to them, the content of those rights is identifiable on the basis of the provisions of the directive and a causal link exists between the breach of the state's obligation and the loss and damage suffered by the injured parties: no other conditions need be taken into consideration.[210]

The questions then arose of whether the directive entailed the grant of rights to individuals and, if so, whether the content of those rights was sufficiently identifiable. The Court held that the purpose of the directive was the protection of consumers[211] and that the fact that it might also have other objectives was irrelevant:

[I]t must be concluded that the result prescribed by . . . the directive entails the grant to package travellers of rights guaranteeing the refund of money that they have paid over and their repatriation in the event of the organizer's insolvency.[212]

These rights were fully defined in the directive, as were the consumers it was intended to protect. It made no difference that the directive left the Member State considerable latitude as to how to achieve its results. The content of the rights conferred was therefore sufficiently identifiable.[213]

---

[210] [1996] ECR I-4845, at 4879–80. See Hervey, '*Francovich* Liability Simplified' (1997) 26 ILJ 74.

[211] If such a general aim is sufficient for this purpose, it being clear from *Francovich* that the instrument need not be precise enough to take direct effect, it is difficult to imagine a provision which would *not* entail the grant of rights to individuals. All legislation is surely enacted with the ultimate goal of benefiting human beings.

[212] [1996] ECR I-4845, at 4883.

[213] See also Tridimas, 'Member State Liability in Damages' [1996] CLJ 412. Considerable uncertainty remains in the UK as to the relevant procedure applicable to *Francovich* actions: are they, for example, subject to the three month limitation period for public law claims or should they be equated to private law claims and thus subject to a six year limitation period? What is the appropriate forum for such an action? For further discussion of the enforcement in the UK of the principles analysed in this section, see Convery, 'State Liability in the United Kingdom after *Brasserie du Pêcheur*' (1997) 34 CMLRev. 603 and Hervey and Rostant, 'After *Francovich*: State Liability and British Employment Law' (1996) 25 ILJ 259.

(vi) The Need to Implement Directives

In the light of all that has now been decided about the direct effect of directives, it might appear that the distinction between regulations and directives has been almost entirely eroded and that, in particular, the requirement of the legislative implementation of directives—at least where those directives take direct effect—has now been dispensed with. After all, if a directive is immediately enforceable by individuals in the national courts, why should the Member States go to the trouble of legislating to give it legal force? One reason for doubting the validity of this argument has already been discussed: a directive cannot of itself take horizontal direct effect so that, in the absence of national legislation, its provisions will not be fully effective and enforceable by everybody who falls within its purview. In order to render it fully enforceable against persons other than the State (where this is envisaged by the terms of the directive itself), national legislation will be required.[214]

Further reasoning supporting the continuing necessity to implement even directly effective directives was provided by the ECJ in *Commission* v. *Belgium*.[215] It held that legal certainty and clarity require that national legislation be enacted because individuals cannot know for sure (without legal proceedings) that the directive is directly effective and they may easily become confused, if similar national legislation remains in force, as to which law actually governs their situation. In addition, without national implementing legislation, it becomes impossible for the Commission to check whether directives are actually being applied in a given Member State. It is therefore necessary for the Member State not only to legislate to implement all directives, but to legislate by means of provisions which are of the same type as those used by the Member State to regulate similar matters domestically. Thus, for example, if ministerial regulations are the normal method in the UK for regulating a particular matter, then an EC directive in the same area should also be implemented by ministerial regulations so as to avoid confusion to the ordinary person. The direct effect of directives is seen by the ECJ as providing only an essential safety net or 'minimum guarantee' where the Member State does not carry out its EC obligations. Furthermore, the Court added that domestic political difficulties, which render it difficult or impossible for a Member State's government to procure the necessary legislation to implement a directive,

---

[214] Query whether a judicial decision could ever suffice as the entire implementation mechanism for a directive; the ECJ left this question open in Joined Cases C-178, 179, 188, 189 & 190/94 *Dillenkofer* v. *Germany* [1996] ECR I-4845. In Case C-382/92 *Commission* v. *UK* [1994] ECR I-2435, however, the ECJ accepted that the scope of national laws (and thus their compatibility with EC law) must be assessed in the light of the interpretation given to them by national courts.

[215] Case 102/79 [1980] ECR 1473.

are not a sufficient excuse. The Member State remains in default until such time as the implementing measures are enacted.[216]

The protection of individuals and their legal rights was also stressed by the ECJ in *Commission* v. *Denmark*,[217] where it was successfully alleged by the Commission that Denmark had not implemented the Equal Pay Directive[218] properly: the relevant domestic law provided only for equal pay for the 'same work' performed by men and women, whereas the directive requires equal pay also where the work performed by the two sexes is of 'equal value'. The ECJ held:

In that respect the Danish law in question does not exhibit the clarity and precision necessary for the protection of the workers concerned. Even accepting the assertions of the Danish government that the principle of equal pay for men and women, in the broad sense required by the Directive, is implemented in collective agreements, it has not been shown that the same implementation of that principle is guaranteed for workers whose rights are not defined in such agreements. Since those workers are not unionized and work in small or medium-sized businesses, particular care must be taken to protect their rights under the directive. The principles of legal certainty and the protection of individuals thus require an unequivocal wording which would give the persons concerned a clear and precise understanding of their rights and obligations and would enable the courts to ensure that those rights and obligations are observed.[219]

It is thus absolutely clear now that, even where a directive takes direct effect, its provisions must nevertheless be carried into full legal force by appropriate implementing measures enacted by the Member States.

(vii) The Principle of Procedural Autonomy

A further issue in relation to direct effect, which is important in practice and has been discussed by the ECJ on a number of occasions, is precisely what is meant when it is said that a provision is 'enforceable' by individuals. Are particular means of enforcement or particular remedies required, and what procedural rules apply to the enforcement? As will be seen in Chapters 2 and 3, the Equal Pay Directive[220] and the Equal Treatment Directive[221] make special provision for the enforcement of their own clauses. However, the ECJ has commented in other contexts on the consequences of direct effect in general terms. In *Rewe-Zentralfinanz, eG and Rewe-Zentral AG* v. *Landwirtschaftskammer für das Saarland*,[222] the ECJ was

---

[216] Similarly, the ECJ held in Case 48/75 *State* v. *Royer* [1976] ECR 497 that '[t]he freedom left to the member States by Article 189 as to the choice of form and methods of implementation of directives does not affect their obligation to choose the most appropriate forms and methods to ensure the effectiveness of the directives' (at 519).

[217] Case 143/83 [1985] ECR 427, discussed further in Chap. 2.

[218] Directive 75/117, OJ [1975] L45/19, discussed in detail in Chap. 2.

[219] [1985] ECR 427, at 435.   [220] Directive 75/117, OJ [1975] L45/19.

[221] Directive 76/207, OJ [1976] L39/40.   [222] Case 33/76 [1976] 2 ECR 1989.

asked whether a time-bar prescribed by national limitation legislation could operate to preclude the recovery of sums paid contrary to a directly effective provision of EC law. In holding that such a situation did not contravene EC law, the ECJ commented:

Applying the principle of co-operation laid down in Article 5 of the Treaty, it is the national courts which are entrusted with ensuring the legal protection which citizens derive from the direct effect of the provisions of Community law. Accordingly, in the absence of Community rules on this subject, it is for the domestic legal system of each Member State to designate the courts having jurisdiction and to determine the procedural conditions governing actions at law intended to ensure the protection of the rights which citizens have from the direct effect of Community law, it being understood that such conditions cannot be less favourable than those relating to similar actions of a domestic nature. Where necessary, Articles 100 to 102 and 235 of the Treaty enable appropriate measures to be taken to remedy differences between the provisions laid down by law, regulation or administrative action in Member States if they are likely to distort or harm the functioning of the Common Market. In the absence of such measures of harmonization the right conferred by Community law must be exercised before the national courts in accordance with the conditions laid down by national rules. The position would be different only if the conditions and time-limits made it impossible in practice to exercise the rights which the national courts are obliged to protect. This is not the case where reasonable periods of limitation of actions are fixed. The laying down of such time-limits with regard to actions of a fiscal nature is an application of the fundamental principle of legal certainty . . .[223]

Warner AG added that this is really a matter of common sense:

Where Community law confines itself to forbidding this or that kind of act on the part of a Member State and to saying that private persons are entitled to rely on the prohibition in their national courts, without prescribing the remedies or procedures available to them for that purpose, there is really no alternative to the application of the remedies and procedures prescribed by national law. The plaintiffs submitted that to allow national law to apply in such circumstances was to allow it to override Community law. I do not think that that is a correct description of the situation. I see it as a situation in which Community law and national law operate in combination, the latter taking over where the former leaves off, and working out its consequences.[224]

Thus it is clear that no special rules or procedures are required for the enforcement of directly effective EC law in the courts of the Member

[223] Ibid. at 1997–8. See also Case 45/76 *Comet BV* v. *Produktschap voor Siergewassen* [1976] ECR 2043; Case 6/60 *Humblet* v. *Belgium* [1960] ECR 559; Case 28/67 *Molkerei-Zentrale Westfalen/Lippe GmbH* v. *Hauptzollamt Paderborn* [1968] ECR 143; Case 13/68 *Salgoil SpA* v. *Italian Ministry of Foreign Trade* [1968] ECR 453; Case 120/73 *Lorenz* v. *Germany* [1973] 2 ECR 1471; Case 60/75 *Russo* v. *AIMA* [1976] ECR 45; Case 35/74 *Mutualités Chrétiennes* v. *Rzepa* [1974] ECR 1241; Case 26/74 *Roquette* v. *Commission* [1976] ECR 677; and Case 61/79 *Amministrazione delle Finanze dello Stato* v. *Denkavit Italiana Srl* [1980] ECR 1205.

[224] [1976] 2 ECR 1989, at 2003.

States. The applicable principle is said to be that of the procedural autonomy of the Member States. This means that national remedies and procedures are satisfactory, so long as they are also applied to similar domestic areas of law (the principle of non-discrimination)[225] and so long as they do not frustrate the enforcement of the EC law in question (the principle of effectiveness).[226] This last element has been expressed somewhat variously by the Court; so, for example, it has held that the national procedural constraints must not be such as to 'render virtually impossible',[227] 'excessively difficult',[228] or 'impossible in practice'[229] the enforcement of the EC right in question. In *Peterbroeck* v. *Belgium*,[230] it refined this element further, saying:

each case which raises the question whether a national procedural provision renders application of Community law impossible or excessively difficult must be analysed by reference to the role of that provision in the procedure, its progress and its special features, viewed as a whole, before the various national instances. In the light of that analysis the basic principles of the domestic judicial system, such as protection of the rights of the defence, the principle of legal certainty and the proper conduct of procedure, must, where appropriate, be taken into consideration.[231]

Heukels has commented that this new formulation of the principle of effectiveness entails a detailed examination of the national procedural rules in question by the ECJ, which 'may bring the Court into the heart of the national judicial systems, a domain traditionally reserved to the Member States'.[232]

---

[225] Clearly a considerable area of discretion surrounds the scope of the comparison implied here, but the ECJ has not given further guidance on its limits; see Case 68/88 *Commission* v. *Greece* [1989] ECR 2965 and Case C-180/95 *Draehmpaehl* v. *Urania Immobilienservice ohG* [1997] ECR I-2195, also discussed in Chap. 3.

[226] See also Steiner, 'How to Make the Action Suit the Case' (1987) 12 ELRev. 102 and *id, Enforcing EC Law* (Blackstone, London, 1995).

[227] Case 199/82 *Amministrazione delle Finanze dello Stato* v. *San Giorgio SpA* [1983] ECR 3595, at 3616.

[228] Cases C-6 and 9/90 *Francovich and Bonifaci* v. *Italy* [1991] ECR I-5357, at 5416.

[229] *Rewe Zentralfinanze eG* v. *Landwirtschaftskammer für das Saarland*, op. cit. n. 222, and Case C-128/93 *Fisscher* v. *Voorhuis Hengelo BV* [1994] ECR I-4583 at 4599. Case C-246/96 *Maggiorian and Cunningham* v. *Eastern Health and Social Services Board*, judgment of 11 Dec. 1997 (nyr), also discussed in Chap. 2, concerned a statutory limitation imposed byUK law which precluded part-time workers from enforcing their right to non-discriminatory access to a pension scheme in respect of a period longer ago than two years before commencement of the action. The ECJ held that this rule rendered enforcement of the Community right to equal access impossible in practice.

[230] Case C-312/93 [1995] ECR I-4599.

[231] Ibid. at 4621. See also Joined Cases C-430 & 431/93 *Van Schijndel* v. *Stichting Pensioenfonds voor Fysiotherapeuten* [1995] ECR I-4705, Hoskins, 'Tilting the Balance: Supremacy and National Procedural Rules' (1996) 21 ELRev. 365, and Szyszczak and Delicostopoulos, 'Intrusions into National Procedural Autonomy: The French Paradigm' (1997) 22 ELRev. 141.

[232] Heukels (1996) 33 CMLRev. 337.

To the principle that normal limitation periods are generally permissible in relation to the enforcement of EC rights there is one important exception. The ECJ held in *Emmott* v. *Minister for Social Welfare*[233] that where a directive has not been correctly implemented in national law, time cannot begin to run against the state in any action based on the direct effect of that instrument. It explained that:

So long as a directive has not been properly transposed into national law, individuals are unable to ascertain the full extent of their rights. That state of uncertainty for individuals subsists even after the Court has delivered a judgment finding that the Member State in question has not fulfilled its obligations under the directive and even if the Court has held that a particular provision or provisions of the directive are sufficiently precise and unconditional to be relied upon before a national court.

Only the proper transposition of the directive will bring that state of uncertainty to an end and it is only upon that transposition that the legal certainty which must exist if individuals are to be required to assert their rights is created.

It follows that, until such time as a directive has been properly transposed, a defaulting Member State may not rely on an individual's delay in initiating proceedings against it in order to protect rights conferred upon him by the provisions of the directive and that a period laid down by national law within which proceedings must be initiated cannot begin to run before that time.[234]

The application and extent of this principle are far from free from doubt;[235] because of the prevalence of directives in this field, such doubt is especially problematic in relation to sex equality law. As a matter of logic, where a Member State implements a directive correctly but some time later than the directive required, an individual who asserts directly effective rights arising between the directive's coming into operation and its implementation would seem to be in no better a position once the implementing legislation was enacted; unless that legislation took retroactive effect, the individual's rights would still flow directly from the directive and would therefore remain as uncertain as ever. In addition, if, as the ECJ asserts, the need for legal certainty lies at the heart of the *Emmott* principle, it is arguable that the principle should also apply to directly effective rights arising from the Treaty whose ambit or effect is not clear until explained by a court.[236] However, far from extending the scope

---

[233] Case C-208/90 [1991] ECR I-4269, noted by Szyszczak in (1992) 29 CMLRev. 604.

[234] Case C-208/90 at 4299.

[235] For example, was the principle affected by the amendment of Art. 191 by the TEU so that it now requires the publication in the Official Journal of most directives? What is the meaning of 'properly transposed'? Can it be said that, where a Member State has adequately implemented one part of a directive but not another, the *Emmott* principle applies with respect to the whole instrument?

[236] For the examples of the kinds of difficulties arising in such a situation, see *Biggs* v. *Somerset County Council* [1996] ICR 364 and *Preston* v. *Wolverhampton Healthcare NHS Trust*

of *Emmott*, recent decisions of the ECJ suggest an inclination to limit it. In *Steenhorst-Neerings*[237] and *Johnson (No.2)*,[238] the Court held that it is permissible for a Member State to limit claims to arrears of a social security benefit, even where entitlement to the benefit concerned depends on a directive which the State has not properly implemented.[239] In addition, in *Denkavit Internationaal BV* v. *Kamer*,[240] Jacobs AG submitted that *Emmott* depended heavily on its own facts:

the judgment in *Emmott*, notwithstanding its more general language, must be read as establishing the principle that a Member State may not rely on a limitation period where a Member State is in default both in failing to implement a directive and in obstructing the exercise of a judicial remedy in reliance upon it, or perhaps where the delay in exercising the remedy—and hence the failure to meet the time-limit—is in some other way due to the conduct of the national authorities. A further factor in *Emmott* was that the applicant was in the particularly unprotected position of an individual dependent on social welfare. Seen in those terms the *Emmott* judgment may be regarded as an application of the well established principle that the exercise of Community rights must not be rendered 'excessively difficult'.[241]

(viii) Balancing the Claims of National Law and EC Law

Another major defect in the doctrine of direct effect was demonstrated before the British courts. It is the absence of any guaranteed interim or emergency remedy where the enforceability of EC law is arguable but not yet determined. *R.* v. *Secretary of State for Transport, Ex p. Factortame* involved a claim that Community rights were being defeated by British legislation. In an attempt to prevent over-fishing, the common fisheries policy had fixed quotas for national fishing fleets. In response, the Merchant Shipping Act of 1988 was passed in the UK, its aim being to define and restrict those vessels whose catch could be considered part of the UK quota. Under the Act, the Secretary of State was empowered to make

[1997] IRLR 233. See also Ellis, 'The Status of European Community Law in the United Kingdom' (1996) XXXI The Irish Jurist 35.

[237] Case C-338/91 *Steenhorst-Neerings* v. *Bestuur van de Bedrijfsvereniging voor Detailhandel, Ambachten en Huisvrouwen* [1993] ECR I-5475, noted by Sohrab in (1994) 31 CMLRev. 875 and discussed in Chap.4.

[238] C-410/92 *Johnson* v. *Chief Adjudication Officer* Case [1994] ECR I-5483, noted by Docksey in (1995) 32 CMLRev. 1447 and also discussed in Chap. 4.

[239] Cf. Case C-246/96 *Magorrian and Cunningham* v. *Eastern Health and Social Services Board*, judgment of 11 Dec. 1997 (nyr).

[240] Case C-2/94 [1996] ECR I-2827.

[241] Ibid. at 2851. See also Coppel, 'Time Up for *Emmott*?' (1996) 25 ILJ 153. For analysis of the efficacy of the principle of procedural autonomy in the field of sex equality law, see McCrudden, 'The Effectiveness of European Equality Law: National Mechanisms for Enforcing Gender Equality Law in the Light of European Requirements' (1993) 13 OJLS 320.

regulations for a new register of British shipping vessels. The resulting Merchant Shipping (Registration of Shipping Vessels) Regulations of 1988 provided that vessels could only be registered if their owners, or their share-holders, were British citizens or domiciled in Britain. The applicants for judicial review of these regulations were the owners of a large number of vessels; most of them were Spanish, but their vessels had under the previous legislation been treated as British because their catch was landed in the UK. Unable to satisfy the nationality requirement of the new regulations, they faced enormous economic difficulties. They were ineligible to fish against the Spanish quota; to lay up their vessels pending the litigation would have been prohibitively expensive; and if they sold the vessels, the price would be disastrously low because the market would be glutted. In these dire circumstances, the applicants sought an interim remedy from the British courts, to protect their right to continue to fish against the British quota, until such time as the ECJ gave a preliminary ruling under Article 177 of the Treaty explaining their rights and the position generally under EC law; such a ruling had been sought already by the Divisional Court but was expected to take two years to obtain. The owners' argument was that EC law gave them an enforceable right to fish against the British quota, and that the newly enacted British legislation attempted unlawfully to defeat that right. Nevertheless, the House of Lords at first unanimously refused to grant them any interim relief. Although conscious of the unsatisfactory nature of this result, Lord Bridge, making the only speech in the House, clearly believed that the only practicable remedy was for the ECJ to expedite the procedures by which it gave its preliminary ruling. He held:

If the applicants fail to establish the rights they claim before the ECJ, the effect of the interim relief granted would be to have conferred upon them rights directly contrary to Parliament's sovereign will and correspondingly to have deprived British fishing vessels, as defined by Parliament, of the enjoyment of a substantial proportion of the UK quota of stocks of fish protected by the common fisheries policy . . . [A]s a matter of English law, the court has no power to make an order which has these consequences.[242]

The House of Lords faced an additional problem in this case too, namely that for it to grant emergency relief here would have meant ordering an interim injunction against the Crown. After reviewing the fairly extensive case law on this matter, in particular since the passage of the Supreme Court Act 1981, their Lordships held that this was impossible as a matter of British law. They thereupon sought a preliminary ruling from the ECJ, asking whether, in circumstances such as those occurring in *Factortame*, EC law either obliges a national court to grant interim

[242] [1989] 2 WLR 997, at 1014.

protection to the Community rights claimed or gives the national court a discretion to grant such interim protection; in the event that the national court merely enjoys a discretion here, the House of Lords also wished for guidance from the ECJ as to the criteria it should apply in exercising that discretion.

The ECJ's reply[243] was disappointingly evasive. It focused its attention on the rule of domestic law preventing the ordering of an interim injunction against the Crown. Reiterating the reasoning it had given in *Amministrazione delle Finanze dello Stato* v. *Simmenthal SpA*,[244] it ruled that a national court which, in a case before it concerning EC law, considers that the sole obstacle which precludes it from granting interim relief is a rule of national law must set aside that rule. This, of course, was not really what the House of Lords was waiting to hear because the rule about interim injunctions against the Crown was not the sole obstacle it faced. The ECJ solved only the simpler and more mechanical part of the problems posed in *Factortame*. It unfortunately made no attempt whatever to deal with the much more difficult issue of the criteria which should guide a national court which is trying to decide whether to grant interim relief for the protection of disputed Community rights. The problem could be particularly acute in a sex discrimination claim, where irreparable harm may well be done to a person's rights in the period intervening between the claim and any preliminary ruling needed to substantiate it.

The case thus returned to the House of Lords with nobody very much the wiser as to what should occur next and with a very real danger of substantial variations in practice developing as between the different Member States. The House itself heard further evidence as to the predicament of the Spanish applicants and then granted them an interim injunction.[245] Its reasoning was given some three months later.[246] Lord Goff's was the leading speech in the House of Lords. He explained that the jurisdiction of the English courts to grant interim injunctions is contained in s. 37 of the Supreme Court Act 1981, by virtue of which the court has power to grant an injunction in all cases in which it appears to it to be just or convenient to do so; guidelines for the exercise of this jurisdiction were laid down by Lord Diplock in the House of Lords in *American Cyanamid Co.* v. *Ethicon Ltd.*[247] As a result, in the words of Lord Goff:

It is now clear that it is enough if [a party seeking an interlocutory injunction] can show that there is a serious case to be tried. If he can establish that, then he has, so to speak, crossed the threshold; and the court can then address itself to the question whether it is just or convenient to grant an injunction.[248]

---

[244] Case C-213/89 [1990] ECR I-2433.
[245] Order of 9 July 1990.
[247] [1975] AC 396.
[244] Case 106/77 [1978] ECR 629.
[246] [1990] 3 WLR 818.
[248] [1990] 3 WLR 818, at 869.

The first issue, according to Lord Goff, is thus the adequacy of damages as a remedy to either party. If damages are an adequate remedy for the plaintiff, this will normally preclude the grant of an injunction. If damages would not provide an adequate remedy for the plaintiff, then the court has to consider whether, if an injunction is granted against the defendant, there will be an adequate remedy in damages to him under the plaintiff's undertaking in damages; if so, there will be no reason on this ground to refuse to grant the interim injunction. The issue assumes special significance in cases where the validity of legislation is at stake. For example, it may not be thought right to impose an undertaking in damages against the Crown. In addition, there is no general right in the UK to indemnity in respect of damage suffered through invalid administrative action, so that no remedy in damages would have been available to the applicant fishermen in this case for loss suffered by them as a result of enforcement of the 1988 Act, should it eventually turn out that that Act was in contravention of EC law. Conversely, a public authority acting in the general public interest cannot normally be protected by a remedy in damages because it will itself have suffered none. It follows, said Lord Goff: '[T]hat, as a general rule, in cases of this kind involving the public interest, the problem cannot be solved at the first stage, and it will be necessary for the court to proceed to the second stage, concerned with the balance of convenience.'[249] In relation to this second stage, in cases of this sort where one party is a public authority performing duties to the public, particular stress has to be placed on the importance of upholding the law. This means that if a public authority seeks to enforce what is on its face the law of the land, and the person against whom such action is taken challenges the validity of that law, 'matters of considerable weight have to be put into the balance to outweigh the desirability of enforcing, in the public interest, what is on its face the law . . .'[250] Nevertheless, Lord Goff was not prepared to go so far as to say that, in such cases, the party challenging the validity of the law must show 'a strong *prima facie* case that the law is invalid'. He concluded that:

[T]he court should not restrain a public authority by interim injunction from enforcing an apparently authentic law unless it is satisfied, having regard to all the circumstances, that the challenge to the validity of the law is, *prima facie*, so firmly based as to justify so exceptional a course being taken.[251]

Applying these principles to the facts of the case, two matters in particular appeared to weigh with the House of Lords. The first was that recent case law of the ECJ[252] reinforced the likely strength in law of the applicants'

---

[249] Ibid. at 870.   [250] Ibid. also at 870.   [251] Ibid. at 871.
[252] In particular, Case 246/89 *R. Commission* v. *UK* [1989] ECR 3125; Case 3/87 *R.* v. *Minister of Agriculture and Fisheries, Ex p. Agegate Ltd.* [1989] ECR 4459; and Case 216/87 *R.* v. *Minister of Agriculture and Fisheries, Ex p. Jaderow Ltd* [1989] ECR 4509.

case.[253] The second was the immensity and the immediacy of the damage they would suffer if the injunction was not granted and the legislation were subsequently to prove invalid. The House was therefore ultimately persuaded to exercise its discretion in favour of the grant of the injunction.

Further light was shed on the issue of the interim protection of alleged Community rights by the ECJ in *Zuckerfabrik Süderdithmarschen AG* v. *Hauptzollamt Itzehoe.*[254] The Court there aligned the principles applicable to the suspension of national law which is alleged to conflict with Community rights with the suspension of national law implementing Community law which is alleged to be invalid:

The interim legal protection which Community law ensures for individuals before national courts must remain the same, irrespective of whether they contest the compatibility of national legal provisions with Community law or the validity of secondary Community law, in view of the fact that the dispute in both cases is based on Community law itself.[255]

It went on to hold that suspension of enforcement of a national measure adopted in implementation of Community legislation may be granted by a national court only:

(i) if that court entertains serious doubts as to the validity of the Community measure and, should the question of the validity of the contested measure not already have been brought before the Court, itself refers that question to the Court;
(ii) if there is urgency and a threat of serious and irreparable damage to the applicant;
(iii) and if the national court takes due account of the Community's interests.[256]

THE CONSTITUTIONAL SCOPE OF EC LAW

When the two qualities of supremacy and direct effect of EC law are considered together and in the light of the case law of the ECJ, it is obvious that they are of the utmost potential significance from the viewpoint of individuals claiming equality of opportunity. Together they make it possible for EC law to confer a 'constitutional' type of protection for the principle of the equality of the sexes. There is a parallel here to be drawn with the attempts made some years ago in the USA to add an 'equal

---

[253] As eventually demonstrated in Case C-221/89 *R* v. *Secretary of State for Transport, Ex p. Factortame Ltd. (No.3)* [1991] ECR I-3905.
[254] Joined Cases C-143/88 & C-92/89 [1991] ECR I-415.
[255] Ibid. at 541.
[256] Ibid. at 544.

rights' amendment to the Federal Constitution, which would have protected citizens against unequal treatment by any of the States of the Union. Not only can the EC principle of equality be invoked by individuals in actions before their national courts, but it must prevail over any conflicting legislative provision in the Member States, even one contained in the country's constitution.

There can be little doubt that the EC equality provisions have already produced dramatic practical as well as theoretical effects in individual instances. As will be seen in Chapters 2 and 3, they have rendered equal pay a reality in situations where national law did not, especially in relation to part-time workers and to pension provision, and they have radically altered people's employment rights, in particular in the areas of dismissal, retirement and remedies. In addition, as discussed in Chapter 4, they have produced some notable consequences for social security laws. However, all this is at present of relatively limited scope, since all the existing EC provisions on sex equality are in some way related either directly or indirectly to the subject of employment and cannot be said to manifest a coherent, overall strategy for the achievement of opportunity. The possible scope for future developments of EC law in this area will be discussed in Chapter 5.

2

Equal Pay

Article 119 begins with the words:

Each Member State shall ensure that the principle of equal pay for male and female workers for equal work or work of equal value is applied.[2]

It is to be found under Title VIII of the EC Treaty: 'Social Policy, Education, Vocational Training and Youth', which was substantially amended by the Amsterdam Treaty. The opening provision of this Title, Article 117, sets the agenda:

The Community and the Member States, having in mind fundamental social rights such as those set out in the European Social Charter signed at Turin on 18 October 1961 and in the 1989 Community Charter of the Fundamental Social Rights of Workers, shall have as their objectives the promotion of employment, improved living and working conditions, so as to make possible their harmonization while the improvement is being maintained, proper social protection, dialogue between management and labour, the development of human resources with a view to lasting high employment and the combating of exclusion . . .

That the improvement of the quality of life for the peoples of the Communities is a fundamental ideal underlying the Treaties is also clear from the Preamble and from the aspirations of the founders of the Communities discussed in Chapter 1. However, at the time the EC Treaty was being drafted, there were two radically opposed conceptions of the relationship between social policy and the establishment and functioning of the Common Market. The French view was that the harmonization of the 'social costs' of production was necessary in order to make sure that businesses competed on a fair and equal basis once the barriers to the free movement of persons and capital were removed. At the time of the negotiations, there were important differences in the scope and content of the social legislation in force in the states concerned. France, in particular, had on her statute book a number of rules which favoured workers and were consequently expensive for employers. For example, legislation of 1957 mandated equal pay for men and women. Workers in

---

[1] {Art. 141}.

[2] Before its amendment by the Amsterdam Treaty, it read: 'Each Member State shall during the first stage ensure and subsequently maintain the application of the principle that men and women should receive equal pay for equal work'.

France also had longer paid holidays than in the other States, normally a minimum of 24 days. They were, in addition, entitled to overtime pay after fewer hours of work at basic rates than elsewhere. All this meant that the French feared that the indirect costs of production of goods in France would make French goods uncompetitive in the Common Market and would damage French industry. They therefore sought to persuade the other negotiating States that social costs should be equalized throughout the Common Market. Germany, however, took a very different line, arguing that the harmonization of indirect or social costs would inevitably follow from the setting up of the Common Market. The Germans were also strongly committed to a minimum level of government interference in the area of wages and prices. A compromise was ultimately reached and this is the reason why the two differing viewpoints are both reflected in the Treaty's social policy provisions. In particular, the French delegation succeeded in persuading the others to accept two specific provisions, which would protect French industry from the kind of social dumping of which it was afraid. These are Article 119 on equal pay for men and women[3] and Article 119a,[4] which provides that the Member States will 'endeavour to maintain the existing equivalence between paid holiday schemes'.[5] That the debate between the two positions is not yet over has been shown in more recent times by the altercations between those who would seek to deregulate employment and their opponents who advocate harmonized social policy legislation as the only route to real future progress in Europe.[6]

In the years since the Treaty was drafted, social policy has come to play an increasingly prominent role in practice. It has provided a useful mechanism by which to emphasize the human face of the Community, against a background of criticism that it was exclusively economic, capitalist, and uncaring. Social policy legislation has also been made more

---

[3] See Forman, 'The Equal Pay Principle under Community Law' (1982) 1 LIEI 17. Note that despite its legislative history, Art. 119 makes no suggestion (and neither has the subsequent case law of the ECJ) that it protects only women and not men.

[4] {Art. 142}.

[5] Similarly, the Third Protocol on 'Certain Provisions Relating to France', which was annexed to the EC Treaty, provided that the Commission could authorize France to take protective measures where the establishment of the Common Market did not result, by the end of the first stage, in the basic number of hours beyond which overtime was paid, and the average rate of additional payment for overtime in industry, corresponding to the average in France in 1956; see Forman, op. cit., n. 3.

[6] A recent example of the practical issues involved can be seen in the decision of Hoover, a US company, to close their factory in Dijon and transfer production to Scotland where the burden of social protection provisions was perceived to be less than that in France: see Editorial Comment, 'Are European Values Being Hoovered Away?' (1993) 30 CMLRev. 445. Commission President Jacques Santer maintains on the other hand that the EC's social policy legislation actually strengthens competitiveness by fostering good industrial relations: see The Week in Europe, 6 February 1997.

necessary as a result of economic recession and mass unemployment. So, by 1972, the communiqué issued by the Paris Summit Meeting stated that the Heads of State or Government attached 'as much importance to vigorous action in the social field as to the achievement of monetary and economic union'. A 'Social Action Programme' followed in 1973,[7] which was approved by the Council in January 1974.[8] The Social Action Programme had three main aims: the attainment of full and better employment, the improvement of living and working conditions, and the increased involvement of management and labour in the economic and social decisions of the Community and of workers in the life of undertakings. Among other things its objectives included the bringing about of a 'situation in which equality between men and women obtains in the labour market throughout the Community, through the improvement of economic and psychological conditions, and of the social and educational infrastructure'. Gradually, equality of opportunity as between the sexes has emerged in the forefront of EC social policy.[9] In addition to the enactment of a series of directives on the subject,[10] four 'Action Programmes' have been mounted covering the periods 1982–5, 1986–90, 1991– 5, and 1996–2000.[11] These have been designed to enforce the equality legislation on a practical level in a number of ways. An 'Advisory Committee on Equal Opportunities for Women and Men' has been established to help the Commission to formulate and implement policy on the advancement of women's employment and equal opportunities and to arrange for the exchange of information between interested bodies in this field. In addition, a European Women's Lobby has been established, with the aim of facilitating dialogue between the Commission and national women's groups[12] and the Amsterdam Treaty has recently given a strong new emphasis to equality of opportunity.[13]

Quite why sex equality has been accorded this sort of priority by the Community is open to speculation. On an economic level, it is clearly important to prevent competitive distortions in a now quite highly integrated market. On the political level, perhaps it has been selected because it provides a relatively innocuous, even high-sounding, platform

[7] 24 Oct. 1973, COM(73) 1600.

[8] OJ [1974] C13/1.

[9] For an account of the processes at work to achieve this end, see Harlow, 'A Community of Interests? Making the Most of European Law' (1992) 55 MLR 331.

[10] To be discussed in the remaining Chapter of the present work.

[11] Action Programme 1982-5, OJ [1982] C186/3, Bull. EC 5-1982, point 2.1.48 and Bull. EC 7/8-1982, point 2.1.67; Equal Opportunities for Women Medium-term Community Programme 1986-90, Bull. EC Supplement 3/86 and Bull. EC 6-1986, point 2.1.116; Third Medium-term Community Action Programme COM(90) 449 final; Fourth Equality Action Programme 1996-2000, OJ [1995] L335/37, discussed further in Chap. 5.

[12] See CREW Reports (1990), Vol. 10, No. 2, 4.

[13] See in particular Chaps. 1, 3 and 5 of the present work, as well as below in this chapter.

by means of which the Community can demonstrate its commitment to social progress.

The part played by the European Parliament in the process will provide an interesting study for the historians of future generations. The Parliament, which has a higher proportion of women members than have the national parliaments,[14] has since 1984 possessed an influential Standing Committee on Women's Rights and has on several occasions provided the impetus for Community action in this field.[15] To some extent, it may be that to accede to demands made by the Parliament in the sphere of equal rights between the sexes has provided the Community's executive with a useful way out of heeding its advice in other fields.[16] However, even though it may be due more to political chance than to conscious planning that sex equality has emerged as such an important issue in the Community, it is now firmly on the legal and political agenda and those committed to its practical realization would be foolish to ignore the potential offered by EC law in this area today.

Article 119 is thus an unusual type of Treaty provision. On the one hand, it represents a social ideal and an instrument at least indirectly with which to harmonize social policy. On the other hand, it States a complete legal obligation, a social and economic end in its own right. Its wording is based on that of Article 2(1) of International Labour Organization (ILO) Convention No. 100, 1951,[17] which provides:

[E]ach Member State shall, by means appropriate to the methods in question for determining rates of remuneration, promote and, in so far as is consistent with such methods, ensure the application to all workers of the principle of equal remuneration for men and women workers for work of equal value.[18]

The major difference between Article 119 as it was originally phrased and the ILO Convention lay in the use of the phrases 'equal work' (Article

[14] See Valance, 'Do Women Make a Difference? The Impact of Women MEPS on Community Equality Policy' in *Women, Equality and Europe*, eds. Buckley and Anderson (Macmillan, London, 1988), and CREW Reports (1990), Vol. 10, No. 5, 11. After the 1994 elections, women represented 25.7 per cent of the membership of the European Parliament. By 1996, this percentage had increased to 27.6. This is to be compared with the average percentage of women in the national parliaments of the Member States, which stood at 15 in 1996, notwithstanding the accessions of Sweden and Finland which both have an exceptionally high number of women in parliament: see *Equal Opportunities for Women and Men in the European Union: Annual Report 1996*, Commission, Luxembourg, 1997.

[15] See e.g. its Resolution of 11 Feb. 1981 on the Situation of Women in the EC (Bull. EC 2-1981, point 2.3.7) which prompted the production of the first 'Action Programme'.

[16] See O'Donovan and Szyszczak, *Equality and Sex Discrimination Law* (Blackwell, Oxford, 1988), in particular Chap. 7.

[17] UNTS, Vol. 165, 303.

[18] The Editor of the Common Market Law Reports points out in [1976] 2 CMLR at 114 that the authentic English text of Art. 119 was translated from the original languages of the EEC Treaty and the translators did not, in doing so, pay any regard to the English authentic text of the ILO Convention.

119) and 'work of equal value' (ILO Convention). As seen above, the Amsterdam Treaty has now added 'work of equal value' to the EC text.

The ECJ has made it clear that it regards Article 119 as creative of both immediately enforceable legal rights and also of an important general principle whose scope requires further clarification and development. In *Defrenne* v. *Sabena*,[19] it held:

> The question of the direct effect of Article 119 must be considered in the light of the nature of the principle of equal pay, the aim of this provision and its place in the scheme of the Treaty. Article 119 pursues a double aim. First, in the light of the different stages of the development of social legislation in the various Member States, the aim of Article 119 is to avoid a situation in which undertakings established in States which have actually implemented the principle of equal pay suffer a competitive disadvantage in intra-Community competition as compared with undertakings established in States which have not yet eliminated discrimination against women workers as regards pay. Secondly, this provision forms part of the social objectives of the Community, which is not merely an economic union, but is at the same time intended, by common action, to ensure social progress and seek the constant improvement of the living and working conditions of their peoples, as is emphasized by the Preamble to the Treaty. This aim is accentuated by the insertion of Article 119 into the body of a Chapter devoted to social policy whose preliminary provision, Article 117, marks 'the need to promote improved working conditions and an improved standard of living for workers, so as to make possible their harmonization while the improvement is being maintained.' This double aim, which is at once economic and social, shows that the principle of equal pay forms part of the foundations of the Community. Furthermore, this explains why the Treaty has provided for the complete implementation of this principle by the end of the first stage of the transitional period.[20]

This passage explains two vital elements of the ECJ's reasoning in relation to Article 119. First, it sees the Article as part, but only part, of the social objectives of the Community. This has enabled it in later cases to develop an allied general principle of equality as between the sexes, which will be discussed in Chapter 3.[21] It has also undoubtedly contributed to the Court's purposive reading of the secondary legislation on sex discrimination. France's 'foot-in-the-door' negotiating stance when the EC Treaty was being drafted has therefore paid off in a way which could hardly have been anticipated in 1957. Secondly, because Article 119 is an important element in the development of Community social policy, it must never be read

---

[19] Case 43/75 [1976] ECR 455, the so-called *Second Defrenne case*, noted in (1976) Journal of Business Law 296. See also Wyatt, 'Article 119 EEC: Direct Applicability' (1975-6) 1 ELRev. 418, and Crisham, 'Annotation on Case 43/75' (1977) 14 CMLRev. 108.

[20] Case 43/75 at 471-2.

[21] That the principle of equal pay for men and women was the progenitor of the other Community rules on employment equality is further evidenced by the insertion into Art. 119 by the Amsterdam Treaty of an enabling power (discussed in Chap. 1) authorizing secondary legislation on equal opportunities and equal treatment as well as equal pay.

narrowly or restrictively;[22] its meaning and effects must be understood in the light of its purposes and this can lead to very much more extensive constructions of its terms than would normally be expected. Coupled with the principle of the supremacy of EC law, the potential significance of Article 119 is thus very great.

THE MEANING OF 'PAY'

Since its amendment by the Amsterdam Treaty, Article 119 is clearly concerned with equality between the sexes generally in working life;[23] however, its first paragraph articulates the principle specifically in relation to 'pay'. The ECJ's statements as to the underlying objectives of the Article lead to the supposition that 'pay' is to be given a broad and purposive interpretation. The Article itself contains the following definition: 'For the purposes of this Article, "pay" means the ordinary basic or minimum wage or salary and any other consideration, whether in cash or in kind, which the worker receives, directly or indirectly, in respect of his employment from his employer.'[24] Certain immediate conclusions can be drawn from the wording of this paragraph. For example, it is clear that the material form of the consideration is irrelevant for the purpose of Article 119; thus, all perks provided for employees by their employers are likely to constitute 'pay', so that Article 119 catches such things as company cars, and health and other insurance cover paid for by employers. It also follows that Article 119 must cover compensatory payments made by an employer to an employee, such as the refund of expenses incurred in travelling or entertaining. In *Garland* v. *British Rail*,[25] Article 119 was held to extend to concessionary rail fares provided for employees and ex-employees. Similarly, the notion of 'pay' is not confined to basic pay, but covers overtime pay[26] and special bonus payments made by employers.[27]

---

[22] See, for example the comment of Darmon AG in Joined Cases C-399, 409 and 425/92, C-34, 50 and 78/93 *Stadt Lengerich* v. *Helmig* [1994] ECR I-5727, at 5731. See also Case C-1/95 *Gerster* v. *Freistaat Bayern* (nyr), in which the ECJ held that Art. 119 applies to employment relationships in the public service.

[23] See the reference in Art. 119(3) to 'equal opportunities and equal treatment of men and women in matters of employment and occupation' and the reference in Art. 119(4) to 'full equality in practice between men and women in working life'.

[24] Art. 119(2).

[25] Case 12/81 [1982] ECR 359. See also the case note by Bradley in (1982) 19 CMLRev. 625.

[26] This was assumed by the ECJ in Joined Cases C-399, 409 and 425/92, C-34, 50 and 78/93 *Stadt Lengerich* v. *Helmig* [1994] ECR I-5727; Darmon AG said that it was 'agreed that overtime supplements constitute pay for the purposes of the first paragraph of Art. 119' (at 5731).

[27] See Case 58/81 *Commission* v. *Luxembourg* [1982] ECR 2175 where the ECJ held a special 'head of household' allowance to be 'pay'.

Article 119 spells out specifically that, whatever the basis of payment, arbitrary differences must not be made between the sexes. Thus, it provides: 'Equal pay without discrimination based on sex means: (a) that pay for the same work at piece rates shall be calculated on the basis of the same unit of measurement; (b) that pay for work at time rates shall be the same for the same job.'[28] Most of the cases so far litigated have involved alleged discrimination where work is paid at time rates. However, *Specialarbejderforbundet i Danmark* v. *Dansk Industri, acting for Royal Copenhagen A/S*[29] raised questions relating to discrimination in a piece work system. For work paid at time rates, it is established that if the average pay of a group of workers consisting predominantly of women is lower than that of a comparable group of male workers, this may raise an inference of sex discrimination.[30] The ECJ explained in *Royal Copenhagen* that this kind of group comparison cannot usually as a matter of logic be applied in piece work systems:

[I]n a piece-work pay scheme the principle of equal pay requires that the pay of two groups of workers, one consisting predominantly of men and the other predominantly of women, is to be calculated on the basis of the same unit of measurement. Where the unit of measurement is the same for two groups of workers carrying out the same work or is objectively capable of ensuring that the total individual pay of workers in the two groups is the same for work which, although different is considered to be of equal value, the principle of equal pay does not prohibit workers belonging to one or the other group from receiving different total pay if that is due to their different individual output.

It follows that in a piece-work pay scheme the mere finding that there is a difference in the average pay of two groups of workers, calculated on the basis of the total individual pay of all the workers belonging to one or the other group, does not suffice to establish that there is discrimination with regard to pay.

It is for the national court, which alone is competent to assess the facts, to decide whether the unit of measurement applicable to the work carried out by the two groups of workers is the same or, if the two groups carry out work which is different but considered to be of equal value, whether the unit of measurement is objectively capable of ensuring that their total pay is the same. It is also for that court to ascertain whether a pay differential relied on by a worker belonging to a group consisting predominantly of women as evidence of sex discrimination against that worker compared with a worker belonging to a group consisting

---

[28] Art. 119(2). In Case 96/80 *Jenkins* v. *Kingsgate (Clothing Productions) Ltd.* [1981] ECR 911, Warner AG commented at 933 that he did not consider that the phrase 'same job' in this paragraph meant the same as 'equal work' in para. (1) of Art. 119. Thus, he thought that a part-time worker and a full-time worker (engaged on the same process) do not have the 'same job', even though they may do 'equal work'.

[29] Case C-400/93 [1995] ECR I-1275; see Bourn, 'The Devil is in the Detail' (1995) 20 ELRev. 612 and Hervey, 'The Rise and Rise of Conservatism in Equal Pay' (1996) 18 JSWFL 107.

[30] See discussion below.

predominantly of men is due to a difference between the units of measurement applicable to the two groups or to a difference in individual output.[31]

The Article refers specifically to consideration which the worker receives 'in respect of his employment'. This indicates that the payment must arise out of the worker's employment, but that it is not necessarily confined to payment for the work actually done.[32] One type of situation in which such a distinction may become relevant was highlighted in *Sabbatini* v. *European Parliament*.[33] Two Community employees brought a staff action before the ECJ asking to have overturned the decisions of the Community institutions denying them 'expatriation allowances'. These allowances were paid to people having to live in a foreign country in order to work for the EC. One of the applicants' arguments was that the denial of these allowances amounted in the circumstances to a breach of Article 119. The issue therefore arose as to whether the allowances constituted 'pay'. The Commission argued that they were not 'pay' because they represented, not payment for work done, but compensation for having to live away from home in order to work; they were therefore payable quite independently of the work done. The ECJ decided the case on a different basis,[34] but the Advocate General dealt with this issue. He submitted that account should be taken not just of wages *stricto sensu* but also of all other payments made by reason of the links binding workers to their employers. Expatriation allowances fell within the notion of 'pay' because they were so closely linked with the employee's work.

Similarly, the Court has held that payments made by an employer to an employee who is absent from work can also constitute 'pay';[35] thus,

---

[31] [1995] ECR I-1275, at 1305-6.

[32] In Case 19/81 *Burton* v. *British Railways Board* [1982] ECR 555, Van Themaat AG said '[T]he decisive question is whether the benefits are received by the worker concerned from his employer owing to his employment. The French and Italian texts of Article 119 containing the words "en raison de l'emploi" and "in regione dell' impiego" also show that the test is not whether the payment is consideration for work performed. Only the English text of Article 119, which contains the words "in respect of his employment", might perhaps point to a more restrictive meaning. What is required for the purposes of the final words of the second paragraph of Article 119, and what incidentally I believe is also required by the English text logically construed, is rather an unseverable causal link between the payment and a worker's employment' (at 588-9). See also the remarks of Lamothe AG in Case 80/70 *Defrenne* v. *Belgium* [1971] ECR 445. In Case C-342/93 *Gillespie* v. *Northern Health and Social Services Board* [1996] ECR I-475, the ECJ stated: '. . . the concept of pay . . . includes all consideration which workers receive directly or indirectly from their employers in respect of their employment. The legal nature of such consideration is not important for the purposes of the application of Article 119 provided that it is granted in respect of employment . . . ' (at 498).

[33] Case 32/71 [1972] ECR 345.   [34] See Chap. 3.

[35] See e.g. Case C-360/90 *Arbeiterwohlfahrt der Stadt Berlin* v. *Bötel* [1992] ECR I-3589, Case C-457/93 *Kuratorium fur Dialyse und Nierentransplantation eV* v. *Lewark* [1996] ECR I-243 and Case C-278/93 *Freers* v. *Deutsche Bundespost* [1996] ECR I-1165. Cf. the decision of the Employment Appeal Tribunal in *Manor Bakeries Ltd.* v. *Nazir* [1996] IRLR 604.

maternity benefit paid by an employer pursuant to legislation or to the woman's contract of employment is 'pay' because it is 'based on the employment relationship'[36] and, therefore, a woman is subjected to unlawful sex discrimination where she does not receive a pay rise awarded to her colleagues during the period of her maternity pay.[37]

In order to constitute 'pay', it is established that there need be no contractual obligation on the employer to provide the benefit in question. This was made clear by the ECJ in *Worringham* v. *Lloyds Bank Ltd.*[38] As Warner AG explained:

The phrase 'consideration, whether in cash or in kind', seems to me one of wide import. It was suggested to us that it would not cover anything to which the worker concerned was not entitled under his or her contract of employment. Perhaps that suggestion was based on the meaning of the word 'consideration' in English law. At all events it is in my opinion wrong. Let me give an example. An employer may, in prosperous times, voluntarily distribute Christmas bonuses to his staff. No employee has a contractual right to such a bonus. But Article 119 would, in my opinion, clearly preclude an employer from discriminating between men and women in the distribution of it.[39]

The fact that the payment is notional only and never actually passes into the hands of the employee does not prevent it from falling within Article 119. This also was evident from *Worringham* v. *Lloyds Bank Ltd.* where the Bank had separate pension schemes for its male and female employees. The schemes were contributory for all male employees but only for those female employees who were over 25. In order to maintain pay parity with the other clearing banks, Lloyds added an extra five per cent, corresponding to the cost of the contribution, to the salaries of all its contributing employees. This sum passed straight to the pension fund and was thus in effect merely a notional payment to the employee. However, if a man left the Bank before qualifying for a pension benefit, he received a refund of the contributions paid on his behalf, whereas if a woman under 25 left she received nothing. Two women under 25 complained that this treatment breached Article 119 and the ECJ held that it did. The five per cent additions were included in an employee's gross salary and directly

---

[36] Case C-342/93 *Gillespie* v. *Northern Health and Social Services Board* [1996] ECR I-475, at 499. See McGlynn, 'Equality, Maternity, and Questions of Pay' (1996) 21 ELRev. 327.

[37] *Gillespie* v. *Northern Health and Social Services Board*, n. 36.

[38] Case 69/80 [1981] ECR 767. See also Snaith, 'Article 119 EEC and Private Occupational Pension Schemes' (1981) 6 ELRev. 193; Crisham, 'The Equal Pay Principle: Some Recent Decisions of the ECJ' 18 CMLRev. 601; Post, 'New Decisions of the European Court on Sex Discrimination' (1981) 1 LIEI 77; Plender, 'Equal Pay for Men and Women: Two Recent Decisions of the European Court' (1982) 30 American Journal of Comparative Law 627; and Szyszczak, 'Occupational Pension Schemes and Article 119 EEC' (1981) 131 NLJ 527.

[39] Case 69/80 at 805.

determined the calculation of other advantages linked to salary (such as redundancy payments, unemployment benefits, family allowances, and credit facilities). It did not matter that they were immediately deducted by the employer and paid into the pension fund.

Similarly, in *Liefting* v. *Directie van het Academisch Ziekenhuis bij Universiteit van Amsterdam*[40] the ECJ held:

[A]lthough the portion which employers are liable to contribute to the financing of statutory social security schemes to which both employees and employers contribute does not constitute pay within the meaning of Article 119 of the Treaty, the same is not true of sums which are included in the calculation of the gross salary payable to the employee and which directly determine the calculation of other benefits linked to the salary such as redundancy payments, unemployment benefits, family allowances and credit facilities. This is also the case if the amounts in question are immediately deducted by the employer and paid to a pension fund on behalf of the employee.[41]

Can this principle be extended to compulsory deductions from salary demanded by an employer on a discriminatory basis, where the gross salary itself does not vary according to sex? In *Newstead* v. *Department of Transport*,[42] a male civil servant, who described himself as 'a confirmed bachelor', complained of discrimination contrary to Article 119 in the requirement contained in the civil service pension scheme that all male employees contribute one and a half per cent of their gross salary to a fund for widows' pensions. If the employee never married, his contribution was returned to him with interest when he left the civil service or was paid to his estate if he died before then, but no such contribution was required of his female colleagues. He therefore contended that he was denied the immediate enjoyment of his full salary, unlike his female colleagues. The ECJ held that this situation did not breach Article 119, since gross pay was not affected and, unlike the situation in *Worringham* and *Liefting*, there was no consequential effect as regards other salary-related benefits. Critical to this ruling seems to have been the fact that the deduction was made for the purpose of providing a survivor's benefit in an occupational pension scheme which substituted for a part of the state scheme, a matter over which EC law appeared at the time of this case to permit sex discrimination.[43] It would seemingly have been otherwise had the purpose of the deduction been unrelated to an area where sex discrimination was permitted. So, for example, it would

[40] Case 23/83 [1984] ECR 3225.
[41] Ibid. at 3239.
[42] Case 192/85 [1987] ECR 4753. See Arnull, 'Widows' Mite' (1988) 13 ELRev. 135.
[43] The ECJ's decisions in Case C-262/88 *Barber* v. *Guardian Royal Exchange Assurance Group* [1990] ECR I-1889 and succeeding pensions cases subsequently made it clear that sex discrimination was not permissible in such situations. See discussion below.

certainly appear to constitute a breach of Article 119 where an employer requires his male employees only to donate a percentage of their gross salaries to the local cats' home.

Are Pensions 'Pay' within Article 119?

It was seen above that Article 119 provides that, in order to be 'pay', the consideration must come, either directly or indirectly, from the employer. This requirement has presented a problem in relation to the practically very important issue of whether pension benefits fall within Article 119, a matter which has now been raised before the ECJ on a number of occasions.[44] Probably the first real hint from the ECJ itself that they might sometimes be within Article 119 came in *Burton* v. *British Railways Board*.[45] The question here was whether the provision of early retirement pensions under a voluntary redundancy scheme contravened EC law because women became eligible at 55, but men only at 60. The Court held that:

the question of interpretation which has been referred to the Court concerns not the benefit itself, but whether the conditions of *access* to the voluntary redundancy scheme are discriminatory. This is a matter covered by the provisions of Council Directive 76/207 . . . and not by those of Article 119.[46]

Later, it pointed out specifically that:

The option given to workers by the provisions at issue . . . enables a worker who leaves his employment at any time during the five years before he reaches normal pensionable age to receive certain allowances for a limited period. The allowances are calculated in the same manner regardless of the sex of the worker.[47]

Commenting on this case in the Employment Appeal Tribunal, Browne-Wilkinson J said that he considered its implication to be that 'the quantum of benefit payable under a retirement scheme may be "pay" within the meaning of Article 119'.[48]

Razzouk and Beydoun v. *Commission*[49] concerned sex discrimination contained in the Community's own Staff Regulations as regards the provision of survivors' benefits to the relatives of deceased employees. Slynn AG submitted that a retirement pension received by a Community employee, and also a survivor's pension received by such a person's

---

[44] The issue was originally ducked by the ECJ in Case 69/80 *Worringham* v. *Lloyds Bank Ltd.* [1981] ECR 767. For further discussion, see Curtin, 'Occupational Pension Schemes and Article 119: Beyond the Fringe?' (1987) 24 CMLRev. 215.

[45] Case 19/81 [1982] ECR 555, noted by Bradley in (1982) 19 CMLRev. 625.

[46] Case19/81 at 575. (Emphasis supplied.)

[47] Ibid. at 576-7.

[48] *Barber* v. *Guardian Royal Exchange Assurance Group* [1983] IRLR 240, at 243.

[49] Cases 75 and 117/82 [1984] ECR 1509.

widow or widower, was 'pay' and subject to a principle 'analogous' to Article 119. He explained that:

In substance the official's entitlement to, for example, a retirement pension is part of the consideration (albeit deferred) which he receives in respect of his employment . . . The same can, in my view, be said of the survivor's pension even though it is not received directly by the official himself but is paid to his surviving spouse. It is still consideration received in respect of the official's employment for which in part he also makes general pension contributions.[50]

The Court itself preferred to base its conclusion in this case on the general principle of equal treatment of the sexes and said that:

[I]n relations between the Community institutions on the one hand and their employees and those claiming under them on the other, the requirements arising from this principle are by no means limited to those flowing from Article 119 . . .[51]

The Court was much more forthcoming on the pensions issue in *Bilka-Kaufhaus GmbH* v. *Weber Von Hartz*.[52] Bilka was part of a chain of department stores in Germany which employed several thousand people. Ms Weber Von Hartz, who had been employed by the company for a number of years, alleged that its occupational pension scheme discriminated against female employees because of the conditions it imposed for entry into the scheme. Darmon AG submitted that each pension scheme has to be examined individually in order to test whether it falls within the scope of Article 119, in particular in the light of the relevant national legislation. However, he considered that the pension provided by Bilka was within Article 119:

[I]t is a voluntary scheme which complements and 'tops up' the statutory scheme, even if it was encouraged or organized by the authorities, and . . . it applies only in so far as it is incorporated in the employment relationship, after negotiations between the employer and the employees.[53]

The Court itself agreed, saying:

[T]he occupational pension scheme at issue in the main proceedings, although adopted in accordance with the provisions laid down by German legislation for such schemes, is *based on an agreement between Bilka and the staff committee representing its employees* and has the effect of supplementing the social benefits paid under national legislation of general application *with benefits financed entirely by the employer. The contractual rather than the statutory nature of the scheme in question is confirmed by the fact that, as has been pointed out above, the scheme and rules governing it are regarded as an integral part of the contracts of employment between Bilka and its*

[50] Ibid. at 1540.
[51] Ibid. at 1530.
[52] Case 170/84 [1986] ECR 1607. See Arnull, 'Sex Discrimination in Occupational Pension Schemes' (1986) 11 ELRev. 363.
[53] Case 170/84 at 1614.

employees. It must therefore be concluded that the scheme . . . does not constitute a social security scheme governed directly by statute and thus outside the scope of Article 119. Benefits paid to employees under the scheme therefore constitute consideration received by the worker from the employer in respect of his employment, as referred to in the second paragraph of Article 119.[54]

It followed that there were in essence two requirements for payments under this type of supplementary pension scheme to fall within Article 119: the scheme must be funded in part at least by the employer, because otherwise payments would not represent consideration received from the employer within the wording of Article 119; and the scheme must be contractual in origin rather than set up by statute.[55]

The second of these criteria represented an attempt by the ECJ to differentiate between social security payments and pay. Such a distinction appears to be implied by the social policy provisions of the EC Treaty, since they make separate reference to the harmonization of social security systems. The first case to explore the dividing-line was *Defrenne* v. *Belgium*.[56] Ms Defrenne had been an air hostess employed by Sabena Airlines. In common with her other female colleagues, the company required her to retire at the age of 40. She then found that she faced discrimination in relation to her pension arrangements. A Belgian Royal Decree established a pension scheme for 'all members of air crews with the exception of air hostesses'; this special scheme was far more lucrative than the general state pension and payable at the age of 55. Under the general state scheme, women could not claim their pensions until the age of 60. Ms Defrenne voiced two objections in particular: her years of service with Sabena before she reached the age of 40 were only taken into consideration under the less favourable general scheme, and she could not claim any pension at all until she was 60. The Belgian court before which she brought proceedings asked the ECJ whether a 'retirement pension granted under a social security scheme financed by workers' and employees' contributions, as well as by state grants', constituted 'pay'

[54] Ibid. at 1625-6. (Emphases supplied.) It is noteworthy (particularly with the benefit of hindsight) that the Court did not follow the argument of the UK government in this case to the effect that this was a problem of 'access' to benefits and therefore within the principle of Case 19/81 *Burton* v. *British Railways Board* [1982] ECR 555. For further discussion of this issue, see Chap. 3.

[55] Provided that the origin of the payment is not statutory, it has long been clear that it is not taken outside the scope of Art. 119 simply because statute regulates certain of the aspects of the payment. Van Themaat AG commented in Case 19/81 *Burton* v.*British Railways Board* [1982] ECR 555: 'I do not think that it is relevant, for the purpose of determining whether Article 119 applies, that the method of calculating the amount of the benefits partly depends on statutory provisions. As was rightly pointed out in the course of the proceedings, such a criterion would mean that statutory minimum wages which discriminated between the sexes would not fall under Article 119 either' (at 588).

[56] Case 80/70 [1971] ECR 445, the so-called *First Defrenne* case. See also the remarks of Mayras AG in Case 207/78 *Ministère Public* v. *Even* [1979] ECR 2019, at 2038-9.

within the meaning of Article 119. The ECJ ruled that both general and special state pension schemes are excluded from the ambit of Article 119.

Although payments in the nature of social security benefits are therefore in principle not alien to the concept of pay, there cannot be brought within this concept, as defined in Article 119, social security schemes or benefits, in particular retirement pensions, directly governed by legislation without any element of agreement within the undertaking or the occupational branch concerned, which are obligatorily applicable to general categories of workers. These schemes assure for the workers the benefits of a legal scheme, to the financing of which workers, employers and possibly the public authorities contribute in a measure determined less by the employment relationship between the employer and the worker than by considerations of social policy. Accordingly, the part due from the employers in the financing of such schemes does not constitute a direct or indirect payment to the worker. Moreover, the worker will normally receive the benefits legally prescribed not by reason of the employer's contribution but solely because the worker fulfils the legal conditions for the grant of benefits.[57]

A social security payment thus appeared to be one whose qualifying conditions were exclusively laid down by legislation and which was payable irrespective of whether the particular employer concerned had in fact contributed to its financing. In the words of Lamothe AG: '[T]here is no relationship at all between the employer's contribution and the pension and it is this absence of relationship which in this case as in that of the general scheme prevents the pension from being regarded as consideration which the employed person receives from his employer within the meaning of the provisions of Article 119.'[58] In more graphic terms, he explained that social security benefits are: '[N]o more consideration received indirectly from the employer than are the road, water mains or sewer, the benefit of which the employed person has as a citizen and to finance which the taxes and duties paid by the employer have contributed.'[59]

However, this analysis proved to be deceptively simple. In reality, there is considerable overlap between the notions of 'pension' and 'social security', in particular in the UK where occupational pension schemes may be 'contracted-out' of the earnings-related element of the state pension scheme, provided that they satisfy certain statutory requirements.

---

[57] Case 80/70 at 451. The Court appears today to consider that the *origins* of a particular scheme are relevant in helping it to decide whether it falls within the definition of a social security scheme: in Case C-109/91 *Ten Oever* v. *Stichting Bedrijfspensioenfonds voor het Glazenwassers- en Schoonmaakbedrijf* [1993] ECR I-4879, a scheme was differentiated from that in the *Defrenne* case where 'the rules . . . were not laid down directly by law but were the result of an agreement between both sides of the industry concerned' notwithstanding that 'at the request of such employers' and trade union organisations as were considered to be representative, . . . the scheme [was declared] compulsory for the whole of the industry concerned' (at 4943).

[58] Case 80/70 at 461.

[59] Ibid. at 458.

The occupational pension in such a situation thus substitutes, at least in part, for the state pension. Is such a contracted-out pension therefore removed from the scope of Article 119? This question was first put to the ECJ in *Worringham* v. *Lloyds Bank Ltd.*[60] The ECJ itself managed to avoid answering the question on this occasion. However, Warner AG did deal with it. He considered that benefits under the Lloyds Bank scheme would have fallen within Article 119 were it not for the 'contracting-out' element. It had been argued that the rights under such a contracted-out scheme were not received, even indirectly, from the employer because others were concerned in their elaboration and financing. However, the Advocate General submitted:

In my view the circumstances that the terms of a scheme have to be discussed with and to be approved by others does not detract from the fact that, at the end of the day, its adoption is the act of the employer. Nor is the element of tax saving in my opinion relevant. Wages and salaries, which are undoubtedly 'pay', are also deductible in computing the employer's profits for tax purposes; and I hardly think that the circumstance that a member of the scheme is taxable on benefits he receives from it and not on contributions he makes to it can affect the issue. It was also pointed out that some of the benefits under the scheme were payable not to the member but to his dependants. The conferment of the right to those benefits on his dependants can, however, in my opinion, properly be regarded as an advantage to the member arising from his employment.[61]

But he went on to add:

To hold that Article 119 applied in relation to [these] schemes would mean holding that ever since that Article took effect (i.e. since the end of the first stage of the transitional period in the case of the original Member States and since 1 January 1973 in the case of the [UK]) a Member State operating such a system was under an obligation to ensure that a contracted-out scheme afforded equal rights for men and women whilst it was under no such obligation as regards its state scheme. That would, it seems to me, be an unbalanced result to reach, as well as one calculated to deter contracting-out. In my opinion, where a privately established pension scheme is designed, not as a supplement to the state social security scheme . . . but as a substitute for it or for part of it, it must be regarded as outside the scope of Article 119 and as falling to be dealt with under the broader headings in Article 118.[62]

---

[60] Case 69/80 [1981] ECR 767.   [61] Ibid. at 805.
[62] Ibid. at 806. Cf. Joined Cases 75 and 117/82 *Razzouk and Beydoun* v. *Commission* [1984] ECR 1509, where Slynn AG commented: 'The judgment of the Court in Case 80/70 *Defrenne* v. *Belgium* excluded from the scope of Article 119 "social security schemes or benefits, in particular retirement pensions, directly governed by legislation without any element of agreement within the undertaking or the occupational branch concerned, which are obligatorily applicable to general categories of workers." That description cannot, in my view, be applied to the benefits and pensions made available under pension schemes entered into by employers and employees outside a national system of social security. Nor does it in my view fit the benefits provided under the Staff Regulations. True,

The full ECJ itself ultimately reached a different conclusion on this matter in *Barber* v. *Guardian Royal Exchange Assurance Group*.[63] The effect of its forthright ruling in the latter case was to bring contracted-out pensions squarely within the scope of Article 119. It held:

[T]he second question must be understood as seeking in substance to ascertain whether a retirement pension paid under a contracted-out private occupational scheme falls within the scope of Article 119 of the Treaty, in particular where that pension is awarded in connection with compulsory redundancy. It must be pointed out in that regard that [in the *First Defrenne case*] the Court stated that consideration in the nature of social security benefits is not in principle alien to the concept of pay. However, the Court pointed out that this concept, as defined in Article 119, cannot encompass social security schemes or benefits, in particular retirement pensions, directly governed by legislation without any element of agreement within the undertaking or the occupational branch concerned, which are compulsorily applicable to general categories of workers. The Court noted that those schemes afford the workers the benefit of a statutory scheme, to the financing of which workers, employers and possibly the public authorities contribute in a measure determined less by the employment relationship than by considerations of social policy. In order to answer the second question therefore it is necessary to ascertain whether those considerations also apply to contracted-out private occupational schemes . . .

[I]t must be pointed out first of all that the schemes in question are the result either of an agreement between workers and employers or of a unilateral decision taken by the employer. They are wholly financed by the employer or by both the employer and the workers without any contribution being made by the public authorities in any circumstances. Accordingly, such schemes form part of the consideration offered to workers by the employer.

Secondly, such schemes are not compulsorily applicable to general categories of workers. On the contrary, they apply only to workers employed by certain undertakings, with the result that affiliation to those schemes derives of necessity from the employment relationship with a given employer. Furthermore, even if the schemes in question are established in conformity with national legislation and consequently satisfy the conditions laid down by it for recognition as contracted-out schemes, they are governed by their own rules.

Thirdly, it must be pointed out that, even if the contributions paid to those schemes and the benefits which they provide are in part a substitute for those of

they are independent of and replace social security legislation for the officials concerned. On the other hand, although based on Community "legislation", i.e. a Council Regulation, the scheme in the Staff Regulations applies only to persons employed by the institutions and is therefore closer to a scheme applicable to employees rather than to citizens or workers generally. In substance the official's entitlement to, for example, a retirement pension is part of the consideration (albeit deferred) which he receives in respect of his employment . . . ' (at 1540).

[63] Case C-262/88 [1990] ECR I-1889. See Honeyball and Shaw, 'Sex, Law and the Retiring Man' (1991) 16 ELRev. 47 and Fitzpatrick, 'Equality in Occupational Pensions—The New Frontiers After *Barber*' (1991) 54 MLR 271.

the general statutory scheme, that fact cannot preclude the application of Article 119. It is apparent from the documents before the Court that occupational schemes such as that referred to in this case may grant to their members benefits greater than those which would be paid by the statutory scheme, with the result that their economic function is similar to that of the supplementary schemes which exist in certain Member States, where affiliation and contribution to the statutory scheme is compulsory and no derogation is allowed. In its judgment [in the *Bilka-Kaufhaus* case] the Court held that the benefits awarded under a supplementary pension scheme fell within the concept of pay, within the meaning of Article 119.

It must therefore be concluded that, unlike the benefits awarded by national statutory social security schemes, a pension paid under a contracted-out scheme constitutes consideration paid by the employer to the worker in respect of his employment and consequently falls within the scope of Article 119 of the Treaty. That interpretation of Article 119 is not affected by the fact that the private occupational scheme in question has been set up in the form of a trust and is administered by trustees who are technically independent of the employer, since Article 119 also applies to consideration received indirectly from the employer.[64]

The consequence of *Barber* was that both supplementary and contracted-out occupational pension schemes were clearly subject to the principle of equality as between the sexes and discrimination within their terms was therefore actionable via Article 119 itself.[65]

The full Court subsequently analysed the relationship between state social security schemes and occupational pension schemes in the *Beune* case.[66] The main question referred to the ECJ was whether a statutory pension scheme for civil servants in the Netherlands fell within Article 119. The Court referred to Jacobs AG's exhaustive and lucid exposition of the factors which had been regarded as relevant in the earlier case law. It summed them up as follows:

[T]he statutory nature of a pension scheme, negotiation between employers and employees' representatives, the fact that the employees' benefits supplement social security benefits, the manner in which the pension scheme is financed, its applicability to general categories of employees and, finally, the relationship between the benefit and the employees' employment.[67]

---

[64] Case C-262/88 at 1950-2. Part of the Commission's motivation for its arguments in the *Barber* case, and probably part of the Court's motivation in reaching its ultimate decision, was the aim of ensuring equality of treatment as between the Member States in this matter; in other words, if German employers operating *Bilka-Kaufhaus* supplementary pension schemes were to be bound by Art. 119, then so ought British employers operating under the British system of contracted-out pensions.

[65] The relationship between Art. 119 and the Equal Treatment Directive (Directive 76/207, OJ [1976] L39/40) will be discussed in Chap. 3.

[66] Case C-7/93 *Bestuur van Het Algemeen Burgerlijk Pensioenfonds* v. *Beune* [1994] ECR I-4471. This was followed in Case C-147/95 *DEI* v. *Evrenopoulos* (nyr).

[67] Case C-7/93 at 4512.

However, it went on to point out that most of these criteria do not, at least taken alone, provide a conclusive answer to whether the payment is within Article 119. Thus, the fact that a scheme is directly governed by statute may provide an indication that it is a social security scheme but both the *Barber* and *Second Defrenne* cases expressly included as within Article 119 discrimination which was statutory in origin. The Court stated that it has attached more importance to the criterion of whether the scheme is a result of a formal agreement. As to the supplementary nature of schemes, the Court pointed out that the *Barber* case itself demonstrates that this is not invariably required. In relation to funding arrangements, even though a pension is funded by employers' and employees' contributions and is managed independently in accordance with rules similar to those applicable to occupational pension funds, this does not in truth differentiate it from a social security scheme; the Court added that even the fact of a contribution to the scheme by the State is not necessarily decisive. The applicability of the scheme to a 'general category of employees', which *First Defrenne* indicates is typical of a social security scheme, is a difficult test to apply in practice. All this led the Court to conclude:

[T]he only possible decisive criterion is whether the pension is paid to the worker by reason of the employment relationship between him and his former employer, that is to say the criterion of employment based on the wording of Article 119 itself.

Admittedly, as the Court has recognised ever since *Defrenne I*, the employment criterion cannot be regarded as exclusive. Thus, as regards the inception and determination of pension rights, the pensions paid by statutory social security schemes may reflect, wholly or in part, pay in respect of work, but nevertheless fall outside the scope of Article 119.

On the other hand, considerations of social policy, of state organisation, or of ethics or even budgetary preoccupations which influenced, or may have influenced, the establishment by the national legislature of a scheme such as the scheme at issue cannot prevail if the pension concerns only a particular category of workers, if it is directly related to the period of service and if its amount is calculated by reference to the civil servant's last salary. The pension paid by the public employer is therefore entirely comparable to that paid by a private employer to his former employees.

It follows from all the foregoing considerations that a civil service pension scheme of the type at issue in the main proceedings, which essentially relates to the employment of the person concerned, forms part of the pay received by that person and comes within the scope of Article 119.[68]

---

[68] Ibid. at 4518. This decision renders highly doubtful that of the Employment Appeal Tribunal in *Griffin* v. *London Pension Fund Authority* [1993] ICR 564 to the effect that pension payments made under the Local Government Superannuation Scheme are not pay.

It is submitted that this is a far from helpful ruling; it is unacceptably vague both in not defining what indicia are to be applied to determine whether a payment is made by reason of an employment relationship and also in saying that the employment criterion is not exclusive. It is important that legal certainty be provided in this area by the Court remedying these deficiencies as soon as possible.

The Principle of Equality as applied to Pensions[69]

The ECJ's decision in *Barber* left a number of issues unresolved.[70] First, there were problems as to the temporal scope of Article 119 in relation to pensions. It will be seen below that Article 119 generally takes direct effect in relation to pay and has been able to be relied upon since 8 April 1976.[71] However, in this specific context, the Court took a restrictive stance:

[T]he direct effect of Article 119 of the Treaty may not be relied upon in order to claim entitlement to a pension with effect from a date prior to that of this judgment, except in the case of workers or those claiming under them who have before that date initiated legal proceedings or raised an equivalent claim under the applicable national law.[72]

The date of the judgment was 17 May 1990. The Court gave unusually full reasons for reaching this conclusion, saying that it could:

[B]y way of exception, taking account of the serious difficulties which its judgment may create as regards events in the past, be moved to restrict the possibility for all persons concerned of relying on the interpretation which the Court, in proceedings on a reference to it for a preliminary ruling, gives to a provision . . .

With regard to this case, it must be pointed out that Article 7(1) of [the Social Security Directive[73]] authorized the Member States to defer the compulsory implementation of the principle of equal treatment with regard to the determination of pensionable age for the purposes of granting old-age pensions and the possible consequences thereof for other benefits. That exception has been incorporated in Article 9(a) of [the Occupational Social Security Directive[74]] which may apply to contracted-out schemes such as the one at issue in this case.

---

[69] For general discussion of this matter, see Whiteford, 'Lost in the Mists of Time: the ECJ and Occupational Pensions' (1995) 32 CMLRev. 801, *id, Adapting to Change: Occupational Pension Schemes, Women and Migrant Workers* (Kluwer, the Hague, 1997), and Fredman, 'The Poverty of Equality: Pensions and the ECJ' (1996) 25 ILJ 91.

[70] See Moore, '"Justice Doesn't Mean a Free Lunch": The Application of the Principle of Equal Pay to Occupational Pension Schemes' (1995) 20 ELRev. 159.

[71] The date of the ECJ's decision in Case 43/75 *Defrenne* v. *Sabena* [1976] ECR 455.

[72] [1990] ECR I-1889, at 1956. In Case C-147/95 *DEI* v. *Evrenopoulos* (nyr), Jacobs AG submitted that 'the exception in favour of those who [have] already introduced a claim should not be narrowly construed. Rather, it is the temporal limitation introduced by the *Barber* judgment which, as a departure from the normal canons of interpretation, should be subject to strict construction' (at para. 45).

[73] Directive 79/7, OJ [1979] L6/24, discussed in Chap. 4.

[74] Directive 86/378, OJ [1986] L225/40, subsequently amended in this respect and discussed further below.

In the light of those provisions, the Member States and the parties concerned were reasonably entitled to consider that Article 119 did not apply to pensions paid under contracted-out schemes and that derogations from the principle of equality between men and women were still permitted in that sphere.

In those circumstances, overriding considerations of legal certainty preclude legal situations which have exhausted all their effects in the past from being called in question where that might upset retroactively the financial balance of many contracted-out pension schemes. It is appropriate, however, to provide for an exception in favour of individuals who have taken action in good time in order to safeguard their rights. Finally, it must be pointed out that no restriction on the effects of the aforesaid interpretation can be permitted as regards the acquisition of entitlement to a pension as from the date of this judgment.[75]

It was far from clear how the Court's formulation of this prospective direct effect would actually work on the facts of particular cases involving occupational pension schemes. The editors of the Equal Opportunities Review, for example, commented that the Court's statement was capable of being read in at least five different ways.[76] The financial implications were so serious for the pensions industry that the Member States took the unprecedented step of legislating directly on the matter. The TEU annexed the so-called 'Barber Protocol' to the EC Treaty, providing:

For the purposes of Article 119 of this Treaty, benefits under occupational social security schemes shall not be considered as remuneration if and in so far as they are attributable to periods of employment prior to 17 May 1990, except in the case of workers or those claiming under them who have before that date initiated legal proceedings or introduced an equivalent claim under the applicable national law.

The ECJ subsequently ruled that this was what it had intended in *Barber*;[77] in *Ten Oever* v. *Stichting Bedrijfspensioenfonds voor het Glazenwassers- en Schoonmaakbedrijf*,[78] it held:

[75] [1990] ECR I-1889, at 1955-6. (Emphasis supplied.) The French text of the same passage omits the word 'all' in the emphasized section: 'Dans ces conditions, des considérations impérieuses de sécurité juridique s'opposent à ce que des situations juridique qui ont épuisé leurs effets dans le passé soient remises en cause alors que, dans un tel cas, l'équilibre financier de nombre de régimes de pensions conventionellement exclus risquerait d'être rétroactivement bouleversé.'

[76] In 'Occupational Pensions are Pay under EEC Law' (1990) 32 EOR 30. See also the analysis of Van Gerven AG in Joined Cases C-109, 110, 152 and 200/91 *Ten Oever* v. *Stichting Bedrijfspensioenfonds voor het Glazenwassers- en Schoonmaakbedrijf, Moroni* v. *Collo GmbH, Neath* v. *Hugh Steeper Ltd* and *Coloroll Pension Trustees Ltd* v. *Russell* [1993] ECR I-4879.

[77] This was fortunate in the sense that a battle between the EC's legislature and its judiciary would have had disastrous consequences for the rule of law in the Community; on the other hand, it was unfortunate in that it meant that full equality in the area of pensions will not be achieved until about 2030.

[78] Case C-109/91 [1993] ECR I-4879. Van Gerven AG commented in his submissions that the Protocol had not been intended to alter the meaning to be placed on the Court's words in *Barber*; his view was that this is clear from the fifth indent of Art. B {Art. 2} of the TEU which states that one of the Union's objectives is 'to maintain in full the "acquis communautaire" and build on it'.

The Court's ruling [in *Barber*] took account of the fact that it is a characteristic of this form of pay that there is a time lag between the accrual of entitlement to the pension, which occurs gradually throughout the employee's working life, and its actual payment, which is deferred until a particular age. The Court also took into consideration the way in which occupational pension funds are financed and thus of the accounting links existing in each individual case between the periodic contributions and the future amounts to be paid. Given the reasons explained in . . . the *Barber* judgment for limiting its effects in time, it must be made clear that equality of treatment in the matter of occupational pensions may be claimed only in relation to benefits payable in respect of periods of employment subsequent to 17 May 1990, . . . subject to the exception in favour of workers or those claiming under them who have, before that date, initiated legal proceedings or raised an equivalent claim under the applicable national law.[79]

The consequence of this interpretation is that pension-providers must now calculate the proportions of each pension which are attributable to service before and after 17 May 1990 and make the necessary mathematical adjustments to ensure equality of treatment for the later period and not the earlier one. Where a particular pension benefit is not linked to length of service, such as a lump sum paid on the death of an employee during employment, then whether or not the principle of equality applies depends upon whether the triggering event occurred before or after 17 May 1990.[80]

The complexity surrounding this area is increased by the fact that the Court has also ruled that the temporal limitation contained in *Barber* applies only to claims for pension payment, not to claims in relation to the right to join a pension scheme; the right to join a scheme on non-discriminatory terms had been established in *Bilka-Kaufhaus GmbH* v. *Weber Von Hartz*[81] and in *Fisscher* v. *Voorhuis Hengelo BV*[82] the Court held that this

---

[79] Ibid. at 4944-5. Case C-110/91 *Moroni* v. *Collo GmbH* [1993] ECR I-6591 and Case C-200/91 *Coloroll Pension Trustees Ltd* v. *Russell* [1994] ECR I-4389 established that the same temporal limitation applies to non-contracted-out pension schemes; the logic of this holding is dubious in the light of the Court's reasoning in *Barber* because it has been known since Case 170/84 *Bilka-Kaufhaus Gmbh* v. *Weber Von Hartz* [1986] ECR 1607 (discussed above) that pensions paid under such schemes fall within Art. 119; Van Gerven AG got over this difficulty by arguing that in *Bilka* the Court had ruled only on the questions of whether a scheme of the type in point fell within Art. 119 and whether the exclusion of part-timers constituted unlawful discrimination and that it was not until *Barber* that the Court addressed the lawfulness of an age condition which was different for men and women. In Case C-152/91 *Neath* v. *Hugh Steeper Ltd* [1993] ECR I-6935, the Court added: 'As regards transfer benefits and lump-sum options . . . since by virtue of the *Barber* judgment Article 119 cannot be invoked to call in question the financial basis of pension rights accrued before 17 May 1990 on the basis of different retirement ages, it follows . . . that its capital equivalent must necessarily be subject to the consequences of that temporal limitation' (at 6959).

[80] Case C-200/91 *Coloroll Pension Trustees Ltd* v. *Russell* [1994] ECR I-4389.

[81] Case 170/84 [1986] ECR 1607.

[82] Case C-128/93 [[1994] ECR I-4583. The pension scheme in this case excluded married women from membership at the material date. See also Case C-57/93 *Vroege* v. *NCIV Instituut voor Volkshuisvesting BV* [1994] ECR I-4541 where part-time workers were excluded;

made it impossible to argue that it was thereafter unclear that Article 119 applied to this situation:

[T]he limitation of the effects in time of the *Barber* judgment concerns only those kinds of discrimination which employers and pension schemes could reasonably have considered to be permissible, owing to the transitional derogations for which Community law provided and which were capable of being applied to occupational pensions . . . [A]s far as the right to join an occupational pension is concerned, there is no reason to suppose that the professional groups concerned could have been mistaken about the applicability of Article 119. It has indeed been clear since the judgment in the *Bilka* case that a breach of the rule of equal treatment committed through not recognising such a right is caught by Article 119.

Moreover, since the Court's judgment in the *Bilka* case included no limitation of its effect in time, the direct effect of Article 119 can be relied upon in order retroactively to claim equal treatment in relation to the right to join an occupational pension scheme and this may be done as from 8 April 1976, the date of the *Defrenne* judgment in which the Court held for the first time that Article 119 has direct effect.[83] . . . [T]he limitation of the effects in time of the *Barber* judgment does not apply to the right to join an occupational pension scheme.[84]

Furthermore, the Court also held in this case and in *Vroege* v. *NCIV Instituut voor Volkshuisvesting BV*[85] that the Barber Protocol did not apply to claims in relation to the right to join a pension scheme; in the latter case, it explained that:

It is clear that Protocol No.2 is linked to the *Barber* judgment, since it refers to the date of that judgment . . . While extending it to all benefits payable under occupational social security schemes and incorporating it into the Treaty, Protocol No.2 essentially adopted the same interpretation of the *Barber* judgment as did the *Ten Oever* judgment. It did not, on the other hand, any more than the *Barber* judgment, deal with, or make any provision for, the conditions of membership of such occupational schemes.[86]

the Court reached the same conclusions as in *Fisscher*, the only significant difference between the two cases being that the discrimination alleged in *Vroege* was indirect whilst that in *Fisscher* was direct. (For discussion of the concepts of direct and indirect discrimination, see below). See also Case C-7/93 *Bestuur Van Het Algemeen Burgerlijk Pensioenfonds* v. *Beune* [1994] ECR I-4471.

[83] Case 43/75 *Defrenne* v. *Sabena* [1976] ECR 455, as to which see discussion below.

[84] [1994] ECR I-4583, at 4595-6.

[85] Case C-57/93 [1994] ECR I-4541. See to the same effect Case C-435/93 *Dietz* v. *Stichting Thuiszorg Rotterdam* [1996] ECR I-5223.

[86] Case C-57/93 at 4579. In Case C-246/96 *Magorrian and Cunningham* v. *Eastern Health and Social Services Board*, judgment of 11 Dec. 1997 (nyr), the ECJ categorised the inability of part-time workers to qualify as 'Mental Health Officers', and therefore to receive enhanced pension benefits, as discrimination in relation to access to the scheme; in consequence, the *Barber* temporal limitation was not relevant and the claims could be backdated to 1976.

This was a perceptive ruling on the part of a Court which did not wish its earlier decision in *Bilka* to be effectively restricted by later legislation. It was seen in Chapter 1 that national rules on limitation of action may be applied to individual claims to join pension schemes, provided that they do not have the effect of frustrating the Community right and that they are not less favourable than the rules applied to similar domestic law claims.[87] However, in *Maggorian and Cunningham* v. *Eastern Health and Social Services Board*,[87A] the ECJ held that a two-year limit on backdating a claim to pension entitlement (the usual limit on backdating equal pay claims in the UK) was contrary to EC law because it rendered it impossible in practice to exercise the right conferred by EC law.

The fact that a worker can claim retroactively to join an occupational pension scheme is somewhat undermined in practice by the fact that this does not permit the worker to escape paying contributions in relation to the period in question.[88]

The meaning of 'workers or those claiming under them who have [before 17 May 1990] initiated legal proceedings or introduced an equivalent claim under the applicable national law' was in issue in *DEI* v. *Evrenopoulos*.[89] The ECJ held that such proceedings must be brought in accordance with the procedural rules applicable in the relevant Member State. The plaintiff had applied to the Director of the Insurance Fund governing the Greek electricity industry for a pension on the death of his wife, a pensioner of the Fund. His letter remained unanswered, so he brought an action before the Greek Administrative Court of First Instance against the implied rejection of his claim on 12 June 1989. While this action was pending, the Director of the Fund refused his application. By a judgment of November 1990, the Greek Administrative Court rejected his action on the ground that he had not first lodged an objection against the rejection of his claim by the Director with the Staff Insurance Board. However, because the Director had not informed him of the possibility of lodging such an objection, the Court granted him a further three months in which to do so. He then lodged his objection with the Insurance Board in February 1991, and it too was rejected. Against this rejection the plaintiff successfully appealed and, in the course of these appellate proceedings, a ruling was sought from the ECJ. The ECJ held that the

---

[87] See also Occupational Social Security Directive, Dir. 86/378, OJ [1986] L225/40, Art. 2(2), discussed below. Cf. yhe Court of Appeal in *Preston* v. *Wolverhampton Healthcare NHS Trust* [1997] IRLR 233 which held that neither the two-year back-dating limit nor a rule of domestic law requiring equal pay claims to be brought within six months of the ending of the relevant contract of employment contravened EC law. Similar issues are also raised in Case C-305/95 *Université Catholique de Louvain* v. *Plapied* and Case C-326/96 *Levez* v. *Jennings Ltd.* [1996] IRLR 499 (both pending before the ECJ at the time of writing).

[87A] Op. cit. n. 86.   [88] *Fisscher* op. cit. n. 82.

[89] Case C-147/95 (nyr).

judicial proceedings between the plaintiff and the defendant began with the original action, namely the proceedings of 12 June 1989, and were thus commenced before the crucial date of the ruling in the *Barber* case.

Further problems have arisen with respect to transitional arrangements where, pursuant to *Barber*, pension schemes changed their rules so as to stipulate the same pension age for men and women. These problems highlight the mixed blessing which sex equality in pension schemes has proved to be from the point of view of women.[90] In *Smith* v. *Avdel Systems Ltd*,[91] the Court held that, until equalising measures are adopted by a pension scheme, the only way in which there can be compliance with Article 119 is to grant to persons in the disadvantaged class the advantages of those in the favoured class;[92] thus, where a scheme had pension ages of 60 for women and 65 for men, between 17 May 1990 and the date on which the fund rules were changed, the pension rights of men must be calculated on the basis of a pension age of 60. However, after the fund rules changed, the Court held weakly and with little explanation that Article 119 did not preclude measures producing equality by reducing the advantage of the persons formerly favoured, so that from this date onwards it was permissible to have a common pension age of 65. As to the period before 17 May 1990, the Court held that, since Article 119 did not affect the matter, Community law did not justify the retroactive reduction of the advantages which women at that time enjoyed. It added that:

[O]nce discrimination has been found to exist, and an employer takes steps to achieve equality for the future by reducing the advantages of the favoured class, achievement of equality cannot be made progressive on a basis that still maintains discrimination, even if only temporarily ... [T]herefore ... the step of raising the retirement age for women to that for men, which an employer decides to take in order to remove discrimination in relation to occupational pensions as regards benefits payable in respect of future periods of service, cannot be accompanied by measures, even if only transitional, designed to limit the adverse consequences which such a step may have for women.[93]

A second series of difficulties which emerged from *Barber* concerned precisely what amounts to unlawful discrimination within a pension scheme. In *Barber* itself, the discrimination took the seemingly blatant

---

[90] For an interesting analysis of the effect of EC pension equality provisions on the financial position of older people, see Luckhaus and Moffat, *Serving the Market And People's Needs?* (Joseph Rowntree Foundation, York), 1996.

[91] Case C-408/92 [1994] ECR I-4435.

[92] See below for more general discussion of the principle of 'equalisation upwards' in relation to Art. 119.

[93] [1994] ECR I-4435 at 4467. See also Case C-28/93 *Van Den Akker* v. *Stichting Shell Pensioenfonds* [1994] ECR I-4527 and Case C-200/91 *Coloroll Pension Trustees Ltd* v. *Russell* [1994] ECR I-4389.

form of setting different pensionable ages for men and women.[94] The Court had held:

. . . Article 119 prohibits any discrimination with regard to pay as between men and women, whatever the system which gives rise to such inequality. Accordingly, it is contrary to Article 119 to impose an age condition which differs according to sex in respect of pensions paid under a contracted-out scheme, even if the difference between the pensionable age for men and that for women is based on the one provided for by the national statutory scheme.[95]

Does the notion of discrimination extend to more subtle differentiation,[96] such as the payment of a survivor's pension to widows but not to widowers? The Court gave an affirmative answer to this in the *Ten Oever* case, saying that 'entitlement to such a benefit is a consideration deriving from the survivor's spouse's membership of the scheme, the pension being vested in the survivor by reason of the employment relationship between the employer and the survivor's spouse and being paid to him or her by reason of the spouse's employment . . . [A] survivor's pension . . . [therefore] falls within the scope of Article 119'.[97] It added in *Coloroll Pension Trustees Ltd.* v. *Russell*[98] that the survivor's rights are directly effective. Furthermore, Article 119 can be relied upon against the trustees of an occupational pension scheme, even though the trustees are not technically party to the employment relationship since 'the effectiveness of Article 119 would be considerably diminished and the legal protection required to ensure real equality would be seriously impaired if an employee or an employee's dependants could rely on that provision only as against the employer . . .'[99] The temporal limitation in *Barber* also applies to a survivor's pension.[100]

[94] But the setting of different pensionable ages for the two sexes is less obviously discrimination forbidden by Art. 119 if a rigid separation is maintained as between the quantum of a pension and the terms of access to it. See further discussion of this distinction in Chap. 3.

[95] [1990] ECR I-1889, at 1953. For the same principle in relation to supplementary pension schemes, see Case C-110/91 *Moroni* v. *Collo GmbH* [1993] ECR I-6591.

[96] An example is provided by *Davies* v. *Girobank plc* (1997) 75 EOR 43, in which an industrial tribunal has referred to the ECJ the issue of whether the non-recognition of a period of unpaid maternity leave in determining pension entitlement breaches Art. 119.

[97] [1993] ECR I-4879, at 4944. The Editors of the EOR have made the interesting point that this principle might be extended so as to outlaw private medical insurance schemes provided for the spouses of employees (as well as employees themselves) which exclude pregnancy coverage: see (1994) 53 EOR 48.

[98] Case C-200/91 [1994] ECR I-4389. See also Case C-147/95 *DEI* v. *Evrenopoulos* (nyr).

[99] Case C-200/9 at 4411. See also Case C-128/93 *Fisscher* v. *Voorhuis Hengelo BV* [1994] ECR I-4583 and Case C-435/93 *Dietz* v. *Stichting Thuiszorg Rotterdam* [1996] ECR I-5223.

[100] Case C-200/91 at 4419-20. Cf. the view of Van Gerven AG, who had proposed a temporal limitation on the survivor's rights from the date of the *Ten Oever* judgment itself (rather than from the date of the *Barber* judgment). In his submissions in *Vroege* and *Fisscher*, the Advocate General said that he had only one explanation for the Court's choice of the date of the *Barber* judgment: 'the Court is disposed to consider that the temporal limitation

The *Coloroll* case also established that, although Article 119 applies to all benefits payable to an employee by an occupational pension scheme irrespective of whether that scheme is contributory or non-contributory, it does not apply to additional benefits consequent on additional voluntary contributions made by the employee since these do not arise out of employment.[101]

Neither does the equality principle contained in Article 119 apply to an employer's contributions paid under a defined-benefit scheme and these may therefore vary as between male and female employees as a result, for example, of the use of gender-specific actuarial tables. This emerged from *Neath* v. *Hugh Steeper Ltd.*[102] which involved a scheme providing employees with a pension corresponding to one-sixtieth of their final salary for each year of service. The scheme was contributory on the part of both employees and the employer. The employees' contributions consisted of a percentage of salary and in this there was no distinction as between men and women. However, the employer's contributions had to cover the balance of the cost of the pensions promised and so varied over time; they were also higher for female employees than for male employees because the actuarial tables used reflected the fact that women, on average, live longer than men. Where an employee left employment before reaching the prescribed age, acquired pension rights could either be transferred into another fund or the former employee could receive a capital sum by way of commutation; however, in calculating such transfer value or a capital sum, gender-specific actuarial calculations would again be used, with the result that a man would receive less than a woman. The Court held:

> The assumption . . . is that the employer commits himself, albeit unilaterally, to pay his employees defined benefits or grant them specific advantages and that the employees in turn expect the employer to pay them those benefits or provide them with those advantages. Anything that is not a consequence of that commitment and does not therefore come within the corresponding expectations of the employees falls outside the concept of pay.
>
> In the context of a defined-benefit occupational pension scheme . . ., the employer's commitment to his employees concerns the payment, at a given moment in time, of a periodic pension for which the determining criteria are already known at the time when the commitment is made and which constitutes pay within the meaning of Article 119. However, that commitment does not

of the effects of the *Barber* judgment is also applicable in the other situations for which Directive 86/378 allows exceptions to the application of the principle of equal treatment . . . ': [1994] ECR I-4541, at 4560.

[101] Case C-200/91 at 4427-8.

[102] Case C-152/91 [1993] ECR I-6935. See also Case C-200/91 *Coloroll Pension Trustees Ltd* v. *Russell* [1994] ECR I-4389.

necessarily have to do with the funding arrangements chosen to secure the periodic payment of the pension, which thus remain outside the scope of application of Article 119.

In contributory schemes, funding is provided through the contributions made by the employees and those made by the employers. The contributions made by the employees are an element of their pay since they are deducted directly from an employee's salary, which by definition is pay (see the judgment in Case 69/80 *Worringham* v. *Lloyds Bank* [1981] ECR 767). The amount of those contributions must therefore be the same for all employees, male and female, which is indeed so in the present case. This is not so in the case of the employer's contributions which ensure the adequacy of the funds necessary to cover the cost of the pensions promised, so securing their payment in the future, that being the substance of the employer's commitment.

It follows that, unlike periodic payment of pensions, inequality of employers' contributions paid under funded defined-benefit schemes, which is due to the use of actuarial factors differing according to sex, is not struck at by Article 119.

That conclusion necessarily extends to the specific aspects referred to in the questions submitted, namely the conversion of part of the periodic pension into a capital sum and the transfer of pension rights, the value of which can be determined only by reference to the funding arrangements chosen.[103]

The answer to be given to the national court must therefore be that the use of actuarial factors differing according to sex in funded defined-benefit occupational pension schemes does not fall within the scope of Article 119 . . .[104]

In *Coloroll Pension Trustees Ltd.* v. *Russell*[105] the Court extrapolated from its reasoning in *Neath* to defined-benefit schemes in the situations involved in the later case, namely:

. . . [W]here a reversionary pension is payable to a dependant in return for the surrender of part of the annual pension and where a reduced pension is paid when the employee opts for early retirement. [In these cases too] the funding arrangements chosen must also be taken into account. Since those arrangements are not covered by Article 119, any inequality in the amounts of those benefits, arising from the use of actuarial factors in the funding of the scheme, is not struck at by that Article.[106]

---

[103] It is submitted that this is a particularly obscure passage in the Court's judgment; it is far from clear why it is a 'necessary' extension from the mathematics adopted to calculate the employer's contribution to the scheme that the capital equivalent of a payment which certainly falls within the equality principle contained in Art. 119 should cease to be subject to this principle.

[104] [1993] ECR I-6935, at 6962-3. The apparently general nature of the final paragraph quoted in the text must, it is submitted, be read in the context of the preceding paragraphs; thus, it is restricted to the use of sex-specific actuarial calculations in relation to employer contributions only and does not permit their use in relation to employee contributions or benefits. Query the applicability of the *Neath* ruling in the case of defined-contribution schemes, as to which see further discussion below.

[105] Case C-200/91 [1994] ECR I-4389.

[106] Ibid. at 4425-6.

The acceptability of such gender-specific actuarial calculations to the ECJ is regrettable,[107] especially since it means that, in these cases, it is more expensive to employ women than men, which clearly constitutes an obstacle to the principle of equal treatment. In addition, it may be seen as evidence of the Court's diminishing sensitivity to the demands of an effective anti-discrimination law. It is submitted that there is considerable force in the arguments expressed by the Commission:

[T]he principle of equal pay for men and women must be applied individually and not on a category basis. The fact that women generally live longer than men has no significance at all for the life expectancy of a specific individual and it is not acceptable for an individual to be penalised on account of assumptions which are not certain to be true in his specific case.[108] Moreover, there are a number of risk factors which are not taken into account: risks associated with certain occupations, smoking, state of health and so on. Finally, there is no technical necessity for pension schemes to have a distinction based on life expectancies: some pension schemes, and all state pension schemes, use a system of risk compensation which covers differences in the probable lifespan of men and women . . . [T]he Supreme Court of the United States has held that similar discrimination in pension schemes is incompatible with the Civil Rights Act 1964.[109]

Van Gerven AG himself likewise rejected the use of such calculations:

The unequal treatment of men and women may . . . not constitute unlawful discrimination if the difference in treatment is based on objective differences which are relevant, that is to say which bear an actual connection with the subject of the rules entailing unequal treatment. In this regard, I could for instance imagine that factors having a direct impact on the life expectancy of a specific individual, such as risks associated with a particular occupation, smoking, eating and drinking habits and so forth, would be taken into account, if this is technically possible, in order to justify individual differences in contributions and/or benefits. As regards differences in average life expectancy between men and women, the situation is different, however. These differences bear no relation to the life expectancy of a specific individual and are thus irrelevant for the calculation of the contributions and/or benefits which may be ascribed to that individual.[110]

Birds Eye Walls Ltd. v. *Roberts*[111] concerned the legality of a so-called 'bridging pension' in the UK. The bridging pension was intended to

---

[107] See also Curtin, 'Occupational Pension Schemes and Article 119: Beyond the Fringe?' (1987) 27 CMLRev. 215.

[108] It might be added that statistics which held good for a past generation might well not do so for later generations: for example, it would not be surprising if a generation of women who have been subject to the stresses and strains of paid employment (as well as their seemingly inevitable domestic responsibilities) proved to have a shorter average longevity than their male counterparts.

[109] See the submissions of Van Gerven AG in *Ten Oever* [1993] ECR I-4879, at 4913.

[110] Ibid. at 4919.

[111] Case C-132/92 [1993] ECR I-5579.

equalise the financial package received by male and female employees retiring early but, in order to achieve this result, smaller sums were paid to women aged between 60 and 65 than to men of the same age because of the women's entitlement to a state pension. Mrs Roberts argued that this amounted to a breach of Article 119 but the ECJ disagreed. It held that, albeit that the bridging pension constituted pay, like must be compared with like in order to establish discrimination:

It should be noted that the principle of equal treatment laid down by Article 119 of the Treaty, like the general principle of non-discrimination which it embodies in a specific form, presupposes that the men and women to whom it applies are in identical situations. However, that would not appear to be so where the deferred payment which an employer makes to those of his employees who are compelled to take early retirement on grounds of ill health is regarded as a supplement to the financial resources of the man or woman concerned.

It follows clearly from the mechanism for calculating the bridging pension that the assessment of the amount thereof is not frozen at a particular moment but necessarily varies on account of changes occurring in the financial position of the man or woman concerned with the passage of time.

Accordingly, although until the age of 60 the financial position of a woman taking early retirement on grounds of ill health is comparable to that of a man in the same situation, neither of them as yet entitled to payment of the state pension, that is no longer the case between the ages of 60 and 65 since that is when women, unlike men, start drawing that pension. That difference as regards the objective premise, which necessarily entails that the amount of the bridging pension is not the same for men and women, cannot be considered discriminatory.[112]

The Occupational Social Security Directive

Before it became clear just how extensive was the protection extended by Article 119 to the various types of pension schemes, the Council legislated specifically to deal with this matter. The legislation took the form of the so-called Occupational Social Security Directive.[113] The expressed objective

---

[112] Ibid. at 5604-5. Cf. the reasoning of Van Gerven AG, discussed below in relation to the possible justification of direct discrimination. For comment on the post-*Barber* cases, see also Hanlon, 'Some Backward Steps for Equality' (1995) 17 JSWFL 237 and id., 'Some Further Backward Steps for Equality' (1995) 17 JSWFL 399.

[113] Directive 86/378, OJ [1986] L225/40. The Directive was foreshadowed by Art. 3(3) of the Social Security Directive (Directive 79/7, OJ [1979] L6/24, as to which see Chap. 4), which provides: 'With a view to ensuring implementation of the principle of equal treatment in occupational schemes, the Council, acting on a proposal from the Commission, will adopt provisions defining its substance, its scope and the arrangements for its application'. In Case C-7/93 *Bestuur Van Het Algemeen Burgerlijk Pensioenfonds* v. *Beune* [1994] ECR I-4471, Jacobs AG commented that 'at first sight the combination of the terms "occupational", apparently in the sense of "non-statutory", and "social security" may seem surprising' (at p. 4481).

of this instrument was to 'implement' the principle of equal treatment in occupational social security schemes.[114] Ironically, in the light of the treatment later accorded by the ECJ to Article 119 in relation to pensions, the chief effect of the Directive has actually been a negative one; as seen above, its existence and in particular the exemptions which it contained in its original form, provided an important part of the reasoning which underlay the Court's temporal restriction of the effect of the Treaty in the *Barber* case.

The Directive was subsequently amended by Directive 96/97,[115] so as to reflect the substance of the Court's rulings in *Barber* and its later jurisprudence on pensions equality; the main changes that this entailed were to make it clear that the substantive right to equality in this field flows from Article 119, not the Directive,[116] and to reduce the number of exceptions permitted. The Member States were required by this later instrument to legislate to comply with its terms by 1 July 1997.[117]

The Occupational Social Security Directive defines 'occupational social security schemes' as:

schemes not governed by Directive 79/7/EEC whose purpose is to provide workers, whether employees or self-employed, in an undertaking or group of undertakings, area of economic activity, occupational sector or group of such sectors with benefits intended to supplement the benefits provided by statutory social security schemes or to replace them, whether membership of such schemes is compulsory or optional.[118]

Although both the *Bilka-Kaufhaus*-type supplementary pension scheme and the *Barber*-type substitutive pension scheme are thus within the scope of the Directive, the practical importance of the instrument was largely undermined by the Court's rulings that Article 119 also applies to such schemes. Article 119 has proved to be a far more potent weapon, in part because it is not handicapped by the Directive's lack of horizontal direct effect,[119] and in part because the original version of the Directive provided for a number of exceptions not contained in Article 119.[120]

---

[114] Art. 1 of the Directive. According to Jacobs AG in the *Beune* case, referred to in the preceding note, Article 119 and the Directive were not intended to be mutually exclusive.

[115] OJ [1997] L46/20.

[116] There is a parallel to be drawn with the Equal Pay Directive, Dir. 75/117, OJ [1975] L45/19. As discussed below, this merely fleshes out the bare principles contained in Article 119.

[117] Art. 3(1) of the amending Directive.

[118] Art. 2(1) of the Occupational Social Security Directive.

[119] See Chap. 1 for discussion of the concept of horizontal direct effect.

[120] The Occupational Social Security Directive however, unlike Art. 119, covers the self-employed, as regards whom the exceptions contained in its original version (viz. for pensionable age, survivors' benefits and actuarial calculations) are maintained by Art. 9. See further below.

The Directive does not apply to:

(a) individual contracts for self-employed workers;
(b) schemes for self-employed workers having only one member;
(c) insurance contracts to which the employer is not a party, in the case of salaried workers;
(d) optional provision of occupational schemes offered to participants individually to guarantee them:
     —either additional benefits,[121] or
     —a choice of date on which the normal benefits for self-employed workers will start, or a choice between several benefits;
(e) occupational schemes in so far as benefits are financed by contributions paid by workers on a voluntary basis.[122]

Legislative blessing is given to the ruling in *Birds Eye Walls Ltd.* v. *Roberts*[123] by Article 2(3), which States:

This Directive does not preclude an employer granting to persons who have already reached the retirement age for the purposes of granting a pension by virtue of an occupational scheme, but who have not yet reached the retirement age for the purposes of granting a statutory retirement pension, a pension supplement, the aim of which is to make equal or more nearly equal the overall amount of benefit paid to these persons in relation to the amount paid to persons of the other sex in the same situation who have already reached the statutory retirement age, until the persons benefiting from the supplement reach the statutory retirement age.

The Directive governs the treatment of members of the working population 'including self-employed persons, persons whose activity is interrupted by illness, maternity, accident or involuntary unemployment and persons seeking employment, to retired and disabled workers and to those claiming under them, in accordance with national law and/or practice'.[124]

The hazards against which the scheme must provide protection in order to fall within the ambit of the Directive are defined, apparently exhaustively:

This Directive shall apply to:

(a) occupational schemes which provide protection against the following risks:

     —sickness,
     —invalidity,

---

[121] As to which, see Case C-200/91 *Coloroll Pension Trustees Ltd* v. *Russell* [1994] ECR I-4389, discussed above.   [122] Art. 2(2) of the Directive.
[123] Case C-132/92 [1993] ECR I-5579, discussed above.
[124] Art. 3 of the Directive.

—old age, including early retirement,
—industrial accidents and occupational diseases,
—unemployment,

(b)   occupational schemes which provide for other social benefits, in cash or in
      kind, and in particular survivors' benefits and family allowances, if such
      benefits are accorded to employed persons and thus constitute a considera-
      tion paid by the employer to the worker by reason of the latter's employ-
      ment.[125]

The principle of non-discrimination is spelled out in similar but not
wholly identical terms to those in the Equal Treatment Directive;[126] there
must be no discrimination 'on the basis of sex, either directly or indirectly,
by reference in particular to marital or family status'.[127] As in the case of
the Equal Treatment Directive, it is unclear from this formulation whether
discrimination on the basis of marital or family status on its own is caught
by the Directive, or whether it is only prohibited where it also constitutes
discrimination on the ground of sex. It is provided that there must be no
such discrimination:

especially as regards:

—the scope of the schemes and the conditions of access to them;
—the obligation to contribute and the calculation of contributions;
—the calculation of benefits, including supplementary benefits due in respect of a spouse or dependants, and the conditions governing the duration and retention of entitlement to benefits.[128]

The word 'especially' of course indicates that any other form of
discrimination, unless specifically excepted elsewhere in the Directive, is
also forbidden. Special protective provisions for women relating to
maternity are, however, permitted.[129] The words used here are substantially
identical to those used in the Social Security Directive[130] and they are
presumably intended to mean that especially favourable benefits can be
extended to women having babies. However, the wording used is somewhat
unclear in at least two respects. First, unlike the formula adopted in the
Equal Treatment Directive, there is no reference to pregnancy as well as
maternity. It may be thought that maternity necessarily implies pregnancy
and the ECJ certainly might interpret the provision in this way; if it did not
do so, however, problems could develop, for instance, in relation to
counting periods of leave from work prior to the birth of a baby.[131]

---

[125] Ibid. Art. 4.
[126] Directive 76/207, OJ [1976] L39/40, discussed in detail in Chap. 3.
[127] Occupational Social Security Directive, Art. 5.
[128] Ibid. Art. 5(1).   [129] Ibid. Art. 5(2).
[130] Directive 79/7, OJ [1979] L6/24, discussed in detail in Chap. 4.
[131] This matter is raised in the reference pending before the ECJ in *Davies* v. *Girobank plc*
(1997) 75 EOR 43.

Secondly, it is unclear from the wording of the Directive just how far the maternity exception really goes.[132] The ECJ of course usually gives a narrow reading to exceptions to general principles which themselves confer fundamental liberties. But here it might not analyse the exception in this way and might instead see the fundamental right as the right to maternity and thus be persuaded to give this provision a broad reading, so as to confer the maximum protection on mothers. The extent of the discretion intended to be left to the Member States by the maternity exception is thus far from clear.[133] In the view of the present writer the Court ought to countenance the legality of positive measures in favour of pregnant women and those who have recently given birth, since otherwise equality is not accorded to the sexes as a matter of reality. Furthermore, the issue is more one of construing the basic right to equality than of implying exceptions into the text of the Article.[134]

Article 6(1) of the Directive, as amended,[135] contains considerable detail as regards the ways in which sex discrimination may arise:

Provisions contrary to the principle of equal treatment shall include those based on sex, either directly or indirectly, in particular by reference to marital or family status, for:

(a) determining the persons who may participate in an occupational scheme;

(b) fixing the compulsory or optional nature of participation in an occupational scheme;

(c) laying down different rules as regards the age of entry into the scheme or the minimum period of employment or membership of the scheme required to obtain the benefits thereof;

(d) laying down different rules, except as provided for in points (h) and (i), for the reimbursement of contributions when a worker leaves a scheme without having fulfilled the conditions guaranteeing a deferred right to long-term benefits;

(e) setting different conditions for the granting of benefits or restricting such benefits to workers of one or other of the sexes;

(f) fixing different retirement ages;

(g) suspending the retention or acquisition of rights during periods of

---

[132] Does it, for example, extend to adoption?

[133] Whether any such positive measures in favour of pregnancy and maternity are permitted under Art. 119 has not yet been decided by the ECJ. For discussion of Art. 119(4), added by the Amsterdam Treaty and apparently permitting certain measures of positive action, see Chap. 3.

[134] Some support for this view is to be derived from the comments of Slynn AG in Case 318/86 *Re Sex Discrimination in the Civil Service, Commission* v. *France* [1988] ECR 3559, esp. at 3572, where he said: 'Pregnancy of female staff has to be accommodated by employers as one of the consequences of . . . equal treatment.' Cf. Case 177/88 *Dekker* v. *Stichting Vormingscentrum Voor Jonge Volwassen Plus* [1990] ECR I-3941, discussed below.

[135] In particular, so as to put into statutory form the decisions in Case C-152/91 *Neath* v. *Hugh Steeper Ltd.* [1993] ECR I-6935 and Case C-200/91 *Coloroll Pension Trustees Ltd.* v. *Russell* [1994] ECR I-4389, discussed above.

maternity leave or leave for family reasons which are granted by law or agreement and are paid by the employer;

(h) setting different levels of benefit, except in so far as may be necessary to take account of actuarial calculation factors which differ according to sex in the case of defined-contribution schemes. In the case of funded defined-benefit schemes, certain elements (examples[136] of which are annexed) may be unequal where the inequality of the amounts results from the effects of the use of actuarial factors differing according to sex at the time when the scheme's funding is implemented;

(i) setting different levels for workers' contributions; setting different levels for employers' contributions, except:

—in the case of defined-contribution schemes if the aim is to equalise the amount of the final benefits or to make them more nearly equal for both sexes,

—in the case of funded defined-benefit schemes where the employer's contributions are intended to ensure the adequacy of the funds necessary to cover the cost of the benefits defined;

(j) laying down different standards or standards applicable only to workers of a specified sex, except as provided for in points (h) and (i), as regards the guarantee or retention of entitlement to deferred benefits when a worker leaves a scheme.

The Annex provides:

Examples of elements which may be unequal, in respect of funded defined-benefit schemes, as referred to in Article 6(h):

—conversion into a capital sum of part of a periodic pension,
—transfer of pension rights,
—a reversionary pension payable to a dependant in return for the surrender of part of a pension,
—a reduced pension where the worker opts to take early retirement.

Even following its amendment, the Directive therefore continues to permit the use of gender-specific actuarial calculations in certain circumstances.[137] It was seen above that the ECJ's decision in *Neath* v. *Hugh Steeper Ltd.*[138] outlawed inequality over pension payments and employee contributions in defined-benefit schemes, but permitted unequal employer contributions consequent on gender-specific actuarial calculations in such schemes. The Directive today confirms this position. The Court has not, however, dealt with these matters in relation to contribution-defined schemes; whilst accepting that employee contributions must be equal in such schemes, the Directive permits specified exceptions to the equality principle in relation

---

[136] Note the use of the word 'examples' here; the list is clearly not exhaustive.

[137] Cf. the Commission's proposal for the original Directive which prohibited the determination of benefit amounts or rates of contribution by reference to such factors: see OJ [1983] C134/7.

[138] Case C-152/91 [1993] ECR I-6935.

to employers' contributions and pension payments in contribution-defined schemes. The vulnerability of these exceptions to successful challenge for breaching Article 119 thus remains to be tested before the Court. The continued scope for gender-specific actuarial tables sparked considerable controversy between the Commission and the European Parliament during the legislative process of the amending Directive and was only ended on the Commission giving its undertaking to give further consideration to this matter.

Article 6(2) of the Directive States that '[w]here the granting of benefits . . . is left to the discretion of the scheme's management bodies, the latter must take account of the principle of equal treatment'. In response to the argument that it was to be implied from this provision that Article 119 itself was not directly effective as against the trustees of a pension fund, Van Gerven AG commented in *Coloroll Pension Trustees Ltd.* v. *Russell*:[139]

I see in that provision merely a confirmation of the Community legislature's intention to give effect to the principle of equal treatment as effectively as possible and certainly not any argument *a contrario* according to which the worker or the person (or persons) claiming under him could not, as regards pay discrimination directly caught by Article 119, rely on Article 119 against trustees as well. In any case, that directive [viz. the Occupational Social Security Directive] cannot detract from the effect of Article 119 . . .[140]

Article 8(1) used to provide that the Member States were to take all necessary steps to ensure that the provisions of occupational schemes contrary to the principle of equal treatment were revised by 1 January 1993. However, the ruling of the ECJ in *Barber* that, albeit subject to the temporal limitation set out in that decision, Article 119 takes direct effect in relation to pension schemes rendered Article 8(1) nugatory; the Court later explained in *Moroni* v. *Collo GmbH*:[141]

By its second question, the national court wishes to know whether or not Article 8(1) of Directive 86/378 prevents the legal consequences of the incompatibility with Article 119 of the Treaty of the setting of different retirement ages for men and women for the purposes of the payment of company pensions from being drawn before 1 January 1993 . . .

This question is essentially concerned with the relationship between Article 119 and Directive 86/378.

It is sufficient to point out in this regard that it is settled law that Article 119 applies directly to all forms of discrimination which may be identified solely with the aid of the criteria of equal work and equal pay referred to by that Article, without national or Community measures being required to define them with greater precision in order to permit their application . . .[142]

---

[139] Case C-200/91, AG's submissions at [1993] ECR I-4879.
[140] Ibid. at 4940-1.   [141] Case C-110/91 [1993] ECR I-6591.
[142] For further discussion of the direct effect of Art. 119, see below.

Since with the aid of the constitutive elements of the pay in question and of the criteria laid down in Article 119 discrimination may be directly identified as arising from the setting of different retirement ages for men and women in the matter of company pensions, the effects of the Directive do not matter, for its provisions cannot in any way restrict the scope of Article 119.

It follows that, subject to [the temporal limitation contained in the *Barber* case] a worker who is discriminated against by the setting of different retirement ages for men and women may in principle assert his rights to payment of the company pension at the same age as his female counterpart and any reduction in the event of early departure from the service of the undertaking must be calculated on the basis of that age.

The answer to the second question . . . must therefore be that, subject to [the temporal limitation contained in *Barber*], Council Directive 86/378 cannot prevent Article 119 of the Treaty from being relied upon directly and immediately before national courts.[143]

Similarly, although Article 8(2) used to provide that the Directive was not to preclude 'rights and obligations relating to a period of membership of an occupational scheme prior to revision of that scheme from remaining subject to the provisions of the scheme in force during that period', the Court held in the *Beune* case[144] that:

. . . Article 8(2) . . . cannot limit the scope of Article 119 in relation to pension rights in respect of periods of membership prior to revision of the scheme concerned.[145]

Article 8 is today restricted in its scope so as to provide:

1. Member States shall take the necessary steps to ensure that the provisions of occupational schemes *for self-employed workers* contrary to the principle of equal treatment are revised with effect from 1 January 1993 at the latest.

2. This Directive shall not preclude rights and obligations relating to a period of membership of an occupational scheme *for self-employed workers* prior to revision of that scheme from remaining subject to the provisions of the scheme in force during that period.[146]

Furthermore, Article 2(1) of the amending Directive 96/97 mandates that:

Any measure implementing this Directive, as regards paid workers, must cover all benefits derived from periods of employment subsequent to 17 May 1990 and shall apply retroactively to that date, without prejudice to workers or those claiming under them who have, before that date, initiated legal proceedings or raised an equivalent claim under national law. In that event, the implementation

---

[143] [1993] ECR I-6591, at 6616-7.

[144] Case C-7/93 *Bestuur Van Het Algemeen Burgerlijk Pensioenfonds* v. *Beune* [1994] ECR I-4471.

[145] Ibid. at 4523.   [146] Emphases supplied.

measures must apply retroactively to 8 April 1976 and must cover all the benefits derived from periods of employment after that date . . .

Article 2(2) of the amending instrument goes on to spell out the Court's customary position in relation to the procedural autonomy of the Member States:[147]

The second sentence of paragraph 1 shall not prevent national rules relating to time limits for bringing actions under national law from being relied on against workers or those claiming under them who initiated legal proceedings or raised an equivalent claim under national law before 17 May 1990, provided that they are not less favourable for that type of action than for similar actions of a domestic nature and that they do not render the exercise of Community law impossible in practice.

Article 9 of the original Directive contained exceptions, in particular for pensionable age and survivors' benefits, which were later ruled by the ECJ to fall within the scope of Article 119. The amended Article 9 is therefore restricted to the self-employed and provides:

As regards schemes for self-employed workers, Member States may defer compulsory application of the principle of equal treatment with regard to:
(a) determination of pensionable age for the granting of old-age or retirement pensions, and the possible implications for other benefits:
 —either until the date on which such equality is achieved in statutory schemes,
 —or, at the latest, until such equality is prescribed by a directive;
(b) survivors' pensions until Community law establishes the principle of equal treatment in statutory social security schemes in that regard;
(c) the application of the first subparagraph of point (i) of Article 6(1) to take account of the different actuarial calculation factors, at the latest until 1 January 1999.

A new Article 9(a) of the Directive also now provides that, where men and women may claim a flexible pension age under the same conditions, 'this shall not be deemed to be incompatible with this Directive'.

The Directive concludes with provisions guaranteeing the right to legal redress for breaches of its terms[148] and protecting workers against victimization in the form of dismissal where they have complained of a breach of the Directive.[149]

---

[147] See Chap. 1.　　[148] Art. 10 of the Directive.　　[149] Ibid. Art. 11.

Other Statutorily Regulated Payments made by Employers to their Employees

Once the ECJ had conceded in *Bilka-Kaufhaus GmbH* v. *Weber Von Hartz*[150] that an element of statutory regulation of a payment made by employer to employee did not deprive the payment of its status as 'pay' under Article 119,[151] the way was clear for that Article to be extended to a variety of payments made as a result of statutory obligations cast on employers.[152]

Very importantly in practice, the issue arose as to the applicability of Article 119 to redundancy payments. These were involved in *Burton* v. *British Railways Board*[153] but, since the issue was not discrimination in relation to the amount of the payments receivable, the Court did not there decide whether they fell within the Article 119 notion of 'pay'. However, in *Worringham* v. *Lloyds Bank Ltd.*,[154] the Court commented that: 'Sums . . . which are included in the calculation of the gross salary payable to the employee and which directly determine the calculation of other advantages linked to the salary, *such as redundancy payments* . . . form part of the worker's pay . . .'[155] The position was finally clarified as a matter of EC law[156] by *Barber* v. *Guardian Royal Exchange Assurance Group*.[157] The ECJ there held all forms of redundancy payment, whether contractual, statutory or *ex gratia*, to be within the scope of Article 119:

[T]he concept of pay . . . comprises any other consideration, whether in cash or in kind, whether immediate or future, provided that the worker receives it, albeit indirectly, in respect of his employment from his employer . . . Accordingly, the fact that certain benefits are paid after the termination of the employment relationship does not prevent them from being in the nature of pay, within the meaning of Article 119 of the Treaty.

As regards, in particular, the compensation granted to a worker in connection with his redundancy, it must be stated that such compensation constitutes a form

---

[150] Case 170/84 [1986] ECR 1607, discussed above.

[151] See also Jacobs AG in Case C-7/93 *Bestuur Van Het Algemeen Burgerlijk Pensioenfonds* v. *Beune* [1994] ECR I-4471 at 4486.

[152] The ECJ had, in fact, pointed the way to this conclusion many years earlier in Case 43/75 *Defrenne* v. *Sabena* [1976] ECR 455 where it held that 'Article 119 may be relied upon before the national courts and . . . these courts have a duty to ensure the protection of the rights which this provision vests in individuals, in particular as regards those types of discrimination *arising directly from legislative provisions* or collective labour agreements . . .' (at 476. Emphasis supplied.)

[153] Case 19/81 [1982] ECR 555. See also Snaith, 'Equal Pay and Sex Discrimination' (1982) 7 ELRev. 301.

[154] Case 69/80 [1981] ECR 767.

[155] Ibid. at 790. (Emphasis supplied.)

[156] The UK government implicitly acknowledged the applicability of Art. 119 to redundancy payments when, in s. 16 of the Employment Act 1989, it removed the discriminatory age limits applying to eligibility for statutory redundancy pay.

[157] Case C-262/88 [1990] ECR I-1889.

of pay to which the worker is entitled in respect of his employment, which is paid to him on termination of the employment relationship, which makes it possible to facilitate his adjustment to the new circumstances resulting from the loss of his employment and which provides him with a source of income during the period in which he is seeking new employment.

It follows that compensation granted to a worker in connection with his redundancy falls in principle within the concept of pay for the purposes of Article 119 of the Treaty.

At the hearing, the UK argued that the statutory redundancy payment fell outside the scope of Article 119 of the Treaty because it constituted a social security benefit and not a form of pay. In that regard it must be pointed out that a redundancy payment made by the employer . . . cannot cease to constitute a form of pay on the sole ground that, rather than deriving from the contract of employment, it is a statutory or *ex gratia* payment.

In the case of statutory redundancy payments it must be borne in mind that, as the Court held in its judgment of 8 April 1976 in Case 43/75 . . . Article 119 of the Treaty also applies to discrimination arising directly from legislative provisions. This means that benefits provided for by law may come within the concept of pay for the purposes of that provision . . . [B]enefits paid by an employer to a worker in connection with the latter's compulsory redundancy fall within the scope of the second paragraph of Article 119, whether they are paid under a contract of employment, by virtue of legislative provisions or on a voluntary basis.[158]

The Court also made another significant statement of general principle in *Barber*. It held that:

Although it is true that many advantages granted by an employer also reflect considerations of social policy, the fact that a benefit is in the nature of pay cannot be called in question where the worker is entitled to receive the benefit in question from his employer by reason of the existence of the employment relationship.[159]

Once it had become clear that redundancy payments were within Article 119, a large part of the UK's employment protection legislation fell under suspicion. Those covered by the legislation were divided into two classes: employees working for more than 16 hours a week were protected after two years' continuous employment with the same employer, whereas those working between 8 and 16 hours a week were entitled to protection only after five years' of such employment. The argument was that, since the first group of workers was predominantly male and the second predominantly female, this constituted unlawful indirect sex discrimination.[160] The Equal Opportunities Commission (EOC) therefore brought judicial review proceedings against the Secretary of State for

---

[158] Ibid. at 1949-50. This decision was followed shortly afterwards by that of the ECJ in Case 33/89 *Kowalska* v. *Freie und Hansestadt Hamburg* [1990] ECR I-2591.

[159] Case C-262/88 [1990] ECR I-1889, at 1950.

[160] See discussion below as to the concept of indirect discrimination.

Employment, alleging that this discrimination in relation to the availability of statutory redundancy pay and compensation for unfair dismissal contravened EC law.[161] The House of Lords[162] granted declarations that the discrimination in relation to redundancy pay contravened Article 119 and that the discrimination in relation to compensation for unfair dismissal contravened the Equal Treatment Directive;[163] in the absence of any ruling on the matter by the ECJ, the House left open the question of whether compensation for unfair dismissal constituted pay within the meaning of Article 119, though it was conceded that there is 'much to be said in favour' of this view.[164] However, in *Mediguard Services Ltd.* v. *Thame*,[165] the Employment Appeal Tribunal held that such compensation is within Article 119, so entitling a worker with two years' service of between 8 and 16 hours a week to bring an action for unfair dismissal. Eventually, the issue was referred to the ECJ in *R.* v. *Secretary of State for Employment, Ex p. Seymour-Smith*,[166] where the House of Lords asked whether compensation for unfair dismissal constitutes pay within the meaning of Article 119 and, if so, whether the right to complain of unfair dismissal also falls under Article 119.[167]

Another important decision of the ECJ in this context was that in *Rinner-Kuhn* v. *FWW Spezial-Gebaudereinigung GmbH*.[168] This concerned sick pay under the German statutory scheme. Under this scheme, an employer was obliged to pay an employee's full salary for the first six weeks of sickness, after which the social security system took over payments at the level of 80 per cent of normal earnings for a statutorily defined period. The employer was not entitled to be reimbursed by the state in respect of the first six weeks, unless there were fewer than 20 employees in the enterprise concerned, in which case the state reimbursed 80 per cent of the payments. In a terse judgment, making very little mention of its other relevant jurisprudence, the ECJ held that the employer's payments under this scheme constituted 'pay' for the purpose of Article 119. It stated simply that: '[T]he continued payment of wages to a worker in the event

---

[161] It emerged in the course of the proceedings that no other Member State, apart from Ireland, had similar thresholds; Ireland, where statute had at one time provided for an 18 hours per week threshold, had recently introduced legislation reducing this to 8 hours.

[162] [1994] 2 WLR 409. See also Chaps. 1 and 3.

[163] Directive 76/207, OJ [1976] L39/40, discussed further in Chap. 3. The legislation was subsequently amended so as to remove the qualifying thresholds.

[164] See the remarks of Lord Keith of Kinkel in [1994] 2 WLR 409, at 423. In the Court of Appeal, Dillon LJ commented: ' . . . compensation for unfair dismissal, which is compensation payable by the employer for the unfair premature determination of the contract of employment, must, in my judgment, fall within the definition of "pay"': [1993] 1 WLR 872, at 884.

[165] [1994] IRLR 504.

[166] [1997] 1 WLR 473.

[167] At the time of writing, the reference was pending before the ECJ.

[168] Case 171/88 [1989] ECR 2743, also discussed below.

of illness falls within the definition of "pay" within the meaning of Article 119 of the Treaty'.[169] What was unclear from this judgment was whether the Court regarded the ultimate source of the payment as significant (under the German scheme, of course, all employers had to make at least a contribution to the first six weeks' sick pay). It was seen earlier that the Court laid stress in the *Bilka-Kaufhaus* case on the fact that the benefits concerned there were financed solely by the employer, and in *Barber* it noted specifically that the schemes were either wholly financed by the employer or by both the employer and the workers. It adopted a similar approach in *Commission* v. *Belgium*.[170] A scheme, which originated in a collective agreement but was subsequently given statutory force, established special payments for elderly workers on redundancy; however, eligibility for the payments depended upon eligibility for unemployment benefit. Since women were not entitled to unemployment benefit after the age of 60, although men remained so entitled until the age of 65, women were correspondingly excluded from the special redundancy payment after 60. The payments were made by the worker's last employer. The Belgian government argued that the payments were in the nature of social security since they supplemented the state unemployment benefit and that the difference between male and female entitlement reflected the difference in state pension age, so that the situation was exempted by the Social Security Directive. The ECJ rejected this contention:

[t]he additional payment at issue, although *sui generis* in certain respects, must be deemed to constitute 'pay' within the meaning of Article 119 of the Treaty. It is clear from Collective Agreement No. 17 that that payment is to be received from the redundant worker's last employer . . . and that it is payable by reason of the employment relationship which existed between those two persons, the agreement being applicable only to workers employed in pursuance of a contract of employment and their employers . . . It is also apparent that the additional payment is contractual since it is the result of negotiations between employers and employees. The fact that it was subsequently made compulsory *erga omnes* by legislation cannot therefore detract from its contractual nature . . .

The Belgian government's argument that the additional payment and the unemployment benefit form an indivisible unit, namely the 'contractual early-retirement pension', and that consequently the additional payment should, like unemployment benefit, be regarded as a social security benefit cannot be upheld. It must be observed, first, that whilst it is true that the amount of the payment is dependent both on the reference wage and on the unemployment benefit, the additional payment nevertheless constitutes consideration received by the worker from the employer in respect of the employment relationship which existed between them. Secondly, the fact that the payment supplements a social security benefit such as unemployment benefit is not decisive. Under Collective Agreement No. 17, the additional payment, although linked to the unemployment

[169] Ibid. at 2759.   [170] Case C-173/91 [1993] ECR I-673.

benefit as regards the manner in which it is made, is independent of the general social security scheme as regards both its structure and its financing, *the latter being the responsibility of the employer alone.*[171]

On the other hand, in its ruling in *Barber* in relation to redundancy pay, the Court appeared unconcerned as to the original source of the funds involved, provided only that the payment was actually made by the employer and received by the employee in respect of his or her employment. In addition, it has also been seen that in the *Beune* case[172] in relation to pension schemes, the Court pointed out that none of the criteria for distinguishing between pay and social security payments is decisive when taken alone, but that the fundamental issue is whether the payment is made to the worker by reason of the employment relationship between the worker and the employer. This view was confirmed by the Court's decision in *Gillespie*[173] that maternity pay in the UK[174] is within Article 119; the Court arrived at this conclusion without making any explicit reference to the fact that employers making statutory maternity payments are to all intents and purposes totally reimbursed by the State and it based its decision wholly on the payment's foundation in the employment relationship. It must therefore now be concluded that a payment can constitute pay within the meaning of Article 119 even if it is not funded to any extent at all by the employer.

Are all Employment Benefits 'Pay'?

Unlike the British Equal Pay Act of 1970, which in s. 1(2) refers to discrimination in respect of any term of a contract of employment, Article 119 paragraphs (1) and (2) refer specifically only to the term 'pay'. However, as has been seen above, 'pay' is not to be confined to the physical contents of the wage packet, but clearly extends to many other forms of consideration granted even indirectly by the employer to the employee in respect of the employment. This being so, is not any benefit extended to the employee via the contract of employment to be regarded as 'pay'? Such benefits as holiday entitlements, periods of sick leave, access to canteen facilities, and so on would also appear to fall within an extended notion of 'pay': the employer does not grant them out of the goodness of his or her heart but as a reward for the job done. Such an

[171] Ibid. at 698-9. (Emphasis supplied.)

[172] Case C-7/93 *Bestuur Van Het Algemeen Burgerlijk Pensioenfonds* v. *Beune* [1994] ECR I-4471, discussed above.

[173] Case C-342/93 *Gillespie* v. *Northern Health and Social Services Board* [1996] ECR I-475, also discussed above.

[174] The Court was actually asked in this case about both statutory and contractual maternity pay. Since it drew no distinction between the two categories it seemingly attached no significance to the provenance of the payments.

argument found favour with the House of Lords in *Hayward* v. *Cammell Laird Shipbuilders (No. 2)*.[175] It remains to be seen whether it would also commend itself to the ECJ[176] but, if it did so, the scope of Article 119 would of course be enormously widened and in this context the difficulties arising as regards the direct enforcement of the Equal Treatment Directive[177] against persons other than organs of the State would be avoided.[178]

Perhaps the nearest that the ECJ has come to dealing with such an argument was in *Barber* v. *Guardian Royal Exchange Assurance Group*[179] where, as the House of Lords had been in the *Hayward* case, the Court was pressed to apply a global type of assessment to the pay received by each sex. The Court of Appeal had asked the ECJ whether, in EC law, equal pay must be ensured at the level of each element of remuneration or only on the basis of a comprehensive assessment of the consideration paid to the workers concerned. The ECJ, demonstrating considerable sensitivity to the risk of subconscious bias on the part of those carrying out such an assessment, replied that it had already:

[E]mphasized the fundamental importance of transparency and, in particular, of the possibility of a review by the national courts in order to prevent 'and, if necessary, eliminate any discrimination based on sex. With regard to the means of verifying compliance with the principle of equal pay, it must be stated that if the national courts were under an obligation to make an assessment and a comparison of all the various types of consideration granted, according to the circumstances, to men and women, judicial review would be difficult and the effectiveness of Article 119 would be diminished as a result. It follows that genuine transparency, permitting an effective review, is assured only if the principle of equal pay applies to each of the elements of remuneration granted to men or women.[180]

---

[175] [1988] 2 WLR 1134. The employers in that case had convinced the Court of Appeal that a distinction could be drawn for the purposes of the British Equal Pay Act 1970 between those terms of a contract of employment relating to the general category of 'pay', and other terms. The House of Lords rejected this argument and Lord Goff said: '[A]lmost any, indeed perhaps any, benefit will fall within "pay" in the very wide sense favoured by[the Court of Appeal]' (at 1145).

[176] Certain remarks of the ECJ in Case 149/77 *Defrenne* v. *Sabena* [1978] ECR 1365 seem at first sight to reject this argument. However, the issue before the Court there was the enforced retirement of female employees only at the age of 40 and thus concerned working conditions generally, not consideration passing from the employer to the employee. See also Case C-1/95 *Gerster* v. *Freistaat Bayern* (nyr) and further discussion in Chap. 3.

[177] Directive 76/207, OJ [1976] L39/40, discussed in detail in Chap. 3.

[178] See Chap. 1 for discussion of the impossibility of enforcing directives horizontally.

[179] Case C-262/88 [1990] ECR I-1889.

[180] Ibid. at 1953.

THE MEANING OF EQUAL WORK

Article 119 expressly mandates equal pay where men and women perform 'equal work'. The clearest and most obvious case where equal work is performed is, of course, where, as in *Defrenne* v. *Sabena*,[181] a man and a woman perform identical jobs for the same employer in a single establishment. Does the Article extend also to the performance of identical jobs for the same employer in different establishments, or to the performance of identical jobs for different employers? These questions have not yet received a direct answer from the ECJ. However, it is submitted that the answer should be 'yes' to both questions. The underlying issue concerns what precisely is being valued when two jobs are classified as constituting equal work. Broadly, there are two approaches: to analyse the value of the jobs in terms of their content and the demands they place on workers or, alternatively, to measure the value of the jobs to the employer by means of measuring, for example, the benefits they bring to the business or the cost that the employer would incur by buying in other services to replace the jobs in issue. Both approaches have their drawbacks. The job content approach involves the elusive task of putting a price on particular skills and requirements and, moreover, carries with it the risk that in so assessing job factors subconscious prejudices and discrimination are allowed to creep into the calculation. So, for example, if heavy manual work (performed in the past at least largely by men) has traditionally been rewarded at higher rates than repetitive tasks requiring considerable manual dexterity (largely the domain of women workers), then there is a real danger that a job evaluator may be swayed in the direction of rating heavy work more highly than dexterous work. On the other hand, if the approach taken is value to the employer then the legislation's potential for radically changing women workers' economic status is wholly undermined: where there is job segregation according to sex, and the women's jobs have come to be paid less than the men's, then the cost of finding another woman to perform the job in issue will be correspondingly depressed. Putting it another way, the 'market value' of women's jobs is the very thing which Article 119 seeks to address and to remedy.

For this reason, the first approach is to be preferred. The ECJ has made it clear that this is its preference too. So, for example, in *Macarthys Ltd.* v. *Smith*[182] it held:

---

[181] Case 43/75 [1976] ECR 455.
[182] Case 129/79 [1980] ECR 1275, at 1288-9. See also Crisham, 'The Equal Pay Principle: Some Recent Decisions of the ECJ' (1981) 18 CMLRev. 601.

[T]he decisive test lies in establishing whether there is a difference in treatment between a man and a woman performing 'equal work' within the meaning of Article 119. The scope of that concept . . . is entirely qualitative in character in that it is exclusively concerned with the nature of the services in question . . .[183]

It follows that it does not matter where or for whom equal work is performed. If the nature of the services is identical then it must be rewarded equally. In its early judgments on the subject, the ECJ did not appear to recognize this argument and in *Defrenne* v. *Sabena*[184] it said:

[T]he principle of equal pay contained in Article 119 may be relied upon before the national courts and . . . these courts have a duty to ensure the protection of the rights which this provision vests in individuals, in particular as regards those types of discrimination arising directly from legislative provisions or collective labour agreements, as well as in cases in which men and women receive unequal pay for equal work *which is carried out in the same establishment or service*, whether public or private.[185]

However, as will be discussed later in the present Chapter, the ECJ was concerned in this passage to distinguish between those situations in which Article 119 takes direct effect and those in which it does not. Furthermore, the factual situation with which it was presented in *Defrenne* v. *Sabena* of course involved identical work in the same establishment or service.[186] Later cases have suggested that the ECJ may believe that Article 119 does extend to comparisons with colleagues in other establishments belonging to the same employer, or even with comparators working for different employers.[187] This matter is particularly significant in Britain where the scope of comparison permitted under s. 1(6) of the Equal Pay Act 1970 is limited to cases where the man and woman are either working in the same establishment or else at different establishments of the same employer at

---

[183] Case 129/79 at 1288-9. As Lord Bridge explained in *Leverton* v. *Clwyd County Council* [1989] 2 WLR 47, this involves examining the nature of what is done, not the hours at which or frequency with which the tasks are performed. He commented: '[I]n job evaluation studies the demands made by different jobs have in practice always been assessed under whatever headings are adopted on a qualitative, not a quantitative, basis. That this is the correct basis, if English law is to conform to Community law, seems to be amply borne out by the judgment of the ECJ in *Macarthys Ltd* v. *Smith* . . . have no doubt that demand in terms of hours worked is not only beyond the expertise of the job evaluator but is, on the true construction of s. 1(2) (c) and (5) [of the Equal Pay Act 1970], a factor which is outside the scope of job evaluation' (at 74-5).

[184] Case 43/75 [1976] ECR 445.

[185] Ibid. at 476. (Emphasis supplied.)

[186] In Case 96/80 *Jenkins* v. *Kingsgate (Clothing Productions) Ltd.* [1981] ECR 911 the ECJ also appeared to confine its remarks to discrimination within a particular 'undertaking', but that again was the situation presented to it on the facts of the case.

[187] In *Hasley* v. *Fair Employment Agency* [1989] IRLR 106, Lord Lowry in the Northern Ireland Court of Appeal said: 'It has to be observed that neither the *Defrenne* nor the *Macarthy* judgment treats the remedy given by Article 119 as *confined* to work carried out *in the same establishment or service*' (at 111).

which common terms and conditions apply.[188] This restriction is self-evidently even narrower than a requirement that the claimant and the comparator must have a common employer. The Employment Appeal Tribunal has held that the scope of s. 1(6) is narrower than that permitted under Article 119 and allowed a claimant to enforce the Treaty directly so as to make a pay comparison with a comparator doing a similar job for another employer.[189] The scope of comparison under Article 119 was raised, but not answered by the ECJ, in *Commission* v. *Denmark*;[190] Van Themaat AG did, however, comment that in his opinion Article 119 extended to comparisons outside the worker's immediate work-place.[191] And the Court's statements in relation to the Equal Pay Directive[192] have contained at least the suggestion that this instrument requires comparisons outside the employer's establishment; for example, in *Commission* v. *UK*,[193] it held that the Directive requires that a worker 'be entitled to claim before an appropriate authority that his work has the same value *as other work*'.[194] When coupled with its frequent statements that the Directive does not extend, but merely gives greater articulation to, Article 119,[195] it would appear to follow that the Court may mean that Article 119 itself sometimes requires comparisons with the pay of employees outside the claimant's immediate working environment. Quite how far this notion may extend is obviously a matter to be addressed in future litigation before the ECJ. It is to be hoped, however, that in such litigation the Court would not be over-influenced by arguments based on the potential of such claims to generate inflation. As the Court itself made clear in *Defrenne* v. *Sabena*,[196] the object of Article 119 is both economic and social; its very existence in the Treaty indicates a recognition that women have suffered pay discrimination in the past and the remedying of this discrimination

[188] However, this provision has in recent times been receiving an increasingly broad interpretation by the higher courts; see in particular *Leverton* v. *Clwyd County Council* [1989] 2 WLR 47, *British Coal Corporation* v. *Smith* [1996] 3 All ER 97, and *North Yorkshire County Council* v. *Ratcliffe* [1994] ICR 810; in the last-named, for example, the Court of Appeal held that the employees of a local authority direct service organisation, set up to enable the council to engage in compulsory commercial tendering pursuant to the Local Government Act 1988, could compare their pay with persons who were directly employed by the council.

[189] See *Scullard* v. *Knowles* [1996] IRLR 344. The Tribunal emphasised that the phrase used in *Defrenne* v. *Sabena* was 'same establishment *or service*' and it proceeded to initiate further inquiries as to whether the claimant could be said to be in the same service as her comparator.

[190] Case 143/83 [1985] ECR 427.

[191] See also the remarks of Capotorti AG in Case 129/79 *Macarthys Ltd.* v. *Smith* [1980] ECR 1275, esp. at 1293-4.

[192] Directive 75/117, OJ [1975] L45/19, discussed in detail below.

[193] Case 61/81 [1982] ECR 2601.

[194] Ibid. at 2615-6. (Emphasis supplied.)

[195] See e.g. Case 96/80 *Jenkins* v. *Kingsgate (Clothing Productions) Ltd.* [1981] ECR 911, esp. at 927, and see also further discussion below.

[196] Case 43/75 [1976] ECR 455.

inevitably involves the upgrading in financial terms of particular categories of work.

One aspect of the meaning of 'equal work' which is clear is that the concept is not restricted to jobs held simultaneously. In *Macarthys Ltd.* v. *Smith*,[197] the company employed a man as manager of their stockroom until 1975 and paid him £60 per week. After he left, his job was unfilled for four months and then Ms Smith was appointed to it. However, she was paid only £50 per week. The situation was apparently not covered by the British Equal Pay Act of 1970, since that extended only to contemporaneous comparisons between employees.[198] However, the ECJ held that Article 119 did cover this situation and that its ambit 'could not be restricted by the introduction of a requirement of contemporaneity'.[199] It ruled that:

The principle of equal pay enshrined in Article 119 applies to the case where it is established that, having regard to the nature of her services, a woman has received less pay than a man who was employed prior to the woman's period of employment and who did equal work for the employer.[200]

It will be observed that this ruling makes no reference to the length of time which has elapsed between the two periods of employment. It would therefore appear that this is not a relevant factor and that, other things being equal, the comparison can be made even if there has been a very long interval between the two periods of employment. If this is correct then presumably a domestic court applying Article 119 would be entitled to take into account the effect of inflation during the interval, since otherwise there would be little point in seeking parity with a wage paid a number of years before.

Although a comparison may be made under Article 119 with the wage of a predecessor, the ECJ was not prepared in *Macarthys Ltd.* v. *Smith* to go further than this and permit hypothetical comparisons.[201] Ms Smith had argued that Article 119 also extends to workers who cannot compare their work with that of persons of the opposite sex because the employer has segregated the jobs into 'women's work' and 'men's work'; she therefore wanted the ECJ to adopt an interpretation of Article 119 which would

---

[197] Case 129/79 [1980] ECR 1275, also discussed in Chap. 1. See Wyatt, 'Article 119 EEC: Equal Pay for Female Successor to Male Worker' (1980) 5 ELRev. 374.

[198] See the judgment of the Court of Appeal at [1979] 3 CMLR 44.

[199] [1980] ECR 1275, at 1289.

[200] Ibid. at 1290. In *Diocese of Hallam Trustee* v. *Connaughton* [1996] IRLR 505, the Employment Appeal Tribunal permitted an applicant to rely on Art. 119 to compare her pay rate with that of a male successor.

[201] Thus Trabucchi AG exaggerated in Case 43/75 *Defrenne* v. *Sabena* [1976] ECR 455 when he said: '[A]s regards the abolition, in connection with pay, of *all discrimination* based on sex, Article 119 imposes an obligation which is clear, precise and unconditional' (at 486). (Emphasis supplied.)

encompass comparison with a hypothetical, as well as an actual, male worker doing the same job.[202] The Court held that this situation:

[I]s to be classed as indirect and disguised discrimination, the identification of which . . . implies comparative studies of entire branches of industry and therefore requires, as a prerequisite, the elaboration by the Community and national legislative bodies of criteria of assessment. From that it follows that, in cases of actual discrimination falling within the scope of the direct application of Article 119, comparisons are confined to parallels which may be drawn on the basis of concrete appraisals of the work actually performed by employees of different sex within the same establishment or service.[203]

It is unfortunate that the Court took this view, but it is to be noted that its remarks on the subject were confined to the context of the direct effect of Article 119.[204] In *Dekker* v. *Stichting Vormingscentrum Voor Jonge Volwassen Plus*[205] in relation to the Equal Treatment Directive[206] the ECJ held that the existence of a comparator was essentially an evidential matter, so that where direct discrimination could be proved without such a comparator this should be enough to satisfy a court.[207] If the ECJ were prepared to hold at least that the theoretical scope of Article 119 (but preferably also the area within which it takes direct effect) extends to hypothetical comparisons, the utility of the Article would be hugely extended. As presently formulated, the Article forbids discrimination only as between comparable jobs and so does not cater for the situation where unfair differentials are found between two admittedly different jobs. For example, where a woman is employed to perform a very much more highly skilled job than a male comparator, she cannot complain under Article 119 as presently understood if she is paid more than him, but only slightly more.[208] If hypothetical comparisons were permitted under Article

---

[202] The possibility of making such a comparison has become somewhat less important as a consequence of the extension of Art. 119 to equal value claims. See discussion below.

[203] [1980] ECR 1275, at 1289.

[204] As to which see below.

[205] Case 177/88 [1990] ECR I-3941.

[206] Directive 76/207, OJ [1976] L39/40, discussed in detail in Chap. 3.

[207] See also the somewhat obscure reasoning of the Court in Case C-342/93 *Gillespie* v. *Northern Health and Social Services Board* [1996] ECR I-475, in which it held that a woman on maternity leave is entitled to receive a pay rise enjoyed by the rest of her colleagues even though her situation was 'not comparable either with that of a man or with that of a woman actually at work' (at 499). In *Davies* v. *Girobank plc* (1997) 75 EOR 43, an industrial tribunal has referred to the ECJ the question whether it is contrary to EC law if a woman on maternity leave, having exhausted her full entitlement to maternity pay, does not receive any further contractual maternity pay in circumstances where an employee on sick leave for the same period as the woman is on maternity leave would receive contractual sick pay. *Boyle* v. *EOC* EOR Discrimination Case Law Digest No. 30 Winter 1996, p. 11, has also been referred to the ECJ by an industrial tribunal; it raises a number of questions about the standard of employment-related treatment to which a woman on maternity leave is entitled. See also McGlynn, 'Equality, Maternity and Questions of Pay' (1996) 21 ELRev. 327.

[208] See Case 157/86 *Murphy* v. *Bord Telecom Eireann* [1988] ECR 673, also discussed below.

119, she could argue that, were she a man, she would be paid much more, even though she could not demonstrate this directly by pointing to an actual male comparator. From the point of view of improving the economic lot of women, such an argument would also represent a considerable advance on the redress generally available under domestic law, certainly on that available under UK law.[209]

Work of Equal Value

It was seen at the beginning of this chapter that the Amsterdam Treaty amended the original version of Article 119 so as expressly to mandate equal pay for work of equal value. However, even before this express insertion of the principle, it seems that the ECJ accepted that the term 'equal work' embraced the situation where two jobs were of equal value,[210] as well as the situation where the two jobs compared were identical.[211] In the early days it did not take this view and it stated in *Defrenne* v. *Sabena*[212] that Community secondary legislation:

[i]mplements] Article 119 from the point of view of *extending* the narrow criterion of 'equal work', in accordance in particular with the provisions of Convention 100 on equal pay concluded by the International Labour Organization in 1951, Article[2] of which establishes the principle of equal pay for work 'of equal value'.[213]

However, in its later decision in *Jenkins* v. *Kingsgate (Clothing Productions) Ltd.*,[214] it said of the Equal Pay Directive,[215] which expressly requires equal pay for work to which equal value is attributed:

As may be seen from the first recital in the Preamble the primary objective of the above-mentioned Directive is to implement the principle that men and women

---

[209] However, it has to be admitted that most recent judgments of the ECJ do not suggest any enthusiasm for the idea of permitting hypothetical comparisons under Art. 119. In Case C-200/91 *Coloroll Pension Trustees Ltd* v. *Russell* [1994] ECR I-4389, the Court held: '. . . a worker cannot rely on Article 119 in order to claim pay to which he could be entitled if he belonged to the other sex in the absence, now or in the past, in the undertaking concerned of workers of the other sex who perform or performed comparable work. In such a case, the essential criterion for ascertaining that equal treatment exists in the matter of pay, namely the performance of the same work and receipt of the same pay, cannot be applied' (at 4430-1).

[210] This principle has not, however, received full recognition in all the Member States. In its *Memorandum on Equal Pay for Work of Equal Value* (COM(94) 6 final), the Commission noted that there had by 1994 been no litigation on the matter in France, Luxembourg, Greece or Italy, that in other Member States there had been little litigation in which truly different jobs had been compared, and that the legislation in Luxembourg, Italy, Belgium, Spain, Greece and Portugal did nothing to clarify the scope of the principle.

[211] The same query exists in this area as in relation to identical jobs, namely, whether Art. 119 permits comparison with workers outside the claimant's immediate work-place.

[212] Case 43/75 [1976] ECR 455.　　　　[213] Ibid. at 472-473. (Emphasis supplied.)

[214] Case 96/90 [1981] ECR 911.

[215] Directive 75/117, OJ [1975] L45/19, discussed in detail below.

should receive equal pay which is 'contained in Article 119 of the Treaty.' For that purpose the fourth recital states that 'it is desirable to reinforce the basic laws by standards aimed at facilitating the practical application of the principle of equality.' The provisions of Article 1 of that Directive are confined, in the first paragraph, to restating the principle of equal pay set out in Article 119 of the Treaty and specify, in the second paragraph, the conditions for applying that principle where a job classification system is used for determining pay. It follows, therefore, that Article 1 of Council Directive 75/117 which is principally designed to facilitate the practical application of the principle of equal pay outlined in Article 119 of the Treaty in no way alters the content or scope of that principle as defined in the Treaty.[216]

Again, it said in *Worringham v. Lloyds Bank Ltd.*[217] that 'Article 1 of the Directive explains that the concept of "same work" contained in the first paragraph of Article 119 of the Treaty includes cases of "work to which equal value is attributed" '.[218]

A curious twist in this development occurred in *Murphy v. Bord Telecom Eireann.*[219] Ms Murphy was employed by the Bord as a factory worker maintaining telephones. She claimed the right to be paid at the same rate as a male colleague employed in the same factory as a stores labourer. The Irish Equality Officer, to whom the claim had been referred under the national Anti-Discrimination (Pay) Act 1974, found that Ms Murphy's work was actually of a higher value than that of her comparator and so it did not constitute 'like work' within the meaning of the Act. The Equality Officer therefore considered that she could not lawfully recommend that Ms Murphy receive equal pay with the comparator. The Irish High Court, to which the issue came on appeal, asked the ECJ whether:

the Community law principle of equal pay for equal work extend[s] to a claim for equal pay on the basis of work of equal value in circumstances where the work of the claimant has been assessed to be of higher value than that of the person with whom the claimant sought comparison.

As Lenz AG pointed out, this was not a claim for pay proportionate to the work performed (as fairness in the circumstances would certainly seem to have justified). It amounted in effect to a claim for 'less than equal pay for equal work'. Nevertheless, the Court held that Article 119 caught the situation:

---

[216] [1981] ECR 911, at 926–7. The cynic might be tempted to reflect that, by the date of the judgment in *Jenkins,* the ECJ was becoming aware that its reasoning in relation to the direct effect of directives was unlikely to enable it to grant them horizontal effect. (See Chap. 1.) Article 119 thus became a more versatile and therefore more attractive basis for its decision.

[217] Case 69/80 [1981] ECR 767.

[218] Ibid. at 790–1. See also Case 157/86 *Murphy* v. *Bord Telecom Eireann* [1988] ECR 673, discussed below.

[219] Case 157/86 [1988] ECR 673.

It is true that Article 119 expressly requires the application of the principle of equal pay for men and women solely in the case of equal work or, according to a consistent line of decisions of the Court, in the case of work of equal value, and not in the case of work of unequal value. Nevertheless, if that principle forbids workers of one sex engaged in work of equal value to that of workers of the opposite sex to be paid a lower wage than the latter on grounds of sex, it *a fortiori* prohibits such a difference in pay where the lower-paid category of workers is engaged in work of higher value. To adopt a contrary interpretation would be tantamount to rendering the principle of equal pay ineffective and nugatory. As the Irish Government rightly emphasized, in that case an employer would easily be able to circumvent the principle by assigning additional or more onerous duties to workers of a particular sex, who could then be paid a lower wage . . . Article 119 must be interpreted as covering the case where a worker who relies on that provision to obtain equal pay within the meaning thereof is engaged in work of higher value than that of the person with whom a comparison is to be made.[220]

An important practical issue in this area which the ECJ has not yet confronted is how precise it is necessary to be in assessing equality. The problem is to know whether substantial equality is all that is required by Article 119, or whether there must be absolute mathematical equality. The latter seems unlikely, since the whole business of assessing the value of work is essentially imprecise, but what degree of divergence will be allowed? British industrial tribunals, faced with this issue, have so far reached conflicting conclusions.[221]

THE ARTICLE 119 CONCEPT OF 'DISCRIMINATION'

Article 119, it will be recalled, requires application of the principle of equal pay for male and female workers for equal work or work of equal value. It thus *prima facie* requires simply the identical treatment of men

---

[220] Case 157/86 [1988] ECR 673, at 689. This case is sometimes taken as suggesting that the ECJ was not on this occasion prepared to require 'proportionate' pay and it is contrasted with its later decision in Case C-127/92 *Enderby* v. *Frenchay Health Authority* [1993] ECR I-5535 (discussed below) where it stated: 'If . . . the national court has been able to determine precisely what proportion of the increase in pay is attributable to market forces, it must necessarily accept that the pay differential is objectively justified to the extent of that proportion. When national authorities have to apply Community law, they must apply the principle of proportionality' (at 5575). In the view of the present writer, this apparent inconsistency is to be explained by the fact that in *Murphy* the true rate of pay due to the plaintiff was not revealed by the evidence and therefore any upward adjustment would have resulted in the court acting as a wage-fixer; it is otherwise where it is clear what the rate of pay would be were a disproportionate adjustment not being made for market forces. Such a distinction, though regrettable from the point of view of achieving substantive sex equality, is understandable both in terms of the drafting of Art. 119 and of the constitutional role of the ECJ.

[221] See for example *Wells and Others* v. *Smales Ltd.* (1985) 2 EOR 24 and *Brown and Royle* v. *Cearns and Brown Ltd.* (1986) 6 EOR 27.

and women as regards pay; nothing whatsoever is to be permitted to create a differential between the two groups. So formulated, the Article does not appear to distinguish between sex-related distinctions and others. It simply forbids all distinctions.

However, and this is probably the only practicable line to take, this is not how the ECJ has come to apply the Article. It has instead interpreted it as meaning that there must be no discrimination between the sexes over pay where they perform equal work or work of equal value, a conclusion reinforced by the wording of the second paragraph of Article 119(2) and reflected in the national legislation of the Member States. In other words, the Court holds that there must be no distinction made on the basis of sex within the scope of the Article.[222] This necessarily indicates that certain other distinctions over pay will be permitted, provided only that they are not in any way based on sex. It thus opens up the possibility of a causation-based defence to a claim under Article 119, but it is important to notice that no other excuses or defences are articulated by Article 119. It has also led the Court to have to define what it means by 'discrimination'.

Discrimination is a concept encountered elsewhere in the EC Treaty, in particular in relation to nationality.[223] In that context, the Court has defined it as:

[T]he application of different rules to comparable situations or the application of the same rule to different situations.[224]

It is also a concept which has been considerably refined in the national laws of the Member States. From both these sources it is clear that there are essentially two forms which discrimination can take. The first is commonly known as 'direct discrimination'. This occurs where, on the ground of sex, one person is treated differently from or less favourably than another person; in some jurisdictions, the concept of direct discrimination also extends to hypothetical comparisons with how another person would be treated.[225] The more subtle form of discrimination, the 'indirect' kind, is encountered where some requirement is demanded, some practice is applied or some other action is taken which produces an 'adverse impact' for one sex. In *Jenkins* v. *Kingsgate (Clothing Productions) Ltd.*,[226] Warner AG,

---

[222] See also the remarks of Lord Lowry in *Hasley* v. *Fair Employment Agency* [1989] IRLR 106, at 111.

[223] See Art. 6 {Art. 12} and Title III relating to the freedom of movement of workers, the right of establishment, and the freedom to provide services.

[224] Case C-279/93 *Finanzampt Koln-Altstadt* v. *Schumacker* [1995] ECR I-225, at 259.

[225] E.g. under the Sex Discrimination Act 1975, s. 1(1)(a).

[226] Case 96/80 [1981] ECR 911. See also Crisham, 'The Equal Pay Principle: Some Recent Decisions of the ECJ' (1981) 18 CMLRev. 601; Post, 'New Decisions of the European Court on Sex Discrimination' (1981) 1 LIEI 77; and Plender, 'Equal Pay for Men and Women: Two Recent Decisions of the European Court' (1982) 30 American Journal of Comparative Law 627.

referring to earlier cases before the ECJ on the nationality provisions, defined indirect discrimination as follows:

These cases . . . establish that a rule which, on the face of it, differentiates between people on the basis of a criterion other than nationality nonetheless infringes a provision of Community law forbidding such discrimination if its application leads in fact to the same result, unless the differentiation is justifiable on 'objective' grounds. I can see no reason for applying a different principle to sex discrimination.[227]

Both direct and indirect discrimination have emerged as conduct forbidden by Article 119 in relation to pay and the Court has refined their respective definitions for this purpose in a succession of cases.[228] In *Defrenne* v. *Sabena*[229] the ECJ held:

[A] distinction must be drawn within the whole area of application of Article 119 between, first, direct and overt discrimination which may be identified solely with the aid of the criteria based on equal work and equal pay referred to by the Article in question and, secondly, indirect and disguised discrimination which can only be identified by reference to more explicit implementing provisions of a Community or national character. It is impossible not to recognize that the complete implementation of the aim pursued by Article 119, by means of the elimination of all discrimination, direct or indirect, between men and women workers, not only as regards individual undertakings but also entire branches of industry and even of the economic system as a whole, may in certain cases involve the elaboration of criteria whose implementation necessitates the taking of appropriate measures at Community and national level.[230]

This early attempt to explain the difference between direct and indirect discrimination was confusing; direct discrimination is here linked with overt conduct, while indirect discrimination is linked with disguise. Yet, notionally at least, either sort of discrimination can be either overt or disguised; and, in practice, it is more often direct discrimination which is disguised by its perpetrator, whilst indirect discrimination is frequently quite overt. To take an example, an employer will rarely openly admit to preferring to appoint a man, even if this is in fact the reality of the position. Conversely, where an employer is guilty of indirect discrimination, say through the imposition of an unnecessary qualification for a particular job, the insistence on the qualification will often be quite overt. In addition, in relation to nationality at least, the Court has never

---

[227] [1981] ECR 911, at 937. The concept of adverse impact discrimination was articulated by the US Supreme Court in *Griggs* v. *Duke Power Co.* (1971) 401 US 425. For the somewhat restrictive definitions of direct and indirect discrimination for the purposes of British sex discrimination law, see the Sex Discrimination Act 1975, s. 1(1).

[228] On the meaning of indirect discrimination, see Prechal 'Combating Indirect Discrimination in the Community Law Context' [1993-4] LIEI 81.

[229] Case 43/75 [1976] ECR 455.

[230] Ibid. at 473.

refused to apply EC law directly just because the discrimination was covert.[231] Furthermore, the distinction that the ECJ appeared to be making did not correspond to the generally recognized categories of direct and indirect discrimination. In reality, the distinction which the Court seems to have been trying to make in *Defrenne* was simply between discrimination which can be identified without the need for further explanatory legislation and that which cannot. Van Themaat AG explained this in *Burton* v. *British Railways Board*,[232] saying:

[T]he distinction drawn in the *Second Defrenne* judgment between overt and disguised discrimination which is important in determining whether or not Article 119 is directly applicable, does not coincide with a factual distinction between direct discrimination or discrimination in form, on the one hand, and indirect discrimination or discrimination in substance, on the other.[233]

Nevertheless, the Court repeated its original formula in *Macarthys Ltd.* v. *Smith*.[234] A year later, in *Worringham* v. *Lloyds Bank Ltd.*,[235] however, it had begun to change its wording and, whilst still making the same distinction,[236] it had dropped the expressions 'direct and overt' and 'indirect and disguised'. In *Jenkins* v. *Kingsgate (Clothing Productions) Ltd.*,[237] it held that Article 119 outlaws indirect discrimination in the sense of 'adverse impact' discrimination, and thus brought the EC concept closer to that of British and American anti-discrimination law. The case concerned a complaint by a woman part-time employee that she received some ten per cent less pay per hour than a male colleague employed full-time on the same work. At the time of the proceedings, the part-time workers employed by Kingsgate were all female, with the exception of one male part-timer who had just retired and who had, exceptionally and for short periods, been allowed to go on working. This situation generally reflected the employment pattern of the UK, where the great majority of part-time workers both at the date of the case and today are women.[238] The

---

[231] See the remarks of Warner AG in Case 69/80 *Worringham* v. *Lloyds Bank Ltd.* [1981] ECR 767, at 802-3.

[232] Case 19/81 [1982] ECR 555.

[233] Ibid. at 582.

[234] Case 129/79 [1980] ECR 1275.

[235] Case 69/80 [1981] ECR 767.

[236] Which, as will be seen below, is relevant to the issue of direct effect.

[237] Case 96/80 [1981] ECR 911. See also Snaith, 'Sex Discrimination and the Part-Time Worker' (1981) 6 ELRev. 196.

[238] See Robinson, 'Part-Time Employment in the European Community' (1979) 118 International Labour Review 299 and the evidence presented to the ECJ by the Commission in Case 171/88 *Rinner-Kuhn* v. *FWW Spezial Gebaudereinigung GmbH* [1989] 1RLR 493. The 1995 New Earnings Survey showed that 80 per cent of part-time workers in the UK at that date were female. In the EU as a whole over 80 per cent of those working part-time are women: see *Equal Opportunities for Women and Men in the European Union: Annual Report 1996*, Commission, Luxembourg, 1997.

Employment Appeal Tribunal wanted to know from the ECJ whether Article 119 forbids paying part-time workers less than full-time workers, when the category of part-timers is exclusively or predominantly composed of women. The ECJ ruled that:

[T]he purpose of Article 119 is to ensure the application of the principle of equal pay for men and women for the same work. The differences in pay prohibited by that provision are therefore exclusively those based on the difference of the sex of the workers. Consequently the fact that part-time work is paid at an hourly rate lower than pay for full-time work does not amount *per se* to discrimination prohibited by Article 119 provided that the hourly rates are applied to workers belonging to either category without distinction based on sex.[239]

However, the Court went on to add:

[I]f it is established that a considerably smaller percentage of women than of men perform the minimum number of weekly working hours required in order to be able to claim the full-time hourly rate of pay, the inequality in pay will be contrary to Article 119 of the Treaty where, regard being had to the difficulties encountered by women in arranging to work that minimum number of hours per week, the pay policy of the undertaking in question cannot be explained by factors other than discrimination based on sex. Where the hourly rate of pay differs according to whether the work is part-time or full-time it is for the national courts to decide in each individual case whether, regard being had to the facts of the case, its history and the employer's intention, a pay policy such as that which is at issue in the main proceedings although represented as a difference based on weekly working hours is or is not in reality discrimination based on the sex of the worker. The reply to the first three questions must therefore be that a difference in pay between full-time workers and part-time workers does not amount to discrimination prohibited by Article 119 of the Treaty unless it is in reality merely an indirect way of reducing the level of pay of part-time workers on the ground that that group of workers is composed exclusively or predominantly of women.[240]

Although this judgment showed that indirect discrimination is forbidden by Article 119, it was less than clear about precisely how indirect discrimination is to be defined for the purposes of EC law. In particular, the ECJ seemed ambivalent about the relevance of the employer's intention: is unintentional indirect discrimination contrary to Article 119, or is it only intentional discrimination which is forbidden? The latter solution would have drastically curtailed the efficacy of Article 119, since it is of the nature of indirect discrimination that it frequently occurs as a result of inadvertence. When *Jenkins* v. *Kingsgate (Clothing Productions) Ltd.* returned to the Employment Appeal Tribunal, that Tribunal decided to construe the Equal Pay Act 1970 so as to cover unintentional indirect discrimination, since the Sex Discrimination Act 1975 covers such discrimination and the two Acts were intended to form a 'code' together.[241]

---

[239] [1981] ECR 911, at 925.   [240] Ibid. at 925-6.   [241] [1981] IRLR 388.

In *Bilka-Kaufhaus GmbH* v. *Weber Von Hartz*,[242] the ECJ itself apparently ruled in favour of Article 119 also extending to unintentional indirect discrimination.[243] Ms Weber complained of indirect discrimination contrary to Article 119 in that her ex-employer's pension scheme conferred rights on part-time workers only where they had been in full-time employment with the company for 15 years out of a total of 20 years. Ms Weber, a part-time worker who could not satisfy this requirement, argued that it worked to the detriment of women workers because they were more likely than their male colleagues to have to opt for part-time work because of their family and child-care commitments. The ECJ held:

Since, as was stated above, such a pension falls within the concept of pay for the purposes of the second paragraph of Article 119 . . . it follows that, hour for hour, the total remuneration paid by Bilka to full-time workers is higher than that paid to part-time workers.

If, therefore, it should be found that a much lower proportion of women than of men work full time, the exclusion of part-time workers from the occupational pension scheme would be contrary to Article 119 of the Treaty where, taking into account the difficulties encountered by women workers in working full time, that measure could not be explained by factors which exclude any discrimination on grounds of sex. However, if the undertaking is able to show its pay practice may be explained by objectively justified factors unrelated to any discrimination on grounds of sex, there is no breach of Article 119. The answer to the first question referred by the national court must therefore be that Article 119 of the EEC Treaty is infringed by a department store company which excludes part-time employees from its occupational pension scheme, where that exclusion affects a far greater number of women than men, unless the undertaking shows that the exclusion is based on objectively justified factors unrelated to any discrimination on grounds of sex.[244]

Since a lack of intention to discriminate cannot sensibly be regarded as an objectively justified factor unrelated to sex discrimination, it followed that the Court was saying here that even unintentional indirect discrimination is caught by Article 119.

This principle was established even more clearly in *Rinner-Kuhn* v. *FWW Spezial-Gebaudereinigung GmbH*.[245] Ms Rinner-Kuhn worked for ten hours a

---

[242] Case 170/84 [1986] ECR 1607.

[243] See also the opinion of Van Gerven AG in Joined Cases C-63 & 64/91 *Jackson and Cresswell* v. *Chief Adjudication Officer* [1992] ECR I-4737, especially at 4770. In Case C-317/93 *Nolte* v. *Landesversicherungsanstalt Hannover* [1993] ECR I-4625, Léger AG submitted: 'There is a presumption that indirect discrimination is present "once an apparently neutral measure in fact has a preponderant effect on workers of a given sex—without there being any need to establish the intention to discriminate"' (at 4632, quoting from Commission DGV 'Equal Treatment in Community Law' Social Europe, 3/91, p. 79).

[244] Case 170/84 at 1626-7. See also Case 33/89 *Kowalska* v. *Freie und Hansestadt Hamburg* [1990] ECR I-2591.

[245] Case 171/88 [1989] ECR 2743.

week. Her employers, strictly in accordance with the relevant German statutory provision, refused to pay her for a period of six days' absence owing to sickness. She complained to her local Labour Court, which referred to the ECJ the question:

Is a legislative provision excluding from the principle of continued payment of salary by the employer during illness those workers whose normal period of work does not exceed 10 hours a week or 45 hours a month compatible with Article 119 of the EEC Treaty and Council Directive 75/117/EEC of 10 February 1975 on the approximation of the laws of Member States relating to the application of the principle of equal pay for men and women—although the proportion of female workers suffering adverse effects from this exclusion is much higher than that of male workers?

The ECJ replied:

[T]he German legal provision in question grants the benefit of the principle of continued payment by the employer in the event of illness only to workers whose employment contracts provide for normal working hours exceeding 10 hours of work a week or 45 hours a month. As such payment falls under the definition of pay within the meaning of the second paragraph of Article 119, it follows that the German legislative provision concerned allows employers to maintain a global difference in pay between two categories of workers, those who carry out the minimum number of hours' work a week or a month and those who, whilst doing the same work, do not carry out that minimum number of hours. It also follows from the Order to refer that a considerably smaller percentage of women than of men carries out the minimum number of hours' work a week or a month which is required to be entitled to the continued payment of wages in the event of incapacity to work because of illness. In such a case, it must be noted that a provision such as the one in question results in practice in discrimination between male and female workers and is, in principle, to be regarded as contrary to the objective pursued by Article 119 of the EEC Treaty. It would only be otherwise if the different treatment between the two categories of workers is justified by objective factors unrelated to any discrimination on grounds of sex . . .[246]

As well as unintentional indirect discrimination, it is clear today that EC law also embraces the concept of unintentional direct discrimination. This is a logical conclusion given that Article 119 was included in the Treaty in order to obviate inequalities in pay which are attributable to sex; it is in principle irrelevant to the Article to examine an employer's motives, if the

---

[246] Ibid. at 495-6. Shaw comments in 'The Burden of Proof and the Legality of Supplementary Payments in Equal Pay Cases' (1990) 15 ELRev. 260 that the Court in *Rinner-Kuhn* effectively grasped the legislative nettle and enacted the long-stalled proposal for a directive granting equality of treatment to part-time employees (OJ [1982] C62/7, and OJ [1983] C18/5); for discussion of the directive on part-time work which was subsequently enacted, see Chap. 3. It is noteworthy that no minimum number of hours of service per week was required by the ECJ in order to trigger the *Rinner-Kuhn* principle.

effect of what has been done is in reality to the disadvantage of one sex. In the words of Lenz AG in *Enderby* v. *Frenchay Health Authority*:[247]

[F]orms of direct sex discrimination are quite conceivable without sex being expressly mentioned in the contract of employment, pay scales or collective agreement as the criterion for the higher or lower pay. The conceptual scheme of that category makes it clear that discrimination does not even have to have been intentional.[248]

This view is also inherent in the ECJ's attitude to so-called 'gender-plus' discrimination. The expression 'gender-plus' was coined by the American courts in the context of sexual harassment.[249] The problem is to know whether the law catches discrimination against a class or sub-class of women, so that the conduct has to be analysed as discrimination on the ground of sex-plus-something-else.[250] In common with their American counterparts, UK courts have come to accept that such conduct breaches the national anti-discrimination legislation: 'but-for' the sex of the victim, the person would have been treated more favourably, and therefore the discrimination is 'on the ground of sex'; questions of intention and motivation are quite irrelevant to such a test.[251] In *Liefting* v. *Directie van het Academisch Ziekenhuis bij de Universiteit van Amsterdam*,[252] where the gender-plus point was argued, the ECJ held that there was a breach of Article 119 where a system of making employer contributions to certain types of pension scheme discriminated against women civil servants who were married to civil servants. There was no allegation that the system discriminated against women generally, or even against women civil servants generally, but only against that class whose husbands were also civil servants. The same analysis can be applied to *Worringham* v. *Lloyds Bank Ltd.*[253] where the discrimination was not against women employees generally but only against those aged under 25. In this later decision, the ECJ made a statement which is really only compatible with an objective test for direct discrimination, unrelated to any requirement of motivation or intention on the part of the employer. It said:

Article 119 of the Treaty applies directly to all forms of discrimination which may be identified solely with the aid of the criteria of equal work and equal pay referred to by the Article in question, without national or Community measures

---

[247] Case C-127/92 [1993] ECR I-5535.   [248] Ibid. at 5558.

[249] The treatment of sexual harassment by EC law is discussed in Chap. 3.

[250] See e.g. *Barnes* v. *Costle* (1977) 15 FEP Cases 345; *Hurley* v. *Mustoe* [1981] IRLR 208; *Horsey* v. *Dyfed District Council* [1982] IRLR 395; and *Hayes* v. *Malleable Working Men's Club* [1985] ICR 703. Cf. *Turley* v. *Allders Department Stores Ltd.* [1980] IRLR 4.

[251] See also the decision of the House of Lords in *James* v. *Eastleigh Borough Council* [1990] 3 WLR 55.

[252] Case 23/83 [1984] ECR 3225.

[253] Case 69/80 [1981] ECR 767.

being required to define them with greater precision in order to permit of their application . . . This is the case where the requirement to pay contributions applies only to men and not to women and the contributions payable by men are paid by the employers in their name by means of an addition to the gross salary *the effect of which* is to give men higher pay within the meaning of the second paragraph of Article 119 than that received by women engaged in the same work or work of equal value.[254]

The ECJ in *Dekker* v. *Stichting Vormingscentrum Voor Jonge Volwassen Plus*[255] also implicitly ruled out the need for intention in relation to direct discrimination, saying that 'If the employer's liability for infringement of the principle of equal treatment were made subject to proof of a fault attributable to him and also to there being no ground of exemption recognized by the applicable national law, the practical effect of those principles would be considerably weakened'.[256]

A further vital point about the concept of direct discrimination was made by the ECJ in *Dekker*. It held that discrimination on the ground of pregnancy is *per se* unlawful sex discrimination; it is adverse treatment of a person for a reason which can only apply to one sex and is therefore necessarily direct discrimination on the ground of sex. This ruling was of special practical as well as theoretical significance in the UK, where the courts had hitherto accepted pregnancy-related discrimination as unlawful discrimination only where the claimant could demonstrate that a man suffering from a temporary medical disorder, 'comparable' to pregnancy, would have been more favourably treated.[257]

In order to establish indirect discrimination in EC law, all that the ECJ appears to require is that one sex be treated less favourably than the other (in circumstances which are not objectively justifiable). For example, in *Gerster* v. *Freistaat Bayern*,[258] national law provided that part-timers whose working hours exceeded two-thirds of normal working hours were deemed to have worked full-time for the purpose of calculating their length of service in relation to promotion. Part-timers whose working hours amounted to at least half of normal working hours were regarded as working two-thirds of normal working hours, but all working time was completely ignored in the case of those working less than half-time. Women accounted for 87 per cent of part-timers in the relevant

---

[254] Ibid. at 792. (Emphasis supplied.) See also Case C-7/93 *Bestuur Van Het Algemeen Burgerlijk Pensioenfonds* v. *Beune* [1994] ECR I-4471, at 4520.

[255] Case 177/88 [1990] ECR I-3941, discussed in Chap. 3.

[256] At 3976. See further discussion below.

[257] *Webb* v. *EMO Air Cargo (UK) Ltd.* [1990] ICR 442; *Hayes* v. *Malleable Working Men's Club* [1985] ICR 703. For further discussion of the present law in relation to discrimination on the ground of pregnancy, see Chap. 3.

[258] Case C-1/95 (nyr).

department. The Court effectively ignored the benefit which this system accorded to some part-timers and concluded:

It is common ground that the provision of national law at issue . . . treats part-time employees less favourably than full-time employees in so far as, since the former accrue length of service more slowly, they perforce gain promotion late . . .

In a situation of that kind, it must be concluded that in practice provisions such as those at issue . . . result in discrimination against women employees as compared with men . . .[259]

The Court has not, however, been very precise or literal in defining the required element of adverse impact, as Léger AG observed in *Nolte* v. *Landesversicherungsanstalt Hannover.*[260]

[I]n order to be presumed discriminatory, the measure must affect 'a far greater number of women than men' (*Rinner-Kühn*) or 'a considerably lower percentage of men than women' (*Nimz, Kowalska*) or 'far more women than men' (*De Weerd*).

Consequently, the proportion of women affected by the measure must be particularly marked. Thus, in the judgment in *Rinner-Kühn*, the Court inferred the existence of a discriminatory situation where the percentage of women was 89%.

In this instance, *per se* the figure of 60% . . . would therefore probably be quite insufficient to infer the existence of discrimination.[261]

In *R* v. *Secretary of State for Employment, Ex p. Seymour-Smith,*[262] the House of Lords referred to the ECJ questions including:

What is the legal test for establishing whether a measure adopted by a Member State has such a degree of disparate effect as between men and women as to amount to indirect discrimination for the purposes of Article 119 . . .?

[And] when must this legal test be applied to a measure adopted by a Member State? In particular at which of the following points in time, or at what other point in time, must it be applied to the measure: (a) when the measure is adopted; (b) when the measure is brought into force; (c) when the employee is dismissed?[263]

It is unnecessary to prove (as the UK demands) that a specific requirement or condition has been laid down which is more difficult for one sex to fulfil

---

[259] Ibid. at paras. 32-4. Cf. Joined Cases C-399, 409 & 425/92 and C-34, 50 and 78/93 *Stadt Lengerich* v. *Helmig* [1994] ECR I-5727, discussed below. The Court did not explain why it accepted in *Gerster* that taking account of the shorter working time accrued by part-timers constituted indirect discrimination in relation to promotion but not (as in *Helmig*) in relation to pay.

[260] Case C-317/93 [1995] ECR I-4625.

[261] Ibid. at 4640.   [262] [1997] 1 WLR 473.

[263] At the time of writing, this reference was pending before the ECJ. See also Case C-243/95 *Hill and Stapleton* v. *Revenue Commissioners*, also pending before the ECJ, in which the issue is whether it is indirectly discriminatory to treat two years' job-sharing as equivalent to one year's full-time work for pay purposes.

than the other.[264] Thus, in the *Bilka-Kaufhaus* case, the Court was satisfied with the existence of a mere 'pay practice' which produced an adverse impact for women.

In similar vein was *Handels-OG Kontorfunktionaerernes Forbund i Danmark* v. *Dansk Arbejdsgiverforening (acting for Danfoss)*.[265] This concerned a collective agreement between a staff union and an employers' association. The same basic minimum was paid to all workers in the same pay grade. Grading was determined by job classification. However, the collective agreement allowed the company to make additional payments to individuals within a grade on the basis of the individual's 'flexibility', vocational training, and seniority. The union argued that the pay system discriminated on the ground of sex because, within a pay grade, the average pay of women was less than that of men: specifically, it produced evidence of a statistical survey covering the pay of 157 Danfoss employees between 1982 and 1986 which showed a differential of 6.85 per cent between the average pay of male and female workers within the relevant pay grades. The industrial arbitration tribunal sent a number of questions to the ECJ.[266] The first issue raised was perceived by the ECJ to be in essence related to the burden of proof in equal pay claims:

[T]he issue between the parties . . . has its origin in the fact that the system of individual supplements applied to basic pay is implemented in such a way that a woman is unable to identify the reasons for a difference between her pay and that of a man doing the same work. Employees do not know what criteria in the matter of supplements are applied to them and how they are applied. They know only the amount of their supplemented pay without being able to determine the effect of the individual criteria. Those who are in a particular wage group are thus unable to compare the various components of their pay with those of the pay of their colleagues who are in the same wage group.

In those circumstances the questions put by the national court must be understood as asking whether . . . where an undertaking applies a system of pay which is totally lacking in transparency, it is for the employer to prove that his practice in the matter of wages is not discriminatory, if a female worker establishes, in relation to a relatively large number of employees, that the average pay for women is less than that for men.[267]

The answer given was that the burden of proof (and it would appear from the context that the Court meant the legal as distinct from merely

---

[264] See s. 1(1)(b) of the Sex Discrimination Act 1975. Cf. the decision of the Employment Appeal Tribunal in *Falkirk Council* v. *Whyte* [1997] IRLR 560 that a 'requirement or condition' does not have to be an absolute bar in order to be challengeable as indirectly discriminatory.   [265] Case 109/88 [1989] ECR 3199.

[266] These questions in fact referred to the principle of equal pay as expressed in the Equal Pay Directive (Directive 75/117, OJ [1975] L45/19), but the ECJ has repeatedly made it clear that the relevant principles are identical under both the Directive and Art. 119 (see below).   [267] [1989] ECR 3199, at 3225.

the evidential burden of proof) is indeed so placed on the employer.[268]
The Court's reasoning was that the employer may not shelter behind the
grading scheme involved:

[I]n a situation where a system of individual pay supplements which is completely
lacking in transparency is at issue, female employees can establish differences
only so far as average pay is concerned. They would be deprived of any effective
means of enforcing the principle of equal pay before the national courts if the
effect of adducing such evidence was not to impose upon the employer the
burden of proving that his practice in the matter of wages is not in fact discriminatory.

Finally, it should be noted that under Article 6 of the Equal Pay Directive
Member States must, in accordance with their national circumstances and their
legal systems, take the measures necessary to ensure that the principle of equal
pay is applied and that effective means are available to ensure that it is observed.
The concern for effectiveness which thus underlies the Directive means that it
must be interpreted as implying adjustments to national rules on the burden of
proof in special cases where such adjustments are necessary for the effective
implementation of the principle of equality.

To show that his practice in the matter of wages does not systematically work to
the disadvantage of female employees the employer will have to indicate how he
has applied the criteria concerning supplements and will thus be forced to make
his system of pay transparent.[269]

Danfoss thus established the principle that, where a system of pay is non-
transparent, the burden of proof is on the employer to show that that
system is not discriminatory, where a woman can establish by comparison
with a 'relatively large' number of employees, that the average pay of
women employees is 'lower' than that of male employees.[270] This formula
of course leaves uncertain how many employees must be involved
(although clearly 157 was enough), for how long (here it was four years),
and what percentage differential is sufficient to reverse the burden of
proof (6.85 per cent being established to be enough).

The Court proceeded to a more general statement of principle in

---

[268] The UK government had intervened in the case and argued in favour of this solution
to the effect that, in the UK in such a situation, the employer would already bear the
burden of proof under the Equal Pay Act 1970. At first sight, this appears ironic since the
UK government vetoed a draft directive on reversal of the burden of proof in sex
discrimination claims in the late 1980s. However, that draft directive was seriously defective
and would probably have increased rather than decreased confusion. In addition, the
government appeared to confine its submissions in *Danfoss* to the equal pay field and would
probably have opposed any extension of the principle to equal treatment generally.

[269] [1989] ECR 3199, at 3226. For the domestic sequel to *Danfoss*, see Precht, '*Danfoss* in
the Danish Courts' (1992) 21 ILJ 323.

[270] Cf. the position in relation to piece-work payment systems: Case C-400/93
Specialarbejderforbundet i Danmark v. *Dansk Industri, acting for Royal Copenhagen A/S* [1995]
ECR I-1275, discussed above.

Enderby v. *Frenchay Health Authority.*[271] A speech therapist employed by the UK National Health Service complained that speech therapists, who were almost all female, were less well paid than clinical psychologists and pharmacists, who were predominantly male, and whom she claimed performed work of equal value to herself. Both the Court and the Advocate General took a pragmatic approach as to how adverse impact might be demonstrated. The Court stated simply that the existence of a '*prima facie* case of discrimination' casts the burden of proving objective justification onto the employer[272] and it added that such a *prima facie* case might be made out where 'significant statistics disclose an appreciable difference in pay between two jobs of equal value, one of which is carried out almost exclusively by women and the other predominantly by men . . .'.[273] Lenz AG explained:

The basic legal position is that Article 119 . . . and the directives adopted for its implementation, as interpreted and applied by the Court of Justice, prohibit all forms of sex-related discrimination. Sex-related pay discrimination takes various forms, the categorization of which can pose a legal problem. In order to render them susceptible to legal categorization, the courts have adopted the categories of direct and indirect discrimination. The conceptual scheme applied should in no way be construed in the sense of any exclusiveness of possible forms of sex discrimination. A glance at the conceptual scheme applied in these proceedings under the laws of the UK bears this out. The reference there to intentional or unintentional direct discrimination and to intentional or unintentional indirect discrimination shows that there are four possible ways of categorizing the same phenomenon for legal purposes.

The purpose of a conceptual scheme is to comprehend methods by which women are placed at a disadvantage in their working lives and not to create additional obstacles to claims being made before the courts in respect of sex-related pay discrimination. For this reason, a formalistic approach should not be adopted when categorizing actual instances where women are placed at a disadvantage at work.[274]

Later he added:

Attention should be directed less to the existence of a requirement or a hurdle by means of which women suffer a disadvantage, and more to the discriminatory result.[275]

It is, however, necesary to raise a *prima facie* case of indirect discrimination before the employer is required to justify a pay

---

[271] Case C-127/92 [1993] ECR I-5535, noted by Fredman in 'Equal Pay and Justification' (1994) 23 ILJ 37, by Wynn in 'Equal Pay and Gender Segregation' (1994) 110 LQR 556, and by the present author in (1994) 31 CMLRev. 387. See also Kentridge, 'Direct and Indirect Discrimination After *Enderby*' [1994] Public Law 198.

[272] See Chap. 3 for further discussion of the proof of discrimination.

[273] [1993] ECR I-5535, at 5573.

[274] Ibid. at 5557.   [275] Ibid. at 5560.

disparity.[276] *Stadt Lengerich* v. *Helmig*[277] concerned a claim by women part-time workers that the denial to them of overtime pay when they exceeded their normal (part-time) working hours constituted indirect discrimination. Under the relevant collective agreements, all employees were entitled to overtime supplements but only after they had worked a full-time week. The Court held that it must be asked, first of all, whether there was different treatment for part-time and full-time employees and whether that difference affected considerably more women than men. Only if those questions were answered in the affirmative would a *prima facie* case arise which would require objective justification. The Court concluded:

There is unequal treatment wherever the overall pay of full-time employees is higher than that of part-time employees for the same number of hours worked on the basis of an employment relation. In the circumstances considered in these proceedings, part-time employees do receive the same overall pay as full-time employees for the same number of hours worked. A part-time employee whose contractual working hours are 18 receives, if he works 19 hours, the same overall pay as a full-time employee who works 19 hours. Part-time employees also receive the same overall pay as full-time employees if they work more than the normal working hours fixed by the collective agreements because on doing so they become entitled to overtime supplements. Consequently, the provisions at issue do not give rise to different treatment as between part-time and full-time employees and there is therefore no discrimination . . .[278]

This decision highlights the essentially non-dynamic nature of the concept of discrimination;[279] as discussed further in Chapter 5. Although indirect discrimination in particular seeks to take note of the hidden obstacles facing women in our society and to set them aside where they are irrelevant to the work performed, neither direct nor indirect discrimination takes an active part in globally dismantling those obstacles or changing customary gendered roles.[280] In short, discrimination provides a corrective, rather than a redistributive, remedy.[281]

---

[276] For an example of a case in which this initial hurdle was not surmounted, see Case C-297/93 *Grau-Hupka* v. *Stadtgemeinde Bremen* [1994] ECR I-5535.

[277] Joined Cases C-399, 409 and 425/92 and C-34, 50 and 78/93 [1994] ECR I-5727.

[278] Ibid. at 5754-5.

[279] For further criticism of the excessive devotion paid by the ECJ in this case to the concepts of formal equality and the male norm, see Holtmaat, 'Overtime Payments for Part-Time Workers' (1995) 24 ILJ 387.

[280] Nevertheless, there would appear to be further potential in the concept than has hitherto been tapped. In particular, a claim combining an allegation of indirect discrimination against a part-timer with a demand for equal pay for work of equal value could produce dramatic effects. It is well known that the vast majority of part-time workers are female and that they often work in gender-segregated occupations. This group encompasses some of the most poorly paid members of our society and many would argue that their pay is unfairly depressed taking into account the importance of the work which they frequently do (e.g. caring for children or elderly patients). A successful equal value claim makes it possible to upgrade pay in gender-segregated occupations and this would be

[*See opposite page for n. 280 cont. and n. 281*].

After a number of unsuccessful attempts during the late 1980s to produce a statutory definition of indirect discrimination for the purposes of EC law, a directive dealing with this matter was eventually adopted by the Council in December 1997.[282] Article 2 of this instrument reflects the existing case law of the ECJ and provides that:

[I]ndirect discrimination shall exist where an apparently neutral provision, criterion or practice disadvantages a substantially higher proportion of the members of one sex unless that provision, criterion or practice is appropriate and necessary and can be justified by objective factors unrelated to sex.[283]

Although the preceding discussion of the meaning of 'discrimination' has been largely in the context of Article 119, it appears that the ECJ accepts the same principles for the purposes of other EC instruments outlawing sex discrimination and accordingly it adopts a unified definition of 'discrimination'.[284] There is also evidence that the UK courts believe there to be a single, integrated EC definition of 'discrimination'. For example, in *R. v. Secretary of State for Education, Ex p. Schaffter*,[285] Schiemann J in the Queen's Bench Division applied the *Bilka-Kaufhaus* objective justification test to indirect discrimination which was contrary to the Equal Treatment Directive.[286] And in *Rainey v. Greater Glasgow Health Board*,[287] Lord Keith of Kinkel said that it did not appear to him that there was any material distinction in principle between the need to demonstrate objectively justified grounds of difference for the purposes of the British Equal Pay Act, as influenced by Article 119 and *Bilka-Kaufhaus*, and the need to justify indirect discrimination under the Sex Discrimination Act 1975, which in turn is influenced by the Equal Treatment Directive.[288]

This approach is largely confirmed by the directive which in Article 3

---

especially potent where the part-timer could make a two-stage claim, alleging first that she is entitled *pro rata* to equal pay with a full-time colleague doing the same work as herself, and then secondly that that colleague is underpaid by comparison with a member of the opposite sex doing a different job.

[281] See also Morris, 'On the Normative Foundations of Indirect Discrimination Law: Understanding the Competing Models of Discrimination Law As Aristotelian Forms of Justice' (1995) 15 OJLS 199.

[282] Directive 97/80, OJ [1998] L14/6.

[283] The objective justification of what appears otherwise to constitute indirect discrimination is discussed below.

[284] See in particular Lenz AG in Case C-127/92 *Enderby v. Frenchay Health Authority* [1993] ECR I-5535, Van Gerven AG in Joined Cases C-63 & 64/91 *Jackson and Cresswell v. Chief Adjudication Officer* [1992] ECR I-4737 and Darmon AG in Case C-189/91 *Kirsammer-Hack v. Sidal* [1993] ECR I-6185. Cf. McGlynn 'Equality, Maternity and Questions of Pay' (1996) 21 ELRev. 327.

[285] [1987] IRLR 53.

[286] Directive 76/207, OJ [1976] L39/40, discussed in detail in Chap. 3.

[287] [1986] 3 WLR 1017.

[288] Ibid. at 1028. Cf. the decision of the Employment Appeal Tribunal in *Tyldesley v. TML Plastics Ltd* [1996] ICR 356.

expressly applies its definition of indirect discrimination to the situations envisaged by Article 119, the Equal Pay Directive,[289] the Equal Treatment Directive,[290] the Pregnancy Directive[291] and the Directive on Parental Leave.[292] The directive also applies to any civil or administrative procedure concerning the public or private sector which provides for means of redress under national law pursuant to these measures, with the exception of out-of-court procedures of a voluntary nature or provided for in national law;[293] it does not apply to criminal procedures, unless otherwise provided by the Member States.[294]

DEFENCES TO A DISCRIMINATION CLAIM[295]

Since it is only discrimination based on sex which is forbidden by Article 119, it follows that differences in the pay of male and female workers which are not attributable to sex remain permissible. Thus, where the allegation is of direct discrimination contrary to Article 119, the way is open for the employer to plead that some factor other than sex is the cause of the pay discrepancy. As the ECJ explained in *Macarthys Ltd.* v. *Smith*:[296] '[I]t cannot be ruled out that a difference in pay between two workers occupying the same post but at different periods in time may be explained by the operation of factors which are unconnected with any discrimination on grounds of sex'.[297] This is in essence a matter of *causation* and not a matter of *justification*; properly analysed, this is a situation where there is no discrimination, not one where proven discrimination can be excused.[298] As has been remarked earlier, Article 119 contains no specific defences, in the sense of excuses for proven discrimination.

There is a logical, though not a verbal, parallel as regards causation in

[289] Directive 75/117, OJ [1975] L45/19, discussed below.

[290] Directive 76/207, OJ [1976] L39/40, discussed in Chap. 3.

[291] Directive 92/85, OJ [1992] L348/1, discussed in Chap. 3.

[292] Directive 96/34, OJ [1996] L145/4, discussed in Chap. 3. Note, however, that the instrument does not extend to the Social Security Directive (Directive 79/7, OJ [1979] L6/24, discussed in Chap. 4), the Occupational Social Security Directive (Directive 86/378, OJ [1986] L225/40, discussed above) or the Directive on the Self-Employed (Directive 86/613, OJ [1986] L359/56, discussed in Chap. 3).

[293] Art. 3(1)(b) of the directive.

[294] Ibid. Art. 3(2).

[295] On this subject generally, see Hervey, *Justifications for Sex Discrimination in Employment* (Butterworths, London, 1993).

[296] Case 129/79 [1980] ECR 1275.

[297] Ibid. at 1289. See also the remarks of Capotorti AG in the same case, especially at 1295.

[298] See also Case 177/88 *Dekker* v. *Stichting Vormingscentrum Voor Jonge Volwassen Plus* [1990] ECR I-3941, where this point was specifically recognized by the ECJ, and Ellis, 'The Definition of Discrimination in European Community Sex Equality Law' (1994) 19 ELRev. 563.

cases of indirect discrimination. Here, the employer can defend the conduct if it can be shown that the discriminatory effect is explicable, in the words of the ECJ in *Bilka-Kaufhaus GmbH* v. *Weber Von Hartz*[299] by 'objectively justified factors which are unrelated to any discrimination based on sex': in other words, where the apparently objectionable effect is in fact not grounded in sex discrimination. The Court went on in that case to explain that:

It falls to the national court, which has sole jurisdiction to make findings of fact, to determine whether and to what extent the grounds put forward by an employer to explain the adoption of a pay practice which applies independently of a worker's sex, but in fact affects more women than men may be regarded as objectively justified [on] economic grounds. If the national court finds that the measures chosen by Bilka correspond to a real need on the part of the undertaking, are appropriate with a view to achieving the objectives pursued, and are necessary to that end, the fact that the measures affect a far greater number of women than men is not sufficient to show that they constitute an infringement of Article 119.[300]

This sets up a formidable hurdle for an employer seeking to justify indirectly discriminatory conduct.[301] The employer must show to the satisfaction of the national court that there is a genuine need on behalf of the enterprise for the discriminatory factor, that the means chosen are suitable for attaining the objective and, most strictly of all, that the means chosen are 'necessary' to attain the objective; it follows that, if reasonable alternative means are available to the employer to attain the objective, the behaviour will breach Article 119.

The Court has made it clear that the subjective beliefs of the employer are not the essence of the matter[302] and in *Enderby* v. *Frenchay Health Authority*,[303] it established the important principle that the justification proved must be proportionate to the particular pay discrepancy in issue:

The state of the employment market, which may lead an employer to increase the pay of a particular job in order to attract candidates, may constitute an objectively justified economic ground . . . How it is to be applied in the circumstances of each case depends on the facts and so falls within the jurisdiction of the national court.

If, as the question referred seems to suggest, the national court has been able to determine precisely what proportion of the increase in pay is attributable to market forces, it must necessarily accept that the pay differential is objectively

---

[299] Case 170/84 [1986] ECR 1607.
[300] Ibid. at 1628.
[301] The burden of proof is borne by the employer; see e.g. the opinion of Léger AG in Case C-317/93 *Nolte* v. *Landesversicherungsanstalt Hannover* [1995] ECR I-4625, at 4641.
[302] See discussion above.
[303] Case C-127/92 [1993] ECR I-5535, also discussed above.

justified to the extent of that proportion. When national authorities have to apply Community law, they must apply the principle of proportionality.

If that is not the case, it is for the national court to assess whether the role of market forces in determining the rate of pay was sufficiently significant to provide objective justification for part or all of the difference.[304]

The fact remains that the Court is accepting the existence in EC law of an economic defence, at least in the field of equal pay,[305] and it has made little attempt to explain where it sees the balance lying as between the commercial profitability of an organization and the elimination of discrimination.[306] The UK courts for a number of years resisted such a defence, on the sensible ground that, if pursued, it would rob the anti-discrimination legislation of all purpose. In the words of Lord Denning MR in *Clay Cross Ltd.* v. *Fletcher*:[307]

[A]n employer cannot avoid his obligations under the [Equal Pay Act] by saying: 'I paid him more because he asked for more', or 'I paid her less because she was willing to come for less'. If such excuses were permitted, the Act would be a dead letter. Those are the very reasons why there was unequal pay before the statute. They are the very circumstances in which the statute was intended to operate. Nor can the employer avoid his obligations by giving the reasons why he submitted to the extrinsic forces. As for instance by saying: 'He asked for that sum because it was what he was getting in his previous job', or 'He was the only applicant for the job so I had no option'. In such cases the employer may beat his breast, and say: 'I did not pay him more because he was a man. I paid it because he was the only suitable person who applied for the job. Man or woman made no difference to me'. Those are reasons personal to the employer. If any such reasons were permitted as an excuse, the door would be wide open. Every employer who wished to avoid the statute would walk straight through it.[308]

The *Bilka-Kaufhaus* decision forced the UK courts to retrench somewhat and to accept the possibility of an economic defence.[309] Nevertheless, the danger pointed out by Lord Denning remains a real one. It is vital that the courts scrutinize cases very carefully to make sure that what looks like an objectively justified factor does not in reality have its roots in sex discrimination; for example, where it is alleged in an equal value case that one skill is rarer and more valuable than another, the court must insist on knowing the background to that statement and must ensure that this is not because women have been discriminated against as regards training for

[304] Ibid. at 5575.

[305] See also Case 96/80 *Jenkins* v. *Kingsgate (Clothing Productions) Ltd.* [1981] ECR 911.

[306] Cf. the position in relation to the justification of indirect discrimination in the field of social security, discussed in Chap. 4.

[307] [1979] ICR 1.

[308] Ibid. at 5.

[309] See in particular *Rainey* v. *Greater Glasgow Health Board* [1986] 3 WLR 1017.

that rarer skill.[310] In general, the ECJ in guiding the national courts must remain vigilant to ensure that, when the 'genuine need' of an enterprise is assessed, it is not merely male-orientated notions of merit and qualifications which are used as the parameters.[311]

There is now a body of case law in which the ECJ has elaborated on the application of the *Bilka-Kaufhaus* criteria. In *Handels-OG Kontorfunktion-aerernes Forbund i Danmark* v. *Dansk Arbejdsgiverforening (acting for Danfoss)* [312] an employer sought to justify pay discrimination on the basis that incremental payments were made to its employees as a reward for 'mobility', vocational training, and seniority. The Court looked at each separately. 'Mobility' had a rather specific meaning here, and did not merely embrace a willingness to work at different hours; it involved the employer making an overall assessment of the quality of the work carried out by the employees and would take into account their 'enthusiasm for work', their sense of initiative, and the amount of work done. In scrutinizing such a factor as providing an objective justification for discrimination, the Court was sensitive to the risks it carries. It held:

[A] distinction must be made according to whether the criterion of mobility is employed to reward the quality of the work done by the employee or is used to reward the employee's adaptability to variable work hours and varying places of work.

In the first case, the criterion of mobility is undoubtedly wholly neutral from the point of view of sex. Where it systematically works to the disadvantage of · women that can only be because the employer has misapplied it. It is inconceivable that the quality of work done by women should generally be less good. The employer cannot therefore justify applying the criterion of mobility, so understood, where its application proves to work systematically to the disadvantage of women.[313]

In such a case, therefore, the employer would invariably lose the claim. However, the Court went on to say:

The position is different in the second case. If it is understood as covering the employee's adaptability to variable hours and varying places of work, the criterion of mobility may also work to the disadvantage of female employees who, because

---

[310] In Case C-127/92 *Enderby* v. *Frenchay Health Authority* [1993] ECR I-5535, Lenz AG observed: 'Since justification of the discriminatory result is called for, it cannot be sufficient to explain the causes leading to the discrimination . . . The historical and social context of a "purely female profession" is most probably sex-related. If an explanatory approach were accepted as sufficient justification, that would lead to the perpetuation of sexual roles in working life. Instead of the equality of treatment which is sought, there would be afforded a legal argument for maintaining the *status quo*' (at 5563). See also Fredman, 'Equal Pay and Justification' (1994) 23 ILJ 37.

[311] See discussion in Townshend-Smith, *Sex Discrimination in Employment Law, Practice and Policy* (Sweet and Maxwell, London, 1989), esp. at 25-6.

[312] Case 109/88 [1989] ECR 3199, also discussed above.

[313] [1989] ECR 3199, at 3227.

of household and family duties for which they are frequently responsible, are not as able as men to organize their working time flexibly . . . [The *Bilka-Kaufhaus* principles] apply in the case of a wages practice which specially remunerates the employee's adaptability to variable hours and varying places of work. *The employer may, therefore, justify the remuneration of such adaptability by showing that it is of importance for the performance of specific tasks entrusted to the employee.*[314]

It took the same line in relation to vocational training, saying:

[It cannot] be excluded that [the criterion of vocational training] may work to the disadvantage of women in so far as they have had less opportunity than men for training or have taken less advantage of such opportunity. Nevertheless, in view of the considerations laid down [in *Bilka-Kaufhaus*], the employer may justify remuneration of special training by showing that it is of importance for the performance of specific tasks entrusted to the employee.[315]

As to seniority, the Court was considerably less perceptive and was perhaps timorous in its approach because of the admitted practical significance of seniority in pay systems and collective bargaining. It held simply:

[It cannot be ruled out that seniority] may involve less advantageous treatment of women than of men, in so far as women have entered the labour market more recently than men or more frequently suffer an interruption of their career. Nevertheless, since length of service goes hand in hand with experience and since experience generally enables the employee to perform his duties better, *the employer is free to reward it without having to establish the importance it has in the performance of specific tasks entrusted to the employee.*[316]

This last is an illogical deduction, since for many jobs experience does not improve performance, a point subsequently recognised by the Court. In *Nimz* v. *Freie und Hansestadt Hamburg*,[317] a collective agreement provided for reclassification into a higher salary grade after a certain number of years for those employed for at least three-quarters of normal working time. For those, predominantly women, employed between one-half and three-quarters of normal working time, double the number of years was required before reclassification into the higher grade.[318] The employers sought to

---

[314] Ibid. at 3227-8. (Emphasis supplied.)

[315] Ibid. at 3228.

[316] Ibid. at 3228. (Emphasis supplied.)

[317] Case C-184/89 [1991] ECR I-297, commented on by Adinolfi in (1992) 29 CMLRev. 637 and by More in 'Seniority Pay for Part-time Workers' (1991) 16 ELRev. 320.

[318] It is noteworthy that this case, like Case C-262/88 *Barber* v. *Guardian Royal Exchange Assurance Group* [1990] ECR I-1889 (discussed above), involved access to pay rather than the quantum of pay, but the Court nonetheless held the situation to fall within the scope of Art. 119. On the other hand, in Case C-1/95 *Gerster* v. *Freistaat Bayern* (nyr), where a similar rule to that operating in *Nimz* disadvantaged part-timers as regards promotion, the ECJ held that the matter fell within the scope of Dir. 76/207 (OJ [1976] L39/40, discussed in Chap. 3) because length of service was merely one factor considered by the employer and therefore only affected pay indirectly.

justify this situation by arguing that full-timers acquired job-related skills more quickly than part-timers. The Court rejected this with some enthusiasm, saying:

Such considerations, in so far as they are no more than generalizations about certain categories of workers, do not make it possible to identify criteria which are both objective and unrelated to any discrimination on grounds of sex . . . Although experience goes hand in hand with length of service, and experience enables the worker in principle to improve performance of the tasks allotted to him, the objectivity of such a criterion depends on all the circumstances in a particular case, and in particular on the relationship between the nature of the work performed and the experience gained from the performance of that work upon completion of a certain number of working hours.[319]

In similar vein, in *Rinner-Kuhn* v. *FWW Spezial-Gebaudereinigung GmbH*,[320] the ECJ held that the *Bilka-Kaufhaus* test for justifying indirect discrimination must be applied to German legislation restricting the payment of sick pay to employees working for longer than 10 hours a week or 45 hours a month. The Court asked the German government to provide information on the reasons which had motivated the legislation, and the government answered that the workers affected by the legislation were not integrated in or connected with the undertaking in a comparable way to that of other workers and that therefore the conditions for recognition of a duty of care from the employer towards them, including an obligation to continue to pay wages, did not exist; in addition, the government pointed out that the statutory exclusion followed earlier legislation.[321] The ECJ firmly rejected this approach:

It should however be stated that those considerations, in so far as they are only generalizations about certain categories of workers, do not enable criteria which are both objective and unrelated to any discrimination on grounds of sex to be identified. However, if the Member State can show that the means chosen meet a necessary aim of its social policy and that they are suitable and requisite for attaining that aim, the mere fact that the provision affects a much greater number of female workers than male workers cannot be regarded as constituting an infringement of Article 119.[322]

A novel aspect of this ruling is that it applies the *Bilka- Kaufhaus* test, not merely to an employer's practices, but to the state's legislation, backed up of course by the principle of the supremacy of EC law. The test therefore

---

[319] [1991] ECR I-297, at 319. See also Case C-1/95 *Gerster* v. *Freistaat Bayern* (nyr) and Case C-100/95 *Kording* v. *Sanator für Finanzen* (nyr).

[320] Case 171/88 [1989] ECR 2743.

[321] These arguments were strikingly similar to those of the British government in *Building Businesses . . . Not Barriers* (Cmnd. 9794) where it was proposed to raise the hours of work qualification for UK statutory rights from 16 to 20.

[322] [1989] ECR 2743, at 2761. Cf. the submissions of Darmon AG in this case.

evolved from the needs of a business to the needs of a State's social policy.[323] It appears to be up to the State to justify the legislation, although:

It is for the national court . . . which has sole jurisdiction to assess the facts and interpret the national legislation, to determine whether and to what extent a legislative provision, which, although applying independently of the sex of the worker, actually affects a greater number of women than men, is justified by reasons which are objective and unrelated to any discrimination on grounds of sex.[324]

This raises considerable practical problems. In the UK, it means that an employer faced with a similar claim to that in *Rinner-Kuhn* must ask the industrial tribunal to join the Secretary of State for Employment as a party to the case in order to justify the relevant legislation.[325] There is also the difficulty that, justification being an issue of fact rather than law as far as the British courts are concerned, different industrial tribunals may well reach different conclusions when presented with the same evidence.[326] This, however, is a general problem as far as the justification of indirect discrimination is concerned. It cannot be denied that the formula chosen by the ECJ entrusts a considerable discretion to the deciding judge. Indeed, Sebba has gone so far as to argue that the assessment of justification is essentially a non-justiciable task: 'The judge can do no more than express his or her personal political opinion on the matter. The personal perspective of the unelected judge therefore shapes . . . social policy . . .'[327]

In addition to this potential for local inconsistencies in its application, the Court's jurisprudence on objective justification has wavered in its underlying principles, the bullish stance evident in cases such as *Nimz* and *Rinner-Kuhn* giving way on occasion to a weaker form of supervision over the national courts. For example, in *Kowalska v. Freie und Hansestadt Hamburg*,[328] the defendants argued that discrimination against part-timers in relation to severance pay was justified because these kinds of workers do not provide for their needs or those of their families exclusively out of their earned income; one might have expected this argument to be dismissed as another mere generalization but instead the Court simply

[323] See also Szyszczak, 'European Court Rulings on Discrimination and Part-Time Work and the Burden of Proof in Equal Pay Claims' (1990) 19 ILJ 114.

[324] [1989] ECR 2743, at 2761.

[325] See also *R. v. Secretary of State for Employment, Ex p. EOC* [1994] 2 WLR 409, discussed above.

[326] See the comments of the editors of the Equal Opportunities Review on the *Rinner-Kuhn* decision in 'Discriminatory Statutory Rights can be challenged under EEC law' (1989) 28 EOR 39.

[327] Sebba, 'The Doctrine of "Direct Effect": A Malignant Disease of Community Law' [1995] LIEI 35.

[328] Case C-33/89 [1990] ECR I-2591, discussed further below.

replied that the assessment of justification was a matter for the national court. This sort of inconsistency of approach is also evident in a series of references from German courts in relation to the employment staff committee system which operates in that country. The first was *Arbeiterwohlfahrt der Stadt Berlin eV* v. *Bötel*.[329] Ms Bötel, a part-time worker, was chair of such a staff committee and exercised her statutory right to paid time off work in order to attend some training courses in connection with this activity which lasted for longer than her normal working hours. Her employers, in accordance with their usual practice, paid her only in respect of her normal working hours. Had she been a full-timer, she would have been reimbursed in respect of all the hours she spent on the courses and this disparity of treatment she alleged to be indirect discrimination against her. After concluding that the sums paid were within Article 119,[330] the Court held:

[T]he argument that compensation for participation in training courses granted under national legislation is calculated solely on the basis of working hours not worked does not alter the fact that staff council members who work on a part-time basis receive less compensation than their full-time colleagues when in fact both categories of workers receive without distinction the same number of hours of training in order to be able effectively to look after the interests of employees for the sake of good working relations and for the general good of the undertaking . . . [S]uch a situation is likely to deter employees in the part-time category, in which the proportion of women is undeniably preponderant, from serving on staff councils or from acquiring the knowledge needed in order to serve on them, thus making it more difficult for that category of worker to be represented by qualified staff council members. To that extent, the difference in treatment in question cannot be regarded as justified by objective factors unrelated to any discrimination on grounds of sex, unless the Member State concerned proves the contrary before the national court.[331]

Kuratorium für Dialyse und Nierentransplantation eV v. *Lewark*[332] raised the same 'delicate' issue as *Bötel*[333] and the Federal Labour Court specifically asked the ECJ to reconsider its position. Both the German court and the German government argued that it was important to the staff council system that those workers serving did so on an unpaid and independent basis; all that therefore ought to be required should be that these workers be reimbursed in respect of the hours that they would have spent at work

---

[329] Case C-360/90 [1992] ECR 3589.
[330] See discussion above as to the meaning of 'pay' in the context of Art. 119.
[331] [1992] ECR I-3589, at 3613-4.
[332] Case C-457/93 [1996] ECR I-243.
[333] See Darmon AG in Case C-278/93 *Freers* v. *Deutsche Bundespost* [1996] ECR I-1165, at 1167. The Advocate General also commented that the 'heated debate provoked by the [*Bötel*] judgment in Germany' had prompted the two further references discussed in the text.

had they not been serving on a staff committee. The Court reiterated that, irrespective of how these payments were perceived within Germany, they nevertheless fell within the Article 119 notion of 'pay'. Furthermore, it held that there was unequal treatment as between full-timers and part-timers because they received unequal pay in respect of their hours devoted to staff committee service. Since this undoubtedly impacted more severely on women than men, there was therefore a *prima facie* case of indirect discrimination and the issue was whether that could be justified. On this last point, the Court compromised its former stance, saying:

It is . . . apparent from the order for reference in the present case that the Bundesarbeitsgericht considers that the German legislature's wish to place the independence of staff councils above financial inducements for performing staff council functions . . . is an aim of social policy. Such a social policy aim appears in itself to be unrelated to any discrimination on grounds of sex. It cannot be disputed that the work of staff councils does indeed play a part in German social policy, in that the councils have the task of promoting harmonious labour relations within undertakings and in their interest. The concern to ensure the independence of the members of those councils thus likewise reflects a legitimate aim of social policy.

If a Member State is able to show that the measures chosen reflect a legitimate aim of its social policy, are appropriate to achieve that aim and are necessary in order to do so, the mere fact that the legislative provision affects far more women workers than men cannot be regarded as a breach of Article 119 . . .

However, it should be noted that, as the Court held in *Bötel*, . . . legislation such as that at issue is likely to deter workers in the part-time category . . . from performing staff council functions . . .

In the light of all those considerations and taking into account the possibility of achieving the social policy aim in question by other means, the difference in treatment could be justified . . . only if it appeared to be suitable and necessary for achieving that aim. It is for the national court to ascertain whether that is so in the present case.[334]

This reasoning is inherently illogical. If the sums in question are 'pay', as the ECJ maintains, then discrimination in relation to them ought not to be able to be justified by an argument which relies on the fact that they are not pay. To argue that inequality over pay is prohibited but not inequality over compensation for loss of pay is purely semantic.[335] Nevertheless, the Court followed its judgment in *Lewark* in *Freers* v. *Deutsche Bundespost*.[336]

---

[334] [1996] ECR I-243, at 269-70.

[335] This factor may have been in the mind of Jacobs AG who submitted: 'I conclude that, as the Court held in *Bötel*, the compensation paid to a staff council member for attendance at training courses . . . is 'pay' for the purposes of Article 119 . . . However, it must be recognised that on the facts of this case that compensation can be regarded as pay only in the broadest sense of the term. Even if the continuance of salary for undertaking such activities during normal working hours can be regarded as pay, it is less clear that payment for undertaking such activities outside working hours can be so regarded' (at 250).

[336] Case C-278/93 [1996] ECR I-1165. Darmon AG, however, submitted that the indirect

Another important practical issue on which the ECJ has not been wholly consistent is whether the existence of two separate collective agreements, applying essentially to male and female workers respectively, is sufficient to satisfy the *Bilka-Kaufhaus* requirement of objective justification.[337] Such a factor ought not in theory to constitute an 'objectively justified factor unrelated to any discrimination based on sex' since, even if the collective agreements in question did not have their roots in earlier sex discrimination, it is more or less inconceivable that their existence could constitute a 'necessary' response to a 'genuine need' of the employer.[338] Uncharacteristically, the UK government, which intervened in the *Danfoss* case, argued that the existence of two separate collective agreements does not by itself justify a pay differential.

The issue was put directly to the ECJ in *Enderby* v. *Frenchay Health Authority*,[339] where separate non-discriminatory collective agreements governed the groups of workers whose pay was the subject of comparison. The Court held robustly that this was not sufficient to establish justification:

The fact that the rates of pay at issue are decided by collective bargaining processes conducted separately for each of the two professional groups concerned, without any discriminatory effect within each group, does not preclude a finding of *prima facie* discrimination where the results of those processes show that two groups with the same employer and the same trade union are treated differently. If the employer could rely on the absence of discrimination within each of the collective bargaining processes taken separately as sufficient justification for the difference in pay, he could, as the German government pointed out, easily circumvent the principle of equal pay by using separate bargaining processes.[340]

However, in the Court's later decision in *Specialarbejderforbundet I Danmark* v. *Dansk Industrie, acting for Royal Copenhagen A/S*,[341] it resiled from this clear-cut position but without substantial reasoning:

[T]he principle of equal pay for men and women . . . applies where the elements of the pay are determined by collective bargaining or by negotiation at local level

---

discrimination was not justified in this case and that *Bötel* should be followed. For comment on *Lewark* and *Freers* see Shaw, 'Works Councils in German Enterprises and Article 119 EC' (1997) 22 ELRev. 256. See also *Manor Bakeries Ltd.* v. *Nazir* [1996] IRLR 604.

[337] It was asked about this matter but declined to answer the question because it found it to be unnecessary in Case C-109/88 *Handels-OG Kontorfunktionaererernes Forbund I Danmark* v. *Dansk Arbejdsgiverforening (acting for Danfoss)* [1989] ECR 3199.

[338] However, this has not always been the view of UK courts. See in particular *Reed Packaging Ltd.* v. *Boozer* [1987] IRLR 26 and *Enderby* v. *Frenchay Health Authority and the Secretary of State for Health* [1991] IRLR 44. Cf. the remarks of Lord Goff in *Hayward* v. *Cammell Laird (No. 2)* [1988] 2 WLR 1134, at 1146.

[339] Case C-127/92 [1993] ECR I-5535, also discussed above.

[340] Ibid. at 5574. Lenz AG drew a distinction, apparently taken up by the Court, between collective agreements concluded for whole branches of industry and those where there is a common employer.

[341] Case C-400/93 [1995] ECR I-1275, also discussed above.

but . . . the national court may take that fact into account in its assessment of whether differences between the average pay of two groups of workers are due to objective factors unrelated to any discrimination on grounds of sex.[342]

As discussed in Chapter 4, the ECJ has considerably relaxed its grip over justification in the field of social security, emphasising in particular the breadth of the discretion which the Member States continue to enjoy in their choice of measures of social policy.[343] Whether this trend towards making it easier to justify otherwise indirectly discriminatory legislation will be extended into the employment field may be revealed when the ECJ gives its preliminary ruling in *R.* v. *Secretary of State for Employment, Ex p. Seymour-Smith.*[344] The House of Lords seeks enlightenment on 'the legal conditions for establishing the objective justification, for the purposes of indirect discrimination under Article 119, of a measure adopted by a Member State in pursuance of its social policy'. It asks, in particular, what material the Member State needs to adduce in support of its grounds for justification.

Can Direct Discrimination be Justified?

It has sometimes been suggested that it is not only indirect discrimination which may be justified, but that this concept may also be applied so as to legalize direct discrimination.[345] For example, in *Birds Eye Walls Ltd.* v. *Roberts,*[346] both the Commission and the defendant-employers argued that the alleged discrimination in relation to bridging pensions against female ex-employees aged between 60 and 65 who had retired early could be justified. Van Gerven AG agreed that 'exceptionally' direct discrimination might be justified, apparently largely on the basis that it can be difficult to distinguish between direct and indirect discrimination.[347] He concluded:

Since I consider that Birds Eye Walls can justify on objective grounds the policy with regard to pensions at issue here, I have come to the conclusion . . . that an employer is not in breach of Article 119 . . . if, taking account of the difference between the pensionable age for men and that for women applied by the state

[342] Ibid. at 1314.

[343] See in particular Case C-317/93 *Nolte* v. *Landesversicherungsanstalt Hannover* [1995] ECR I-4625 and Case C-444/93 *Megner and Scheffel* v. *Innungskrankenkasse Vorderplatz* [1995] ECR I-4741.

[344] [1997] 1 WLR 473. ECJ ruling pending at the time of writing.

[345] See McCrudden, *Equality of Treatment Between Men and Women in Social Security* (Butterworths, London, 1994), especially at 215-7.

[346] Case C-132/92 [1993] ECR I-5579, discussed above.

[347] See the Advocate General's submissions ibid. at 5593. See also the somewhat ambiguous submissions of La Pergola AG in Case C-1/95 *Gerster* v. *Freistaat Bayern* (nyr) and Case C-100/95 *Kording* v. *Senator für Finanzen* (nyr), at para.32, and in Case C-243/95 *Hill and Stapleton* v. *Revenue Commissioners* (pending before the ECJ at the time of writing, AG's submissions delivered 20 Feb. 1997), at para. 21.

and authorized for the time being, he operates an occupational scheme involving payment of a bridging pension using a method of calculation *designed to ensure* the same overall retirement pension (occupational pension and state pension combined) for male and female ex-employees.[348]

As seen above, the Court avoided dealing with the issue in this case by holding that there was no discrimination at all on the facts. This appeared consistent with its earlier holding in *Dekker* v. *Stichting Vormingscentrum Voor Jonge Volwassen Plus*[349] that the concept of justification has no place in the law relating to direct discrimination.[350] However, an indication that the Court might be able to be persuaded of the possibility of justifying direct discrimination was provided in *Smith* v. *Avdel Systems Ltd*.[351] Van Gerven AG had again argued in favour of such a solution:

Such a possibility . . . may be used only in exceptional situations, more specifically in order to take account of circumstances which are entirely unconnected with discrimination on grounds of sex and which meet an *acute* need concerning the very existence of the undertaking or the solvency of its occupational pension scheme.[352]

The Court itself held that Article 119 forbade raising the pension age for women members of the scheme from 60 to 65 in the period intervening between the operative date of the *Barber* judgment and the date on which the scheme rules were equalized for men and women.[353] It went on to add:

Even assuming that it would, in this context, be possible to take account of objectively justifiable considerations relating to the needs of the undertaking or of the occupational scheme concerned, the administrators of the occupational scheme could not reasonably plead, as justification for raising the retirement age for women during this period, financial difficulties as significant as those of which the Court took account in the *Barber* judgment, since the space of time is relatively short and attributable in any event to the conduct of the scheme administrators themselves.[354]

Similarly, in relation to direct discrimination contrary to the Equal Treatment Directive,[355] the Court has recently apparently countenanced

---

[348] Case C-132/92 at 5596; the supplied emphasis suggests that the Advocate General was in fact satisfied with subjective rather than objective justification. See also the same Advocate General's submissions in Case C-152/91 *Neath* v. *Hugh Steeper Ltd* [1993] ECR I-6935, also discussed above.

[349] Case 177/88 [1990] ECR I-3941, also discussed in Chap. 3.

[350] See also Elmer AG inCase C-249/96 *Grant* v. *South-West Trains Ltd* (pending before the ECJ at the time of writing).

[351] Case C-408/92 [1994] ECR I-4435, discussed above.

[352] Ibid. at 4448.

[353] See above.

[354] [1994] ECR I-4435, at 4468.

[355] Directive 76/207, OJ [1976] L39/40.

the possibility of justification but without actually applying the principle.[356]

It is respectfully submitted that this is a misconceived and undesirable route for the ECJ to pursue. It is misconceived because it is based upon a flawed analysis of the concept of discrimination. Sex discrimination occurs where a person is treated adversely on the ground of sex. The concept is a remedial one and, as Lenz AG pointed out in *Enderby* v. *Frenchay Health Authority*,[357] it makes no sense to make technical distinctions between its direct and indirect manifestations. There are, therefore, broadly speaking, two elements of the tort of discrimination, whichever form it takes: adverse treatment (harm) and the grounding of that treatment in sex (causation). It has already been seen that the ECJ recognized expressly in *Macarthys Ltd.* v. *Smith*[358] that where there is no causation there can be no discrimination. It has also been argued that objective justification reflects the element of causation where the discrimination is indirect: if the adverse consequences to one sex can be shown to be attributable to an acceptable and gender-neutral factor, then there is no discrimination. The *cause* of the adverse impact is something other than sex discrimination. When one is dealing with direct discrimination, however, once adverse treatment and causation have been proved, this is the end of the matter; there can logically be no room for any further arguments about the roots of the adverse treatment. Justification is, therefore, not an applicable notion.[359]

The possibility of justifying direct discrimination is also undesirable because it permits a raft of undefined excuses for discrimination which are not articulated in Article 119 or in any other instrument of EC law.[360] This has the potential gravely to undermine the operation of the principle of sex equality and is, furthermore, contrary to the Court's usual rule that exceptions to fundamental principles are to be construed narrowly.[361]

---

[356] See Case C-32/93 *Webb* v. *EMO (Air Cargo) Ltd* [1994] ECR I-3567 and Case C-421/92 *Habermann-Beltermann* [1994] ECR I-1657, discussed in Chap. 3.

[357] Case C-127/92 [1993] ECR I-5535.

[358] Case 129/79 [1980] ECR 1275.

[359] It is submitted that this what was intended by Lenz AG in *Enderby*. Although he spoke of an employer 'justifying' differences of pay in cases of direct discrimination, he was dealing with proof that the pay difference was *caused* by sex discrimination; see the Advocate General's submissions: [1993] ECR I-5535, at 5558-9. For further support for this analysis, see Watson, 'Equality of Treatment: A Variable Concept?' (1995) 24 ILJ 33, Hepple 'Equality and Discrimination' in *European Community Labour Law: Principles and Perspectives*, eds. Davies, Lyon-Caen, Sciarra and Simitis (Clarendon Press, Oxford, 1996), Szyszczak, '"The Status to be Accorded to Motherhood": Case C-32/93 *Webb* v. *Emo Air Cargo (UK) Ltd*' (1995) 58 MLR 860, and Ellis, 'The Definition of Discrimination in European Community Sex Equality Law' (1994) 19 ELRev. 563.

[360] See Hepple, 'Can Direct Discrimination Be Justified?' (1994) 55 EOR 48.

[361] Case 222/84 *Johnston* v. *Chief Constable of the RUC* [1986] ECR 1651, also discussed in Chap. 3.

THE EFFECTS OF ARTICLE 119 AND THE REMEDIES FOR ITS BREACH

The first hint in the ECJ that Article 119 might be directly effective came in the *First Defrenne* case[362] where Lamothe AG said:

[Article 119] is thus not limited, as are Articles 117 and 118, to setting out objectives of harmonization of laws and regulations or co-operation between Member States, but it creates an obligation for the Member States. The question could have been asked whether in addition or as a result of the obligation which it created for the states, it gives rise to individual rights in favour of the nationals of Member States and whether it has a 'direct effect'. But this question no longer arises for two reasons:

1. Although the difficulties of application encountered by certain countries were great and although in particular a conference of Member States extended until 31 December 1964 the period initially laid down, it appears to me certain that at least as from this date Article 119 created subjective rights which the workers of the Member States can invoke and respect for which national courts must ensure.

2. It is even more certain in Belgium since, to avoid any difficulty of interpretation by the courts and give additional publicity to this provision of the treaty, the Belgian government by an initiative which was legally superfluous but the intentions of which were highly commendable, has insisted on inserting in Royal Decree No. 40 of 27 October 1967 concerning the work of women an Article 14 worded thus:

'In accordance with Article 119 of the Treaty establishing the European Economic Community, adopted by the law of 2 December 1957, any woman worker may institute proceedings in the competent court for the application of the principle of equal pay for men and women workers. '

In these circumstances the reasons may be well understood why the Belgian Conseil d'Etat does not even seem to have considered and in any event has not asked us to consider whether Article 119 had a direct effect or not. This appeared to it, as it does to me, to be obvious.[363]

However, to others the conclusion that the Article takes direct effect was probably less obvious. It was seen in Chapter 1 that, in order to take direct effect, a provision must satisfy certain criteria of precision; specifically, the scope of the obligation it creates must be clear; and it must also be unconditional, non-discretionary, and final. Arguably, at least three of these conditions could not be said to be satisfied by Article 119. The scope of the obligation might be said to be somewhat vague, in particular since the concepts of 'equal work' and 'equal pay' require clarification. Such clarification might confer a discretion on the Member States and might also mean that the Article could not be regarded as 'final'. Nevertheless, the ECJ in its dramatic ruling in the *Second Defrenne* case[364] agreed with

---

[362] Case 80/70 *Defrenne* v. *Belgium* [1971] ECR 445.   [363] Ibid. at 456.
[364] Case 43/75 *Defrenne* v. *Sabena* [1976] ECR 455.

Lamothe AG's earlier conclusion. In reaching this result, it clearly showed its frustration with the non-compliance with Article 119 by the Member States and with the weak-willed attitude towards this non-compliance demonstrated by the Commission. It was a proactive ruling given by a Court intent on ascribing useful effect to an important Article of the Treaty. Having explained its belief that Article 119 forms 'part of the foundations of the Community',[365] it went on to say that nothing in the wording of the Article undermined its direct effect:

First of all it is impossible to put forward an argument against its direct effect based on the use in this Article of the word 'principle', since, in the language of the Treaty, this term is specifically used in order to indicate the fundamental nature of certain provisions, as is shown for example by the heading of the first part of the Treaty which is devoted to 'Principles' and by Article 113, according to which the commercial policy of the Community is to be based on 'uniform principles'. If this concept were to be attenuated to the point of reducing it to the level of a vague declaration, the very foundations of the Community and the coherence of its external relations would be directly affected. It is also impossible to put forward arguments based on the fact that Article 119 only refers expressly to 'Member States'. Indeed, as the Court has already found in other contexts, the fact that certain provisions of the Treaty are formally addressed to the Member States does not prevent rights from being conferred at the same time on any individual who has an interest in the performance of the duties thus laid down. The very wording of Article 119 shows that it imposes on states a duty to bring about a specific result to be mandatorily achieved within a fixed period. The effectiveness of this provision cannot be affected by the fact that the duty imposed by the Treaty has not been discharged by certain Member States and that the joint institutions have not reacted sufficiently energetically against this failure to act. To accept the contrary view would be to risk raising the violation of the right to the status of a principle of interpretation, a position the adoption of which would not be consistent with the task assigned to the Court by Article 164 of the Treaty. Finally, in its reference to 'Member States', Article 119 is alluding to those states in the exercise of all those of their functions which may usefully contribute to the implementation of the principle of equal pay. Thus, contrary to the statements made in the course of the proceedings, this provision is far from merely referring the matter to the powers of the national legislative authorities. Therefore the reference to 'Member States' in Article 119 cannot be interpreted as excluding the intervention of the courts in direct application of the Treaty.[366]

Under the original terms of Article 119, it became unconditional as far as the founding Member States were concerned as from the end of the first stage, in other words from the beginning of January 1962. However, as this date approached, it became clear that some of the Member States had not introduced the necessary legislation in time and so had not put the equality principle into practice within their own jurisdictions.

---

[365] Ibid. at 472.   [366] [1976] ECR 455, at 474–5.

Consequently the Member States adopted the Resolution mentioned by Lamothe AG, by which they agreed to postpone the deadline to the end of 1964.[367] The ECJ held that this Resolution was ineffective to modify the time limit stipulated in Article 119, since the Treaty can only be amended by means of the procedure laid down therein.[368]

However, the Court's judgment contained an unfortunate sting in its tail in relation to the operative date of Article 119. Several of the original Member States did not observe even the later time limit agreed in the Resolution. The Commission therefore held a conference, attended by representatives of the governments and the two sides of industry, and produced several reports on the matter. It also declared its intention to take enforcement proceedings under Article 169 against those States remaining in breach, although it in fact took no further action. The UK and Irish governments also argued that the economic repercussions of holding Article 119 to be directly effective from its operative date under the Treaty would be disastrous; undertakings might face bankruptcy as a result of large numbers of backdated claims. This argument seems an exaggerated one in the light of the fact that, as seen in Chapter 1, national rules of procedure relate to directly effective Community provisions and, in the UK at least, the relevant statute provided that no equal pay claim could be backdated further than two years.[369] The ECJ was, however, persuaded by the Member States' arguments and held:

[I]n the light of the conduct of several of the Member States and the views adopted by the Commission and repeatedly brought to the notice of the circles concerned, it is appropriate to take exceptionally into account the fact that, over a prolonged period, the parties concerned have been led to continue with practices which were contrary to Article 119, although not yet prohibited under their national law. The fact that, in spite of the warnings given, the Commission did not initiate proceedings under Article 169 against the Member States concerned on grounds of failure to fulfil an obligation was likely to consolidate the incorrect impression as to the effects of Article 119. In these circumstances, it is appropriate to hold that, as the general level at which pay would have been fixed cannot be known, important considerations of legal certainty affecting all the interests involved, both public and private, make it impossible in principle to reopen the question as regards the past. Therefore the direct effect of Article 119 cannot be relied on in order to support claims concerning pay periods prior to the date of this judgment, except as regards those workers who have already brought legal proceedings or made an equivalent claim.[370]

---

[367] See Warner, 'European Community Social Policy in Practice: Community Action on Behalf of Women and its Impact in the Member States' (1984) 23 Journal of Common Market Studies 141.

[368] [1976] ECR 455 at 478–9. At that time, the relevant procedure was set out in Art. 236 and later in Art. N {Art. 48} of the Treaty on European Union 1993. Cf. the apparently different view of Lamothe AG on this point.

[369] Equal Pay Act 1970, s. 2(5).   [370] [1976] ECR 455, at 480–1.

In terms of principle, this is an illogical conclusion. If Article 119 possesses the qualities required to produce direct effect, then this has been so ever since it ceased to be conditional at the beginning of 1962. To interpose another operative date was a clear example of judicial legislation and highlights the unsatisfactoriness of there being no appeal from decisions of the ECJ.[371] Furthermore, in paying heed to the failure of the Commission to initiate proceedings, the Court was inconsistent in its reasoning, since earlier in its judgment it rejected the notion that the effectiveness of Article 119 could be undermined by the dilatoriness of the Commission.[372] The creation of the concept of prospective effect for Article 119 also produced an unfortunate precedent in practice.[373] The Court does, however, appear to regard prospective direct effect as exceptional and it held in *Amministrazione delle Finanze dello Stato* v. *Denkavit Italiana Srl*:[374]

[I]t is only exceptionally that the Court may, in application of the general principle of legal certainty inherent in the Community legal order and in taking account of the serious effects which its judgment might have, as regards the past, on legal relationships established in good faith, be moved to restrict for any person concerned the opportunity of relying upon the provisions as thus interpreted with a view to calling into question those legal relationships. *Such a restriction may, however, be allowed only in the actual judgment ruling upon the interpretation sought. The fundamental need for a general and uniform application of Community law implies that it is for the Court of Justice alone to decide upon the temporal restrictions to be placed on an interpretation which it lays down.*[375]

The temporal limitation which the Court applies to the enforcement of Article 119 in relation to pensions has been discussed above. It is important to note, however, that the limitation expressed in the *Barber* case[376] does not extend to matters outside the pensions field; as seen above, the Court

---

[371] Even today, despite the existence of the Court of First Instance, there would be no possibility of appeal in a case such as *Defrenne*.

[372] See [1976] ECR 455, at 472–3. On this matter, the Court differed from the Advocate General. Burrows, in 'The Promotion of Women's Rights by the European Economic Community' (1980) 17 CMLRev. 191, comments that 'the Court did in effect what it said the other institutions of the Community were not entitled to do i.e. amended the Treaty by a procedure other than that foreseen in Article 236'.

[373] See Wyatt, 'Prospective Effect of a Holding of Direct Applicability' (1975–6) 1 ELRev. 399, and L. Neville Brown, 'Agromonetary Byzantinism and Prospective Overruling' (1981) 18 CMLRev. 509.   [374] Case 61/79 [1980] ECR 1205.

[375] Ibid. at 1223–4. (Emphasis supplied.) See also Case 33/76 *Rewe-Zentralfinanz eG and Rewe-Zentral AG* v. *Landwirtschaftskammer für das Saarland* [1976] 2 ECR 1989, esp. the remarks of Warner AG at 2005, Cases 66, 127, and 128/79 *Amministrazione delle Finanze dello Stato* v. *Meridionale Industria Salumi Srl* [1980] ECR 1237, Case 69/80 *Worringham* v. *Lloyds Bank Ltd.* [1981] ECR 767, Case 24/86 *Blaizot* v. *University of Liège* [1988] ECR 379, Case C-262/88 *Barber* v. *Guardian Royal Exchange Assurance Group* [1990] ECR I-1889, Case C-163/90 *Administration des Douanes* v. *Legros* [1992] ECR I-4625, Case C-110/91 *Moroni* v. *Collo GmbH* [1993] ECR I-6591 and Case C-57/93 *Vroege* v. *NCIV Instituut Voor Volkshuisvesting BV* [1994] ECR I-4541.

[376] Case C-262/88 [1990] ECR I-1889.

also dealt with non-discrimination in relation to redundancy payments.

The ECJ's ruling in the *Second Defrenne* case[377] also established, very importantly in practice, that Article 119 takes horizontal direct effect; in other words, it may be enforced against employers who are private persons or companies, as well as against organs of the State. The Court held:

[S]ince Article 119 is mandatory in nature, the prohibition on discrimination between men and women applies not only to the action of public authorities, but also extends to all agreements which are intended to regulate paid labour collectively, as well as to contracts between individuals.[378]

In contrast to the width of the class for whom Article 119 creates obligations, it seems that the scope of its direct effect is limited; in other words, there are some circumstances in which the Article obliges the Member States to provide equal pay for equal work but in which, without further implementing legislation, the Article itself cannot be directly enforced. It was seen earlier in the present chapter that the Court in the *Second Defrenne* case drew a distinction between what it then described as 'direct and overt' sex discrimination, as regards which Article 119 does take direct effect, and 'indirect and disguised' discrimination, as to which it does not. 'Direct and overt' discrimination can be identified solely with the aid of the criteria based on equal work and equal pay referred to by Article 119, whilst 'indirect and disguised' discrimination can only be identified by reference to more explicit implementing provisions of a Community or national character. The ECJ went on to hold:

Among the forms of direct discrimination which may be identified solely by reference to the criteria laid down by Article 119 must be included in particular those which have their origin in legislative provisions or in collective labour agreements and which may be detected on the basis of a purely legal analysis of the situation. This applies even more in cases where men and women receive unequal pay for equal work carried out in the same establishment or service, whether public or private. As is shown by the very findings of the judgment making the reference, in such a situation the court is in a position to establish all the facts which enable it to decide whether a woman worker is receiving lower pay than a male worker performing the same tasks.[379]

Although the Court in later cases abandoned the use of the phrases 'direct and overt' and 'indirect and disguised', it has stuck to its original reasoning in relation to the direct effect of Article 119. This is unsurprising given that the concept of direct effect calls for the enforcement of the provision in question by the judges of the national courts; its ambit must

---

[377] Case 43/75 [1976] ECR 455.
[378] Ibid. at 476. See also the remarks of Van Themaat AG in Case 58/81 *Commission* v. *Luxemburg* [1982] ECR 2175.
[379] Case 43/75 [1976] ECR 455, at 473–4.

therefore be clearly defined if there are not to be great discrepancies in application. Warner AG explained the position in *Jenkins* v. *Kingsgate (Clothing Productions) Ltd.*[380] as follows:

A difficulty . . . is . . . caused by certain *dicta* of the Court in Case 43/75 the *Second Defrenne* case and in *Macarthys Ltd.* v. *Smith* . . . Those *dicta* could be interpreted as meaning that the test for determining whether there is 'covert' discrimination, in the sense meant in [the nationality cases] is the same as the test for identifying the kind of discrimination as regards which Article 119 has no direct effect. In my opinion the two tests are not the same and I doubt if the Court can ever have intended to say that they were . . . Article 119 is, in my opinion, more accurately described as not having direct effect where a court cannot apply its provisions by reference to the simple criteria that those provisions themselves lay down and where, consequently, implementing legislation, either Community or national, is necessary to lay down the relevant criteria.[381]

The Court has held that Article 119 is directly effective where male and female workers perform identical jobs simultaneously in the same establishments,[382] where they perform such jobs at different times,[383] where there is indirect discrimination over pay in relation to men and women performing identical jobs,[384] and where there is gender-plus discrimination in relation to identical jobs.[385]

It remains to be determined in what other situations Article 119 takes direct effect. In particular, if the Article does extend to comparisons with workers in other establishments or working for different employers, it is arguable that, so long as the pay discrimination can be ascertained by means of the concepts of pay and work contained in the Article itself, then there is nothing to inhibit direct effect in this situation. Perhaps even more importantly in practice, there is the question of whether the Article is directly effective where the two jobs compared are not identical but are alleged to be of equal value.[386] It was seen earlier in the present chapter that the ECJ changed its mind in this context and came to consider, even before its amendment by the Amsterdam Treaty, that at least the theoretical scope of Article 119 embraced equal value situations. This may well have been because, once it had articulated its position on the horizontal direct effect of directives, it realized that the Equal Pay

[380] Case 96/80 [1981] ECR 911.

[381] Ibid. at 937–8.

[382] Case 43/75 *Defrenne* v. *Sabena* [1976] ECR 455, and Case 69/80 *Worringham* v. *Lloyds Bank Ltd.* [1981] ECR 767.

[383] Case 129/79 *Macarthys Ltd.* v. *Smith* [1980] ECR 1275.

[384] Case 96/80 *Jenkins* v. *Kingsgate (Clothing Productions) Ltd.* [1981] ECR 911, and Case 170/84 *Bilka-Kaufhaus GmbH* v. *Weber Von Hartz* [1986] ECR 1607. Cf. the remarks of Capotorti AG in Case 149/77 *Defrenne* v. *Sabena* [1978] ECR 1365, at 1382.

[385] Case 23/83 *Liefting* v. *Directie van het Academisch Ziekenhuis bij de Universiteit van Amsterdam* [1984] ECR 3225.

[386] See Arnull, 'Article 119 and Equal Pay for Work of Equal Value' (1986) 11 ELRev. 200.

Directive would be of little help in the equal value situation, so that recourse would have to be made to Article 119.[387] *Dicta* from the early cases about the extent of the Article's direct effect are of course misleading today,[388] although the difficulty referred to in those cases appears a real one: namely, how can the Article apply directly when further explanatory legislation is needed before a court can know how equal value is to be assessed? However, notwithstanding this obstacle, by the time of *Worringham* v. *Lloyds Bank Ltd.*[389] the Court seemed prepared to include the equal value situation in its definition of the extent of the direct effect of Article 119:

[Article 119 applies directly] to all forms of discrimination which may be identified solely with the aid of the criteria of equal work and equal pay referred to by the Article in question, without national or Community measures being required to define them with greater precision in order to permit of their application. Among the forms of discrimination which may thus be judicially identified, the Court mentioned in particular cases where men and women receive unequal pay for equal work carried out in the same establishment or service, public or private. In such a situation the court is in a position to establish all the facts enabling it to decide whether a woman receives less pay than a man engaged in the same work *or work of equal value.*[390]

The issue seems to have been settled by *Murphy* v. *Bord Telecom Eireann,*[391] in which the ECJ held that Article 119 is directly effective where the claimant can demonstrate that she is engaged on work of higher value than that of her male comparator. It would seem to follow from the Court's remarks in this case that the same would have been true were the work established to be of equal value. In *Pickstone* v. *Freemans plc,* the Court of Appeal also came to the conclusion that Article 119 is directly effective in equal value cases.[392] The House of Lords decided the case on the basis of British law, but the comments of Lord Oliver are significant:

[T]he cases in the European Court to which your Lordships have been referred clearly establish that there is an area within which [Article 119] is not directly applicable.[393] The bounds of that area are far from clear to me, however, but the

---

[387] See further discussion below.

[388] See e.g. the comments of Trabucchi AG in Case 43/75 *Defrenne* v. *Sabena* [1976] ECR 455, at 485–6.

[389] Case 69/80 [1981] ECR 767. Cf. the opinion of Van Themaat AG in Case 61/81 *Commission* v. *UK* [1982] ECR 2601.

[390] [1981] ECR 767, at 792. (Emphasis supplied.)

[391] Case 157/86 [1988] ECR 673, discussed above.

[392] [1987] 3 WLR 811. Cf. the view of the Court of Appeal in *O'Brien* v. *Sim-Chem Ltd.* [1980] 1 WLR 734.

[393] It is apparent from the context that Lord Oliver is using the expression 'directly applicable' in the same sense as the present writer is using 'directly effective'.

cases appear to indicate that the Article may not be directly applicable in an 'equal value' claim, *at any rate where there is no machinery in the domestic law by which the criterion of what is work of equal value can be readily ascertained.*[394]

The last part of Lord Oliver's statement probably explains the ECJ's change of mind in relation to direct effect in equal value cases: where national implementing legislation has been passed explaining how equal value is to be assessed then Article 119 can in principle take direct effect in such cases within that Member State.[395] However, *Pickstone's case* involved a particular difficulty, as Lord Oliver went on to demonstrate. The assessment of equal value in the UK is the job of industrial tribunals under s. 1(2)(c) of the Equal Pay Act 1970 but their jurisdiction is purely statutory and they possess no inherent powers. The Court of Appeal had held that s. 1(2)(c) did not extend because of its wording to the precise situation in issue in that case and thus, in his Lordship's opinion, there was no national machinery for the assessment of equal value on the Court of Appeal's analysis. Thus, he could not envisage how Article 119 could be enforced either. This is, of course, of critical importance to the enforcement of equal value claims in the UK, although there is now a body of case law which takes the view that directly effective EC law automatically amends UK law.[396] Moreover, it does not detract from the general principle that Article 119 appears now to be directly effective in such cases, at least provided that there is national legislation governing the ascertainment of equal value.

Where a litigant relies in a national court on the direct effect of Article 119, it was seen in Chapter 1 that the same remedies must be available as would be available in a similar domestic claim, provided that these do not actually frustrate the EC claim. The ECJ has added that the effect of a successful Article 119 claim is to raise the lower pay to the level of that of the comparator:

[S]ince Article 119 appears in the context of the harmonization of working conditions while the improvement is being maintained, the objection that the

---

[394]   [1988] 2 All ER 803, at 816. (Emphasis supplied.)

[395]   There is a parallel to be drawn here with the reasoning adopted by the ECJ in Case C-271/91 *Marshall* v. *Southampton and South-West Hants Area Health Authority (No. 2)* [1993] ECR I-4367, discussed in Chap. 3. Essentially, the Court held in *Marshall (No. 2)* that Art. 6 of the Equal Treatment Directive (Directive 76/207, OJ [1976], L39/40) was rendered directly effective so as to provide a remedy for the victim of a discriminatory dismissal where the national legislature had acted to restrict the available remedies in this situation to compensation; the victim was entitled to rely on the direct effect of the otherwise insufficiently specific Art. 6 in order to over-ride a national ceiling on damages, whose effect was to prevent her from recovering in full for the loss which she had sustained.

[396]   See e.g. *Biggs* v. *Somerset County Council* [1996] ICR 364.

terms of this Article may be observed in other ways than by raising the lowest salaries may be set aside.[397]

The strength of this principle has been somewhat diluted in the field of occupational pension schemes where it has been held lawful to re-write the scheme's rules so as to equalize as between men and women, even where such equalization operates downwards.[398]

A rate of pay which violates Article 119 is automatically rendered void and replaced by the higher rate applicable to comparators;[399] this remedy can also be supplemented by national measures imposing penal sanctions on those who disobey the equal pay principle.[400] In *Kowalska* v. *Freie und Hansestadt Hamburg*,[401] this principle was applied to discrimination occurring under the terms of a collective agreement.[402] The agreement in question restricted the payment of severance benefits to workers employed for at least 38 hours a week, thereby indirectly discriminating against women since the large majority of those employed for under 38 hours a week were female. The Court held:

It is apparent from the judgment of 13 December 1989, *Ruzius-Wilbrink* (Case C-102/88 [1989] ECR 4311), that in a case of indirect discrimination the members of the class of persons placed at a disadvantage are entitled to have the same scheme applied to them as that applied to other workers, on a basis proportional to their working time. That ruling applies equally to discriminatory provisions in a collective agreement. It must therefore be stated in reply to the second question that where there is indirect discrimination in a clause in a collective wage agreement, the class of persons placed at a disadvantage by reason of that discrimination must be treated in the same way and made subject to the same scheme, proportionately to the number of hours worked, such scheme remaining for want of correct transposition of Article 119 of the EEC Treaty into national law, the only valid point of reference.[403]

---

[397] Case 43/75 *Defrenne* v. *Sabena* [1976] ECR 455, at 472; Case C-200/91 *Coloroll Pension Trustees Ltd.* v. *Russell* [1994] ECR I-4389, at 4413. See also Case C-147/95 *DEI* v. *Evrenopoulos* (nyr), where it was alleged that a term in a pension scheme discriminating against widowers was unconstitutional and therefore invalid; the ECJ held that this was not correct as a matter of EC law and that the position of widowers must be levelled-up to match that of widows. Cf. the effect of establishing discrimination in a social security scheme contrary to the Social Security Directive, Directive 79/7, OJ [1979], L6/24, where the result may be a general levelling-down of the benefit in question, as discussed in Chap. 4.

[398] See Case C-408/92 *Smith* v. *Avdel Systems Ltd.* [1994] ECR I-4434, discussed above; also Deakin, 'Levelling Down Employee Benefits' [1995] CLJ 35.

[399] See Trabucchi AG in Case 43/75 *Defrenne* v. *Sabena* [1976] ECR 455, at 489.

[400] See Case 14/83 *Von Colson and Kamann* v. *Land of North Rhine-Westfalia* [1984] ECR 1891, discussed further in Chap. 3.

[401] Case 33/89 [1990] ECR I-2591, discussed by Reiland in 'Sex Discrimination in Collective Agreements' (1991) 20 ILJ 79 and by More in 'Severance Pay for Part-time Workers' (1991) 16 ELRev. 58.

[402] As also Case C-184/89 *Helga Nimz* v. *Freie und Hansestadt Hamburg* [1991] ECR I-297 and Joined Cases C-399, 409 and 425/92, C-34, 50 and 78/93 *Stadt Lengerich* v. *Helmig* [1994] ECR I-5727, both discussed above.   [403] [1990] ECR I-2591, at 2613.

In *Nimz* v. *Freie und Hansestadt Hamburg*,[404] the ECJ added:

It should also be pointed out that the Court has consistently held . . . that a national court which is called upon, within the limits of its jurisdiction, to apply provisions of Community law is under a duty to give full effect to those provisions, if necessary by refusing of its own motion to apply any conflicting provision of national legislation, and it is not necessary for the court to request or await the prior setting aside of such provision by legislative or other constitutional means.

It is equally necessary to apply such considerations to the case where the provision at variance with Community law is derived from a collective labour agreement. It would be incompatible with the very nature of Community law if the court having jurisdiction to apply that law were to be precluded at the time of such application from being able to take all necessary steps to set aside the provisions of a collective agreement which might constitute an obstacle to the full effectiveness of Community rules.

. . . [W]here there is indirect discrimination in a provision of a collective agreement, the national court is required to set aside that provision, without requesting or awaiting its prior removal by collective bargaining or any other procedure, and to apply to members of the group disadvantaged by that discrimination the same arrangements as are applied to other employees, arrangements which, failing the correct application of Article 119 . . . in national law, remain the only valid system of reference.[405]

THE EQUAL PAY DIRECTIVE[406]

The Background to the Equal Pay Directive

The Equal Pay Directive was passed in 1975, in an effort to harmonize the laws of the Member States in relation to the principle of equal pay.[407] It was, accordingly, based on Article 100.[408] That the principle of pay equality had by that date emerged as of fundamental importance to the Community is exemplified by the first recital of the Directive's Preamble, which describes the implementation of Article 119 as an 'integral part of the establishment and functioning of the common market'. The Preamble also refers expressly to the Council Resolution of 21 January 1974[409] which 'recognized that priority should be given to action taken on behalf of women as regards access to employment and vocational training and advancement, and as regards working conditions, including pay'.

The record in relation to equal pay in the various Member States during the early 1970s was, to say the least, patchy.[410] Strong feelings began to be

---

[404] Case C-184/89 [1991] ECR I-297.   [405] Ibid. at 321.
[406] Directive 75/117, OJ 1975, L45/19.   [407] See the final recital of the Preamble.
[408] {Art. 94}.   [409] OJ [1974], C13/1.
[410] See e.g. the Commission's comments in its Sixth General Report on the Activities of the Communities, 1972, para. 211. Also the Reports of the Commission to the Council on

expressed, particularly in the European Parliament, that Article 119 had been legally binding for a period of many years (at least in six of the Member States) and yet it had achieved little practical significance.[411] This was attributed in part to a lack of effective monitoring of what was going on in the Member States, and in part to the lack at that time of wider legislative measures to deal with discrimination against women in employment generally. The Equal Pay Directive was therefore seen as providing a valuable additional means of control by the Commission over the Member States in relation to pay equality.[412] The fifth recital of the Directive's Preamble refers to the differences which in 1975 continued 'to exist in the various Member States despite the efforts made to apply the resolution of the conference of the Member States of 30 December 1961 on equal pay for men and women' and implies that the Directive seeks to impose, at the very least, a uniform minimum standard.

As events turned out, the need for the Directive was greatly reduced very shortly after its enactment, when the ECJ ruled in *Defrenne* v. *Sabena*[413] that Article 119 itself was directly effective.[414] This had the very important consequence in practice that the principle of pay equality, at least on some occasions, could be enforced directly in the courts of the Member States and, even more significantly, that national legislation which conflicted with the Treaty Article was automatically rendered inapplicable. A large part of the Commission's job of chasing up offending Member States was thus performed at a stroke.

The Relationship between the Directive and Article 119

The ECJ experienced a change of heart with respect to the relationship between the Equal Pay Directive and Article 119. This may well have been provoked by its development of the doctrine of the direct effect of directives and its ultimate conclusion that they are incapable of horizontal

the Application of the Principle of Equal Pay for Men and Women of 18 July 1973 (SEC(73) 3000 final) and 17 July 1974 (SEC(74) 2721 final), and Sullerot, *The Employment of Women and the Problems it Raises in the Member States of the European Community* (Commission of the European Communities, 1975).

[411] The editors of the Common Market Law Review commented in 1974 that a directive on equal pay was long overdue 'as the failure to give effective enforcement to Article 119 of the EEC Treaty has been the scandal of the stunted development of the social aspect of the Community' ((1974) 11 CMLRev. 1–2).

[412] See Bull. EC 4–1974, point 2420. Also Burrows, 'The Promotion of Women's Rights by the European Economic Community' (1980) 17 CMLRev. 191.

[413] Case 43/75 [1976] ECR 455.

[414] See above. A similar sequence of events occurred in relation to the Occupational Social Security Directive (Directive 86/379, OJ [1986], L225/40), also discussed above, when the ECJ ruled that Art. 119 itself extended to various types of pension schemes.

effect:[415] if the Member States were going to prove recalcitrant in implementing the Directive, then the way to achieve maximum utility for EC law would be via the Treaty Article itself. Its original stance was articulated in *Defrenne* v. *Sabena*,[416] where it commented that Community secondary legislation 'implement[s] Article 119 from the point of view of extending the narrow criterion of "equal work"', thus suggesting that the Directive went further in its provisions than Article 119. However, by the early 1980s, it had decided that this was not so and that the Directive does no more than flesh out the bare bones of Article 119. This view has the logical support of the wording of the Directive itself both in Article 1(1) and in the fourth recital of its Preamble which states that 'it is desirable to reinforce the basic laws by standards aimed at facilitating the practical application of the principle of equality in such a way that all employees in the Community can be protected in these matters'. This enabled the ECJ to hold in *Jenkins* v. *Kingsgate (Clothing Productions) Ltd.*[417] that: 'Article 1 of Council Directive 75/117 which is principally designed to facilitate the practical application of the principle of equal pay outlined in Article 119 of the Treaty in no way alters the content or scope of that principle as defined in the Treaty'.[418] The fact that the Directive does not extend the scope of Article 119 does not, of course, mean that it can diminish it either because, as noted above, a measure of secondary legislation cannot restrict the scope of primary legislation.[419] The ECJ applied this general principle to the present context in *Defrenne* v. *Sabena*,[420] saying:

[T]he principle contained in Article 119 has been fully effective in the new Member States since the entry into force of the Accession Treaty . . . It was not possible for this legal situation to be modified by Directive 75/117, which was adopted on the basis of Article 100 dealing with the approximation of laws and was intended to encourage the proper implementation of Article 119 by means of a series of measures to be taken on the national level, in order, in particular, to eliminate indirect forms of discrimination, *but was unable to reduce the effectiveness of that Article or modify its temporal effect.*[421]

If the Directive therefore merely spells out the detail of Article 119, without in any way undermining its scope, it follows that its chief practical

---

[415] Discussed in Chap. 1.   [416] Case 43/75 [1976] ECR 455, at 473.
[417] Case 96/80 [1981] ECR 911.
[418] Case 96/80 [1981] ECR 911, at 927. See also Case 69/80 *Worringham* v. *Lloyds Bank Ltd.* [1981] ECR 767; Case 192/85 *Newstead* v. *Department of Transport* [1987] ECR 4753; Case 262/88 *Barber* v. *Guardian Royal Exchange Assurance Group* [1990] ECR I-1889 and Joined Cases C-399, 409 and 425/92 and C-34, 50 and 78/93 *Stadt Lengerich* v. *Helmig* [1994] ECR I-5727. And see Arnull, 'Article 119 and Equal Pay for Work of Equal Value' (1986) 11 ELRev. 200.
[419] See the discussion of the relationship between the Occupational Social Security Directive (Directive 86/378, OJ 1986, L225/40) and Art. 119 and the remarks of the ECJ in Case C-110/91 *Moroni* v. *Collo GmbH* [1993] ECR I-6591.
[420] Case 43/75 [1976] ECR 455.   [421] Ibid. at 478–9. (Emphasis supplied.)

effect today is to shed light on the more obscure aspects of Article 119. The major object of the discussion of the Directive which follows is therefore to explore the ways in which it might be said to elucidate Article 119. It should be remembered that the scope of Article 119 is important in two different ways. First, it places obligations on the Member States to ensure that its terms are complied with; and, secondly, it is capable of conferring directly enforceable rights on individuals. The Directive may play a part in each of these processes, both explaining more clearly what duties are cast on the Member States (and therefore conditioning the interpretation to be placed by national courts on any national implementing legislation) and also facilitating the direct effect of the Article.

Given this analysis, and bearing in mind that it may not in any event be enforced horizontally, the possible direct effect of the Directive itself assumes only limited significance. The question whether the Directive takes direct effect has in fact been referred to the ECJ on several occasions[422] but has not been resolved, largely because the more potent effects of Article 119 have proved more useful to litigants.[423]

Content of the Equal Pay Directive

Article 1 (1) of the Directive provides:

The principle of equal pay for men and women outlined in Article 119 of the Treaty, hereinafter called 'principle of equal pay', means, for the same work or for work to which equal value is attributed, the elimination of all discrimination on grounds of sex with regard to all aspects and conditions of remuneration.

There are essentially two aspects of substance to this provision: first is the nature of the work to be compared, and second is the scope of the prohibition on discrimination.

As regards the nature of the work to be compared, the Article refers to the 'same work' or 'work to which equal value is attributed'. These phrases suggest, unfortunately, a necessity for an actual comparator of the opposite sex. Whilst they do not expressly rule out the possibility of hypothetical comparison, they are more appropriate to deal with the situation where a man and a woman are actually engaged on the same work or on work of

---

[422] See in particular Case 129/79 *Macarthys Ltd.* v. *Smith* [1980] ECR 1275; Case 69/80 *Worringham v. Lloyds Bank Ltd.* [1981] ECR 767; Case 96/80 *Jenkins* v. *Kingsgate (Clothing Productions) Ltd.* [1981] ECR 911; Case 12/81 *Garland* v. *British Rail* [1982] ECR 359; Case 192/85 *Newstead* v. *Department of Transport* [1987] ECR 4753; Case 19/81 *Burton* v. *British Railways Board* [1982] ECR 555; and Case 157/86 *Murphy* v. *Bord Telecom Eireann* [1988] ECR 673.

[423] In *Preston* v. *Wolverhampton Healthcare NHS Trust* [1997] IRLR 233, Schiemann LJ commented that it is clear that the Equal Pay Directive is not directly effective (at 239).

equal value to one another. It was seen above that the ECJ has held that the direct effect of Article 119 does not extend to the situation of hypothetical comparison,[424] although it still appears arguable that the Article nevertheless creates binding obligations for the Member States in this respect. Since the Equal Pay Directive may not in any way diminish the scope of Article 119, but is merely intended to facilitate its application, this argument remains open.

The expression 'same work' is presumably designed primarily to cover the case where two people are employed to perform identical jobs. Even this matter is not, however, entirely free from doubt. It follows from *Jenkins* v. *Kingsgate (Clothing Productions) Ltd.*[425] that what is relevant for this purpose is the nature of the tasks performed, rather than the overall job description. Thus, a full-timer and a part-timer engaged on the same process would seem to be performing the same work, even though their job descriptions would vary because of the different hours worked.[426]

Even more elusive is the meaning of 'work to which equal value is attributed'. What is the meaning of 'equal value' for this purpose? By whom, and when, must it be attributed? It has been seen that, for the purposes of Article 119, the ECJ has focused on job content (rather than the market value of the work performed from the point of view of the employer) in assessing the value of work.[427] Logic clearly demands that the Court adopt the same analysis for the purposes of the Equal Pay Directive, and this conclusion is reinforced by Article 1(2) of the Directive,[428] which gives its blessing to the use of non-discriminatory job classification schemes for determining pay. The issues of who must attribute equal value, and when the attribution must take place, for the purposes of the Directive were considered by the ECJ in *Commission* v. *UK.*[429] This was a prosecution of the UK by the Commission under Article 169 of the Treaty for failure to implement the Equal Pay Directive fully. UK legislation at the time of the action provided for equal pay as between the sexes only where the man and woman concerned were engaged on 'like work' (meaning broadly similar work), or where their work had been `rated as equivalent' in a job evaluation study. It made no provision for a claimant to demand equal pay with a colleague of the opposite sex where he or she merely alleged that their work was of equal value, but where no job evaluation study had been conducted. Since a job evaluation study could

[424] Case 129/79 *Macarthys Ltd.* v. *Smith* [1980] ECR 1275; Case C-200/91 *Coloroll Pension Trustees Ltd.* v. *Russell* [1994] ECR I-4389.
[425] Case 96/80 [1981] ECR 911.
[426] See Warner AG in *Jenkins* ibid. at 933, op.cit., n. 28.
[427] See in particular its remarks in Case 129/79 *Macarthys Ltd.* v. *Smith* [1980] ECR 1275.
[428] Discussed below.
[429] Case 61/81 [1982] ECR 2601. See Atkins, 'Equal Pay for Work of Equal Value'(1983) 8 ELRev. 48.

only be conducted with the consent of the employer, this left a considerable lacuna in the legislation: the lacuna was of enormous practical significance because large numbers of women were known to be working in sex-segregated occupations, so that they could not rely on the `like work' provision, but neither could they insist on having a job evaluation study conducted in their organization generally if the employer did not agree. The UK government defended its position by arguing that the requirements of the Directive take effect only *after* the jobs concerned have been found to be of equal value; neither the Directive nor Article 119, it said, gave an individual employee the right to take steps to determine the value of the jobs to be compared. It stressed the precise wording of the Directive in this context, and pointed out that the words 'is attributed' are used; this wording suggests that it is not until equal value *has been* attributed that the claim to equal pay arises. According to the UK government, if the drafters of the Directive had intended otherwise, they would have simply used the words `work of equal value'. In addition, it was pointed out that Article 1(2) of the Directive suggests that equal value has, as a matter of EC law, to be determined on the basis of a job classification system and that that indeed was the only practicable way of comparing the value of two different jobs. Finally, the UK argued that, at the time the Directive was agreed by the Council, the situation under UK legislation was recorded in the minutes of the Council meeting; since neither the Council nor the Commission raised any objections then, it was said that they were subsequently estopped from doing so. Both the Court itself and the Advocate General rejected all the UK's arguments. The Court held that perusal of the Directive showed that job classification is merely one of several methods for determining whether work is of equal value; Article 1(2) begins with the words `*In particular*, where a job classification system is used for determining pay . . .'.[430] Van Themaat AG observed that all sorts of different methods were in use for evaluating jobs in the Member States of the Community in practice and job classification constituted merely one method. The Court went on to hold:

British legislation does not permit the introduction of a job classification system without the employer's consent. Workers in the UK are therefore unable to have their work rated as being of equal value with comparable work if their employer refuses to introduce a classification system. The UK attempts to justify that state of affairs by pointing out that Article 1 of the Directive says nothing about the right of an employee to insist on having pay determined by a job classification system. On that basis it concludes that the worker may not insist on a comparative evaluation of different work by the job classification method, the introduction of which is at the employer's discretion. The UK's interpretation amounts to a denial of the very existence of a right to equal pay for work of equal value where

[430] Emphasis supplied.

no classification has been made. Such a position is not consonant with the general scheme and provisions of the Equal Pay Directive 75/117. The recitals in the Preamble to that Directive indicate that this essential purpose is to implement the principle that men and women should receive equal pay contained in Article 119 of the Treaty and that it is primarily the responsibility of the Member States to ensure the application of this principle by means of appropriate laws, regulations and administrative provisions in such a way that all employees in the Community can be protected in these matters.[431]

To the UK's arguments about the practicality of giving effect to equal value claims, the Court replied:

[W]here there is disagreement as to the application of . . . [the equal value] concept a worker must be entitled to claim before an appropriate authority that his work has the same value as other work and, if that is found to be the case, to have his rights under the Treaty and the Directive acknowledged by a binding decision. Any method which excludes that option prevents the aims of the Directive from being achieved . . . The implementation of the Directive implies that the assessment of the 'equal value' to be 'attributed' to particular work may be effected notwithstanding the employer's wishes if necessary in the context of adversary proceedings. The Member States must endow an authority with the requisite jurisdiction to decide whether work has the same value as other work, after obtaining such information as may be required.[432]

Thus, the Court made it clear that national legislation must not deny a claimant the right to allege that his or her work is of equal value to that of a comparator irrespective of the employer's wishes; and this allegation must be investigated by an 'authority' endowed by the State concerned with the 'requisite jurisdiction'. The right to claim equal pay for work of equal value is therefore certainly not restricted to the period of time subsequent to a finding of equal value through job classification.

Van Themaat AG also rejected the UK's argument about its statement in the Council minutes, saying:

As for the statement itself, I share the Commission's view that it simply explains that in order to determine the equal value of different jobs in the UK a job classification system must be used. As I have already stated, no objection can be taken to that. However, the statement does not indicate in practical terms how far such a system is dependent on the consent of the employer. It is this, in particular, which in my opinion is of crucial importance in this case. The argument that the Commission forfeited its right to take action under Article 169 by not raising any objection against the UK's statement cannot be accepted in my judgment. In my view such conduct on the part of the Commission cannot diminish its responsibility under Article 155 of the Treaty. Nor is it possible in my view to accept the argument that the UK can rely on the statement when construing the provision in question. As the Court has held on several occasions (for instance in Case 39/72

---

[431] [1982] ECR 2601, at 2615.   [432] Ibid. at 2616–7.

Commission v. *Italy* [1973] CMLR 439 at paragraph (22)) such a statement made by a Member State for recording in the minutes of the Council when a decision is adopted cannot modify the objective scope of Community rules enacted by the Community decision.[433]

The Court's final ruling was that:

By failing to introduce into its national legal system in implementation of the provisions of Council Directive 75/117/EEC of 10 February 1975 such measures as are necessary to enable all employees who consider themselves wronged by failure to apply the principle of equal pay for men and women for work to which equal value is attributed and for which no system of job classification exists to obtain recognition of such equivalence, the UK has failed to fulfil its obligations under the Treaty.[434]

This ruling clearly required a change to the national legislation to cover the case of the employee alleging non-equal pay for work of equal value to that of another worker, where the employer was unwilling to commission a job evaluation study. The new legislation took the form of the Equal Pay (Amendment) Regulations 1983.[435]

Denmark has also been prosecuted by the Commission for inadequate implementation of the Directive.[436] The relevant Danish legislation provided:

Every person who employs men and women to work at the same place of work must pay them the same salary for the *same work* under this Act if he is not already required to do so pursuant to a collective agreement.[437]

The Commission argued that this was defective, first, because it made no reference to work to which equal value is attributed and, second, because it did not provide for any means of redress enabling workers alleging unequal pay for work of equal value to pursue their claims. Van Themaat AG took the somewhat eccentric view that, since Article 1 of the Directive merely spells out the detail of Article 119, and since Article 119 can itself be enforced in the national courts, it is unnecessary to implement the precise wording of the Directive as a matter of national law. This approach is inconsistent with that hitherto taken by the ECJ itself, namely that the

---

[433] Ibid. at 2625. [434] Ibid. at 2617–8.

[435] SI 1983, No. 1794, as to which, see in particular Rubenstein, *Equal Pay For Work of Equal Value* (Macmillan, London and Basingstoke, 1984). The Equal Pay Regulations have proved inordinately cumbersome in practice; in 1993 and 1994, the TUC and the EOCs for both Britain and Northern Ireland made formal complaints to the EC Commission to the effect that the inadequacies of the legislation meant that the UK remained in breach of the Equal Treatment Directive. The Commission, however, declined to begin further infringement proceedings. See Ellis 'Equal Pay for Work of Equal Value: the United Kingdom's Legislation Viewed in the Light of Community Law' in *Sex Equality Law in the European Union*, eds. Hervey and O'Keefe (Wiley, Chichester, 1996).

[436] Case 143/83 *Commission* v. *Denmark* [1985] ECR 427.

[437] Emphasis supplied.

fact that a directive takes direct effect does not remove the requirement that it be transformed into national law.[438] The Court itself took a different view. The Danish government had argued that its legislation constituted only a subsidiary guarantee of the principle of equal pay in cases where the principle was not already ensured under collective agreements. Collective agreements governed most contracts of employment in Denmark and they upheld the principle of equal pay for work of equal value. The Court, however, ruled that this was not sufficient and that the Danish legislation should refer specifically to the equal value situation:

It is true that Member States may leave the implementation of the principle of equal pay in the first instance to representatives of management and labour. That possibility does not, however, discharge them from the obligation of ensuring, by appropriate legislation and administrative provisions, that all workers in the Community are afforded the full protection provided for in the Directive. The state guarantee must cover all cases where effective protection is not ensured by other means, for whatever reason, and in particular cases where the workers in question are not union members, where the sector in question is not covered by a collective agreement, or where such an agreement does not fully guarantee the principle of equal pay.[439]

The situation was not saved by Denmark's argument (akin to that of the UK in the earlier case) that it had entered a declaration in the Council minutes when the Equal Pay Directive was passed, saying: 'Denmark is of the view that the expression "same work" can continue to be used in the context of Danish labour law'. The ECJ pointed out that it had:

[C]onsistently held that such unilateral declarations cannot be relied upon for the interpretation of Community measures, since the objective scope of rules laid down by the common institutions cannot be modified by reservations or objections which Member States may have made at the time the rules were being formulated.[440]

Another aspect of the nature of the work to be compared under Article 1(1) of the Directive which remains unclear is the geographical or spatial scope of the comparison which the worker may demand. It was suggested above that Article 119 may well extend to comparisons with workers in other establishments of the same employer, and even to comparisons with workers employed by different employers.[441] Perhaps in consequence of

---

[438] See discussion in Chap. 1.

[439] [1985] ECR 427, at 434–5. The Danish legislation was subsequently amended to reflect the ECJ's decision: see Nielsen, *Equality in Law betwen Men and Women in the European Community: Denmark* (Martinus Nijhoff, The Hague/Boston/London, 1995).

[440] Case 143/83 at 436.

[441] Article 3(2) of the Netherlands Equal Pay Law of 20 March 1975 used to provide: 'Where no work of equal or approximately equal value is done by a worker of the other sex in the undertaking where the worker concerned is employed, the basis shall be the wage that a worker of the other sex normally receives, in an undertaking of as nearly as possible

his national background, Van Themaat AG was prepared in *Commission* v. *Denmark*[442] to submit that the Equal Pay Directive mandates such comparisons. As already noted, the Danish legislation challenged in that case specifically restricted claims for equal pay to men and women working 'at the same place of work'. The Danish government argued that this phrase had been put in in order to permit geographical differences in pay within Denmark, but the Advocate General found this unconvincing because such differences in pay, if genuine and if applied equally to men and women, are not grounded on sex and are therefore not prohibited anyway. He went on to say:

As appears from the second sentence of Article 1 of the Directive . . . a comparison of duties within the same fixed establishment of an undertaking or even within a single undertaking will not always be sufficient. In certain circumstances comparison with work of equal value in other undertakings covered by the collective agreement in question will be necessary. As is correctly observed in the annual report for 1980 of the Danish Council for Equal Treatment of Men and Women ('Ligestillingsradet'), submitted by the Commission in evidence, in sectors with a traditionally female workforce comparison with other sectors may even be necessary. In certain circumstances the additional criterion of 'the same place of work' for work of equal value may therefore place a restriction on the principle of equal pay laid down in Article 119 of the EEC Treaty and amplified in the Directive in question. The mere fact that such a supplementary condition for equal pay which has no foundation in Article 119 or in the Directive has been added must in any event be regarded as an infringement of the Treaty.[443]

The Court itself did not deal with this issue, apparently because the Commission did not formally raise it in its pleadings.[444] As seen above, its remarks on this subject in *Commission* v. *UK*[445] were equivocal. It said merely:

[W]here there is disagreement as to the application of [the concept of non-discrimination] a worker must be entitled to claim before an appropriate authority that his work has the same value as other work and, if that is found to be the case, to have his rights under the Treaty and the Directive acknowledged by a binding decision. Any method which excludes that option prevents the aims of the Directive from being achieved.[446]

The Directive thus, as presently construed by the ECJ, does not cast much light on the question of whether Article 119 requires comparisons outside the worker's immediate work-place.

the same kind in the same sector, for work of equal value or, in the absence of such work, for work of approximately equal value'. However, this provision was repealed by the Equal Treatment Act of 1986 since, according to the government, it had never been utilized.

[442] Case 143/83 [1985] ECR 427.　　　　　　　　　　　[443] Ibid. at 430.
[444] Case 143/83 [1985] ECR 427, at 436.
[445] Case 61/81 [1982] ECR 2601.　　　　　　　　　　　[446] Ibid. at 2616.

The second limb of Article 1(1) of the Directive is concerned with the scope of the prohibition of discrimination. It refers first of all to 'the elimination of all discrimination'. This strongly suggests that indirect, as well as direct, discrimination is outlawed by the combined forces of Article 119 and the Directive, and this conclusion was first confirmed by the ECJ's decision in *Jenkins* v. *Kingsgate (Clothing Productions) Ltd.*[447] However, the discrimination in question must of course be 'on grounds of sex', which means that it must be proved to the satisfaction of the court or tribunal that sex is the cause of the differential treatment of the man and woman. This element will not be established where it can be shown that there is some wholly independent cause for the differentiation.[448] Thus far, this part of the Directive appears to say little which could not be deduced from Article 119 itself. However, it goes on to add that sex discrimination is forbidden 'with regard to all aspects and conditions of remuneration'.[449] Although Article 119 explains that 'pay' may be expected to embody a wide variety of forms and to arise in various circumstances, it does not explicitly focus on its 'aspects' and 'conditions'. Two specific consequences might be said to follow from these words. First, the word 'aspects' provides reinforcement for the argument suggested in relation to Article 119 to the effect that any benefit extended to an employee by an employer via the contract of employment could be regarded as 'pay' and therefore could be argued to fall within Article 119. For example, a generous contractual holiday entitlement might be said to be an 'aspect' of 'pay', since it enters into the calculation of the size of the worker's pay packet. The word 'conditions' suggests that the Directive enables a worker to challenge the *way* in which, or the *terms* on which, pay is made available. In other words, this part of the wording of the Directive reinforces the view taken in *Barber* v. *Guardian Royal Exchange Assurance Group*[450] and the later pensions equality cases that Article 119 forbids discriminatory access to pay, as well as discrimination in relation to the quantum of pay received.

Article 1(2) provides: 'In particular, where a job classification system is

[447] Case 96/80 [1981] ECR 911. See also Case 170/84 *Bilka-Kaufhaus GmbH* v. *Weber Von Hartz* [1986] ECR 1607 and Joined Cases C-399, 409 and 425/92 and C-34, 50 and 78/93 *Stadt Lengerich* v. *Helmig* [1994] ECR I-5727, both discussed above. For an ingenious, though ill-fated, attempt to establish indirect discrimination over pay in relation to the qualifications required in order to receive an expatriation allowance where the Commission was the employer, see Case 246/83 *De Angelis* v. *Commission* [1985] ECR 1253.

[448] See e.g. Van Themaat AG's argument mentioned above in Case 143/83 *Commission* v. *Denmark* [1985] ECR 427 in relation to geographically determined pay differences. And see also the discussion of this matter in relation to Art. 119.

[449] In Case 69/80 *Worringham* v. *Lloyds Bank Ltd.* [1981] ECR 767, at 807, Warner AG commented: 'Nothing turns on the change from the use of the word "pay" in Article 119 to the use of the word "remuneration" in the Directive. That is a feature of the English texts only. In all the other texts the same word is used in Article 119 and in the Directive: "remuneration" in French, "Entgelt" in German, and so forth'.

[450] Case C-262/88 [1990] ECR I-1889.

used for determining pay, it must be based on the same criteria for both men and women and so drawn up as to exclude any discrimination on grounds of sex'. The opening phrase 'in particular' underlines a point made clear by the ECJ in *Commission* v. *UK*,[451] namely that job classification systems merely constitute one of the permissible ways in which equal value can be established. The meaning and effect of this provision were tested in *Rummler* v. *Dato-Druck GmbH*.[452] Ms Rummler brought proceedings against her employer, a printing firm, with the object of having herself placed in a higher category in the pay scale relating to the printing industry. This pay scale, which was nationally agreed, provided for seven wage groups varying according to the work carried out and determined on the basis of degree of knowledge required, concentration, muscular demand or effort, and responsibility. The activities in Wage Group II were those which could be executed with slight previous knowledge and after brief instruction or training, required little accuracy, placed a slight to moderate demand on the muscles, and involved slight or occasionally moderate responsibility. Group III comprised activities which could be executed with moderate previous knowledge and instruction or training related to the particular job, required moderate accuracy, required moderate or occasionally great muscular effort, and involved slight or occasionally moderate responsibility. Group IV covered activities requiring previous knowledge on the basis of instruction or training related to the particular job, occasionally a fair degree of occupational experience requiring moderate accuracy, moderate and occasionally great effort of different kinds particularly as a result of work dependent on machines, and involved moderate responsibility. It was specified that the evaluation criteria must not be regarded as cumulative in all cases. Ms Rummler was classified in Group III, but argued that she ought to be placed in Group IV, in particular since she was required to pack parcels weighing more than 20 kg, which for her represented heavy physical work. Her employer disagreed, contending that because her job in fact made only slight muscular demands she ought to be classified in Group II. The national court dealing with the case sought a preliminary ruling from the ECJ, asking whether the Equal Pay Directive permits a job classification system to include muscular effort as a criterion of evaluation and, if so, whether account must be taken of the amount of such effort required of women in particular. The practical point at issue was, of course, that certain types of physical work require more effort from women on average than men; it might be said to follow from this that women should be more highly remunerated for such tasks than men, but this might in turn produce the unfortunate consequence that

---

[451] Case 61/81 [1982] ECR 2601.
[452] Case 237/85 [1986] ECR 2101. See Arnull, 'Equal Treatment and Job Classification Schemes (1987) 12 ELRev. 62.

women would become more expensive to employ than men and so might in practice find themselves excluded from the type of work in question.

The ECJ avoided this trap. The employers argued, in accordance with generally accepted theories of the role of job evaluation, that pay criteria must be established to reflect the duties actually performed and not by reference to the personal attributes of the worker who carries them out. They therefore took the view that the criteria of muscle demand and the heaviness of work were not discriminatory in so far as they corresponded to the characteristics of the work actually performed and were used in a system which also referred to the criteria of ability, mental effort, and responsibility. The UK government, which submitted observations, added its view that the principle of non-discrimination does not preclude the use of a criterion in relation to which one sex has greater natural ability than the other, so long as that criterion is representative of the range of activities involved in the job in question. The Commission pointed out that what has to be judged is whether the classification system as a whole is or is not discriminatory, in other words whether because of the factors it takes into account it is in reality loaded in favour of one sex. With these submissions the Court overall agreed, saying:

Where a job classification system is used in determining remuneration, that system must be based on criteria which do not differ according to whether the work is carried out by a man or by a woman and must not be organized, as a whole, in such a manner that it has the practical effect of discriminating generally against workers of one sex. Consequently, criteria corresponding to the duties performed meet the requirements of Article 1 of the Directive where those duties by their nature require particular physical effort or are physically heavy. In differentiating rates of pay, it is consistent with the principle of non-discrimination to use a criterion based on the objectively measurable expenditure of effort necessary in carrying out the work or the degree to which, reviewed objectively, the work is physically heavy. Even where a particular criterion, such as that of demand on the muscles, may in fact tend to favour male workers, since it may be assumed that in general they are physically stronger than women workers, it must, in order to determine whether or not it is discriminatory, be considered in the context of the whole job classification system, having regard to other criteria influencing rates of pay. A system is not necessarily discriminatory simply because one of its criteria makes reference to attributes more characteristic of men. In order for a job classification system as a whole to be non-discriminatory and thus to comply with the principles of the Directive, it must, however, be established in such a manner that it includes, if the nature of the tasks in question so permits, jobs to which equal value is attributed and for which regard is had to other criteria in relation to which women workers may have a particular aptitude. It is for the national courts to determine on a case-by-case basis whether a job classifi-cation system as a whole allows proper account to be taken of the criteria neces-

sary for adjusting pay rates according to the conditions required for the performance of the various duties throughout the undertaking.[453]

The only difficulty with this view is that the concept of the 'objective'
measurement of the amount of physical effort demanded by a particular
job is an obscure one. It postulates the existence of an inter-sex person
whose characteristics and abilities are neither all-male nor all-female. This
is a problem encountered in connection with all analytical systems of job
evaluation and carries within it the inherent risk that the assessment will
be biased in favour of traditional values, rather than being truly neutral
and `objective'.[454] The difficulty becomes even more marked in relation to
the second part of the national court's questioning, namely, how precisely
physical demand is to be measured and what value is to be placed on it. In
particular, the national court wanted to know whether values reflecting
the average performance of workers of each sex ought to be used. The
Court held that they should not:

The answer to Questions 2 and 3 . . . follows from what has already been said in
answer to Question 1, that is to say that nothing in the Directive prevents the use
in determining wage rates of a criterion based on the degree of muscular effort
objectively required by a specific job or the objective degree of heaviness of the
job. The Directive lays down the principle of equal pay for equal work. It follows
that the work actually carried out must be remunerated in accordance with its
nature. Any criterion based on values appropriate only to workers of one sex
carries with it a risk of discrimination and may jeopardize the main objective of
the Directive, equal treatment for the same work. That is true even of a criterion
based on values corresponding to the average performance of workers of the sex
considered to have less natural ability for the purpose of that criterion, for the
result would be another form of pay discrimination: work objectively requiring
greater strength would be paid at the same rate as work requiring less strength.

The failure to take into consideration values corresponding to the average
performance of female workers in establishing a progressive pay scale based on
the degree of muscle demand and muscular effort may indeed have the effect of
placing women workers, who cannot take jobs which are beyond their physical
strength, at a disadvantage. That difference in treatment may, however, be objectively justified by the nature of the job when such a difference is necessary in
order to ensure a level of pay appropriate to the effort required by the work and
thus corresponds to a real need on the part of the undertaking (see the judgment
in Case–170/84 *Bilka-Kaufhaus* v. *Von Hartz*).[455]

The answer to the second and third questions must therefore be that it follows
from Directive 75/117 that:

(a) criteria governing pay-rate classification must ensure that work which is
objectively the same attracts the same rate of pay whether it is performed
by a man or a woman;

[453] [1986] ECR 2101, at 2115.
[454] See the remarks of Van Themaat AG in Case 61/81 *Commission* v. *UK* [1982] ECR
2601, at 2624–5.   [455] [1986] ECR 1607.

(b) the use of values reflecting the average performance of workers of one sex as a basis for determining the extent to which work makes demands or requires effort or whether it is heavy constitutes a form of discrimination on grounds of sex, contrary to the Directive;

(c) in order for a job classification system not to be discriminatory as a whole, it must, in so far as the nature of the tasks carried out in the undertaking permits, take into account criteria for which workers of each sex may show particular aptitude.[456]

The practical effect of this judgment is potentially useful. Although it is still far from clear exactly when a job classification system will be discriminatory taken as a whole, not least because there will always be room for argument about what demands a particular job actually makes on the workers carrying it out, there is acknowledged at least the possibility of alleging that a particular classification system falls short of the requirements of EC law. In such a situation, it would be helpful to be able to rely on the direct effect of Article 1(2) of the Directive; whilst this would be impossible, at least as against an employer who was not an organ of the State, if the Directive stood alone,[457] it remains to be seen whether the ECJ would be prepared to enforce Article 119 itself in this situation. It is arguable that, if all the Directive achieves legally is a practical elucidation of the general principle articulated in Article 119, then Article 119 itself extends to forbidding discrimination in job classification systems. A litigant facing an allegedly sex discriminatory job classification system could then rely simply on the direct effect of Article 119 to have it declared inapplicable. A second way in which this provision could prove of practical use is through the doctrine of supremacy of EC law; if a national law precludes challenge or makes excessively difficult challenge to a job classification system on the ground of its being sex discriminatory, then that national law itself could be rendered inapplicable because of the conflict with the Directive and Article 119. Such an argument might, for example, be used in the UK, where the Equal Pay (Amendment) Regulations 1983 make it difficult for a litigant to attack a job evaluation study as discriminatory.[458]

Article 2 provides:

Member States shall introduce into their national legal systems such measures as are necessary to enable all employees who consider themselves wronged by failure to apply the principle of equal pay to pursue their claims by judicial process after possible recourse to other competent authorities. ·

---

[456] [1986] ECR 2101, at 2116–7.

[457] Because of the lack of possible horizontal direct effect for directives, discussed in Chap. 1.

[458] See the Equal Pay Act 1970, s. 2A(2). The EOC might, in such circumstances, bring an action for judicial review of the UK legislation, as discussed in Chap. 1.

Although physically distanced from it, this provision must be read in conjunction with Article 6, which states:

Member States shall, in accordance with their national circumstances and legal systems, take the measures necessary to ensure that the principle of equal pay is applied. They shall see that effective means are available to take care that this principle is observed.

Together, these provisions require a proper judicial hearing for a claim of denial of the equal pay principle and an effective remedy if the claim proves successful at the end of the day. One issue of importance in the present context is the relationship between these provisions and Article 119. It was seen in Chapter 1 that, in so far as Article 119 is directly effective, it may be relied on in the national courts to provide a remedy within the same procedural limitations as parallel national proceedings; and it has also been seen that the direct effect of Article 119 may be relied on to demand an equal pay rate with that of the comparator. Neither Article 119 nor the Directive prescribes remedies or procedures which are more precise than this. Under both measures there exists the possibility, however, of alleging that the relevant national remedies and procedures are *defective*; here, the wording of Article 6 of the Directive might be relied upon to lend weight to the direct effect of Article 119, since it provides expressly for 'effective means' of redress. So, for example, if national equal pay legislation allowed only a small claim for compensation in cases where unequal pay was established, rather than a full claim for the difference between what was received and what ought to have been received, the Directive and Article 119 together might be relied upon to enforce the more effective remedy.[459] The remedies provided in the UK before the passage of the Equal Pay (Amendment) Regulations 1983 were certainly inadequate. The Directive requires that 'all employees who consider themselves wronged by failure to apply the principle of equal pay' shall have a right to judicial redress. As seen above, the Commission's successful prosecution of the UK[460] was provoked by the absence of a remedy in the UK at that date for a complainant alleging work of equal value but where the employer was unwilling to commission a job evaluation study. Whether or not the cumbersome procedures available today in UK equal pay claims fall short of the requirements of the Directive and Article 119 remain to be tested in future litigation.

In cases of sex discrimination over pay which fall outside the scope of

---

[459] This is essentially the same argument as that used successfully in Case C-271/91 *Marshall* v. *Southampton and South-West Hants Area Health Authority* [1993] ECR I-4367, (discussed in Chap. 3), to challenge the UK's statutory ceiling on damages for sex discriminatory treatment contrary to the Equal Treatment Directive (Dir. 76/207, OJ [1976], L39/40).

[460] Case 61/81 *Commission* v. *UK* [1982] ECR 2601.

the direct effect of Article 119, there is nothing in Articles 2 or 6 of the Directive which creates greater precision and which might therefore supply the missing ingredients for direct effect. A person seeking a remedy in such a claim would therefore be unable to enforce the EC equal pay legislation directly, but might be able to rely on the *Francovich* principle[461] in order to claim damages from the state itself for its breach of EC obligations.

An interesting argument which has not yet been addressed by the ECJ is whether, since it is the Directive rather than the Treaty which spells out the requirement of adequate remedies, the *Emmott* principle[462] applies where a proper remedy is not provided in national law for unequal pay; in other words, can any limitation period begin to run in a claim against the State or one of its organs where it can be shown that the national remedies are inadequate?[463] Whilst such a situation seems to be literally within the ambit of the *Emmott* principle, it seems likely that the ECJ would hold that the essential right being claimed arises out of the Treaty rather than the Directive; thus, the non-availability of adequate remedies does not defeat assertion of the right to equal pay and the Member State's inaction does not therefore prevent the victim from bringing a claim, with the result that the 'mischief' addressed by *Emmott* has not occurred.

Article 2 of the Directive also refers to the pursuit of claims by 'judicial process'. This wording implies that the issue must be decided by an independent judge, after the hearing of arguments and representations from both parties and in an established court or tribunal. This provision was influential during the drafting of the UK's Equal Pay (Amendment) Regulations 1983, in particular in relation to the way in which equal value was to be assessed. The Regulations provide for the appointment of an 'independent expert' to assess value, but it was regarded as essential that the expert's report be open to challenge before the industrial tribunal hearing the claim, otherwise the process would not be a 'judicial' one.[464] Similarly, where a job evaluation study has already been conducted and has resulted in a finding that the complainant's work is not of equal value to that of the comparator, this must also be open to challenge on the grounds of the scheme being discriminatory in design or operation, otherwise the assessment of value would not be 'judicial'. The words 'judicial process' clearly elucidate Article 119 in a significant respect and could prove useful to an individual complainant; quite how they would be

---

[461] Discussed in Chap. 1.

[462] Discussed in Chap. 1.

[463] See *Preston* v. *Wolverhampton Healthcare NHS Trust* [1997] IRLR 233 and *Biggs* v. *Somerset County Council* [1996] ICR 364.

[464] The appointment of an independent expert by the tribunal was subsequently made optional: see the Sex Discrimination and Equal Pay (Miscellaneous Amendments) Regulations 1996 (SI 1996 No. 438).

useful would again depend on the type of claim being brought. If it was a claim within the area of direct effect of Article 119, it would appear that the allegation of a denial of proper 'judicial process' could also be made directly. If the matter fell outside the direct effect of Article 119 but the defendant was an organ of the State, then it might be argued that this part of the Directive is vertically directly effective; if the Directive were held not to take direct effect or if the defendant were not an organ of the State, the claimant would need to rely on the *Francovich* principle.

Article 3 requires the repeal of all legislation which conflicts with the equal pay principle: 'Member States shall abolish all discrimination between men and women arising from laws, regulations or administrative provisions which is contrary to the principle of equal pay'. Once again, to the extent to which Article 119 is directly effective, it can of course be relied upon to take precedence over any conflicting national law; this is the practical operation of the doctrine of supremacy of EC law.[465] To the extent that it is not so effective, this provision merely casts a duty on the Member States. This duty is unqualified and so extends even to legislation which pre-dated the Directive. There can therefore be no saving legislative provisions preserving pay inequalities, for example, for historical reasons. If the cause of the pay differential between men and women is their difference of sex, then any legislation approving such a situation, whether directly or indirectly, must be repealed.

Article 4 provides:

Member States shall take the necessary measures to ensure that provisions appearing in collective agreements, wage scales, wage agreements or individual contracts of employment which are contrary to the principle of equal pay shall be, or may be declared, null and void or may be amended.

This wording indicates that all types of pay discrimination on the ground of sex are barred from collective agreements and the rest; the bar is not restricted merely to direct discrimination, or to that which is overt.[466] By analogy with a decision of the ECJ under a parallel provision of the Equal Treatment Directive,[467] it would appear irrelevant that the collective agreement or wage scale itself produced no binding legal effects; pay discrimination on the ground of sex in its terms is still prohibited, since its existence misleads all who are affected by it. This part of the Directive was

---

[465] See Chap. 1.

[466] Unlike the position in the UK under the Equal Pay Act 1970, s. 3, before the latter's repeal by the Sex Discrimination Act 1986. See also *R. v. CAC, Ex p. Hy-Mac Ltd.* [1979] IRLR 461.

[467] Directive 76/207, OJ [1976], L39/40, *Commission v. UK* Case 165/82 [1983] ECR 3431, discussed in Chap. 3.

given effective teeth by the decision of the ECJ in *Kowalska* v. *Freie and Hansestadt Hamburg.*[468]

Article 5 is concerned with victimization of those who allege a breach of the equal pay principle: 'Member States shall take the necessary measures to protect employees against dismissal by the employer as a reaction to a complaint within the undertaking or to any legal proceedings aimed at enforcing compliance with the principle of equal pay.' This provision is broad, in that it mentions those who have merely made 'a complaint within the undertaking', as well as those who have actually launched legal proceedings. However, it is undesirably narrow in its reference merely to protection against dismissal.[469] The Article appears to provide no protection for those who are ill-treated in some way which falls short of dismissal, such as through a wrongful refusal to promote or the denial of some benefit extended to other employees. The possible direct effect of this provision is also a matter of some doubt. This is the type of provision which an individual person might well wish to enforce. The ECJ, in its statements about the Equal Pay Directive and its role merely as the elucidator of Article 119, probably did not have this Article specifically in mind, and thus this might perhaps be a way in which the Directive does in fact extend beyond the scope of Article 119. If this were so, Article 5 could of course only be enforced (if at all) vertically, as against an employer who was an organ of the State.[470] If, on the other hand, the Court were prepared to hold that Article 5 of the Directive simply spells out a principle already contained in Article 119, then, so long as it was regarded as precise enough in its ambit to be capable of direct effect, it could be enforced both vertically and horizontally, in other words, against any type of employer.

Article 7 provides: 'Member States shall take care that the provisions adopted pursuant to this Directive, together with the relevant provisions already in force, are brought to the attention of employees by all appropriate means, for example at their place of work'.

---

[468] Case C-33/89 [1990] ECR I-2591. See also Case C-184/89 *Helga Nimz* v. *Freie und Hansestadt Hamburg* [1991] ECR I-297, Case C-127/92 *Enderby* v. *Frenchay Health Authority* [1993] ECR I-5535, and Joined Cases C-399, 409, and 425/92 and C-34, 50 and 78/93 *Stadt Lengerich* v. *Helmig* [1994] ECR I-5727, all discussed above. This case law was of particular significance in the UK before the enactment of the Trade Union Reform and Employment Rights Act 1993, s. 32 which enables an individual to bring industrial tribunal proceedings to challenge an allegedly discriminatory term of a collective agreement; this amendment to the legislation was introduced in order to settle infringement proceedings which had been threatened by the EC Commission. See also discussion in Chap. 3.

[469] Contrast the UK's domestic victimization provision, contained in the Sex Discrimination Act 1975, s. 4, which states: 'A person ("the discriminator") discriminates against another person ("the person victimized") in any circumstances relevant for the purposes of any provision of this Act if he treats the person victimized less favourably than in those circumstances he treats or would treat other persons . . .'.

[470] Failing this, the *Francovich* principle might provide a remedy.

The Member States were given the unusually short period of one year within which to put into force the legislation necessary to ensure compliance with the Directive:[471] this period was presumably chosen because Article 119 itself had by that time already supposedly been in operation for a number of years. However, there is an essential logical flaw in imposing a time limit in this Directive at all; if, as the Court has maintained, the Directive does no more than spell out the details already required by Article 119, then any action which has to be taken by national legislatures is a response to the Article and not to the Directive.[472] This point was taken by Van Themaat AG in *Commission* v. *Luxembourg*,[473] although not by the Court itself. The Commission had brought an Article 169 enforcement action in respect of legislation which remained in force in Luxembourg after the period for implementing the Equal Pay Directive had expired. The legislation in question granted to central government and local authority officials a 'head of household allowance', but did so on discriminatory terms because it was only in exceptional cases (for example, where her husband was incapacitated) that a female official would qualify for the payment. The Luxembourg government admitted that discrimination was occurring and tried unsuccessfully to defend itself by arguing that it was engaged in procuring the necessary legislative amendments. Van Themaat AG considered that the Commission had made out a successful case of breach of Article 119, rather than of Article 8 of the Equal Pay Directive; he pointed out that, as the Court itself had held in the *Second Defrenne* case,[474] Article 119 became binding as far as the original Member States were concerned as from 1 January 1962.[475] He went on to say:

[T]he terms 'shall ensure . . . and . . . maintain' used in Article 119 do not, in my opinion, stand in the way of the interpretation that the Member States were required to adopt within the said period all the measures needed to ensure the application of that principle, despite the fact that the Article does not expressly refer to 'abolition' or 'the adoption of measures'. That idea is in my view also to be found in the same *Defrenne* judgment in which it is stated, in paragraph 56 of the decision, that as from 1 January 1962 the application of the principle 'was to be fully secured and irreversible' . . .[476]

And he concluded:

[T]he Court ruled in the *Defrenne* judgment and reaffirmed in its recent decisions, for example Case 96/80 *Jenkins*,[477] that the purpose of the Directive was to

---

[471] Art. 8(1) of the Directive.
[472] See above for discussion of the similar situation in relation to Art. 119 and the Occupational Social Security Directive (Directive 86/378, OJ [1986], L225/40).
[473] Case 58/81 [1982] ECR 2175.
[474] Case 43/75 *Defrenne* v. *Sabena* [1976] ECR 455.
[475] See above.
[476] [1982] ECR 2175, at 2185.　　　　　　　　　　　[477] [1981] ECR 911.

ensure the proper implementation of Article 119, but was unable to reduce the effectiveness of that Article or modify its temporal effect. According to paragraph 54 of the decision in the *Defrenne* case, the Directive clarifies certain aspects of the material scope of Article 119 and contains various provisions 'whose essential purpose is to improve the legal protection of workers . . .' In my opinion, however, the present case is not concerned with such measures but with what is laid down by Article 3 of the Directive, namely that 'Member States shall abolish all discrimination between men and women arising from laws, regulations or administrative provisions which is contrary to the principle of equal pay.' However, that provision no longer serves any purpose in relation to Article 119 in the light of the Court's interpretation of the latter. Accordingly, I consider that it was incorrect to seek a declaration from the Court that the Grand Duchy of Luxembourg had failed to fulfil its obligations under Article 119 and the provisions of the Directive. In my view, the Court should confine itself to finding that the Grand Duchy of Luxembourg has infringed Article 119.[478]

The Court itself, in an unusually terse judgment, made no reference to this point at all and merely ruled that Luxemburg was in breach of Article 8(1) of the Directive because of its failure to adopt the necessary legislation within the period prescribed.

The Directive also obliged the Member States to send to the Commission the texts of all the legislation adopted by them by way of implementation of the Directive.[479] Within three years of the Directive's notification they were to forward all necessary information to the Commission to enable it to draw up a report on the application of the Equal Pay Directive for submission to the Council.[480] This report was produced by the Commission on 16 January 1979.[481] It demonstrated clearly that all the Member States had failed in practice to give full implementation to the principle of equal pay and Article 169[482] enforcement proceedings were begun in March 1979 against no fewer than seven Member States. Ultimately, the report resulted in the Commission's prosecutions of the UK and Luxembourg before the ECJ, discussed above. A judicial action was also begun against Belgium[483] but was discontinued after the Belgian government adopted the measures necessary to fulfil its obligations under the Directive.

Even in recent times, however, the principle of equal pay has remained unfulfilled in practice. In 1994, the Commission issued a Memorandum on Equal Pay for Work of Equal Value[484] which demonstrated that the pay gap between men and women remained wide and was, in some cases, still widening. Although it observed that there was an absence of adequate data on this matter, it was able to find some statistical evidence to support

---

[478] [1982] ECR 2175, at 2186.   [479] Art. 8(2) of the Directive.
[480] Ibid. Art. 9.   [481] COM (78) 711 final.
[482] {Art. 226}.   [483] Case 57/81.
[484] COM(94) 6 final.

its claims: it found that in no Member State did women earn more than 84.5 per cent of men's earnings; in the UK, women on average earned 68.2 per cent of the male rate in manual jobs and only 54.2 per cent in non-manual jobs; only two Member States scored worse: 69.1 per cent for manual rates in Ireland and 65.1 per cent for manual rates in Luxembourg. The impoverished position of women in the pay leagues was attributed by the Commission to their vertical and horizontal segregation in the workforce, to a general lack of objectivity in pay evaluation systems and to inequality in collective agreements. It submitted that a strategy to improve matters should focus on better systems for data collection to enable wage comparisons between men and women across broad sectors of activity and on the improved dissemination of information about the law; it also promised to continue to have recourse to its power of prosecution of Member States under Article 169[485] 'where this is considered appropriate'.[486] In addition, it floated the idea of issuing a Code of Practice on the implementation of the equal pay principle, a step it ultimately took in 1996.

The Code of Practice on the Implementation of Equal Pay for Work of Equal Value for Women and Men[487] 'aims to provide *concrete advice* for employers and collective bargaining partners at business, sectoral or intersectoral level to ensure that the principle of equality between women and men performing work of equal value is applied to all aspects of pay. In particular it aims to eliminate sexual discrimination whenever pay structures are based on job classification and evaluation systems'.[488] It proposes that:

[N]egotiators at all levels, whether on the side of the employers or the unions, who are involved in the determination of pay systems, should carry out an *analysis of the remuneration system* and evaluate the data required to detect sexual discrimination in the pay structures so that remedies can be found,

[And] that a *plan for follow-up* should be drawn up and implemented to eliminate any sexual discrimination evident in the pay structures.[489]

The Code goes on to provide details of the kind of information to be collected, how it should be assessed and appropriate courses of follow-up action.[490]

---

[485] {Art. 226}.   [486] COM(94) 6 final, at 40.
[487] COM(96) 336 final.   [488] Ibid. at 4.
[489] Ibid. at 4.
[490] Unfortunately, in making suggestions for the evaluation of follow-up action, the Code appears to sanction transitional introduction of the equality principle, a course of action which is plainly contrary to Art. 119: see the Code, at 14.

3

Equal Treatment

THE GENERAL PRINCIPLE OF EQUAL TREATMENT

General Principles as part of EC Law

General principles of law are an important part of the 'common law' of the Communities. That is to say, they constitute an unwritten source of law which is, where relevant, applied by the ECJ. Unlike the International Court of Justice, which is expressly enjoined by Article 38 of its Statute to apply 'the general principles of law recognized by civilized nations', the ECJ is under no such general, formal obligation.[1] However, as the Court pointed out in its Opinion[2] on the Accession by the Community to the European Convention for the Protection of Human Rights and Fundamental Freedoms,[3] it has relied on the general principles of Community law in particular in its protection of fundamental rights:

[F]undamental rights form an integral part of the general principles of law whose observance the Court ensures. For that purpose the Court draws inspiration from the constitutional traditions common to the Member States and from the guidelines supplied by international treaties for the protection of human rights on which the Member States have collaborated or of which they are signatories. In that regard, the Court has stated that the [European] Convention [on the Protection of Human Rights and Fundamental Freedoms] has special significance (see, in particular, the judgment in Case C-260/89 ERT [1991] ECR I-2925, paragraph 41).[4]

The other institutions of the Communities have likewise endorsed the Court's acknowledgement that EC law is based upon the recognition of

---

[1] Although, Art. 215(2) {Art.288} of the EC Treaty provides in the case of non-contractual liability that 'the Community shall, in accordance with the general principles common to the laws of the Member States, make good any damage caused by its institutions or by its servants in the performance of their duties'. Art. 164 {Art. 220} also provides in extremely broad terms that it is the job of the ECJ to 'ensure that in the interpretation and application of this Treaty *the law* is observed'. (Emphasis supplied.) On the part played by general principles of law in the jurisprudence of the ECJ, see Arnull, *The General Principles of EEC Law and the Individual* (Leicester University Press, London, 1990), and Tridimas, *General Principles of Community Law* (Oxford University Press, Oxford, forthcoming in 1998).

[2] Opinion 2/94 [1996] ECR I-1759.

[3] ETS No. 5.

[4] [1996] ECR I-1759, at 1789. See also Case 4/73 *Nold KG* v. *Commission* [1974] ECR 491, Case 36/75 *Rutili* v. *Minister of the Interior* [1975] ECR 1219, and Case 44/79 *Hauer* v. *Land Rheinland-Pfalz* [1979] ECR 3727.

fundamental human rights. In particular, in a Joint Declaration by the European Parliament, the Council and the Commission of 5 April 1977, it was stressed that these institutions attach 'prime importance . . . to the protection of fundamental rights, as derived in particular from the constitutions of the Member States and the European Convention for the Protection of Human Rights and Fundamental Freedoms', and they promised 'in the exercise of their powers and in pursuance of the aims of the European Communities' to respect these rights.[5]

In legislative terms, the third recital to the Single European Act's (SEA) Preamble pledges the Member States to work together to promote democracy on the basis of the fundamental rights recognized in the constitutions and laws of the Member States, in the European Convention on Human Rights, and in the European Social Charter,[6] notably freedom, equality, and social justice.[7] The TEU, especially after its amendment by the Amsterdam Treaty, gives further support to this process. Thus, the third and fourth recitals to its Preamble state:

Confirming their attachment to the principles of liberty, democracy and respect for human rights and fundamental freedoms and of the rule of law,Confirming their attachment to fundamental social rights as defined in the European Social Charter signed at Turin on 18 October 1961 and in the 1989 Community Charter of the Fundamental Social Rights of Workers . . .

Article F(1)[8] of the Treaty itself lays down that the Union 'is founded on the principles of liberty, democracy, respect for human rights and fundamental freedoms, and the rule of law, principles which are common to the Member States' and F(2)[9] provides:

The Union shall respect fundamental rights, as guaranteed by the European Convention for the Protection of Human Rights and Fundamental Freedoms signed in Rome on 4 November 1950 and as they result from the constitutional traditions common to the Member States, as general principles of Community law.[10]

When it draws on national constitutional provisions, the Court appears not to require completely identical formulation of the principle in question in all the Member States, but rather regards individual national

[5] OJ [1977] C103/1. See also the other acts of the institutions listed by the ECJ in its Opinion 2/94 [1996] ECR I-1759, at 1768.

[6] ETS No. 35. Revised version ETS No. 163.

[7] See also Art. 117 {Art. 136} of the EC Treaty.

[8] {Art. 6(1)}.

[9] {Art. 6(2)}.

[10] Art. L(c) {Art. 46} of the TEU, as amended by the Amsterdam Treaty, confers jurisdiction (in curiously circular language) on the ECJ in relation to Art. F(2) 'with regard to action of the institutions, in so far as the Court has jurisdiction under the Treaties establishing the European Communities and under this Treaty'.

rules as a source of ideas and as a guide to the solution of particular problems. So, in particular, the German principles of 'proportionality' (in other words, the notion that a penalty or sanction must not be out of scale with the wrong committed), and the protection of legitimate business and other interests, have played a very important part in the ECJ's developing jurisprudence.[11] Britain, although a relatively late entrant into the Communities, is also an important provider of such principles. It can be argued, for instance, that the mechanism allowing for the direct effect of directives, discussed in Chapter 1 and formulated by the ECJ in *Pubblico Ministero* v. *Ratti*[12] owes much to the maxims that equity regards that as done which ought to be done, and that a claimant should come to court with 'clean hands'. Similarly, the natural justice principle known as *audi alteram partem* was applied by the Court in *Transocean Marine Paint Association* v. *Commission*.[13]

As regards international treaties, it is evident from the provisions of the SEA and the TEU quoted above that the most prominent sources of general principles are the European Convention for the Protection of Human Rights and Fundamental Freedoms of 1950, the European Social Charter of 1961 and the Community Charter on the Fundamental Social Rights of Workers of 1989.[14]

The first arose directly out of the Hague Congress of the International Committee of Movements for European Unity of May 1948, which resulted in the creation of the Council of Europe in May 1949. The Member States of the Council of Europe drafted the Human Rights Convention, guaranteeing essential civil and political rights, and it became open for signature from November 1950. Economic and social rights proved harder to reach agreement on, in part because they were not embued with the same sense of post-war urgency as civil and political rights, and in part also because they require constructive action, rather than a mere undertaking not to interfere, by States in order to give them content.[15] The European Social Charter was, however, eventually agreed. It was subsequently revised to take account of recent 'fundamental social changes' and so as to include a number of additional rights. Its new version was opened for signature in

[11] See e.g. Case 11/70 *Internationale Handelsgesellschaft GmbH* v. *Einfuhr-und Vorratsstelle für Getreide und Futtermittel* [1070] ECR 1125; Case 44/79 *Hauer* v. *Land Rheinland-Pfalz* [1979] ECR 3727; and Case 81/72 *Commission* v. *Council* [1973] ECR 575. Note also the place of proportionality in establishing the defence of justification in relation to indirect discrimination, discussed in Chap. 2.

[12] Case 148/78 [1979] ECR 1629. See Usher, 'The Direct Effect of Directives' (1979) 4 ELRev. 268.

[13] Case 17/74 [1974] ECR 1063.

[14] The so-called 'Social Charter', Commission of the European Communities, Luxembourg, 1990.

[15] See further Jaspers and Betten, *Twenty-Five Years, European Social Charter* (Kluwer, 1988).

May 1996.[16] The European Community Charter on the Fundamental Social Rights of Workers was signed in December 1989 by all of the then 12 Member States except the UK. It is a formal declaration with no binding legal force but was supported by an action programme containing numerous proposals for legislation, many of which were subsequently acted upon.

Although international instruments inform EC law only indirectly, acting strictly as channels to which the ECJ will turn in its own formulation of the general principles of EC law, their importance should not be underestimated. Thus, despite the Court's holding that the Community has no power to accede to the Human Rights Convention,[17] Jacobs AG commented in *Bosphorus* v. *Hava Yollari*[18] that:

Although the [Human Rights] Convention may not be formally binding upon the Community, nevertheless for practical purposes the Convention can be regarded as part of Community law and can be invoked as such both in this Court and in national courts where Community law is in issue.[19]

The question therefore arises as to whether the Convention or the Charters are in any sense fertile sources on which the ECJ can draw. Do they contribute substantially to broadening the scope of the general principles of EC law? In order to answer this question, each instrument requires separate examination. Taking the Human Rights Convention first, there can be no doubt that the potential scope of its protection for the principle of non-discrimination on the ground of sex is wider than that otherwise to be found in EC law. The governing provision is Article 14, which provides:

The enjoyment of the rights and freedoms set forth in this Convention shall be secured without discrimination on any ground such as sex, race, colour, language, religion, political or other opinion, national or social origin, association with a national minority, property, birth or other status.[20]

It is clear from the wording of this Article that, taken on its own, it confers no substantive rights; it only does so in conjunction with another Article in the Convention or its Protocols.[21] The Convention itself, however, of course guarantees a broad range of fundamental civil and political rights,

---

[16] At the time of writing, the Revised Charter had been signed by Belgium, Denmark, Finland, France, Greece, Italy, Portugal and Sweden; it had not yet been signed by Austria, Germany, Ireland, Luxembourg, the Netherlands, Spain and the UK.

[17] Opinion 2/94 [1996] ECR I-1759.

[18] Case C-84/95 [1996] ECR I-3953.

[19] Ibid. at 3972.

[20] The 'Convention' in this context includes the First and Fourth Protocols (on property, education, political rights, personal liberty, and freedom of movement) since these Protocols themselves stipulate that all provisions of the Convention are to apply to them.

[21] *National Union of Belgian Police* v. *Belgium* [1979–80] 1 EHRR 578.

including the right to life, to humane trial, treatment, and punishment, freedom of the person and of conscience, and the right to privacy.[22] The result is thus that, where the Convention stipulates the enjoyment of a particular right, or expressly permits a specific limitation on a right, the Member States may not confer the right, or phrase the limitation, in a way which discriminates *inter alia* on the ground of sex.[23] It is also evident from Article 14 that it makes no attempt to spell out the meaning of 'discrimination', unsurprisingly in view of the Convention's relative antiquity and the breadth of Article 14. The French version of the Convention contains an even broader formulation than the English: 'Sans distinction aucune'. Although it has dealt with relatively few cases alleging sex discrimination, the Court of Human Rights has explained that:

It is important . . . to look for the criteria which enable a determination to be made as to whether or not a given difference in treatment, concerning of course the exercise of one of the rights and freedoms set forth, contravenes Article 14. On this question the Court, following the principles which may be extracted from the legal practice of a large number of democratic States, holds that the principle of equality of treatment is violated if the distinction has no objective and reasonable justification. The existence of such a justification must be assessed in relation to the aims and effects of the measure under consideration, regard being had to the principles which normally prevail in democratic societies. A difference of treatment in the exercise of a right laid down in the Convention must not only pursue a legitimate aim: Article 14 is likewise violated when it is clearly established that there is no reasonable relationship of proportionality between the means employed and the aim sought to be realized.[24]

---

[22] For an important addition to the procedural weaponry available for the vindication of such rights, see *Schuler-Zgraggen* v. *Switzerland* [1996] 21 EHRR 404. Discussion of the general content of the European Convention on Human Rights is outside the scope of the present work. There is a large body of literature on the subject, including Feldman, *Civil Liberties & Human Rights* (Clarendon Press, Oxford, 1993); *The Law of the European Convention on Human Rights*, eds. Harris, Boyle and Warbrick (Butterworths, London, 1995); Janis, Kay and Bradley, *European Human Rights Law* (Clarendon Press, Oxford, 1995); Jacobs, *The European Convention on Human Rights* (Clarendon Press, Oxford, 2nd ed. 1996); van Dijk and van Hoof, *Theory and Practice of the European Convention on Human Rights* (Kluwer, London, 2nd ed. 1990); and McKean, *Equality and Discrimination Under International Law* (Clarendon Press, Oxford, 1983).

[23] Thus, in *AP* v. *Austria* (1995) 20 EHRR CD 63, the European Commission of Human Rights considered that an Austrian rule limiting parental leave payments to mothers was in breach of Arts. 8 and 14 of the Convention on respect for family life without discrimination on the ground of sex. It is not necessary, in order to invoke Art. 14, to be able to show that one of the other substantive rights in the Convention has itself been violated for some reason other than discrimination: see the *Belgian Linguistic Case (Merits)* [1979–80] 1 EHRR 252.

[24] *Belgian Linguistic Case* op. cit., n. 23, at 284. It repeated these principles in *Abdulaziz, Cabales and Balkandali* v. *UK* (1985) 7 EHRR 471, in which it commented, at 501: '[I]t can be said that the advancement of the equality of the sexes is today a major goal in the Member States of the Council of Europe. This means that very weighty reasons would have to be advanced before a difference of treatment on the ground of sex could be regarded as compatible with the Convention'.

It thus appears that even direct discrimination can in general be excused or 'justified' under the Convention in any case where it pursues an acceptable aim and is not disproportionate to that aim, although the Court has in recent times demanded a more rigorous standard for justification than in its earlier jurisprudence.[25] This is a considerably wider formulation of the law than one which (like the EC's equal treatment provisions, as will be seen later in the present chapter) contains discreet defences to apply in particular situations, although this is probably inevitable given the width of Article 14.[26] It follows that the Convention (at least potentially) erects into a general principle of EC law the right not to be discriminated against on the ground of sex in a number of fields not otherwise governed by EC law, but this gain is partially offset by the standard for determining whether or not discrimination has occurred. In addition, as will be discussed in the following section of the present chapter, the part played by general principles of EC law in the jurisprudence of the ECJ also restricts the importance of the Convention in this context.

The European Social Charter is by nature a somewhat different type of instrument. In particular, it is not drafted in terms of legal rights which can be invoked before judicial authorities by individuals. It is instead supposed to set standards to be achieved by its contracting States, with a fluid, time-consuming, and non-binding supervision procedure. Perhaps for this reason, its content is not generally as well known as that of the European Convention on Human Rights. Part I of the Charter today lists 31 rights and principles in the field of employment and social welfare which are aimed at by the contracting States; of particular importance in the present context are the following:

Article 8: The right of employed women to protection of maternity.
  With a view to ensuring the effective exercise of the right of employed women to the protection of maternity, the Parties undertake:
  1.   to provide either by paid leave, by adequate social security benefits or by benefits from public funds for employed women to take leave before and after childbirth up to a total of at least fourteen weeks;
  2.   to consider it as unlawful for an employer to give a woman notice of dismissal during the period from the time she notifies her employer that she is pregnant until the end of her maternity leave, or to give her notice of dismissal at such a time that the notice would expire during such a period;[27]

---

[25] See *Hoffmann* v. *Austria* (1994) 17 EHRR 293, *Burghartz* v. *Switzerland* (1994) 18 EHRR 101 and *Karlheinz Schmidt* v. *Germany* Ser. A No. 291–B (judgment of 18 July 1994).
[26] For discussion of the argument that direct sex discrimination may be justified in EC law, see Chap. 2.
[27] The appendix to the Charter however adds that this provision is not to be interpreted as laying down an absolute prohibition; it states that '[e]xceptions could be made, for

3. to provide that mothers who are nursing their infants shall be entitled to sufficient time off for this purpose;
4. to regulate the employment in night work of pregnant women, women who have recently given birth and women nursing their infants;
5. to prohibit the employment of pregnant women, women who have recently given birth or who are nursing their infants in underground mining and all other work which is unsuitable by reason of its dangerousness, unhealthy or arduous nature and to take appropriate measures to protect the employment rights of these women.

Article 20: The right to equal opportunities and equal treatment in matters of employment and occupation without discrimination on the grounds of sex.

With a view to ensuring the effective exercise of the right to equal opportunities and equal treatment in matters of employment and occupation without discrimination on the grounds of sex, the Parties undertake to recognize that right and to take appropriate measures to ensure or promote its application in the following fields:

(a) access to employment, protection against dismissal and occupational re-integration
(b) vocational guidance, training, retraining and rehabilitation;
(c) terms of employment and working conditions, including remuneration;
(d) career development, including promotion.

The Appendix however states, in relation to Article 20:

1. It is understood that social security matters, as well as other provisions relating to unemployment benefit, old age benefit and survivor's benefit, may be excluded from the scope of this article.
2. Provisions concerning the protection of women, particularly as regards pregnancy, confinement and the post-natal period, shall not be deemed to be discrimination as referred to in this article.
3. This article shall not prevent the adoption of specific measures aimed at removing *de facto* inequalities.
4. Occupational activities which, by reason of their nature or the context in which they are carried out, can be entrusted only to persons of a particular sex may be excluded from the scope of this article or some of its provisions. This provision is not to be interpreted as requiring the Parties to embody in laws or regulations a list of occupations which, by reason of their nature or the context in which they are carried out, may be reserved to persons of a particular sex.

Article 26: The right to dignity at work.

With a view to ensuring the effective exercise of the right of all workers to protection of their dignity at work, the Parties undertake, in consultation with employers' and workers' organizations:

instance, . . . (a) if an employed woman has been guilty of misconduct which justifies breaking off the employment relationship; (b) if the undertaking concerned ceases to operate; (c) if the period prescribed in the employment contract has expired'.

1. to promote awareness, information and prevention of sexual harassment in the workplace or in relation to work and to take all appropriate measures to protect workers from such conduct;

2. to promote awareness, information and prevention of recurrent reprehensible or distinctly negative and offensive actions directed against individual workers in the workplace or in relation to work and to take all appropriate measures to protect workers from such conduct.[28]

Article 27: The right of workers with family responsibilities to equal opportunities and equal treatment.

With a view to ensuring the exercise of the right to equality of opportunity and treatment for men and women workers with family responsibilities and between such workers and other workers, the Parties undertake:

1. to take appropriate measures:
   (a) to enable workers with family responsibilities to enter and remain in employment, as well as to re-enter employment after an absence due to those responsibilities, including measures in the field of vocational guidance and training;
   (b) to take account of their needs in terms and conditions of employment and social security;
   (c) to develop or promote services, public or private, in particular child daycare services and other childcare arrangements;
2. to provide a possibility for either parent to obtain, during a period after maternity leave, parental leave to take care of a child, the duration and conditions of which should be determined by national legislation, collective agreements or practice;
3. to ensure that family responsibilities shall not, as such, constitute a valid reason for termination of employment.[29]

Article E provides that:

The enjoyment of the rights set forth in this Charter shall be secured without discrimination on any ground such as race, colour, sex, language, religion, political or other opinion, national extraction or social origin, health, association with a national minority, birth or other status'.

But the Appendix provides that 'differential treatment based on an objective and reasonable justification shall not be deemed discriminatory'. As will be seen from the discussion below, these statements of principle

---

[28] The Appendix further provides that this article does not require the enactment of legislation and that para. 2 does not cover sexual harassment.

[29] The Appendix states: 'It is understood that this article applies to men and women workers with family responsibilities in relation to their dependent children as well as in relation to other members of their immediate family who clearly need their care or support where such responsibilities restrict their possibilities of preparing for, entering, participating in or advancing in economic activity. The terms "dependent children" and "other members of their immediate family who clearly need their care and support" mean persons defined as such by the national legislation of the Party concerned'.

reflect the broad thrust of EC law but add little of substance to its provisions.

The Community Social Charter addresses a number of 'Fundamental Social Rights of Workers', one of which is equal treatment for men and women. Its Article 16 states:

Equal treatment for men and women must be assured. Equal opportunities for men and women must be developed.

To this end, action must be intensified to ensure the implementation of the principle of equality between men and women as regards in particular access to employment, remuneration, working conditions, social protection, education, vocational training and career development.

Measures should also be developed enabling men and women to reconcile their occupational and family obligations.

The Role played by General Principles of EC Law

General principles play a part in EC law in two subtly different situations. In the words of Capotorti AG in *Defrenne* v. *Sabena*:[30]

First, the respect for fundamental rights is a limitation on all Community acts: any measure whereby the powers of the Community institutions are exercised is subject to that limitation and in that sense the entire structure of the Community is under an obligation to observe that limitation. Secondly where directly applicable Community measures exist (by the effect of the Treaties or secondary legislation) they must be interpreted in a manner which accords with the principle that human rights must be respected.[31]

The ECJ has summarized the first of these situations thus:

Respect for fundamental rights is . . . a condition of the lawfulness of Community acts.[32]

Judicial review of Community action takes a number of forms. A direct action may lie under Article 173[33] of the EC Treaty or a claim may succeed under Article 184[34] where a regulation is declared inapplicable. A similar jurisdiction is exercised by the ECJ under Article 177[35] when it rules on the validity of Community acts, and under Article 215(2)[36] when it adjudicates tort claims against the Community based on acts of the institutions.

Article 173 permits judicial review of administrative action on four broadly defined grounds, of which the most important in the present

---

[30] Case 149/77 [1978] ECR 1365.   [31] Ibid. at 1385.

[32] Opinion 2/94 on the Accession of the Community to the European Convention on Human Rights and Fundamental Freedoms [1996] ECR I-1759, at 1789. See also Jacobs AG in Case C-84/95 *Bosphorus* v. *Hava Yollari* [1996] ECR I-3953, at 3972.

[33] {Art. 230}.   [34] {Art. 241}.

[35] {Art. 234}.   [36] {Art. 288(2)}.

context is 'infringement of this Treaty *or of any rule of law relating to its application*'.[37] In practice, the Court has fairly frequently exercised its powers of review where the administrative decision in question contravened a general principle of law. However, there are serious limitations on the scope of this jurisdiction in the present context. Where the person seeking judicial review is an individual (whether human or corporate), it is clear that it is the intention of Article 173 to restrict the circumstances in which the action is admissible. However, the Court's jurisprudence as to the extent of any such restriction is disturbingly confused and self-contradictory.[38] First, it is unclear whether it interprets Article 173(2) as conferring on individuals the right only to seek annulment of an instrument that is in substance a 'decision' within the definition contained in Article 189 or whether the individual is entitled also to challenge a true 'regulation'.[39] Secondly, even where the individual can establish that the act impugned is one which he or she may challenge, the Court has made inconsistent statements as to the degree of interest required on the part of the applicant in order for there to be *locus standi*. Article 173(4) provides that it must be shown either that the decision is addressed to the applicant, or else that it is of 'direct and individual concern' to that applicant. This requirement, in particular the element of individual concern, has at times been extremely narrowly construed by the ECJ;[40] in these narrow decisions, far from simply requiring the applicant to demonstrate some sort of interest in the subject-matter of the action over and above that of other members of the public (as a British administrative lawyer might perhaps anticipate), the ECJ has ruled that an applicant will only be individually concerned where he or she belongs to a closed and ascertainable class of people whose interests are particularly affected by the decision in

[37] Emphasis supplied.

[38] See in particular Case 789/79 *Calpak SpA* v. *Commission* [1980] ECR 1949, Cases 239/82 and 275/82 *Allied Corporation* v. *Commission* [1984] ECR 1005, Case C-358/89 *Extramet Industrie* v. *Council* [1991] ECR I-2501 and Case 309/89 *Codorniu* v. *Council* [1994] ECR I-1853. The confusion has been exacerbated by the failure of the Court of First Instance (which inherited this jurisdiction from the ECJ by Council Decision 93/350, OJ [1993] L144/21) to follow the lead provided by the ECJ in *Codorniu*: see for example its decisions in Case T-489/93 *Unifruit Hellas* v. *Commission* [1994] ECR II-1201, Case T-472/93 *Campo Ebro* v. *Council* [1995] ECR II-421 and Case T-585/93 *Stichting Greenpeace Council* v. *Commission* [1995] ECR II-2205 (in which an appeal was pending at the time of writing). For further discussion, see Greaves, 'Locus Standi under Article 173 EEC when Seeking Annulment' (1986) 11 ELRev. 119 and Arnull, 'Private Applicants and the Action for Annulment under Article 173 of the EC Treaty' (1995) 32 CMLRev. 7.

[39] Contrast, for example, the Court's decision in *Calpak SpA* v. *Commission* op. cit. with that in *Codorniu* v. *Council* also op. cit., n. 38. It seems from the wording of Art. 173 that an individual may not seek judicial review of a non-binding act and the CFI has held in Case T-99/94 *Asocarne* v. *Council* [1994] ECR II-871 that an individual has no standing to challenge a directive.

[40] See Cases 106 and 107/63 *Toepfer* v. *Commission* [1965] ECR 405 and Case 62/70 *Bock* v. *Commission* [1971] ECR 897.

question. On the other hand, in some of its more recent decisions, the Court has inclined to the wider view that a close factual connection with the instrument impugned will be sufficient for an applicant to establish *locus standi*.[41]

These procedural uncertainties and limitations have meant in practice that actions brought by members of the Community's own work-force have assumed a particular significance in this field, since Community employees are especially prone to receiving 'decisions' addressed to themselves.

Article 184 is likewise of fairly restricted scope. Known in its parent French as the 'exception d'illégalité', it provides a means of challenge to a decision affecting an individual (or a Member State), where the decision is itself based on an illegal regulation in respect of which the very strict time limit of two months for a direct challenge under Article 173 may well have run out. A successful action under Article 184 results not in the annulment of the regulation, but merely in its being declared 'inapplicable'. Once again, given the dearth of occasions in ordinary life on which an individual is liable to receive a decision addressed to him or herself, this Article has also proved of particular use to Community staff.[42]

The inability of the Community to legislate in defiance of general principles extends itself in certain circumstances to the actions of the Member States.[43] In *Elliniki Radiophonia Tileorassi AE* v. *Dimotiki Etairia Pliroforissis*,[44] the ECJ explained that it had:

[N]o power to examine the compatibility with the European Convention on Human Rights of national rules which do not fall within the scope of Community law. On the other hand, where such rules do fall within the scope of Community law, and reference is made to the Court for a preliminary ruling, it must provide all the criteria of interpretation needed by the national court to determine whether those rules are compatible with the fundamental rights the observance of which the Court ensures and which derive in particular from the European Convention on Human Rights.

In particular, where a Member State relies on the combined provisions of Articles 56 and 66 [of the EC Treaty] in order to justify rules which are likely to obstruct the exercise of the freedom to provide services, such justification, provided for by Community law, must be interpreted in the light of the general principles of law and in particular of fundamental rights. Thus the national rules in question can fall under the exceptions provided for by the combined provi-

---

[41] See in particular *Extramet Industrie* v. *Council* and *Codorniu* v. *Council* op. cit., n. 38.

[42] For general discussion of the scope of judicial review in EC law, see Brown and Kennedy, *The Court of Justice of the European Communities* (Sweet & Maxwell, London, 4th ed. 1994), Chap. 7; Hartley, *The Foundations of European Community Law* (Clarendon Press, Oxford, 3rd ed. 1994), Pt. IV; and Wyatt and Dashwood, *European Community Law* (Sweet & Maxwell, 3rd ed. 1993), Chap. 5.

[43] See Wyatt, 'Article 119 and the Fundamental Principle of Non-discrimination on Grounds of Sex' (1978) 3 ELRev. 483.

[44] Case C-260/89 [1991] ECR I-2925.

sions of Articles 56 and 66 only if they are compatible with the fundamental rights the observance of which is ensured by the Court.

It follows that in such a case it is for the national court and, if necessary the Court of Justice, to appraise the application of those provisions having regard to all the rules of Community law, including freedom of expression, as embodied in Article 10 of the European Convention on Human Rights, as a general principle of law the observance of which is ensured by the Court.

. . . [T]he limitations imposed on the power of the Member States to apply the provisions referred to in Articles 56 and 66 of the Treaty on grounds of public policy, public security and public health, must be appraised in the light of the general principle of freedom of expression embodied in Article 10 of the European Convention on Human Rights.[45]

It is thus clear that the Member States must observe the general principles of EC law when they rely upon a derogation from a Community rule. It is also established that they are constrained by the general principles when they implement Community measures.[46] These are important additions to the armoury of the individual litigant seeking to assert a right protected by a general principle of EC law before a national court. However, a difficult question which remains to be directly addressed by the ECJ is whether there are any additional circumstances in which national rules 'fall within the scope of Community law' and in which the general principles of EC law therefore limit national legislative action. In *R. v. Ministry of Agriculture, Fisheries and Food, Ex p. First City Trading Ltd.*,[47] Laws J analysed the relationship between the EC Treaty, general principles and domestic law thus:

There is a critical distinction to be drawn between these following situations. *On the one hand, a Member State may take measures solely by virtue of its domestic law. On the other a Community institution or Member State may take measures which it is authorized or obliged to take by force of the law of the Community.* In the former situation I contemplate a measure which is neither required of the Member State nor permitted to it by virtue of Community Treaty provisions. It is purely a domestic measure. Even so, it may affect the operation of the Common Market and accordingly be held to be 'within the scope of application' of the Treaty. This was the *Phil Collins* case [Case C-92/92 [1993] ECR 5145]. It is of the first importance to notice that its falling within the Treaty's scope is by no means the same thing as being done under powers or duties conferred or imposed by Community law. The second situation primarily includes (so far as Member States are concerned) measures which Community law requires, such as, for example, law which is made to give effect to a directive. It includes also an act or decision done or taken by a Member State in reliance on a derogation or permission granted by Community

---

[45] Ibid. at 2964.
[46] Case 5/88 *Wachauf v. Germany* [1989] ECR 2609, Case C-351/92 *Graff v. Hauptzollamt Köln-Rheinau* [1994] ECR I-3361, Case C-84/95 *Bosphorus v. Hava Yollari* [1996] ECR I-3953.
[47] [1997] 1 CMLR 250.

law . . . In the first situation, the measure is in no sense a function of the law of Europe, although its legality may be constrained by it. In the second, the measure is necessarily a creature of the law of Europe. Community law alone either demands it, or permits it.

. . . The power of the Court of Justice, as it seems to me, to apply . . . principles of public law which it had itself evolved cannot be deployed in a case where the measure in question, taken by a Member State, is not a function of Community law at all. To do so would be to condition or moderate the internal law of the Member State without that being authorized by the Treaty. Where action is taken, albeit under domestic law, which falls within the scope of the Treaty's application, then of course the Court has the power and duty to require that the Treaty be adhered to. But no more: precisely because the fundamental principles elaborated by the Court of Justice are not vouchsafed by the Treaty, there is no legal space for their application to any measure or decision taken otherwise than in pursuance of Treaty rights or obligations . . . *It follows that in the first situation I have described there is no question of the application of the Community's internal fundamental principles.*

The position is altogether different where a measure is adopted *pursuant* to Community law; this is the second situation. Then the internal law of the Court of Justice applies. Decisions of the Community institutions are plainly subject to it: they have no other domestic law but the Court's internal law. Their very existence is a function of the Treaty, by which the arbiter of their actions is the Court of Justice. *Decisions of the Member States are likewise subject to the Community's internal law when and to the extent that they are taken so as to implement Community law, or must necessarily rely on it* . . . This must be so, since in all such instances the Member State's domestic law is no more than the vehicle for a measure whose validity falls to be tested according to the law of the Community. If the Member State were in such cases permitted to legislate or take other action purely according to its own rules, free from the constraints and disciplines of the Community's internal law, the legal régime of the Community would plainly lack harmony and uniformity.[48]

This is an interesting view but one which, with respect, is not necessarily shared by the ECJ. In particular, it is not clear that that Court would agree that the fundamental or general principles of EC law are not vouchsafed by the Treaty; on the contrary, it might be argued that they owe their very legitimacy to the supposition that the Treaty is predicated upon them, since they are essential to the concept of justice as understood by the Member States in their current state of development. If this were so, then all national legislation falling within the scope of the Treaty would also be subject to the general principles and only legislation which was purely domestic in its ambit and without any overlap with matters governed by the EC Treaty would be exempt from review on this basis.

The second situation in which general principles of law assume

---

[48] Ibid. at 267–9. (Emphases supplied.)

importance is when it comes to construing the EC Treaty or secondary Community law.[49] Although general principles of law will not be permitted by the Court to override specific provisions of the Treaty,[50] they are from time to time utilized by the ECJ to justify a liberal interpretation of what might otherwise seem to be a narrow rule.[51] Here there is considerable potential for improving the lot of the individual, since the provision may of course prove directly effective. The procedure provided by Article 177 of the Treaty for seeking preliminary rulings on interpretation has facilitated this process.[52]

The General Principle of Non-Discrimination on the Ground of Sex

The chief reason for this discussion of general principles of law, and in particular of mention of their effectiveness as a procedural tool in the hands of an individual applicant, is of course that the ECJ regards the principle of non-discrimination between the sexes as one such principle, indeed as a fundamental human right.[53] Thus, in *Defrenne* v. *Sabena*,[54] it stated:

The Court has repeatedly stated that respect for fundamental personal human rights is one of the general principles of Community law, the observance of which it has a duty to ensure. There can be no doubt that the elimination of discrimination based on sex forms part of those fundamental rights.[55]

This approach has moreover been lent greater strength recently by the Amsterdam Treaty which, as seen elsewhere in the present work, has emphasised the importance of the principle of sex equality in a number of its provisions.

The ECJ has relied on the principle both to quash discriminatory administrative decisions and to justify a broad interpretation for various pieces of EC legislation. In the words of Trabucchi AG in *Defrenne* v. *Sabena*:[56]

---

[49] For an example outside the field of sex discrimination, see Case T-93/94 *Becker* v. *Court of Auditors* [1996] ECR II-141.

[50] Case 40/64 *Sgarlata* v. *Commission* [1965] ECR 215.

[51] See for example Case C-260/89 *Elliniki Radiophonia Tileorassi AE* v. *Dimotiki Etairia Pliroforissis* [1991] ECR I-2925.

[52] A general principle may also play an important part in the outcome of a case pending before a national court where the implementation of Community law by a Member State is in issue: see Case C-84/95 *Bosphorus* v. *Hava Yollari* [1996] 3 CMLR 257, in which Jacobs AG submitted: 'Community law cannot release Member States from their obligations under [the European Convention on Human Rights]' (at 286). See also discussion above.

[53] See Docksey, 'The Principle of Equality Between Women and Men As A Fundamental Right Under Community Law' (1991) 20 ILJ 258.

[54] The so-called *Third Defrenne* case, Case 149/77 [1978] ECR 1365.

[55] Ibid. at 1378. See also Case C-13/94 *P* v. *S and Cornwall* [1996] ECR I-2143, discussed below. The CFI confirmed this position in Case T-45/90 *Speybrouck* v. *Parliament* [1992] ECR II-33.   [56] Case 43/75 [1976] ECR 455.

[I]n interpreting Article 119, the Court cannot overlook the fact that the principle of equal treatment is enshrined in the legal system of Member States, the majority of which have erected it into a principle formally underwritten by the constitution itself. In its judgment of 17 December 1970 in Case 11/70, *Internationale Handelsgesellschaft*, the Court stated that respect for fundamental human rights forms an integral part of the general principles of law and that the protection of such rights within the Community can and must be inspired by the constitutional traditions common to the Member States. In view of this it seems to me that the prohibition of all discrimination based on sex (particularly on the subject of pay) protects a right which must be regarded as fundamental in the Community legal order as it is elsewhere.[57]

He went on to add:

Undoubtedly, action by the Member States and by the Community institutions in the form of legislation, regulations or administrative measures is essential for the reason that, if the principle of equal treatment were to apply only to pay in the strict sense of the word or to absolutely identical work, the practical effect of Article 119 would be rather small. This gives the Member States and the Community institutions enormous scope in taking action to put into effect the principle of non-discrimination laid down in Article 119 without having to rely on its direct applicability.[58]

A good example of the use of the principle of non-discrimination on the ground of sex to justify judicial review of administrative action came in *Razzouk and Beydoun* v. *Commission*.[59] The widower of a deceased Commission employee was refused a survivor's pension by the Commission in circumstances in which, under the Staff Regulations, a surviving widow would have received such a pension. He argued that this treatment amounted either to the breach of a principle analogous to Article 119 which applied to Community employees, or else to the breach of a general rule of EC law that employees should be treated equally in like or comparable situations. His claim was, in essence therefore, for the annulment of the Commission's decision which had denied him the pension. Slynn AG commented that there was clearly discrimination between Community employees, and consequently between their spouses, on the ground of sex, since both male and female officials made the same pension contributions during their employment but stood to receive different benefits in the event of predeceasing their spouses. This discrimination, he went on to say, could not be shown to be justified on any objective ground,[60] and he would have annulled it both on the ground

---

[57] Ibid. at 490.

[58] Ibid. at 491.

[59] Cases 75 and 117/82 [1984] ECR 1509, also discussed in Chap. 2.

[60] By this, Slynn AG presumably meant that no other 'cause' for the differential treatment of male and female had been found. See discussion in Chap.2. of the Art. 119 concept of discrimination.

that it offended against the general principle of non-discrimination and the narrower principle akin to Article 119. The Court agreed that the decision should be annulled but based its decision wholly on the general principle of non-discrimination, saying that the Staff Regulations were:

[C]ontrary to a fundamental right and . . . therefore inapplicable in so far as they treat the surviving spouses of officials unequally according to the sex of the person concerned.[61]

Usher has raised the fascinating question of whether this same principle could be used to challenge the Social Security Directive[62] which permits differential state pensionable ages for men and women; he points out that the Court has made no comment on this matter, though it has several times interpreted the relevant provisions of the Directive.[63]

The *Razzouk and Beydoun* case involved direct discrimination on the ground of sex. However, it has been clear since *Sabbatini* v. *European Parliament*[64] that the general principle of non-discrimination can also be useful when indirect discrimination is concerned. Ms Sabbatini was a Community employee who, before her marriage, had received an expatriation allowance to compensate for her having to live in a foreign country in order to work for the Communities. Once married, she ceased to be paid the allowance because of the Civil Service Regulations which at the time provided: 'An official loses entitlement to the allowance, if, marrying a person who, at the time of the marriage, does not fulfil the conditions required for the grant of that allowance, he (or she) does not become the head of the family.' Under the Regulations, the 'head of the family' was normally the husband, except in the event of his disability. Ms Sabbatini contested the decision stopping her allowance on the basis of Article 184, arguing that the decision was based on the Regulations which were invalid because they breached the 'higher' rule prohibiting discrimination on the ground of sex. The discrimination alleged here was of course indirect, since both sexes were subjected to facially neutral treatment but, in reality, that treatment disadvantaged women rather than men. Roemer AG submitted that the claim should be dismissed, in doing so denying that any general principle of non-discrimination on the ground of sex existed in EC law.[65] The Court, however, upheld the claim, saying:

---

[61] [1984] ECR 1509, at 1530.

[62] Directive 79/7, OJ [1979] L6/24, discussed in Chap. 4. Likewise also the Occupational Social Security Directive 86/378, OJ [1986] L225/40, discussed in Chap. 2 which contains a similar exemption in respect of the self-employed.

[63] Usher, 'European Community Equality Law: Legal Instruments and Judicial Remedies', in *Women, Employment and European Equality Law*, ed. McCrudden (Eclipse Publications, London, 1987). See also the submissions of Van Gerven AG in Case C-9/91 *R. v. Secretary of State for Social Security, Ex p. EOC* [1992] ECR I-4297, at 4324.

[64] Case 32/71 [1972] ECR 345, also discussed in Chap. 2.

[65] See esp. his remarks in Case 32/71 [1972] ECR 345, at 355.

[I]t is . . . clear that the provision the validity of which is contested does in fact create a difference of treatment as between male and female officials, in as much as it renders the retention of the expatriation allowance conditional upon the acquisition of the status of head of household within the meaning of the Staff Regulations. It is therefore necessary to examine whether this difference of treatment is such as to affect the validity of the contested provision of the Regulations. The purpose of the expatriation allowance is to compensate for the special expenses and disadvantages resulting from entry into the service of the Communities for those officials who—in the conditions more fully set out in detail in Article 4(1) of Annex VII [to the Regulations]—are thereby obliged to change their place of residence.

Article 4, taken as a whole, indicates that the expatriation allowance is paid to married officials, not only in consideration of the personal situation of the recipient, but also of the family situation created by the marriage. Thus Article 4(3) takes into account the new family situation entered upon by the official when he or she marries a person who does not satisfy the conditions for the grant of the expatriation allowance. The withdrawal of the allowance following the marriage of the recipient might be justified in cases in which this change in the family situation is such as to bring to an end the state of 'expatriation' which is the justification for the benefit in question.

In this respect, the Regulations cannot, however, treat officials differently according to whether they are male or female, since termination of the status of expatriate must be dependent for both male and female officials on uniform criteria, irrespective of sex.

Consequently, by rendering the retention of the allowance subject to the acquisition of the status of 'head of household' . . . the Staff Regulations have created an arbitrary difference of treatment between officials. Consequently the decisions taken with regard to the applicant are devoid of any legal basis and must be annulled . . .[66]

A similar result was arrived at in *Airola* v. *Commission*,[67] where a woman Community employee ceased to be paid an expatriation allowance on her marriage to a national of the country in which she was employed; the local law concerned automatically and irrevocably granted her the husband's nationality which nationality, according to the Staff Regulations, disentitled her to the allowance. The Court upheld her claim to continued payment of the allowance, pointing out that the Regulations operated in a discriminatory fashion since under no national legislation in existence at the time in any of the Member States did a husband automatically acquire his wife's nationality on marriage. It held:

Though 'expatriation' is a subjective state conditioned by the official's assimilation into new surroundings, the Staff Regulations of officials cannot treat officials differently in this respect according to whether they are of the male or female sex

---

[66] [1972] ECR 345, at 350–1.   [67] Case 21/74 [1975] ECR 221.

since, in either case, payment of the expatriation allowance must be determined by considerations which are uniform and disregard the difference in sex. The concept of 'nationals' contained in Article 4(a) must therefore be interpreted in such a way as to avoid any unwarranted difference of treatment as between male and female officials who are, in fact, placed in comparable situations. Such unwarranted difference of treatment between female officials and officials of the male sex would result from an interpretation of the concept of 'nationals' . . . as also embracing the nationality which was imposed by law on an official of the female sex by virtue of her marriage, and which she was unable to renounce. It is therefore necessary to define the concept of an official's present or previous nationality under Article 4(a) of Annex VII as excluding nationality imposed by law on a female official upon her marriage with a national of another state, when she has no possibility of renouncing it.[68]

The efficacy of the notion of indirect discrimination is, however, heavily dependent on the sensitivity of the deciding court as to what is truly adverse to a greater number of women than men. The tenor of the ECJ's remarks, although not its overall conclusion on the facts, in *De Angelis* v. *Commission*[69] suggests that it needed, at least in 1985, to be made more aware of the practical issues in this field. Ms De Angelis became an employee of the Commission in Brussels in December 1982. Although an Italian national, she had been living in Brussels since 1970, when she had gone there in order to accompany her husband who at that earlier date had also become a Commission employee. She contested the Commission's decision not to pay her an expatriation allowance. Her position was governed by Article 4(1)(a) of Annex VII to the Staff Regulations, providing:

An expatriation allowance shall be paid . . . (a) to officials:

—who are not and never have been nationals of the state in whose territory the place where they are employed is situated, and
—who during the five years ending six months before they entered the service did not habitually reside or carry on their main occupation within the European territory of that state. For the purposes of this provision, circumstances arising from work done for another state or for an international organization shall not be taken into account.

Until February 1982, the Commission had interpreted this provision benevolently, especially for the benefit of the spouses and children of

---

[68] Case 21/74 [1975] ECR 221 at 228–9. Cf. Case 37/74 *Van Den Broeck* v. *Commission* [1975] ECR 235, in which the Court rejected such a claim because the applicant in that case had the choice, under the local law concerned, of renouncing the nationality conferred on her by marriage. The Staff Regulations were subsequently retrospectively amended so as to reflect these rulings: Art. 21(2) of Council Regulation 912/78 of 2 May 1978, OJ [1978] L119/1. See also Case 257/78 *Devred* v. *Commission* [1979] ECR 3767 where the situation, though more complicated, was similar to that in *Van Den Broeck*.
[69] Case 246/83 [1985] ECR 1253.

Community officials who were themselves recruited by a Community institution. In practice, what this meant was that a period spent by a wife accompanying her husband to another Member State was not taken into account in relation to the expatriation allowance. However, this construction was abandoned after criticism by the Court of Auditors that it amounted to a rewriting of the Staff Regulations. Ms De Angelis argued that the denial of an expatriation allowance to her amounted to a breach of the principle of equal pay; the Commission's new, restrictive interpretation of the Staff Regulations, she claimed, led to discrimination between male workers, who are free to carry on their occupation without delay, and female workers, who are 'subject to social and cultural pressure to raise their children until they have reached school-age and must therefore delay their careers by several years'.[70] In so constructing her argument, Ms De Angelis would seem to have been misguided; there certainly may be indirect discrimination where an employer stipulates an age or time qualification for applicants for employment.[71] However, there was no attempt made here to prove that age or time had stood in Ms De Angelis's way. What she really appears to have been trying to argue is that, since wives accompany their husbands to the latter's place of work more frequently than occurs vice versa, any employment stipulation which ignores that fact is potentially indirectly discriminatory. The case failed because the Court found, understandably in the circumstances, that discrimination had not been proved. However, both its remarks and those of the Advocate General have a disturbingly unperceptive quality. Darmon AG, for example, commented:

No one has any intention of challenging the sociological and cultural factors relied upon by the applicant. However, neither the provision at issue nor the new application thereof can be criticized on the ground that they do not contribute towards mitigating the effects of those factors. Neither that provision nor the application thereof discriminate, either directly or indirectly, against employed women in the manner complained of by the applicant.

The Staff Regulations must not contain any provisions which give rise to unequal treatment . . . However, the provisions of the Staff Regulations cannot necessarily be expected to correct any pre-existing inequalities.[72]

It is submitted that this demonstrates little or no sympathy with the aims of the anti-discrimination laws. Contrary to what Darmon AG said, the whole purpose of the concept of indirect discrimination is to mitigate the sociological, cultural, and other factors which prevent women from competing even-handedly with men. The Court's remarks are hardly more encouraging:

---

[70] In the words of Darmon AG, ibid. at 1257.
[71] See e.g. the British cases *Price* v. *Civil Service Commission* [1977] IRLR 291 and *Huppert* v. *UGC* (1986) 8 EOR 38. [72] [1985] ECR 1253, at 1257.

[N]either the wording of the provision in question nor the application thereof by the Commission provides the slightest indication of direct or indirect discrimination based on the sex of officials . . . [T]he principle of equal treatment implies that both men and women must be afforded identical working conditions without discrimination but it cannot require the institution to interpret the provisions of the Staff Regulations in a different manner in order to offset any domestic or social expenses or obligations.[73]

It is vital to the efficacy of EC anti-discrimination law that the Court should be made properly conscious of how and when indirect discrimination may occur. As the concept of discrimination becomes more familiar to the population generally, it seems likely that the incidence of direct discrimination can be expected to decline. What people are less likely to be aware of are the ways in which indirect discrimination can take place, and it is on this level that the Court's intervention is probably most needed.

Efforts to persuade the ECJ to regard the principle of non-discrimination on the ground of sex as a positive and enforceable right have, on the whole, not proved so successful as efforts to persuade it to exercise its powers of judicial review on this ground. Of course, of its nature, this is a matter which is not susceptible to precise measurement and, furthermore, there can be little doubt that the Court's liberal interpretations of Article 119 and (as will be seen later in the present chapter) of the Equal Treatment Directive,[74] are attributable in part to a desire to further the general principle of the equality of the sexes. However, this is an area where advances could be made. It is important that the Court's case law be developed so as to articulate the general principle of non-discrimination clearly and to raise the consciousness of both judges and advocates to its presence in the background when any relevant legislation is being construed. One thing which would help this process would be a much clearer indication from the ECJ as to the precise scope of the principle. In the staff cases, of which the most numerous are those dealing with expatriation allowances, and in *Defrenne* v. *Sabena*,[75] although the principle is expressed in broad terms, in reality it boils down to little more in practice than the application of the principle of equal pay for equal work[76] and, since this is guaranteed anyway by Article 119, the Court is only in effect holding that the Staff Regulations infringe the Treaty itself. Nevertheless, it was seen above that the Court on several occasions has referred to the principle of equal treatment, and implied

[73] Ibid. at 1264.

[74] Directive 76/207, OJ [1976] L39/40.

[75] Case 43/75 [1976] ECR 455.

[76] In particular in the light of Roemer AG's words in Case 32/71 *Sabbatini* v. *European Parliament* [1972] ECR 345, discussed in Chap. 2. to the effect that the expatriation allowance constitutes pay.

that it sees pay equality merely as an example of this grander principle.[77] In addition, it is clear from the cases so far decided that the Court will not be satisfied by facially equal treatment but will also concern itself with the notion of indirect discrimination. What is not so clear is how far the principle of equal treatment extends: is it restricted, for example, to employment or does it go further? If it extends, for example, to vocational training, might it not also govern education in other areas, as does the European Convention on Human Rights? Does it, for example, apply to the supply of services, or to taxation? Does a general principle of sex equality in fact influence all law that the Community is empowered to make, as might be implied from the complementary provisions of the European Convention on Human Rights and the European Social Charter? A clear positive response to these questions would be a tremendously important step towards improving the protection afforded by EC sex equality law.

One limitation on the utility of the general principle of equality to shed light on the meaning of EC law is, however, undoubted: there must be some definite EC law for the principle to bite on. This was illustrated by *Defrenne* v. *Sabena*[78] and is reflective of the civil law principle that the judge's role is restricted to the enforcement of enacted law. The redoubtable Ms Defrenne had brought an action before the Belgian courts claiming *inter alia* an increase in the allowance she received on the termination of her service with Sabena as her contract required when she reached the age of 40 (the airline was prepared to pay her a sum equal to 12 months' pay), and compensation for the damage she suffered as regards her old age pension in consequence of her enforced premature retirement. The Cour de Cassation sought a preliminary ruling from the ECJ under Article 177, asking:

Must Article 119 of the Treaty of Rome which lays down the principle that 'men and women should receive equal pay for equal work' be interpreted by reason of the dual economic and social aim of the Treaty as prescribing not only equal pay but also equal working conditions for men and women and, in particular, does the insertion into the contract of employment of an air hostess of a clause bringing the said contract to an end when she reaches the age of 40 years, it being established that no such limit is attached to the contract of male cabin attendants who are assumed to do the same work, constitute discrimination prohibited by the said Article 119 of the Treaty of Rome or by a principle of Community law if that clause may have pecuniary consequences, in particular, as regards the allowance on termination of service and pension?[79]

---

[77] Legislative support for this approach can now be drawn from Art. 119. Since its amendment by the Amsterdam Treaty, it deals in its opening two paragraphs with equal pay, but then continues in its remaining two paragraphs to broaden out to cover the whole field of equal treatment in employment.

[78] Case 149/77 [1978] ECR 1365.   [79] Ibid. at 1367.

The ECJ held, first of all, that Article 119 did not extend to this situation. In so doing, it demonstrated that, despite the fact that it is prepared to interpret EC legislation broadly and teleologically, there are limits beyond which it will refuse to go. Ms Defrenne had argued that Article 119 must be given a wide interpretation because it was only a specific statement of the more general principle of non-discrimination. In particular, she claimed that her enforced retirement at the age of 40 fell within the scope of Article 119, first, because 'a woman worker can receive pay equal to that received by men only if the requirement regarding equal conditions of employment is first satisfied' and, secondly, because 'the age limit imposed on air hostesses by the contract of employment has pecuniary consequences which are prejudicial as regards the allowance on termination of service and pension'. The Court rejected these arguments on the basis that the Treaty's Social Provisions were divisible into those provisions requiring a harmonization of the laws of the Member States in relation to working conditions (Articles 117 and 118) and the more specific and prescriptive, of which Article 119 is an example.[80] It implied that these two categories are mutually exclusive, and then went on to add, in somewhat sinister vein:

[T]he fact that the fixing of certain conditions of employment—such as a special age-limit—may have pecuniary consequences is not sufficient to bring such conditions within the field of application of Article 119, which is based on the close connection which exists between the nature of the services provided and the amount of the remuneration. That is all the more so since the touchstone which forms the basis of Article 119—that is, the comparable nature of the services provided by workers of either sex—is a factor as regards which all workers are 'ex hypothesi' on an equal footing, whereas in many respects an assessment of the other conditions of employment and working conditions involves factors connected with the sex of the workers, taking into account considerations affecting the special position of women in the work process.[81]

As to the allegation that a general principle of EC law was breached in this situation, and that that general principle was specifically enforceable, the Court had this to say:

[A]s regards the relationships of employer and employee which are subject to national law, the Community had not, at the time of the events now before the Belgian court, assumed any responsibility for supervising and guaranteeing the observance of the principle of equality between men and women in working conditions other than remuneration.[82]

[80] See Chap. 2 for discussion of the origins of this distinction.
[81] [1978] ECR 1365, at 1377. In later decisions, particularly Case C-262/88 *Barber* v. *Guardian Royal Exchange Assurance Group* [1990] ECR I-1889, discussed in Chap. 2 and below, the Court has considerably eroded this distinction.
[82] [1978] ECR 1365 at 1378.

In other words, there was at the time of this action no enforceable EC law on working conditions to which the general principle of non-discrimination could be attached. This situation was reversed with the coming into force of the Equal Treatment Directive, to be discussed in the next section of the present chapter.

The potency of the principle of sex equality would, of course, be vastly increased if the Treaty were to be amended so as to contain a provision which articulated it in directly effective terms. The opportunity for such a reform was not made use of when the Amsterdam Treaty was agreed. Were such a directly effective article to be included in some future version of the Treaty, the doctrine of supremacy would enable individual litigants not only to use it to assert a positive right to sex equality throughout the entire field of application of the Treaty but also to impugn national law which sought to deny equality. This would, as discussed in Chapter 1, amount to fundamental constitutional protection for this basic human right.

THE EQUAL TREATMENT DIRECTIVE[83]

Background to the Instrument

In common with the Equal Pay Directive, this Directive was prompted by the Council's Resolution of 21 January 1974[84] concerning a social action programme, which included amongst its priorities 'action for the purpose of achieving equality between men and women as regards access to employment and vocational training and promotion and as regards working conditions, including pay'.[85] The Equal Pay Directive was regarded as carrying forward the programme in the field of pay. The Equal Treatment Directive aimed to regulate the other areas mentioned, with the exception of the 'definition and progressive implementation of the principle of equal treatment in matters of social security', which was to be dealt with by means of later instruments.[86] The Preamble to the Directive explains its specific aims as follows:

Whereas Community action to achieve the principle of equal treatment for men and women in respect of access to employment and vocational training and promotion and in respect of other working conditions also appears to be necessary;
Whereas equal treatment for male and female workers constitutes one of the

---

[83] Directive 76/207, OJ [1976] L39/40.
[84] OJ [1974] C13/1. See also Chap. 2.
[85] See the first recital in the Preamble to the Directive.
[86] See the final recital in the Preamble to the Directive, and also Chaps. 2 and 4 on the legislation subsequently enacted.

objectives of the Community, in so far as the harmonization of living and working conditions while maintaining their improvement are *inter alia* to be furthered.

In view of these far-reaching objectives, Article 100,[87] the 'harmonization' Article, was thought to constitute an insufficient legal authority for the Equal Treatment Directive. It is therefore based instead on Article²35,[88] available where action by the EC proves 'necessary to attain, in the course of the operation of the common market, one of the objectives of the Community, and [the] Treaty has not provided the necessary powers'. As discussed in Chapter 1, such a legal basis in no way inhibits the potential direct effect of a legal provision and indeed, as will be seen later in the present chapter, important parts of the Equal Treatment Directive have been held by the ECJ to confer rights directly on individuals. It is unfortunate, however, that a directive was chosen as the type of instrument to be used here, rather than a regulation; the latter could theoretically have been passed, since Article²35 authorizes the taking of 'appropriate measures', and it would have obviated the problem of lack of horizontal direct effect[89] which presents such a serious practical obstacle to the utility of social policy directives.

Substantive Rights Conferred by the Directive

Article 1 of the Directive enacts the aims of the instrument as expressed in the Preamble:

1. The purpose of this Directive is to put into effect in the Member States the principle of equal treatment for men and women as regards access to employment, including promotion, and to vocational training and as regards working conditions and, on the conditions referred to in paragraph², social security. This principle is hereinafter referred to as 'the principle of equal treatment.'
2. With a view to ensuring the progressive implementation of the principle of equal treatment in matters of social security, the Council, acting on a proposal from the Commission, will adopt provisions defining its substance, its scope and the arrangements for its application.[90]

It would seem to be the intention of Article 1(1) that equal treatment should be the rule throughout the territory covered by the Community. However, it does not make plain the precise geographical scope of the obligations it places on the Member States. At the heart of the difficulty is

---

[87] {Art. 94}.   [88] {Art. 308}.

[89] See discussion in Chap. 1.

[90] The first draft of the Equal Treatment Directive itself included social security as part of the 'working conditions' to which the principle of equal treatment must apply. It was removed from later versions of the instrument because of the complexities involved, but the Commission insisted that a commitment to cover social security in a future piece of legislation be written into the Equal Treatment Directive nevertheless.

the fact that it does not identify the essential constituents of 'treatment' and 'employment'; this leads to potential, but as yet unresolved, difficulties in cases with a multi-national element. For example, does the Directive govern a case where a job offer is made in a Member State but the job is to be performed outside that Member State?[91] If so, does it make any difference whether the job is to be performed inside or outside the Community? Does it make any difference where a job offer is actually made if the prospective employer is based in a Member State? In the light of the fundamental importance which the ECJ attaches to the principle of equality of the sexes,[92] it is arguable that the principle of equality demanded by the Directive should be engaged whenever there is a factual link between the employment and a Member State; thus, where a job offer (or other potentially discriminatory act) takes place on the territory of a Member State, or where the employer is based in that Member State, or where the job is to be performed in that Member State, then the requirements of the Directive should have to be complied with by the State concerned.

The exclusion of social security schemes from the ambit of the Directive in consequence of Article 1(2) is not complete.[93] The ECJ held in *Marshall v. Southampton and South-West Hants Area Health Authority*[94] that since the Equal Treatment Directive expresses a principle of fundamental importance, the derogation from it contained in Article 1(2) must be strictly construed.[95] Indeed, as Lenz AG has pointed out,[96] 'If matters of social security were to be excluded entirely from the scope of the Directive, the express reference to social security in Article 1(1) would make no sense'.[97] This is important in view of the limitations on the scope of the Social Security Directive,[98] discussed in Chapter 4. In *Meyers v. Adjudication Officer*,[99] the Court held that a social security scheme falls within the Equal Treatment Directive 'if its subject-matter is access to employment, including vocational training and promotion, or working conditions'.[100] Thus, the payment of family credit in the UK is governed by the Equal Treatment Directive because, albeit within the formal scheme of social

[91] This is of significance in the UK because the effect of ss. 6 and 10 of the Sex Discrimination Act 1975 is to exclude from the ambit of the Act job offers made in the UK where the work is to be performed wholly or mainly outside the UK.

[92] See the discussion above, and also below in relation to discrimination on the ground of transsexuality.

[93] Cf. Case 192/85 *Newstead* v. *Department of Transport* [1987] ECR 4753.

[94] Case 152/84 [1986] ECR 723, discussed further below.

[95] Ibid. at 746.

[96] In Case C-116/94 *Meyers* v. *Adjudication Officer* [1995] ECR I-2131, at 2136.

[97] See also Van Gerven AG in Joined Cases C-63 & 64/91 *Jackson and Cresswell* v. *Chief Adjudication Officer* [1992] ECR I-4737, at 4767.

[98] Directive 79/7, OJ [1979] L6/24.   [99] Op.cit., n. 96.

[100] Ibid. at 2149. But cf. the comments of Jacobs AG in Joined Cases C-245 & 312/94 *Hoever* v. *Land Nordrhein-Westfalen* [1996] ECR I-4895.

security, family credit is linked to the employment relationship; it is payable only where, at the time of making the claim, the claimant or his or her spouse or partner is employed,[101] and the purpose of the benefit is to encourage low-paid workers to remain in employment.[102] Its status is not undermined, according to the Court, by the fact that the benefit is always payable to the female partner, even where it is the male partner who is employed, nor by the fact that entitlement to the benefit lasts for 26 weeks irrespective of the earnings of the family during that period. Conversely, the Court held in *Jackson and Cresswell* v. *Chief Adjudication Officer*[103] that income support in the UK is not within the scope of the Equal Treatment Directive because the 'subject-matter' of the scheme is not access to employment; rather its purpose is exclusively the support of people in receipt of low incomes.

Article 2(1) goes on to spell out the scope of the equal treatment principle: 'For the purposes of the following provisions, the principle of equal treatment shall mean that there shall be no discrimination whatsoever on grounds of sex either directly or indirectly by reference in particular to marital or family status.' This provision, on its own, would appear to be incapable of taking direct effect, since it does not explain the circumstances in which it is to operate. When combined with the later provisions of the Directive, however, outlawing discrimination in relation to specifically defined matters, there is no doubt that this paragraph can be relied upon by individual litigants to show that both direct and indirect discrimination are forbidden.[104]

The wording of Article 2(1) is notably far-reaching in at least two respects. The first is that it provides that there must be no sex discrimination 'whatsoever'. This is a very much more powerful formulation than one which merely prohibits discrimination as between two identically or comparably placed individuals, as Article 119 appears to do. Discrimination may, of course, occur where one person receives more favourable treatment than that received by a colleague in the same circumstances. But it may occur in other cases as well, such as where there is no other colleague in similar circumstances but, if there were, that colleague would be more favourably treated.[105] This is the case of the hypothetical comparator, discussed in Chapter 2. There is also the

---

[101] In addition, the claimant's income must not exceed a stated level and there must be a child or other dependent person in the household.

[102] See also Case C-78/91 *Hughes* v. *Chief Adjudication Officer* [1992] ECR I-4839.

[103] Op.cit., n. 97.

[104] See the Court's comments to this effect in particular in Case 152/84 *Marshall* v. *Southampton and South West Hants Area Health Authority* [1986] ECR 723; and Case 222/84 *Johnston* v. *Chief Constable of the RUC* [1986] ECR 1651.

[105] See in particular Case 177/88 *Dekker* v. *Stichting Vormingscentrum Voor Jonge Volwassen Plus* [1990] ECR I-3941, discussed further below.

related case, again mentioned in Chapter 2, where two workers perform admittedly different tasks, such as where one task requires greater skill than the other, and the differential between the two pay levels or the two sets of working conditions is inordinately great. If the Court were at some future date to hold that Article 119 extends to hypothetical comparison (contrary to most of the indications it has so far given), these cases would be remediable via Article 119 in so far as they relate to pay, but not otherwise. All these situations, however, appear to fall within the scope of Article²(1) of the Equal Treatment Directive because of its ban on all discrimination 'whatsoever'. If this is correct, a further difficulty is, however, raised: what is the relationship between Article 119 and the Equal Treatment Directive? Are they mutually exclusive, as the British Equal Pay and Sex Discrimination Acts are expressed by their terms to be, or can there be an overlap between their spheres of operation? Unfortunately, the ECJ held in *Gillespie* v. *Northern Health and Social Services Board*[106] that they are mutually exclusive and that the Equal Treatment Directive does not apply to pay.[107] This conclusion throws into sharp focus the meaning of 'pay' for the purposes of Article 119.[108] On the one hand, the ability of Article 119 to take horizontal direct effect and to override the pensionable age exception contained in the Social Security Directive[109] encourages litigants to argue for a broad interpretation of 'pay' as therein defined; on the other hand, the ability of the Equal Treatment Directive to accommodate claims for hypothetical comparison may drive litigants to argue that the less obviously financial aspects of a contract of employment, though they could in a broad sense be regarded as consideration provided for the employee by the employer, are not 'pay' within the meaning of Article 119. The relationship between Article 119 and the Directive is discussed in greater detail below in relation to discrimination over dismissal.

As well as providing the basis for hypothetical comparisons, the expression 'no discrimination whatsoever on grounds of sex' has enabled a successful claim to be made in respect of discrimination on account of

---

[106] Case C-342/93 [1996] ECR I-475, also discussed in Chap. 2. See also the submissions of Elmer AG in Case C-139/95 *Balestra* v. *INPS* [1997] ECR I-549.

[107] Case C-342/93 at 501. This was said to be clear from the second recital to the Directive's Preamble, which provides: 'Whereas, with regard to pay, the Council adopted [the Equal Pay Directive] . . .'. Cf. the view expressed by Van Gerven AG in Case C-262/88 *Barber* v. *Guardian Royal Exchange Assurance Group* [1990] ECR I-1889, at 1925, and see also *Hammersmith and Queen Charlotte's Special Health Authority* v. *Cato* [1988] 1 CMLR 3.

[108] Discussed in Chap. 2.

[109] Directive 79/7, OJ [1979] L6/24, discussed further in Chap. 4; Art. 7 excludes from the scope of the instrument the determination of state pensionable age 'for the purposes of granting old-age and retirement pensions and the possible consequences thereof for other benefits'.

transsexuality. The word 'whatsoever' has led the Court to what has been described as the 'courageous' decision[110] that the scope of the Directive is not confined to discrimination against someone simply on account of their being biologically either female or male, but that it extends also to other discrimination which is more remotely connected with their sexual identity.[111] Thus, in *P* v. *S and Cornwall County Council*,[112] it held that the Directive prohibited the dismissal[113] of an employee where the true reason for the dismissal had been found by the referring court to be the employee's proposal to undergo gender reassignment.[114] The Court explained that the Directive:

. . . is simply the expression, in the relevant field, of the principle of equality, which is one of the fundamental principles of Community law. Moreover, . . . the right not to be discriminated against on grounds of sex is one of the fundamental human rights whose observance the Court has a duty to ensure . . .

Accordingly, the scope of the Directive cannot be confined simply to discrimination based on the fact that a person is of one or other sex. In view of its purpose and the nature of the rights which it seeks to safeguard, the scope of the Directive is also such as to apply to discrimination arising, as in this case, from the gender reassignment of the person concerned.

Such discrimination is based, essentially if not exclusively, on the sex of the person concerned. Where a person is dismissed on the ground that he or she intends to undergo, or has undergone, gender reassignment, he or she is treated unfavourably by comparison with persons of the sex to which he or she was deemed to belong before undergoing gender reassignment.

To tolerate such discrimination would be tantamount, as regards such a person, to a failure to respect the dignity and freedom to which he or she is entitled, and which the Court has a duty to safeguard.[115]

---

[110] See the opinion of Tesauro AG in Case C-13/94 *P* v. *S and Cornwall County Council* [1996] ECR I-2143, at 2157.

[111] Some would identify this as gender-based discrimination; for further discussion of the distinction between sex and gender and the reflection of this distinction in law, see Skidmore, 'Sex, Gender and Comparators in Employment Discrimination' (1997) 26 ILJ 51.

[112] Op cit., n. 110. See also Campbell and Lardy, 'Discrimination Against Transsexuals in Employment' (1996) 21 ELRev. 412 and Flynn's comments in (1997) 34 CMLRev. 367.

[113] See discussion below of Art. 5 of the Directive, prohibiting discrimination in relation to dismissal.

[114] This conclusion was of particular significance in the UK where the Sex Discrimination Act 1975 had not been interpreted hitherto as extending to this situation on the basis that the treatment received by the applicant would have been no different whether the gender reassignment had been male to female or *vice versa*. See *White* v. *British Sugar Corporation* [1977] IRLR 121. However, subsequently in *Chessington World of Adventures Ltd.* v. *Reed* [1997] IRLR 556, the Employment Appeal Tribunal held that the Sex Discrimination Act could be construed so as to cover unfavourable treatment on the ground of a declared intention to undergo gender reassignment.

[115] [1996] ECR I-2143, at 2165.

Tesauro AG added:

I regard as obsolete the idea that the law should take into consideration, and protect, a woman who has suffered discrimination in comparison with a man, or *vice versa*, but denies that protection to those who are also *discriminated against*, again by reason of sex, merely because they fall outside the traditional man/woman classification.[116]

This broad interpretation of the concept of 'sex' for the purposes of the Directive, combined with the Court's references to the fundamental right to equality and to dignity and freedom, lend considerable force to the view that the Directive also extends to discrimination on the ground of homosexuality.[117]

This issue has been referred to the ECJ by a Southampton industrial tribunal in *Grant* v. *South West Trains*[118] and by the High Court in *R.* v. *Secretary of State for Defence, Ex p. Perkins*.[119] In the latter, Lightman J held:

After the decision in the *Cornwall* case, it is scarcely possible to limit the application of the Directive to gender discrimination, as was held in the *Smith* case,[120] and there must be a real prospect that the European Court will take the further courageous step to extend protection to those of homosexual orientation, if a courageous step is necessary to do so. I doubt, however, whether any courage is necessary, for all that may be required is working out and applying in a constructive manner the implications of the Advocate General's Opinion and the judgment in the *Cornwall* case.[121]

In *Grant*, which concerns travel concessions granted by an employer in respect of the common law opposite-sex cohabitant of an employee but refused to a lesbian employee who was living with a female partner, Elmer

[116] Ibid. at 2153. See Barnard, '*P* v. *S*: Kite Flying or a New Constitutional Approach?' in *The Principle of Equal Treatment in EC Law*, eds. Dashwood and O'Leary (Sweet and Maxwell, London, 1997).

[117] Support might also be derived for the application of the Directive to discrimination on account of homosexuality from the fact that Art. 2(1) refers to discrimination on 'grounds' plural 'of sex'. On the other hand, Art. 6a {Art. 13} of the EC Treaty, added by the Amsterdam Treaty, appears to distinguish discrimination on the ground of sex from discrimination on the ground of sexual orientation. In *R.* v. *Ministry of Defence, Ex p. Smith* [1996] IRLR 100 (noted by Skidmore in 'Homosexuals Have Human Rights Too' (1996) 25 ILJ 63) and *Smith* v. *Gardner Merchant Ltd* [1996] ICR 790, UK courts have held that UK sex equality legislation does not protect homosexuals against discrimination on grounds of sexual orientation. For further discussion, see Wintermute, 'Recognising New Kinds of Direct Sex Discrimination: Transsexualism, Sexual Orientation and Dress Codes' (1997) 60 MLR 334 and *Homosexuality: A European Community Issue*, eds. Kees Waaldijk and Andrew Clapham (Martinus Nijhoff, Dordrecht, 1993).

[118] (1996) 69 EOR 2. Case C-249/96, pending before the ECJ at the time of writing.

[119] [1997] IRLR 297. The *Perkins* case challenges the Ministry of Defence's policy of dismissing all members of the armed services who have a homosexual orientation. The ECJ's ruling in this case was also pending at the time of writing.

[120] Op. cit., n. 117.

[121] [1997] IRLR 297, at 303.

AG has submitted that discrimination on the ground of sexual orientation is forbidden by EC law.[122] Although the *Cornwall* case technically concerned the Equal Treatment Directive, he argued that it had equal significance for Article 119 'which sets out the basic principle prohibiting discrimination based on sex'. In order to give full effect to that principle, he reasoned that Article 119 must be construed so as to preclude forms of discrimination against employees based on gender and he continued:

The provision must, in order to be effective, be understood as prohibiting discrimination against employees not solely on the basis of the employee's own gender but also on the basis of the gender of the employee's child, parent or other dependant. The provision must therefore also be regarded as precluding an employer from, for instance, denying a household allowance to an employee for sons under 18 living at home when such an allowance in otherwise equivalent circumstances was given for daughters living at home.[123]

His conclusion was that:

[A] provision in an employer's pay regulations under which the employee is granted travel concessions for a cohabitant of the opposite sex to the employee but refused such concessions for a cohabitant of the same sex as the employee constitutes discrimination on the basis of gender which falls within the scope of Article 119 . . .[124]

A second respect in which the wording of Article[2](1) is extensive is in its reference to discrimination in relation to marital or family status. The ECJ has never ruled specifically on the meaning of this part of the Directive, which is somewhat obscurely drafted. Discrimination on the basis of 'marital status' would appear to embrace any type of marital status, so that it seems to protect alike those who are married, those who have never been married, and those who were once married but whose marriage has ended because of death, divorce, or nullity.[125] The meaning of discrimination on the basis of 'family status' is less obvious, but this provision is perhaps designed to cover discrimination on the basis of a person's position within a family, for example as a parent, a child, or a grandparent. As discussed below, the ECJ has also held that discrimination based on pregnancy falls within the scope of Article[2] of the Directive.[126]

---

[122] Submissions of 30 September 1997.　　　　　　　[123] Ibid. at para. 16.

[124] Ibid. at para. 26. It remains to be seen, of course, whether the Court will follow the AG's submissions; *P* v. *Cornwall* required the Court to give a broad construction to the meaning of 'sex' for the purpose of determining whether a person has been discriminated against on the ground of his or her sex. In *Grant*, however, another step is needed, namely, to extend the scope of the principle of non-discrimination so as to cover discrimination against one person on account of *another* person's sex.

[125] Cf. the British Sex Discrimination Act 1975, s. 3, which forbids discrimination on the basis of marital status only as far as married persons are concerned.

[126] In Case 177/88 *Dekker* v. *Stichting Vormingscentrum Voor Jonge Volwassen Plus* [1990] ECR I-3941.

However, what remains unclear about this part of the Directive is whether discrimination on the grounds of marital and family status are prohibited *per se*, or whether they are only prohibited where they also constitute some form of sex discrimination, whether direct or indirect. The latter construction is probably the more likely; the main object of the Directive is, after all, to prohibit sex discrimination; and the phrase 'by reference in particular to marital or family status' suggests that these are merely examples of situations in which sex discrimination can occur.

It is also noteworthy that Article²(1) refers expressly to the two forms which discrimination may take, direct and indirect. As discussed in Chapter², both the Court's existing case law and the directive defining indirect discrimination[127] assume a consistent definition of discrimination for the purposes of most instruments of EC sex discrimination law. As will be seen below, a majority of the cases to date on the Equal Treatment Directive have actually involved direct discrimination.

Article 3 of the Directive is concerned with access to employment. It provides:

1. Application of the principle of equal treatment means that there shall be no discrimination whatsoever on grounds of sex in the conditions, including selection criteria, for access to all jobs or posts, whatever the sector or branch of activity, and to all levels of the occupational hierarchy.
2. To this end, Member States shall take the measures necessary to ensure that:
    (a) any laws, regulations and administrative provisions contrary to the principle of equal treatment shall be abolished;
    (b) any provisions contrary to the principle of equal treatment which are included in collective agreements, individual contracts of employment, internal rules of undertakings or in rules governing the independent occupations and professions shall be, or may be declared, null and void or may be amended;[128]
    (c) those laws, regulations and administrative provisions contrary to the principle of equal treatment when the concern for protection which originally inspired them is no longer well founded shall be revised; and that where similar provisions are included in collective agreements, labour and management shall be requested to undertake the desired revision.

Paragraph (1) of this provision was held by the ECJ in *Johnston* v. *Chief Constable of the RUC*,[129] in conjunction with Article²(1) of the Directive, to take direct effect. 'Access' to employment has a wide meaning; in *Meyers* v.

---

[127] Directive 97/80, OJ [1998] L14/6.

[128] For discussion of the importance of collective bargaining in the process of achieving sex equality, see Bercusson, *European Labour Law* (Butterworths, London, 1996), esp. Chap. 14.   [129] Case 222/84 [1986] ECR 1651.

Chief Adjudication Officer,[130] the Court held that it is 'not only the conditions obtaining before an employment relationship comes into being' which are covered by the concept of 'access' to employment; it also extends to factors which influence a person's decision as to whether or not to accept a job offer. Thus, 'the prospect of receiving family credit if he accepts low-paid work encourages an unemployed worker to accept such work, with the result that the benefit is related to considerations governing access to employment'.[131] On the other hand, in *Jackson and Cresswell* v. *Chief Adjudication Officer*,[132] the Court held that where a social security benefit scheme is merely intended to provide income support for those with insufficient means:

[T]he assertion that the method of calculating claimants' actual earnings, which are used as the basis for determining the amount of the benefits, might affect sole mothers' ability to take up access to vocational training or part-time employment, is not sufficient to bring such schemes within the scope of Directive 76/207.[133]

In practice, a particularly important instance of the application of Article 3(1) is in relation to pregnancy. In *Dekker* v. *Stichting Vormingscentrum Voor Jonge Volwassen Plus*[134] the ECJ held that the Article forbade an employer to refuse to employ a pregnant woman, who was otherwise suitable for the job. The fact of her pregnancy was the most important reason for her non-employment and, since this is a condition which can only apply to members of the female sex, this meant that the employer's action necessarily constituted direct discrimination on the ground of sex.[135] In *Handels-OG Kontorfunktionaerernes Forbund i Danmark* v. *Dansk Arbejdsgiverforening (acting for Aldi Marked K/S)*,[136] the Court added that this principle holds good throughout the relevant period of maternity leave.[137] It is clear from *Dekker* and also from the ECJ's subsequent decision in *Webb* v. *EMO (Air Cargo) Ltd.*[138] that there is no need to resort to comparison with the treatment afforded, or which would be afforded, to a member of the opposite sex where the detrimental treatment complained of can be shown to be referable to pregnancy; thus, it is incorrect to draw comparisons between the treatment received by a pregnant woman and that which

[130] Case C-116/94 [1995] ECR I-2131.
[131] Ibid. at 2151.
[132] Joined Cases C-63 & 64/91 [1992] ECR I-4737, also discussed in Chap. 4.
[133] Ibid. at 4782. Consider also Case C-77/95 *Züchner* v. *Handelskrankenkasse Bremen* [1996] ECR I-5689, also discussed in Chap. 4.
[134] Case 177/88 [1990] ECR I-3941, noted by Asscher-Vonk in (1991) 20 ILJ 152.
[135] See also Chap. 2.
[136] Case 179/88 [1990] ECR I-3979; both *Dekker* and *Aldi* are noted by Nielsen in (1992) 29 CMLRev. 160. See also More, 'Reflections on Pregnancy Discrimination under EC law' [1992] JSWFL 48.
[137] See also discussion below of the Pregnancy Directive.
[138] Case C-32/93 [1994] ECR I-3567.

would be received by a male comparator suffering from some temporary medical ailment.

The second paragraph of Article 3 provided the basis for a successful infringement action brought by the Commission against the UK under Article 169.[139] The Commission alleged that, at the date of the action (1982), no legislative instrument in force in the UK provided that discriminatory provisions contained in collective agreements, rules of undertakings, or rules governing independent occupations and professions were, or could be declared, void, or could be amended. The UK government replied that s. 18 of the Trade Union and Labour Relations Act 1974 provided that collective agreements were presumed not to have been intended by the parties to be legally enforceable unless they were in writing and contained a provision in which the parties expressed their intention that the agreements were to be legally enforceable. Collective agreements, it said, were not usually legally binding in the UK in practice for this reason. Accordingly, to require them to be annulled would be like 'beating the air'. In any event, it pointed out that, even if collective agreements containing sex discriminatory terms did exist, those terms would be rendered void by s. 77(1) of the Sex Discrimination Act 1975, which provides:

A term of a contract is void where:

   (a) its inclusion renders the making of the contract unlawful by virtue of this
        Act, or
   (b) it is included in furtherance of an act rendered unlawful by this Act, or
   (c) it provides for the doing of an act which would be rendered unlawful by
        this Act.

Similarly, said the government, any discriminatory provisions contained in the internal rules of an undertaking, or of an occupational body, would be void if they were incorporated into an individual's contract of employment; and if any discrimination in employment were to result from the existence of such a discriminatory provision in the internal rules of an undertaking or of an occupational or professional body, that discrimination would be caught by s. 6 of the Sex Discrimination Act 1975, which outlaws discrimination by employers against their employees as regards all aspects of the employment relationship. The government also pointed to s. 13(1) of the Sex Discrimination Act, which makes it unlawful for a body which can confer an authorization or qualification to discriminate on the ground of sex. However, both the Advocate General and the Court rejected these contentions. Rozès AG submitted:

---

[139] Case 165/82 *Commission* v. *UK* [1983] ECR 3431. Art. 4(b) and 5(b) also make identical
provision to Art. 3(b) in their fields of application; see below.

[W]orkers have easier access to collective agreements, the internal rules of undertakings and the rules governing the independent occupations and professions than to Directive 76/207 or to the UK laws depriving those documents, in general, of legal binding force. Thus, workers may believe that because their contracts of employment reproduce possibly discriminatory provisions from the types of document referred to they are legal and may not be challenged at law and the workers may therefore be deprived of the advantages of a Directive which was in fact adopted for their benefit. In order to avoid such risks of confusion, the best course is to make it possible for such discriminatory provisions to be removed from those documents, as required by the Directive.[140]

The Court held:

The Directive . . . covers all collective agreements without distinction as to the nature of the legal effects which they do or do not produce. The reason for that generality lies in the fact that, even if they are not legally binding as between the parties who sign them or with regard to the employment relationships which they govern, collective agreements nevertheless have important *de facto* consequences for the employment relationships to which they refer, particularly in so far as they determine the rights of the workers and, in the interests of industrial harmony, give undertakings some indication of the conditions which employment relationships must satisfy or need not satisfy. The need to ensure that the Directive is completely effective therefore requires that any clauses in such agreements which are incompatible with the obligations imposed by the Directive upon the Member States may be rendered inoperative, eliminated or amended by appropriate means.[141]

The UK responded to this ruling by enacting s. 6 of the Sex Discrimination Act 1986, providing for the automatic invalidity of discriminatory provisions contained in collective agreements, employers' rules and the rules of trades unions, employers' associations, professional organizations, and qualifying bodies. In its original form, this was merely a declaratory provision and it was not until its amendment by s. 32 of the Trade Union Reform and Employment Rights Act 1993 (following the threat of further infringement proceedings against the UK by the Commission) that a statutory remedy was prescribed by means of which an affected individual could ascertain the nullity of a discriminatory collective provision.

This provision, however, merely enables a litigant to establish the nullity of a discriminatory provision but not to have it replaced by a non-discriminatory one; the ECJ's decision in *Kowalska* v. *Freie and Hansestadt Hamburg*,[142] is consequently of particular importance. The Court held, in apparently general terms, that:

---

[140] [1983] ECR 3431, at 3454.

[141] Ibid. at 3447.

[142] Case 33/89 [1990] ECR I-2591. See also Case C-184/89 *Helga Nimz* v. *Freie und Hansestadt Hamburg* [1991] ECR I-297 and Joined Cases C-399, 409 and 425/92, C-34, 50 and 78/93 *Stadt Lengerich* v. *Helmig* [1994] ECR I-5727, all discussed in Chap. 2.

[W]here there is indirect discrimination in a clause in a collective wage agreement, the class of persons placed at a disadvantage by reason of that discrimination must be treated in the same way and made subject to the same scheme, proportionately to the number of hours worked, as other workers . . .[143]

Although the Court ultimately based its ruling in this case on Article 119, it would appear that precisely the same principle would apply to terms of the agreement other than pay. However, the problem of lack of horizontal direct effect would arise for the Equal Treatment Directive, where the collective agreement was sought to be enforced against a body other than an organ of the State.[144]

Article 4 provides:

Application of the principle of equal treatment with regard to all types and to all levels of vocational guidance, vocational training, advanced vocational training and retraining, means that Member States shall take all necessary measures to ensure that:

(a) any laws, regulations or administrative provisions contrary to the principle of equal treatment shall be abolished;

(b) any provisions contrary to the principle of equal treatment which are included in collective agreements, individual contracts of employment, internal rules of undertakings or in rules governing the independent occupations and professions shall be, or may be declared, null and void or may be amended;

(c) without prejudice to the freedom granted in certain Member States to certain private training establishments, vocational guidance, vocational training, advanced vocational training and retraining shall be accessible on the basis of the same criteria and at the same levels without any discrimination on grounds of sex.

This Article was held by the ECJ in *Johnston* v. *Chief Constable of the RUC*[145] to be directly effective, so as to confer an enforceable right on a policewoman to the same type of firearms training as was provided to her male colleagues.

Article 5 applies to working conditions generally, including dismissal, which has of course assumed a heightened significance in recent recessionary times. It provides:

1. Application of the principle of equal treatment with regard to working conditions, including the conditions governing dismissal, means that men and women shall be guaranteed the same conditions without discrimination on grounds of sex.

---

[143] Case 33/89 at 2613.
[144] See discussion in Chap. 1.
[145] Case 222/84 [1986] ECR 1651, discussed further below. See also Morris, 'Sex Discrimination, Public Order and the European Court' (1987) Public Law 334, and Arnull, 'The Beat Goes On' (1987) 12 ELRev. 56.

2. To this end, Member States shall take the measures necessary to ensure that:

    (a) any laws, regulations and administrative provisions contrary to the principle of equal treatment shall be abolished;

    (b) any provisions contrary to the principle of equal treatment which are included in collective agreements, individual contracts of employment, internal rules of undertakings or in rules governing the independent occupations and professions shall be, or may be declared, null and void or may be amended;

    (c) those laws, regulations and administrative provisions contrary to the principle of equal treatment when the concern for protection which originally inspired them is no longer well founded shall be revised; and that where similar provisions are included in collective agreements labour and management shall be requested to undertake the desired revision.

'Working conditions' are not confined to those set out in the contract of employment or applied by the employer in respect of a worker's employment. Having established this principle, the Court was able to go to hold in *Meyers* v. *Chief Adjudication Officer*[146] that family credit in the UK, although a social security benefit, also constitutes part of a person's 'working conditions'.

France has been found by the ECJ to be in breach of Article 5 by maintaining in force a law prohibiting night work in industry by women (but not men).[147] Article 5 has also been held to take direct effect in these circumstances.[148] In accordance with the Court's usual reasoning in this regard, the direct effect of the Article does not excuse a Member State from legislating to give effect to the Directive.[149]

The ECJ has applied the same principle in relation to pregnancy for the purpose of Article 5 as for Article 3;[150] so, for example, it held in *Habermann-Beltermann* v. *Arbeiterwohlfahrt*[151] that the termination of an employment contract on account of the employee's pregnancy, whether by

---

[146] Case C-116/94 [1995] ECR I-2131.

[147] Case C-197/96 *Commission* v. *France* (nyr). See also Case C-207/96 *Commission* v. *Italy*, (nyr).

[148] Case C-345/89 *Stoeckel* [1991] ECR I-4047. Cf.Case C-158/91 *Levy* [1993] ECR I-4287 and Case C-13/93 *Office National de l'Emploi* v. *Minne* [1994] ECR I-371 where, as discussed in Chap. 1, France was permitted to rely on Art. 234 {Art. 307} to preserve national legislation which conflicted with Art. 5 of the Directive but which was necessary in order to comply with a pre-existing international obligation pursuant to ILO Convention No. 89 which France had not at the relevant date yet renounced. See also Wuiame, 'Night Work for Women—*Stoeckel* Revisited' (1994) 23 ILJ 95 and Kilpatrick, 'Production and Circulation of EC Night Work Jurisprudence' (1996) 25 ILJ 169.

[149] *Commission* v. *France*, op. cit., n. 147; see also Chap. 1.

[150] See Case 179/88 *Handels-OG Kontorfunktionaerernes Forbund i Danmark* v. *Dansk Arbejdgiverforening (acting for Aldi Marked K/S)* [1990] ECR I-3979.

[151] Case C-421/92 [1994] ECR I-1657.

annulment or avoidance, concerns women alone and therefore constitutes direct discrimination on the ground of sex. Unfortunately however, as discussed in Chapter², the Court has recently hinted that such direct discrimination may sometimes be justifiable, though without actually expressing the view that this principle applied in the cases referred to it. Thus, in *Habermann-Beltermann* it held that, where a woman's contract of employment is for an indefinite period, termination on account of her pregnancy is not 'justified' by a statutory provision prohibiting pregnant women from engaging in nightwork.[152] Similarly, in *Webb* v. *EMO (Air Cargo) Ltd,*[153] where a woman employee was dismissed on account of pregnancy because she would be absent from work during the leave of another employee whom she had been engaged to replace, it held:

[D]ismissal of a pregnant woman recruited for an indefinite period cannot be justified on grounds relating to her inability to fulfil a fundamental condition of her employment contract. The availability of an employee is necessarily, for the employer, a precondition for the proper performance of the employment contract. However, the protection afforded by Community law to a woman during pregnancy and after childbirth cannot be dependent on whether her presence at work during maternity is essential to the proper functioning of the undertaking in which she is employed. Any contrary interpretation would render ineffective the provisions of the Directive.

In circumstances such as those of Mrs Webb, termination of a contract for an indefinite period on grounds of the woman's pregnancy cannot be justified by the fact that she is prevented, on a purely temporary basis, from performing the work for which she has been engaged . . .[154]

The corollary of this holding is, of course, that, had Mrs Webb been engaged on a temporary contract, her dismissal might have been 'justified' and thus lawful.[155]

Doubts have also lingered in the area of pregnancy discrimination as to the scope for comparisons with male colleagues. It was seen above that the Court held in *Dekker*[156] that there is no need to compare a woman's treatment with that of a male colleague where her non-appointment can be shown to be referable to pregnancy. Furthermore, in *Webb*, the Court added:

---

[152] See also further discussion in relation to Art. 2(3) of the Directive.

[153] Case C-32/93 [1994] ECR I-3567, commented on by More in 'Sex, Pregnancy and Dismissal' (1994) 19 ELRev. 653, by Boch in (1996) 33 CMLRev. 547, and by Fredman in 'Parenthood and the Right to Work' (1995) 111 LQR 220.

[154] Case C-32/93 at 3587-8.

[155] See also discussion below in relation to Art. 10 of the Pregnancy Directive, Directive 92/85, OJ [1992] L348/1, prohibiting dismissal of a worker on the ground of her pregnancy. On the relationship between the Equal Treatment Directive and the Pregnancy Directive, see Jacqmain, 'Pregnancy As Grounds for Dismissal' (1994) 23 ILJ 355.

[156] Case 177/88 *Dekker* v. *Stichting Vormingscentrum Voor Jonge Volwassen Plus* [1990] ECR I-3941.

[T]here can be no question of comparing the situation of a woman who finds herself incapable, by reason of pregnancy discovered very shortly after the conclusion of the employment contract, of performing the task for which she was recruited with that of a man similarly incapable for medical or other reasons.

As Mrs Webb rightly argued, pregnancy is not in any way comparable with a pathological condition, and even less so with unavailability for work on non-medical grounds . . .[157]

On the other hand, once the protected period of maternity leave has expired, the treatment received by a woman may be compared with that receivable by a colleague of the opposite sex, even where pregnancy continues to play a causative role in the matter. Thus, in *Aldi*,[158] a woman dismissed for prolonged absence from work some time after her maternity leave had expired but because of an illness which had its roots in her earlier pregnancy did not experience unlawful discrimination, since a man who was away from work for comparable periods on account of illness would also have been dismissed. In *Larsson*,[159] this principle was extended to cover a case where the woman's illness began during her pregnancy and was a consequence of that pregnancy but continued after her statutory period of maternity leave had expired. The Court repeated its remarks in *Aldi*, saying:

[I]n the case of an illness manifesting itself after the maternity leave, there is no reason to distinguish an illness attributable to pregnancy or confinement from any other illness, and . . . such a pathological condition is therefore covered by the general rules applicable in the event of illness.[160]

It went on to say that it did not mean by that to draw a distinction:

[O]n the basis of the moment of onset or first appearance of the illness. It merely held that, in the factual situation submitted to it on that occasion, there was no reason to distinguish, from the point of view of the principle of equal treatment enshrined in the Directive, between an illness attributable to pregnancy or confinement and any other illness . . .

[M]ale and female workers are equally exposed to illness. Although certain disorders are, it is true, specific to one or other sex, the only question is whether a woman is dismissed on account of absence due to illness in the same circumstances as a man; if that is the case, then there is no direct discrimination on grounds of sex . . .

The Directive therefore does not preclude dismissal on the ground of periods

---

[157] [1994] ECR I-3567, at 3586-7. See also McGlynn, 'Equality, Maternity and Questions of Pay' (1996) 21 ELRev. 327.

[158] Case 179/88 *Handels-OG Kontorfunktionaerernes Forbund i Danmark* v. *Dansk Arbejdsgiverforening (acting for Aldi Marked K/S)* [1990] ECR I-3979.

[159] Case C-400/95 *Handels-OG Kontorfunktionaerernes Forbund i Danmark, acting on behalf of Helle Elisabeth Larsson* v. *Dansk Handel & Service, acting on behalf of Fotex Supermarked A/S* (nyr). [160] Ibid. at para. 16.

of absence due to an illness attributable to pregnancy or confinement, even where such illness first appeared during pregnancy and continued during and after the period of maternity leave.[161]

Ms Larsson argued that it was discriminatory to take into account her absence from work due to sickness in the interval between the beginning of her pregnancy and the beginning of her maternity leave. If those absences were discounted, together with her annual leave which she had tacked onto the end of her maternity leave, she would have been absent on account of her illness for less than four weeks prior to her dismissal. The Court accepted that during whatever period was permitted to her as maternity leave under national law, she was protected from dismissal on account of absence from work. However:

Outside the periods of maternity leave laid down by the Member States to allow female workers to be absent during the period in which the problems inherent in pregnancy and confinement occur, . . . and in the absence of national or, as the case may be, Community provisions affording women specific protection, a woman is not protected under the Directive against dismissal on grounds of periods of absence due to an illness originating in pregnancy . . . [A]s male and female workers are equally exposed to illness, the Directive does not concern illnesses attributable to pregnancy or confinement.

The principle of equal treatment enshrined in the Directive does not, there-fore, preclude account being taken of a woman's absence from work between the beginning of her pregnancy and the beginning of her maternity leave when calculating the period providing grounds for her dismissal under national law.[162]

The only mitigation offered by the Court was that today the situation would be dealt with by the Pregnancy Directive:[163]

[T]he Community legislature subsequently provided . . . for special protection to be given to women, by prohibiting dismissal during the period from the begin-ning of their pregnancy to the end of their maternity leave, save in exceptional cases unconnected with their condition . . . It is clear from the objective of that provision that absence during the protected period, other than for reasons un-connected with the employee's condition, can no longer be taken into account as grounds for subsequent dismissal. However, Directive 92/85 had not yet been adopted when Ms Larsson was dismissed.[164]

It is submitted that, despite its rigour and its apparent divergence from the Court's statement about comparisons in *Webb*, its decision in *Larsson* is analytically correct. The statutory tort of sex discrimination occurs where

[161] Ibid. at paras. 17-20.   [162] Ibid. at paras. 23-4.

[163] Directive 92/85, OJ [1992] L348/1, discussed below.

[164] *Larsson* judgment, op. cit., n. 159, para. 25. It remains significant nevertheless, for the purposes of UK law, whether the claim is for sex discrimination or for unfair dismissal on account of pregnancy: in the latter, but not in the former, cases there is a cap on the level of compensation receivable.

a person receives adverse treatment on the ground of sex. As has already been argued in Chapter², this means that there must be essentially two constituent elements of the tort: causation and adverse treatment. In holding that detrimental treatment of a woman because she is pregnant is necessarily direct discrimination, the Court appears to be asserting no more than that the element of causation is satisfied in such cases: the treatment is grounded on sex. However, it is also necessary to go on and to establish the adverse character of that treatment and that, in the view of the present writer, can only be demonstrated by a comparison with how a similarly situated member of the opposite sex would be treated. Before the advent of the Pregnancy Directive, the Court's zeal to protect pregnant women led it to concentrate its attention exclusively on the element of causation in these cases, to the exclusion of the element of adverse treatment. The effect of this was to establish a core principle which was later partially reflected in the Pregnancy Directive: namely, that non-appointment or dismissal on account of pregnancy is unlawful. The Court's zeal was not, however, unlimited and it has returned to a more principled approach in the cases dealing with adverse treatment resulting from illness, even where that illness has its roots in pregnancy; thus, in *Aldi* and *Larsson*, there is no doubt that the dismissals could be described as grounded in sex (since they were inextricably connected with pregnancy), but they did not amount to discrimination because they were not adverse treatment by comparison with that which would have been received by a temporarily incapacitated man.[165]

At the core of all these difficulties is the tension between the essentially even-handed concept of discrimination and the wholly one-sided situation of pregnancy. The cases analysed above show that to use the concept of discrimination as the law's chief method of reconciling pregnancy with employment risks corrupting the underlying principles of discrimination law. It is therefore very much preferable, both for the welfare of pregnant women and for the coherence of discrimination law, that a separate régime be maintained conferring positive rights in relation to pregnancy, as the Pregnancy Directive has begun to do.[166]

Difficult problems have also manifested themselves as regards the

---

[165] The distinction between pregnancy and sickness arising out of pregnancy is shortly to be tested. In *Brown* v. *Rentokil Ltd.* (pending before the ECJ at the time of writing), the House of Lords has referred the question of whether it is unlawfully discriminatory to dismiss a sick pregnant woman in circumstances where a man absent from work for the same length of time would also have been dismissed: see (1996) 68 EOR 2 and (1997) 73 EOR 47. Cf. in *Stephenson* v. *Wellworth Ltd* (1997) 73 EOR 46, where the Northern Ireland Court of Appeal held that an illness arising out of pregnancy and occurring before the birth is to be equated with pregnancy itself and therefore that a woman dismissed in this situation did not have to show that a sick man would have been treated more favourably.

[166] See Fredman, 'A Difference With Distinction: Pregnancy and Parenthood Reassessed' (1994) 110 LQR 106.

relationship between Article 5 of the Directive and certain other provisions of EC law. First of all, how is the principle of equality as regards 'dismissal' to be reconciled with continuing permissible differential state pensionable ages and their knock-on effects as regards other benefits? The ECJ's case law in this area is really only comprehensible on the basis that it has shifted its ground to a more radical approach over recent years. The issue was first raised before the ECJ in *Burton* v. *British Railways Board*.[167] British Rail had decided to pay voluntary redundancy benefits to certain of its employees, provided that they were aged 55 or over in the case of women and 60 or over in the case of men. Mr Burton was 58 years of age. He wished to take advantage of the scheme and argued that he was being discriminated against unlawfully. Since this issue was at the time of the action excluded from the ambit of the British Sex Discrimination Act 1975 by s. 6(4) of that Act, the effect of the Equal Treatment Directive became crucial. The case was sent to the ECJ for a preliminary ruling and it held that 'dismissal' must be 'widely construed so as to include termination of the employment relationship between a worker and his employer, even as part of a voluntary redundancy scheme'.[168] Access to such a scheme was therefore held to be potentially within the scope of Article 5 of the Directive; however, on the facts, this situation did not fall foul of the Directive, it was held, because the qualifying ages for access to the scheme were linked to the differential state retirement pension ages for men and women; both men and women became eligible for entrance to the scheme five years before each reached the state retirement pension age. Since the Social Security Directive[169] permits differential state retirement pension ages to continue for the present, the Court said that it followed that EC law had not been breached.[170]

Marshall v. *Southampton and South-West Hants Area Health Authority*[171] then made it clear that compulsory retirement also falls within the ambit of Article 5. Ms Marshall, who had been employed as a dietician by the Health Authority, was dismissed by the Authority when she was 62 years of age. The Authority had a policy, which had become an implied term of Ms Marshall's contract of employment, that employees were to retire at the age at which they became entitled to draw the state retirement pension (that is to say, at 65 for men and 60 for women). Ms Marshall did not want to retire at 60 and the Authority waived its normal policy in her case for

[167] Case 19/81 [1982] ECR 555.

[168] Case 19/81 [1982] ECR 555, at 575.

[169] As to which see Chap. 4.

[170] It seems unlikely that the ECJ would today decide this case in the same way in the light of its decision in Case-262/88 *Barber* v. *Guardian Royal Exchange Assurance Group* [1990] ECR I-1889. See the comments of the Court of Appeal to this effect in *Thomas* v. *Adjudication Officer and Secretary of State for Social Security* [1990] IRLR 436.

[171] Case 152/84 [1986] ECR 723.

two years. She complained that her dismissal caused her financial loss because of the difference between her earnings as a dietician and her pension, and she also complained of the premature loss of job satisfaction. Her allegation that the situation contravened the national anti-discrimination legislation was met with the answer that it was saved by the then very broadly drafted s. 6(4) of the Sex Discrimination Act 1975. The issue became, as in *Burton*, whether or not the case fell foul of EC law, particularly Article 5 of the Equal Treatment Directive. The Health Authority argued that, as in *Burton*, account must be taken of the link between the retirement ages it stipulated contractually and the state retirement pension ages. The laying down of different ages for the compulsory termination of a contract of employment, it argued (with considerable logic on its side), merely reflected the minimum ages fixed by the state scheme: a male employee was allowed to continue in employment until the age of 65 precisely because he was not protected by the provision of a state pension until that age, whereas a female employee could draw a state pension at the age of 60. The ECJ, however, rejected this argument, in doing so drawing a somewhat artificial distinction between retirement age and pensionable age.[172] With the benefit of hindsight, this case can be identified as the beginning of a trend in which the ECJ began to erode the Social Security Directive's exception for state pensionable age and its knock-on effects. It held:

Article 5(1) of Council Directive 76/207/EEC provides that application of the principle of equal treatment with regard to working conditions, including the conditions governing dismissal, means that men and women are to be guaranteed the same conditions without discrimination on grounds of sex. In its judgment in the *Burton* case . . . the Court had already stated that the term 'dismissal' contained in that provision must be given a wide meaning. Consequently, an age limit for the compulsory dismissal of workers pursuant to an employer's general policy concerning retirement falls within the term 'dismissal' construed in that manner, even if the dismissal involves the grant of a retirement pension.

As the Court emphasised in its judgment in the *Burton* case, Article 7 of Council Directive 79/7/EEC [the Social Security Directive] expressly provides that the Directive does not prejudice the right of Member States to exclude from its scope the determination of pensionable age for the purposes of granting old age and retirement pensions and the possible consequences thereof for other benefits falling within the statutory social security schemes. The Court thus acknowledged that benefits tied to a national scheme which lays down a different minimum pensionable age for men and women may lie outside the ambit of the aforementioned obligation.

---

[172] In *Duke v. Reliance Systems Ltd* [1988] 2 WLR 359, at 373, Lord Templeman protested that the respondent in that case 'could not reasonably be expected to appreciate the logic of Community legislators in permitting differential retirement pension ages but prohibiting differential retirement ages'.

However, in view of the fundamental importance of the principle of equality of treatment, which the Court has reaffirmed on numerous occasions, Article 1(2) of Council Directive 76/207/EEC, which excludes social security matters from the scope of that Directive, must be interpreted strictly. Consequently, the exception to the prohibition of discrimination on grounds of sex provided for in Article 7(1)(a) of Council Directive 79/7/EEC applies only to the determination of pensionable age for the purposes of granting old age and retirement pensions and the possible consequences thereof for other benefits.

In that respect it must be emphasised that, whereas the exception contained in Article 7 of Council Directive 79/7/EEC concerns the consequences which pensionable age has for social security benefits, this case is concerned with dismissal within the meaning of Article 5 of Council Directive 76/207/EEC.

Consequently, the answer to the first question referred to the Court by the Court of Appeal must be that Article 5(1) of Council Directive 76/207/EEC must be interpreted as meaning that a general policy concerning dismissal involving the dismissal of a woman solely because she has attained the qualifying age for a state pension, which age is different under national legislation for men and for women, constitutes discrimination on grounds of sex, contrary to that Directive.[173]

The Court went on to conclude that Article 5(1) was also directly effective, so as to confer on Ms Marshall rights which she could enforce 'vertically' against an organ of the state.[174]

It therefore appeared after *Marshall* that the ECJ regarded as vital the question of whether the age prescribed governed access to retirement benefits (apparently excluded from the scope of the Directive) or merely dismissal (covered by the Directive). This distinction has, however, come to be blurred in part as a result of the Court's decision in *Roberts* v. *Tate and Lyle Ltd*.[175] This case clearly demonstrates the impossibility of simultaneously respecting the notion of equality in the context of retirement and preserving differential state retirement pension ages. Ms Roberts was made redundant by Tate and Lyle when she was aged 53, as part of a mass redundancy which followed the closure of the depot at which she worked. She was a member of the Tate and Lyle occupational pension scheme, which was contracted out of the state scheme and thus in a sense constituted a substitute for a state social security benefit.[176] It provided for compulsory retirement with a pension at the age of 65 for men and 60 for women. On the closure of the depot, the employers had agreed severance terms with Ms Roberts's trade union, by virtue of which all employees made redundant were to be offered either a cash payment or an early

---

[173] [1986] ECR 723, at 745-6.
[174] See Chap. 1 for discussion of direct effect in relation to directives.
[175] Case 151/84 [1986] ECR 703, noted by Arnull in 'Some More Equal than Others?' (1986) 11 ELRev. 229.
[176] See Chap. 2.

pension up to five years before the date of their entitlement under the scheme; thus, the pension would have been payable to women over 55 and to men over 60. The male employees, however, protested that this constituted discrimination against them, so eventually the employers agreed to pay an immediate pension to both men and women over 55. Ms Roberts in turn protested against this solution, arguing that the situation contravened EC law because a male employee was now entitled to receive a pension ten years before his normal retirement age whereas a female employee only received the pension five years before her normal retirement age. The Court, however, chose to treat this as essentially a dismissal case, saying:

[T]he question of interpretation which has been referred . . . does not concern the conditions for the grant of the normal old-age or retirement pension but the termination of employment in connection with a mass redundancy caused by the closure of part of an undertaking's plant. The question therefore concerns the conditions governing dismissal and falls to be considered under Council Directive 76/207.

Article 5(1) of Council Directive 76/207 provides that application of the principle of equal treatment with regard to working conditions, including the conditions governing dismissal, means that men and women are to be guaranteed the same conditions without discrimination on grounds of sex.

In its judgment in the *Burton* case the Court has already stated that the term 'dismissal' contained in that provision must be given a wide meaning. Consequently, an age limit for the compulsory redundancy of workers as part of a mass redundancy falls within the term 'dismissal' construed in that manner, *even if the redundancy involves the grant of an early retirement pension*.[177]

The Court went on to hold:

Even though the retirement scheme at issue does not 'prima facie' discriminate between men and women with regard to the conditions for dismissal, it is still necessary to consider whether the fixing of the same age for the grant of an early pension nevertheless constitutes discrimination on grounds of sex in view of the fact that under the UK statutory social security scheme the pensionable age for men and women is different . . . As the Court emphasised in its judgment in the *Burton* case, Article 7 of Council Directive 79/7 expressly provides that the Directive does not prejudice the right of Member States to exclude from its scope the determination of pensionable age for the purposes of granting old-age and retirement pensions and the possible consequences thereof for other benefits falling within the statutory social security schemes. The Court thus acknowledged that benefits linked to a national scheme which lays down a different minimum pensionable age for men and women may lie outside the ambit of the aforementioned obligation.

However, in view of the fundamental importance of the principle of equality of

[177] [1986] ECR 703, at 720. (Emphasis supplied.)

treatment, which the Court has reaffirmed on numerous occasions, Article 1(2) of Council Directive 76/207, which excludes social security matters from the scope of that Directive, must be interpreted strictly. Consequently, the exception to the prohibition of discrimination on grounds of sex provided for in Article 7(1)(a) of Council Directive 79/7 applies only to the determination of pensionable age for the purposes of granting old-age and retirement pensions and to the consequences thereof for other social security benefits.

In that respect it must be emphasised that, whereas the exception contained in Article 7 of Council Directive 79/7 concerns the consequences which pensionable age has for social security benefits, this case is concerned with dismissal within the meaning of Article 5 of Council Directive 76/207. In those circumstances the grant of a pension to persons of the same age who are made redundant amounts merely to a collective measure adopted irrespective of the sex of those persons in order to guarantee them all the same rights.[178]

Again with the benefit of hindsight, it is probably implicit in this judgment that the ECJ was not concerned about the early retirement pensions granted here, since they were granted to both sexes at the same age. This development was explicitly articulated in *Barber* v. *Guardian Royal Exchange Assurance Group*,[179] in which the ECJ ruled that it is contrary to Article 119 for an occupational pension scheme to adopt different retirement ages for men and women and for redundancy payments to be related to different ages for the two sexes. The effect of this ruling was clearly to take much of the force and significance out of the ECJ's former distinction between retirement age and pensionable age.

However, a second line of demarcation which remains difficult to draw in this area is that between Article 5 of the Equal Treatment Directive and Article 119 of the Treaty. One group of cases before the ECJ seemed to support a distinction between the quantum of the benefit involved (an Article 119 issue) and the conditions under which access to the benefit was granted (an Equal Treatment Directive issue). For example, in the *Burton*, *Marshall*, and *Roberts* decisions, the Court ruled that, where an age limit was applied in relation to selection for compulsory retirement, that fell within the Equal Treatment Directive, even though there were financial implications for the litigants involved. However, in *Bilka-Kaufhaus GmbH* v. *Weber Von Hartz*,[180] the Court held that the conditions of access to a supplementary pension scheme were challengeable via Article 119,[181] and

---

[178] Ibid. at 720-1.
[179] Case C-262/88 [1990] ECR I-1889, also discussed in Chap. 2 and below.
[180] Case 170/84 [1986] ECR 1607, also discussed in Chap. 2.
[181] In Case C-57/93 *Vroege* v. *NCIV Instituut voor Volkshuisvesting BV* [1994] ECR I-4541 and Case C-128/93 *Fisscher* v. *Voorhuis Hengelo BV* [1994] ECR I-4583, the ECJ repeated that it followed from *Bilka* 'that Article 119 covers not only entitlement to benefits paid by an occupational pension scheme but also the right to be a member of such a scheme' (at 4573 and 4593 respectively).

in *Rinner-Kuhn* v. *FWW Spezial-Gebaudereinigung GmbH*[182] it ruled that an hours-based exclusion from the right to sick pay fell within Article 119.[183] *Barber* v. *Guardian Royal Exchange Assurance Group*[184] also takes this approach. Mr Barber was a member of a pension fund established by Guardian which operated a non-contributory, contracted-out[185] occupational pension scheme. Normal pensionable age under the scheme was 62 for men and 57 for women but employees' contracts of service also provided that, in the event of redundancy, members of the pension fund were entitled to an immediate pension provided only that they had reached the age of 55 in the case of men and 50 in the case of women. Staff who did not fulfil these conditions received cash benefits calculated on the basis of the number of years of their service and a deferred pension payable at normal pensionable age. Mr Barber was made redundant when he was 52. Guardian paid him the cash benefits just referred to, a statutory redundancy payment, and an *ex gratia* payment. He complained of unlawful sex discrimination on the basis that a woman of his age and in his position would have received an immediate retirement pension, as well as the statutory redundancy payment, and that the total value of these benefits would have been greater than the amount Mr Barber in fact received. One of the questions referred by the Court of Appeal to the ECJ asked whether this was contrary to Article 119, in particular in the light of the fact that the age conditions imposed by Guardian reflected the differential contained in the state pension scheme. The ECJ did not explain how it distinguished this situation from its earlier decisions in *Burton, Marshall,* and *Roberts,* which of course suggested that this was an Equal Treatment Directive issue rather than an Article 119 issue; it simply held:

Article 119 prohibits any discrimination with regard to pay as between men and women, whatever the system which gives rise to such inequality. Accordingly, it is contrary to Article 119 to impose an age condition which differs according to sex in respect of pensions paid under a contracted-out scheme, even if the difference between the pensionable age for men and that for women is based on the one provided for by the national statutory scheme.[186]

Van Gerven AG was considerably more analytical in his treatment of this matter, although it is not clear whether the Court accepted his analysis since it made no reference to it. He submitted:

---

[182] Case 171/88 [1989] ECR 2743.
[183] Note also Case C-184/89 *Nimz* v. *Freie und Hansestadt Hamburg* [1991] ECR I-297 (discussed in Chap. 2) and Case C-1/95 *Gerster* v. *Freistaat Bayern* (nyr), (also discussed in Chap. 2).
[184] Case C-262/88 [1990] ECR I-1889.
[185] See Chap. 2 for further discussion of 'contracted-out' pension schemes.
[186] [1990] ECR I-1889, at 1953.

The judgments in *Defrenne III, Burton, Marshall, Beets-Proper,* and apparently in *Roberts* as well, are all connected with an (age) condition or (age) limit regarding the termination of an employment relationship. That condition or limit was intended to select employees with whom the employment relationship was to be terminated on certain financial conditions. Viewed in those terms, the age condition or age-limit is clearly revealed as a working condition, more particularly as a condition governing dismissal or, in a wider context, termination, that is to say a condition for the selection of employees whose employment relationship is to be terminated . . . If, on the other hand, the age condition or limit does not play such a role but relates, as in this case, to the grant of a terminal payment or a pension to employees the termination of whose employment relationship has already been decided upon on the basis of other (supposedly non-discriminatory) factors, then it constitutes a condition governing pay which comes within Article 119. The *Bilka-Kaufhaus* case, in which no age condition was involved, was also concerned with the grant of entitlement to a pension (as was the recent judgment in *Rinner-Kuhn* where a condition for the payment of remuneration in the event of illness was brought within Article 119).

Essentially, the distinction does amount to bringing within Article 119 working conditions (including conditions governing dismissal or other forms of redundancy) which directly govern access to, that is to say the grant of, remuneration (including a payment or pension benefit in connection with redundancy), but not the conditions precedent thereto which govern the inception, continuation or termination of the employment relationship, even though those conditions are attended by financial consequences or accompanied by financial provisions (such as terminal payments or pension benefits).[187]

It remains to be seen from future case law whether the Court is merely changing its mind and broadening the scope of Article 119 in a more or less untrammelled fashion, or whether on the other hand it accepts the Advocate General's distinction between a condition governing the grant of a payment and a condition governing the continuation of the employment relationship.[188]

Another important practical issue is the applicability of Article 5(1) of the Directive to instances of 'sexual harassment' in employment. There is of course no universally accepted definition of this term. The issue has been widely litigated in the USA where the Equal Employment Opportunity Commission has issued guidelines to explain the circumstances in which sexual harassment becomes unlawful discrimination.[189] These provide:

---

[187] Ibid. at 1926-7.

[188] The question has been referred to the ECJ by the House of Lords in *R. v. Secretary of State for Employment, Ex p. Seymour-Smith* [1997] 1 WLR 473, where the Court has been asked whether, if compensation for unfair dismissal constitutes 'pay' within Art. 119, the conditions determining whether a worker has the right not to be unfairly dismissed fall within Art. 119 or the Equal Treatment Directive.

[189] EEOC Guidelines on Sexual Harassment, 1980, 29 CFR, s. 1604, 11(f).

Unwelcome sexual advances, requests for sexual favours, and other verbal or physical conduct constitute sexual harassment when

1. Submission to such conduct is made either explicitly or implicitly a term or condition of an individual's employment,
2. Submission to or rejection of such conduct by an individual is used as the basis for employment decisions affecting such individual, or
3. Such conduct has the purpose or effect of unreasonably interfering with an individual's work performance or creating an intimidating, hostile, or offensive working environment.

The gist of the offence is unwanted sexual behaviour in the work-place, which causes some kind of damage or detriment to its victim.

Because of the lack of a standard definition, it is difficult to assess the extent of the problem posed in practice by sexual harassment, although most estimates suggest that it is considerable. The first empirical evidence as to incidence came from the USA, where the problem was orginally articulated and given a name; the US Merit Systems Protection Board questioned 3,000 Federal civil servants (both male and female) and found that 42 per cent of the female employees reported having experienced sexual harassment during the two-year period from May 1978 to May 1980; 15 per cent of males also reported having been sexually harassed during the same period.[190] This picture is roughly reflected by the findings of more recent European surveys. The most extensive study of the situation within the EC was conducted by Rubenstein for the EC Commission,[191] who concluded:

Whatever its precise incidence, all the available data now indicates that sexual harassment at work is not an isolated phenomenon perpetuated by the odd socially-deviant man. On the contrary, it is clear that for millions of women in the EEC today, sexual harassment is an unpleasant and unavoidable part of their working lives.[192]

Empirical studies suggest a clear link between status and the likelihood of being harassed. The US Merit Systems Protection Board Study found that the most sexual harassment was experienced by young women, and especially those who were well-educated and trying to break out of traditional occupational confines. In most instances, the harasser was the woman's supervisor, which obviously compounds the difficulty she faces in making a complaint within the organization concerned. Similarly, the

---

[190] 'Sexual Harassment in the Federal Workplace', US Merit Systems Protection Board Study, 1981.

[191] Rubenstein, *The Dignity of Women at Work* (Commission of the European Communities, 1988). See this study for details of empirical data on the incidence of sexual harassment within the Member States of the EC. The galvanising effect of the report on the governments of the Member States is recounted by Rubenstein in 'Sexual Harassment: European Commission Recommendation and Code of Practice' (1992) 21 ILJ 70.

[192] *The Dignity of Women at Work* at 16.

European evidence collected by Rubenstein suggests that 'sexual harassment is disproportionately perpetrated by male supervisors or managers upon female subordinates'.[193] The cost of sexual harassment to society in general, and to businesses in particular, is likely to be colossal. Again, the empirical studies show that it frequently damages the victim's health, causing anxiety and depression which leads to her taking time off work, and sometimes to her leaving her employment altogether. These sorts of consequences of sexual harassment led the US Merit Systems Protection Board to conclude that sexual harassment had cost the US Federal government $189 million over the two years surveyed.

There seems little doubt that most forms of sexual harassment in the work-place are forbidden by Article 5 of the Equal Treatment Directive: to subject a woman employee to sexual harassment is not to grant her equal working conditions to those enjoyed by her male colleagues, without discrimination on grounds of sex.[194] Rubenstein found, however, that at the date of his study, even though the majority of Member States had passed national legislation ostensibly carrying out their obligations under the Equal Treatment Directive, the principle that sexual harassment constitutes unlawful discrimination had yet to receive recognition by the courts.[195] In addition, as will be seen later in the present chapter, the remedies mandated for breach of the Equal Treatment Directive are not specific and thus do not guarantee an appropriate remedy in cases of sexual harassment. Rubenstein therefore concluded that there was a need for a separate directive dealing with sexual harassment, which would declare that sexual harassment at work is contrary to the Equal Treatment Directive, but would contain certain further provisions as well. If such a directive could not, however, be agreed by the Member States, litigants should be reminded of the existence of Article 5 of the Equal Treatment Directive: it can probably be enforced directly against the State where the State as employer is vicariously liable for sexual harassment perpetuated by one of its employees, and it can on general principles be used to shed

---

[193] Ibid. at 15. The Commission's Code of Practice on sexual harassment, discussed below, comments: 'Some specific groups are particularly vulnerable to sexual harassment. Research in several Member States, which documents the link between sexual harassment and the recipient's perceived vulnerability, suggests that divorced and separated women, young women and new entrants to the labour market and those with irregular or precarious employment contracts, women in non-traditional jobs, women with disabilities, lesbians and women from racial minorities are disproportionately at risk. Gay men and young men are also vulnerable to harassment'.

[194] But see Dine and Watt, 'Sexual Harassment: Moving Away From Discrimination' (1995) 58 MLR 343 for the argument that discrimination law provides an inadequate theoretical basis for the remedying of sexual harassment.

[195] He found, in fact, that it was only in the UK and Ireland that there was relatively unequivocal judicial acceptance that sexual harassment constitutes unlawful sex discrimination.

light on the meaning which should be ascribed by the national courts to national measures implementing the Equal Treatment Directive.

Rubenstein's proposed directive would have focused on preventing sexual harassment from occurring in the first place, or from recurring. This is in contrast to existing EC anti-discrimination legislation which concentrates on remedying unlawful discrimination after it has taken place. It would have defined sexual harassment as 'verbal or physical conduct of a sexual nature which the perpetrator knew or should have known was offensive to the victim'. Under the scheme, sexual harassment would become unlawful if:

(a)   rejection of, or submission to, such conduct by the victim is used, or is threatened to be used, as a basis for a decision affecting her employment or her terms and conditions of employment or

(b)   the victim can reasonably complain that such conduct harmed her working environment.[196]

In addition, it would become the duty of every employer to take reasonably practicable steps to maintain a work-place free of the risk to employees of sexual harassment, and employers would be liable for any unlawful sexual harassment committed by their employees at the work-place unless they could show that reasonably practicable steps had been taken to prevent harassment. In addition, the Commission would be deputed to publish a Code of Practice giving guidance on reasonably practicable steps to prevent and deal with sexual harassment at work. As to sanctions for unlawful sexual harassment, the proposed directive would have required Member States to ensure that the relevant courts or tribunals were empowered to provide 'assistance' where appropriate to those found liable for unlawful sexual harassment by requiring them to present to the court or tribunal for its approval a suitable plan outlining the corrective and preventive action to be taken to ensure that similar acts did not occur in the future. In the view of the present writer, the directive should also require that courts and tribunals dealing with sexual harassment claims be given specifically enforceable powers to enjoin harassment, breach of any such an order being a serious offence (such as contempt of court); whilst a preventive and educative role for a directive on sexual harassment is clearly a laudable aim, there is also an overriding need to protect victims who actually suffer such harassment.

The proposed directive would also have recognized the potential embarrassment and humiliation suffered by the victim of sexual harassment who makes a legal claim. Accordingly, it would have provided for Member States to take appropriate measures to ensure that the utilization of the judicial process is not deterred by unjustified publicity

---

[196] Rubinstein, *The Dignity of Women at Work*, 104.

and does not entail an unwarranted intrusion into the claimant's private life. As will be seen later in the present chapter, the protection against victimization provided by the Equal Treatment Directive is undesirably limited, and so the proposed directive contained a broader formulation for cases of sexual harassment; it required:

Member States to take such measures as are necessary to protect employees against dismissal, transfer or other detrimental treatment by the employer as a reaction to a complaint within the undertaking or to any legal proceedings aimed at enforcing compliance with the right to be protected against the risk of sexual harassment at work.[197]

A formal response to the Rubenstein Report came on[2]9 May 1990, when the Council of Ministers passed, not a directive, but a resolution on the dignity of women and men at work.[198] It is of course both legally and politically significant that a binding legal instrument was not used here, but the importance of 'soft law' as an aid to the construction of domestic legislation should be borne in mind.[199] The Resolution endorses many of Rubenstein's proposals. Part I contains a definition of sexual harassment:

The Council affirms that conduct of a sexual nature, or other conduct based on sex affecting the dignity of women and men at work, including conduct of superiors and colleagues, constitutes an intolerable violation of the dignity of workers or trainees and is unacceptable if:

(a)   such conduct is unwanted, unreasonable and offensive to the recipient;[200]
(b)   a person's rejection of or submission to such conduct on the part of employers or workers (including superiors or colleagues) is used explicitly or implicitly as a basis for a decision which affects that person's access to vocational training, access to employment, continued employment, promotion, salary or any other employment decisions; and or
(c)   such conduct creates an intimidating, hostile or humiliating work environment for the recipient.

In Part II, the Council stresses that sexual harassment may well amount, in particular circumstances, to a breach of Articles 3, 4, and 5 of the Equal Treatment Directive, and it goes on to:

3.   Remind employers that they have a responsibility to seek to ensure that the work environment is free from:

(a)   unwanted conduct of a sexual nature or other conduct based on sex affecting the dignity of women and men at work;
(b)   victimization of a complainant or of a person wishing to give, or giving, evidence in the event of a complaint . . .

---

[197] Rubenstein, *The Dignity of Women at Work*, 104.
[198] OJ [1990] C157/3.
[199] See discussion in Chap. 1.
[200] Notice the subjective nature of this definition.

It urges action by the Member States to develop awareness on the part of both employers and workers to counter sexual harassment, to develop measures to deal with the issue in the public sector which can serve as an example to the private sector, and to encourage appropriate anti-sexual harassment clauses in collective agreements.

The Commission was charged with the production of a Code of Conduct on the matter by 1 July 1991, the specific aim of the Code being to 'provide guidance based on examples and best practice in the Member States on initiating and pursuing positive measures designed to create a climate at work in which women and men respect one another's human integrity'. It adopted a Recommendation on the protection of the dignity of women and men at work on 27 November 1991, and annexed a 'Code of Practice'[201] to this Recommendation.[202] The Code spells out in full a definition of sexual harassment, illustrates circumstances in which it occurs and then explains the contraventions of law which it may constitute.[203] It focuses, however, on harassment as a form of discrimination and emphasises that the prime objective should be to change behaviour and attitudes to prevent it from occurring. It therefore recommends a number of practical steps, to be taken in the main by employers, including the issuing of detailed policy statements condemning sexual harassment and explaining complaints procedures, the provision of training for managers and supervisors, and the articulation of effective internal practices to help employees to utilize complaints procedures.[204]

The Member States were required by the Recommendation to inform the Commission within three years of the measures taken by them in pursuance of it, to enable the Commission to draw up a report on the overall position within the Community.[205] That subsequent report showed 'a clear lack of progress' on the matter.[206] Few Member States were found to have taken coherent action and, in particular, only Belgium, France and the Netherlands had enacted specific legislation requiring employers to be proactive in combating sexual harassment. In other Member States the

---

[201] *Sic.*

[202] Commission Recommendation 92/131, OJ [1992] L49/1. Michael Rubenstein and the Dutch social affairs journalist, Ineke de Vries, acted as consultants to the Commission in the drafting of the Code. Rubenstein has pointed out in 'Sexual Harassment: European Commission Recommendation and Code of Practice' (1992) 21 ILJ 70 that the Code was annexed to a Recommendation in order to enhance its status.

[203] The Code was referred to by the Employment Appeal Tribunal in *Wadman* v. *Carpenter Farrer Partnership* [1993] IRLR 374 as a means of elucidating the law on sexual harassment to be applied by an industrial tribunal. See also Lester, 'Some Reflections on the EC's Code of Conduct on Sexual Harassment' [1994] JSWFL 354.

[204] See Dine and Watt, 'Sexual Harassment: Hardening the Soft Law' (1994) 19 ELRev. 104.

[205] Article 4 of the Recommendation.

[206] 'Consultation of management and labour on the prevention of sexual harassment at work' COM(96) 373 final.

existing legislation was found to be inadequate and the Commission also questioned whether national collective agreements had been implemented at local level. In view of these disappointing findings, the Commission suggested a new 'global approach', involving comparison of different national policies to try to identify a strategy for improving the efficacy of existing measures; significantly, it also reverted to the original view of Rubenstein that a binding instrument might be required.[207] The Commission began a new round of negotiations with the two sides of industry in 1997 in an attempt to draw up a collective EU-wide agreement to combat sexual harassment in the work-place; the social partners were charged with reaching an agreement within nine months on what constitutes sexual harassment, how it can be prevented and on a possible system of confidential counsellors. If such an agreement could not be arrived at, the Commission warned that it would pursue other ways of preventing work-place harassment, including possibly a new directive.[208]

Article 6 of the Equal Treatment Directive provides:

Member states shall introduce into their national legal systems such measures as are necessary to enable all persons who consider themselves wronged by failure to apply to them the principle of equal treatment within the meaning of Articles 3, 4 and 5 to pursue their claims by judicial process after possible recourse to other competent authorities.

Its importance was revealed in *Von Colson and Kamann* v. *Land Nordrhein-Westfalen*.[209] Women social workers had applied for vacant posts in a German prison for male offenders. Although they were placed at the top of the list of candidates by the social workers' committee, they were moved down by the recruiting authority, which eventually selected two male candidates. The local labour court found that it was quite clear from the attitude of the authority that the female candidates had been discriminated against on the ground of their sex. Their problems were compounded by the fact that, under German law, they were not entitled to demand that the jobs be offered to them and, indeed, even their right to compensation appeared to be severely limited: they were entitled only to be reimbursed their expenses incurred in making the unsuccessful job applications (for example, postage and travel expenses, and the cost of compiling a *curriculum vitae*). The German court sought a preliminary ruling from the ECJ, asking essentially what remedies are mandated by the

---

[207] See also the Fourth Action Programme on Equal Opportunities for Women and Men (1996-2000) OJ [1995] L335/37, discussed further in Chap. 5.

[208] See 'EC Consultation on Sexual Harassment' (1997) 75 EOR 33 and CREW Reports (1997) 17, No. 5/6, p. 13.

[209] Case 14/83 [1984] ECR 1891, noted by Arnull in 'Sanctioning Discrimination' (1984) 9 ELRev. 267. See also Curtin, 'Effective Sanctions and the Equal Treatment Directive: The *Von Colson* and *Hartz* Cases' (1985) 22 CMLRev. 505.

Equal Treatment Directive in such a situation. The ECJ pointed out that, although Article 189 leaves Member States freedom to choose the ways and means of ensuring that a directive is implemented, they nevertheless remain under an obligation to ensure that the substance of the directive is complied with; they must see that 'the directive is fully effective, in accordance with the objective which it pursues'.[210] It went on to hold that the Equal Treatment Directive does not prescribe any specific remedies for sex discrimination, so that it does not, for example, entitle a victim of discrimination to demand a contract of employment where the non-selection was on grounds of sex. However, since Article 6 of the Directive requires there to be proper judicial remedies, what remedies there are must be sufficient to fulfil the objectives of the legislation. Thus:

Although . . . full implementation of the directive does not require any specific form of sanction for unlawful discrimination, it does entail that that sanction be such as to guarantee real and effective judicial protection. Moreover it must also have a real deterrent effect on the employer. It follows that where a Member State chooses to penalize the breach of the prohibition of discrimination by the award of compensation, that compensation must in any event be adequate in relation to the damage sustained. In consequence it appears that national provisions limiting the right to compensation of persons who have been discriminated against as regards access to employment to a purely nominal amount, such as, for example, the reimbursement of expenses incurred by them in submitting their application, would not satisfy the requirements of an effective transposition of the directive.[211]

It follows from this that Article 6 can be used by litigants in national courts to challenge undue restrictions placed on national remedies; the only proviso to this is the usual one in the case of directives, namely that the directive itself can only be enforced directly against organs of the State.[212] Thus, in *Dekker* v. *Stichting Vormingscentrum Voor Jonge Volwassen Plus*[213] the ECJ held that 'when the sanction chosen by a Member State is contained within the rules governing an employer's civil liability, any breach of the prohibition of discrimination must, in itself, be sufficient to make the employer liable, without there being any possibility of invoking the grounds of exemption provided by national law'.[214] The presence or absence of fault, which was normally relevant in Netherlands law, was therefore irrelevant here.[215] Similarly, the ECJ held in *Draehmpaehl* v. *Urania Immobilienservice ohG*[216] that:

---

[210] Case 14/83 at 1905-6.

[211] Ibid. at 1908. When the case returned to the local court, compensation amounting to six months' pay was awarded.

[212] But note the technique relied on in *Von Colson* itself whereby a national court interprets what national legislation there is so as to accord with the terms of a directive; this may be done whether or not the defendant is an organ of the State. See discussion in Chap. 1.

[213] Case 177/88 [1990] ECR I-3941.   [214] Ibid. at 3976.

[215] In the UK, s. 66(3) of the Sex Discrimination Act 1975 originally provided that no

[*See next page for n. 215 (cont.) and n. 216*]

[T]he Directive precludes provisions of domestic law which . . . make reparation of damage suffered as a result of discrimination on grounds of sex in the making of an appointment subject to the requirement of fault.[217]

It went on to add:

That conclusion cannot be affected by the German government's argument that proof of such fault is easy to adduce since, in German law, fault entails liability for deliberate or negligent acts. It must be pointed out in this regard that . . . the Directive does not provide for any ground of exemption from liability on which the person guilty of discrimination could rely and does not make reparation of such damage conditional on the existence of fault, no matter how easy it would be to adduce proof of fault.[218]

In *Marshall* v. *Southampton and South-West Hants Area Health Authority (No. 2)*,[219] an industrial tribunal assessing the compensation due to Ms Marshall following her enforced discriminatory retirement found that the existing UK statutory maximum for such compensation,[220] which was £6,250 at the time of Ms Marshall's dismissal and £8,500 at the date of the hearing, was 'inadequate' within the meaning intended by the ECJ in *Von Colson*. The case was appealed up to the House of Lords, which sought a preliminary ruling from the ECJ on the matter. The ECJ held:

Article 6 does not prescribe a specific measure to be taken in the event of a breach of the prohibition of discrimination, but leaves Member States free to choose between the different solutions suitable for achieving the objective of the Directive, depending on the different situations which may arise.

However, the objective is to arrive at real equality of opportunity and cannot therefore be attained in the absence of measures appropriate to restore such equality when it has not been observed . . . [T]hose measures must be such as to guarantee real and effective judicial protection and have a real deterrent effect on the employer.

Such requirements necessarily entail that the particular circumstances of each breach of the principle of equal treatment should be taken into account. In the event of discriminatory dismissal . . ., a situation of equality could not be restored without either reinstating the victim of discrimination or, in the alternative, granting financial compensation for the loss and damage sustained.

---

damages were available in respect of unintentional indirect discrimination; in view of the argument that this breached the principles of adequate compensation and full liability, this limitation was removed by the Sex Discrimination and Equal Pay (Miscellaneous Amendments) Regulations 1996, SI 1996, No. 438.

[216] Case C-180/95 [1997] ECR I-2195.

[217] Ibid. at para. 19.

[218] Ibid. paras. 20-1.

[219] [1988] IRLR 325.

[220] Under s. 65(2) of the Sex Discrimination Act 1975. The statutory maximum was removed after the decision in *Marshall (No. 2)* by the Sex Discrimination and Equal Pay (Remedies) Regulations 1993, SI 1993, No. 2798.

Where financial compensation is the measure adopted in order to achieve the objective indicated above, it must be adequate, in that it must enable the loss and damage actually sustained as a result of the discriminatory dismissal to be made good in full in accordance with the applicable national rules.[221]

Later it added:

[T]he fixing of an upper limit of the kind at issue in the main proceedings cannot, by definition, constitute proper implementation of Article 6 of the Directive, since it limits the amount of compensation *a priori* to a level which is not necessarily consistent with the requirement of ensuring real equality of opportunity through adequate reparation for the loss and damage sustained as a result of discriminatory dismissal.

. . . [F]ull compensation for the loss and damage sustained . . . cannot leave out of account factors, such as the effluxion of time, which may in fact reduce its value. The award of interest, in accordance with the applicable national rules, must therefore be regarded as an essential component for the purposes of restoring real equality of treatment.[222]

However, in its later decision in *Draehmpaehl* v. *Urania Immobilienservice ohG*,[223] the Court resiled somewhat from its tough stance that an upper limit on damages contravenes Article 6. The German legislation involved limited to three months' salary the compensation payable for discrimination over appointment to a job; it also limited to six months' salary the total compensation payable in such a situation where claims were made by several people. The Court held that these limitations were in most cases precluded by the Directive, in particular since there were no similar limitations to be found in analogous provisions of German law. Nevertheless, despite repeating its earlier comments that compensation must guarantee real and effective judicial protection, have a real deterrent effect on the employer and be adequate in relation to the damage sustained, it conceded that the ceiling on compensation was permissible where the applicant would not have got the job even had there been no discrimination:

---

[221] Case C-271/91 [1993] ECR I-4367, at 4407-8. Cf. the view of Van Gerven AG that 'compensation must be adequate in relation to the damage sustained but does not have to be equal thereto' (at 4390). The ECJ's judgment is analyzed by Curtin in (1994) 31 CMLRev. 63, by Grief in 'Compensation for Sex Discrimination' (1993) 22 ILJ 314, and by Fitzpatrick and Szyszczak in 'Remedies and Effective Judicial Protection in Community Law' (1994) 57 MLR 434.

[222] Case C-271/91 at 4409. As More points out in 'Compensation for Discrimination?' (1993) 18 ELRev. 533, the judgment does not provide an answer to the question of whether national courts can restrict the period over which interest is payable, by excluding the time between the unlawful conduct and the date when the claim is brought, if this delay can be attributed to the conduct of the applicant. See also the editorial comment on this decision in (1993) 18 ELRev. 365.

[223] Case C-180/95 [1997] ECR I-2195.

[R]eparation may take account of the fact that, even if there had been no discrimination in the selection process, some applicants would not have obtained the position to be filled since the applicant appointed had superior qualifications. It is indisputable that such applicants, not having suffered any damage through exclusion from the recruitment process, cannot claim that the extent of the damage they have suffered is the same as that sustained by applicants who would have obtained the position if there had been no discrimination in the selection process.

Consequently, the only damage suffered by [such] an applicant . . . is that resulting from the failure, as a result of discrimination on grounds of sex, to take his application into consideration . . .

[I]t does not seem unreasonable for a Member State to lay down a statutory presumption that the damage suffered by [such] an applicant . . . may not exceed a ceiling of three months' salary.

In this regard, it must be made clear it is for the employer, who has in his possession all the applications submitted, to adduce proof that the applicant would not have obtained the vacant position even if there had been no discrimination.[224]

This unprincipled and unimaginative conclusion does not respect the Court's own rule that compensation must be an adequate reflection of the loss sustained in the particular circumstances; where, for example, an employer discriminates in such a way as to cause extreme distress and injury to feelings, there is no logical reason to suppose that the amount of damages which would properly compensate for that head of loss would necessarily be limited in such an arbitrary fashion.

In *Marshall (No. 2)*,[225] the Court also held Article 6 to be directly effective so as to enable a victim of discrimination to rely on it as against an authority of the State.[226] To the argument that this frustrated the discretion entrusted to the Member States by the Directive in relation to remedies, the Court replied:

The fact that Member States may choose among different solutions in order to achieve the objective pursued by the Directive depending on the situations which may arise, cannot result in an individual's being prevented from relying on Article 6 in a situation such as that in the main proceedings where the national authorities have no degree of discretion in applying the chosen solution.

---

[224] Ibid. at paras. 33-6.

[225] Op. cit., n. 221.

[226] The editors of the *Equal Opportunities Review* in (1993) 51 EOR 51 make an interesting point in relation to people who contemplate relying retrospectively on the direct effect of Art. 6 to claim larger amounts of damages than they were awarded in sex discrimination claims; they face the difficulty that their cases are already decided and the matter is thus *res judicata*. However, the *Emmott* principle (discussed in Chap. 1) suggests that limitation periods barring those who have not made a claim do not begin to run until proper implementation of the Directive. The editors conclude that 'it is difficult to see why the law should treat those who did not make a claim at all more favourably than it treats those who did make a successful claim but were incorrectly compensated'.

It should be pointed out in that connection that, as appears from the judgment in Joined Cases C-6 & 9/90 *Francovich* v. *Italy* [1991] ECR I-5357, at paragraph 17, the right of a state to choose among several possible means of achieving the objectives of a directive does not exclude the possibility for individuals of enforcing before national courts rights whose content can be determined sufficiently precisely on the basis of the provisions of the directive alone.[227]

Putting this in a slightly different way, the Member State had constrained its own discretion in this situation by choosing the remedy of damages; having done so, Article 6 was directly effective so as to ensure the efficacy of this remedy.[228]

The emphasis placed by the ECJ in *Von Colson, Marshall (No.2)* and *Draehmpaehl* on the element of deterrence is interesting; deterrence is not normally regarded as one of the objectives of the civil law, which traditionally concentrates its attention on restitution and compensation rather than on seeking to change future behaviour patterns. The express mention of deterrence in the context of remedies for sex discrimination seems to underline what a serious view the ECJ takes of the issue of sex equality. It remains to be seen from the future case law of the Court whether it also indicates that exemplary, as well as purely compensatory, damages should be available in appropriate cases of unlawful sex discrimination.[229]

Johnston v. *Chief Constable of the RUC*[230] also cast important light on the meaning of Article 6. Ms Johnston, who was a member of the Royal Ulster Constabulary's full-time Reserve, complained that the Chief Constable's refusal to renew her contract of employment was unlawfully discriminatory. Her action before the Belfast industrial tribunal was obstructed by the Secretary of State issuing a certificate under Article 53 of the Sex Discrimination (Northern Ireland) Order 1976, stating that Ms Johnston's contract was not renewed in order to safeguard national security and to

---

[227] Case C-271/91 [1993] ECR I-4367 at 4410.

[228] It is therefore strongly arguable that, where a Member State chooses to make some sort of specific enforcement available in sex discrimination cases, as the UK does in providing for a recommendation that the employer take certain action under the Sex Discrimination Act 1975, s. 65(1)(c), that specific enforcement must be effective. A recommendation is, however, not effective, because there are very limited sanctions for its non-observance under the Sex Discrimination Act, s. 65(3). It follows that more effective specific remedies such as reinstatement, engagement, and injunctions to restrain continuing acts of discrimination must be granted by UK courts and tribunals as a result of Art. 6 of the Directive. Injunctions are today available in the UK in the limited sphere of application of the Protection From Harassment Act 1997.

[229] If so, UK law remains in breach of Art. 6, since exemplary damages are not available in domestic sex discrimination claims: *AB* v. *South West Water Services* [1993] 1 All ER 609, *Deane* v. *London Borough of Ealing* [1993] IRLR 209, *Ministry of Defence* v. *Cannock* [1994] IRLR 509 and *Ministry of Defence* v. *Meredith* [1995] IRLR 539; see further Arnull, 'EC Law and the Dismissal of Pregnant Servicewomen' (1995) 24 ILJ 215.

[230] Case 222/84 [1986] ECR 1651.

protect public safety and public order. The effect of such a certificate under Northern Ireland law was to withdraw the matter from the consideration of courts and tribunals. Ms Johnston argued that this contravened Article 6 of the Directive. The ECJ agreed with her, saying:

The requirement of judicial control stipulated by [Article 6 of the Equal Treatment Directive] reflects a general principle of law which underlies the constitutional traditions common to the Member States. That principle is also laid down in Articles 6 and 13 of the European Convention for the Protection of Human Rights and Fundamental Freedoms of 4 November 1950 (1953) (Cmd. 8969). As the European Parliament, Council and Commission recognized in their joint declaration of 5 April 1977 (OJ 1977 No.C 103, p. 1) and as the Court has recognized in its decisions, the principles on which that Convention is based must be taken into consideration in Community law.

By virtue of Article 6 of Council Directive 76/207/EEC, interpreted in the light of the general principle stated above, all persons have the right to obtain an effective remedy in a competent court against measures which they consider to be contrary to the principle of equal treatment for men and women laid down in the Directive. It is for the Member States to ensure effective judicial control as regards compliance with the applicable provisions of Community law and of national legislation intended to give effect to the rights for which the Directive provides.

A provision which, like Article 53(2) of the Sex Discrimination (Northern Ireland) Order 1976, requires a certificate such as the one in question in the present case to be treated as conclusive evidence that the conditions for derogating from the principle of equal treatment are fulfilled allows the competent authority to deprive an individual of the possibility of asserting by judicial process the rights conferred by the Directive. Such a provision is therefore contrary to the principle of effective judicial control laid down in Article 6 of the Directive.[231]

Exactly as in *Von Colson* and *Marshall (No. 2)*, although the complainant here could not enforce her rights under the Directive within the sphere of freedom of action allowed to the Member States, she could enforce the instrument directly (against an organ of the State) when the State outstepped the limits of the discretion conferred on it. It was, in other words, directly effective where the State attempted to withdraw from her all possible routes to judicial redress.

A further important issue in relation to remedies concerns the burden of proof required to be discharged before a remedy can be granted. A complainant in any discrimination claim normally faces considerable difficulties in proving the case. If the law places the entire burden of proof throughout the proceedings upon the complainant, then all the respondent needs to do in practice is to produce a colourable story which casts doubt on the complainant's version of events. Thus, for example,

---

[231] Ibid. at 1682-3.

where a man has been chosen for a job in preference to a woman candidate who has slightly better qualifications than him on paper, the employer will escape liability for discrimination if the tribunal can be convinced that the man had a more appropriate personality for the particular job. This may be quite untrue, or at least an example of subconscious gender-stereotyping on the employer's part, yet it will save the case for the employer provided only that the tribunal does not conclude that the employer is lying. The real problem from the complainant's point of view is that it is extremely difficult, and sometimes quite impossible, to prove why she was *not* selected. This is a matter which is peculiarly within the employer's own knowledge which is why, arguably, the legal burden of proof should be reversed once a *prima facie* case has been made out and the employer should then be required to prove to the satisfaction of the tribunal the reason for the relevant decision.[232]

The ECJ has considered the issue of burden of proof on a number of occasions and, although the matter is complicated by differences between the adversarial and inquisitorial approaches to be found in the various Member States, the underlying difficulty is, as indicated above, to know what is the kind and weight of evidence from which a court or tribunal should infer discrimination. Specific questions were put to the ECJ in *Von Colson and Kamann* v. *Land Nordrhein-Westfalen*[233] concerning the facts which would have to be proved in order to entitle a claimant to the remedy of actually ordering the employer to conclude a contract of employment with the person discriminated against. For example, Question 2(a) asked:

Is the employer required to conclude a contract of employment only if, in addition to the finding that he made a subjective decision on the basis of criteria relating to sex, it can be established that the candidate discriminated against is objectively—according to acceptable selection criteria—better qualified for the post than the candidate with whom a contract of employment was concluded?

In the light of the ECJ's overall response to the questions in this case, namely that Article 6 of the Equal Treatment Directive does not prescribe any particular remedies, the Court found it unnecessary to answer questions such as these.

A similar issue, however, arose in *Delauche* v. *Commission*.[234] Ms Delauche sought annulment of a Commission decision rejecting her application to be appointed a Head of Division and of the Commission's decision to appoint a male candidate, a Mr Capogrossi, to the post instead. She also

---

[232] But for distinguished opinion to the opposite effect, see the 17th Report (Session 1988-9) of the House of Lords Select Committee on the European Communities, 'Burden of Proof in Sex Discrimination Cases', July 1989, HL Paper 76, and especially the view of Anthony Lester QC expressed therein.

[233] Case 14/83 [1984] ECR 1891, also discussed above.

[234] Case 111/86 [1987] ECR 5345.

claimed compensation for the damage she had suffered as a result of these decisions and as a result of the general lack of provisions within the Commission to prevent sex discrimination. She argued first that, if there are several candidates who are acknowledged to be equally suitable to fill a post and one sex is considerably under-represented in posts of that level, then preference should in principle be given to candidates of the under-represented sex. She produced evidence showing the very small percentage of women in Commission posts at the level in question. The Court rejected this contention saying that Ms Delauche had not proved the first part of this argument:

[T]he Commission did not consider Mrs Delauche to be as suitable as Mr Capogrossi to occupy the post in question. On the contrary, the Commission considered that the interests of the service would be better served by the appointment of Mr Capogrossi than by the appointment of Mrs Delauche.[235]

It left tantalizingly open the question of what its conclusion would have been had she established that she was as suitable a candidate as Mr Capogrossi, concluding: '[I]t is not necessary to examine the question whether, if the conditions set out by Mrs Delauche are fulfilled, the candidate belonging to the under-represented sex is in fact entitled to preference'.[236] The claimant's second argument was that the contested decisions were illegal because they contained no statement of reasons. In particular she argued that, in the light of the principle of equal treatment for men and women, the Commission had been under an obligation to provide a statement of reasons when rejecting a female applicant if the circumstances gave rise to a presumption of sex discrimination, as here. In the absence of such an obligation to provide a statement of reasons, a female candidate who wished to prove sex discrimination would, she pointed out, be subject to an impossible burden of proof. The ECJ gave short shrift to this argument on this occasion, referring to its earlier decision in *Bonino* v. *Commission*[237] to the effect that the principle of equal treatment of the sexes does not give rise to a duty to provide a statement of reasons for decisions on promotion even though some of the candidates are women. However, in its later decisions in the *Danfoss* case,[238] in *Re Sex Discrimination in the Civil Service, Commission* v. *France*,[239] and in *Enderby*,[240] which are discussed below, the Court has effectively reversed this part of its ruling.

A third argument for Ms Delauche was that the Commission had discriminated in not selecting her. She had worked for some time

---

[235] Ibid. at 5360.　　　　　　　　　　　　　[236] Ibid. at 5361.
[237] Case 233/85 [1987] ECR 739.　　[238] Case 109/88 [1989] ECR 3199.
[239] Case 318/86 [1988] ECR 3559.
[240] Case C-127/92 *Enderby* v. *Frenchay Health Authority* [1993] ECR I-5535.

previously within the Commission and she claimed that her periodic reports showed that she had all the qualifications needed for appointment to a post of Head of Division. She had several times been rejected for such a post, however, and argued that this could not be explained otherwise than by a deliberate intention on the part of the Commission to avoid any female appointments at that level. The Court took a somewhat weak and insensitive line here and held that the Commission had a wide discretion in the matter of who it promoted, so that: '[T]he Court must restrict its review to consideration of the question whether the appointing authority has used its power in a manifestly incorrect way'.[241] It is submitted that this is inconsistent with the previous case law on discrimination[242] and that, as a matter of policy, the Court ought not to resile from investigating whether there has been covert discrimination. It will, after all, be highly unusual for an appointing authority to broadcast the fact that it has arrived at a decision on discriminatory grounds, so that if the Court cannot examine the use it has made of its powers in some detail there will be no hope of ever proving direct discrimination. Ms Delauche also lost her claim to compensation, since she was unable to prove an illegal act on the part of the Commission.

However, the Court's approach in *Handels-OG Kontorfunktionaerernes Forbund i Danmark* v. *Dansk Arbejdsgiverforening (acting for Danfoss)*[243] was more encouraging. As seen in Chapter 2, the Court held that when an undertaking applies a totally non-transparent pay system (that is to say, one in which the workers concerned do not know how and why increments are applied), the burden of proof is on the employer to show that the pay practice is not discriminatory where the average pay of female workers can be demonstrated to be lower than the average pay of male workers. There were three reasons for concluding that the Court meant this as a general statement of the reversal of the burden of proof when a *prima facie* case has been demonstrated in any anti-discrimination claim. First, the legislative peg on which the judgment was hung was Article 6 of the Equal Pay Directive,[244] whose message (particularly in conjunction with Article 2) is very similar to that of Article 6 of the Equal Treatment Directive. Secondly, the rationale for the reversal of the burden of proof in non-transparent cases is that otherwise the courts would not be able to intervene effectively in discrimination cases, which is equally true of 'treatment' cases as of pay cases. And thirdly, the Court drew for authority on its own previous statement in an equal treatment case, *Re Sex Discrimination in the Civil Service, Commission* v. *France*,[245] in which it had:

---

[241] [1987] ECR 5345, at 5362.   [242] See discussion in Chap. 2.
[243] Case 109/88 [1989] ECR 3199.
[244] Directive 75/117, OJ [1975] L45/19, discussed in Chap. 2.
[245] Case 318/86 [1988] ECR 3559.

[C]ondemned a system of recruitment, characterized by a lack of transparency, as being contrary to the principle of equality of access to employment, on the ground that the lack of transparency prevented any form of supervision by the national courts.[246]

This conclusion was reinforced by *Enderby* v. *Frenchay Health Authority*[247]. As seen in Chapter 2, the Court here generalised its formula and held that proof of a *prima facie* case of discrimination casts the burden of proof onto the employer; it seems clear, both from the attribution of this rule by the Court to the necessity for effective means of enforcing the equality principle and from the submission of Lenz AG, that this statement was intended to extend to any type of discrimination, whether as to pay or as to other conditions of employment.

This represents a considerable advance on the position under UK law alone where a claimant in a sex discrimination case[248] bears the burden of proof throughout the proceedings (except in indirect discrimination cases, where it is up to the employer to justify the conduct once adverse impact has been demonstrated). The usual difficulty remains, however, that where the employer is not an organ of the State, the inability of directives to produce horizontal direct effect would inhibit the application of this principle before the national courts without some relevant national legislation.[249]

A directive regulating the burden of proof in all sex discrimination cases was agreed by the Member States in 1997.[250] This endeavours to express in statutory form the case law so far developed by the ECJ. It provides as follows in Article 4:

1.   Member States shall take such measures as are necessary, in accordance with their national judicial systems, to ensure that, when persons who consider themselves wronged because the principle of equal treatment has not been applied to them establish, before a court or other competent authority, facts from which it may be presumed that there has been direct or indirect discrimination, it shall be for the respondent to prove that there has been no breach of the principle of equal treatment.

2.   This Directive shall not prevent Member States from introducing rules of evidence which are more favourable to plaintiffs.[251]

3.   Member States need not apply paragraph 1 to proceedings in which it is for the court or competent body to investigate the facts of the case.

---

[246] [1989] ECR I-3199, at 3225.   [247] Case C-127/92 [1993] ECR I-5535.
[248] Cf. the position in equal pay claims.

[249] See discussion in Chap. 1. This problem does not arise in relation to equal pay, where the direct effect of Art. 119 of the Treaty can be relied on.

[250] Directive 97/80, OJ [1998] L14/6. The scope of the instrument and its definition of indirect discrimination are discussed in Chap. 2.

[251] Art. 6 of the instrument prohibits regression, that is to say, a reduction in the level of protection already provided to workers in this field.

Article 5 requires the Member States to ensure that measures taken pursuant to the new directive, together with those already in force, are brought to the attention of all persons concerned by all appropriate means.

Article 7 of the Equal Treatment Directive deals with victimization:

Member States shall take the necessary measures to protect employees against dismissal by the employer as a reaction to a complaint within the undertaking or to any legal proceedings aimed at enforcing compliance with the principle of equal treatment.

The wording of this provision is very similar to that of Article 5 of the Equal Pay Directive.[252] Thus, like that Article, it is noticeably broad in its inclusion of those who have merely made a complaint within the undertaking, as distinct from those who have actually launched legal proceedings, and narrow in its protection only against dismissal and not against other forms of detrimental treatment meted out in revenge by an employer. On the other hand, its wording seems to imply that there must be effective protection against dismissal provided in national law; this has led the Commission to argue that the UK is in breach of this part of the Directive, since its Sex Discrimination Act provides only the remedies of compensation, declaration, and recommendation where victimization is proved.[253] The Commission believes that the Directive demands that the remedy of reinstatement be available.[254] Since this part of the Equal Treatment Directive is quite specifically worded, it seems likely that it is directly effective and so could probably be enforced against an employer who was an organ of the State.[255]

Article 8 provides: 'Member States shall take care that the provisions adopted pursuant to this Directive, together with the relevant provisions already in force, are brought to the attention of employees by all appropriate means, for example at their place of employment'.

Article 9 allowed the Member States a period of 30 months from notification of the Directive in which to put into force the laws, regulations, and administrative provisions needed to secure compliance with the bulk of its terms.[256] As will be seen below, some additional time limits were provided for in respect of some of the exceptions to the equal treatment principle. The Member States were also placed under an obligation to communicate to the Commission the texts of the laws, regulations, and administrative provisions adopted by them in response to

---

[252] As to which see Chap. 2.
[253] See Sex Discrimination Act 1975, s. 65.
[254] See COM(78) 711 final, at 136.
[255] See discussion of the parallel point in relation to the Equal Pay Directive in Chap. 2.
[256] See Case 312/86 *Commission* v. *France* [1988] ECR 6315.

the instrument; this was to enable the Commission to check that such legislation was in conformity with the Directive.

Exceptions to the Principle of Equal Treatment Permitted by the Directive[257]

It appears from its decision in *Johnston* v. *Chief Constable of the RUC*[258] that the ECJ is most unlikely to permit exceptions to the Equal Treatment Directive other than those which are expressly mentioned in the instrument itself.[259] The UK government in that case had argued that public safety exonerated the Chief Constable's discriminatory treatment of Ms Johnston. The ECJ, however, held:

[T]he only Articles in which the EEC Treaty provides for derogations applicable in situations which may involve public safety are Articles 36, 48, 56, 223 and 224, which deal with exceptional and clearly defined cases. Because of their limited character those Articles do not lend themselves to a wide interpretation and it is not possible to infer from them that there is inherent in the EEC Treaty a general proviso covering all measures taken for reasons of public safety. If every provision of Community law were held to be subject to a general proviso, regardless of the specific requirements laid down by the provisions of the EEC Treaty, this might impair the binding nature of Community law and its uniform application.

It follows that the application of the principle of equal treatment for men and women is not subject to any general reservation as regards measures taken on grounds of the protection of public safety, apart from the possible application of Article 224 of the EEC Treaty which concerns a wholly exceptional situation . . . [and which the Court later found to be inapplicable on the facts of this case]. The facts which induced the competent authority to invoke the need to protect public safety must therefore if necessary be taken into consideration, in the first place, in the context of the application of the specific provisions of the Directive.

The answer to the first question must therefore be that acts of sex discrimination done for reasons related to the protection of public safety must be examined in the light of the exceptions to the principle of equal treatment for men and women laid down in Council Directive 76/207/EEC.[260]

---

[257] The word 'exceptions' is used here for the sake of verbal simplicity; for argument that they are not really exceptions because they do not involve discrimination, see below in relation to positive action.

[258] Case 222/84 [1986] ECR 1651.

[259] See further Arnull, 'EC Law and the Dismissal of Pregnant Servicewomen' (1995) 24 ILJ 215.

[260] Case 222/84 [1986] ECR 1651, at 1684. This issue is likely to confront the ECJ again in *R.* v. *Secretary of State for Defence, Ex p. Perkins* (pending before it at the time of writing), in which the Ministry of Defence will try to justify its ban on homosexual members of the armed forces. In addition, in *Sirdar* v. *Ministry of Defence* (1997) 73 EOR 3, an industrial tribunal has referred to the ECJ questions concerning the applicability of the Equal Treatment Directive to members of the armed forces.

Furthermore, the Court will usually accord a strict construction to any exception to a general principle, where that general principle exists for the protection of individuals.[261]

The Equal Treatment Directive itself lists three exceptions. The first is contained in Article 2(2), which provides:

This Directive shall be without prejudice to the right of Member States to exclude from its field of application those occupational activities and, where appropriate, the training leading thereto, for which, by reason of their nature or the context in which they are carried out, the sex of the worker constitutes a determining factor.

Article 2(2) was at the root of a Commission prosecution of the UK for defective implementation of the Equal Treatment Directive.[262] The Commission alleged that three of the exceptions contained in the Sex Discrimination Act 1975 conflicted with Article 2(2) of the Directive. The first two were the exceptions then conferred by s. 6(3) of the statute, excusing all employment for the purposes of a private household and also employment where the number of persons employed did not exceed five. The Commission reported that there were no equivalent exceptions provided for by the legislation of any of the other Member States, but the UK government argued that these exceptions were permitted by Article 2(2) since they involve 'close personal relationships between employee and employer, so that it would not be legally possible to prevent the latter from employing persons of a particular sex'. In the case of employment in private households, it contended that the employee often lives in the household, as in the case of resident companions and personal maids, and it also contended (contrary to the Commission's view) that the concept of a 'private household' was perfectly clear. 'Thus, if a chauffeur is not actually employed in his employer's household but for the purposes of his business, the exception will not apply. On the contrary, a family cook or gardener will normally come within that exception.'[263] As to the small business exception, the UK government took as an example female owners and managers of small shops, particularly the elderly, who wish to employ assistants of their own sex. These arguments all have an extraordinarily old-fashioned ring to them and suggest a lack of touch with the modern world of employment. They found no favour with either the Advocate General or with the Court, except that the Advocate General considered that the term 'private household' was susceptible of satisfactory definition through case law. Nevertheless, her general view was that:

---

[261] See e.g. Case 41/74 *Van Duyn* v. *Home Office* [1974] ECR 1337; Case 222/84 *Johnston* v. *Chief Constable of the RUC* [1986] ECR 1651; and Case C-328/91 *Secretary of State for Social Security* v. *Thomas* [1993] ECR I-1247.

[262] Case 165/82 *Commission* v. *UK* [1983] ECR 3431, also discussed above.

[263] These are the words of Rozès AG, ibid. at 3456.

[T]he UK has not furnished proof that in all the cases covered by the exception at issue the conditions in which the work in question is performed make it necessary to allow employers to practise discrimination. It is not true that all occupational and professional activities capable of being covered by the exception contained in that provision involve the close personal relationships which constitute the justification for it. As the Commission rightly points out, the defendant itself admits this in the words it uses: employment for the purposes of a private household frequently (and therefore not always) involves very close personal relationships; close personal relationships often (here too, not always) exist in small undertakings.

I also consider that the terms of s. 6(3) do not satisfy the condition laid down in Article 2(2) by virtue of which the exclusion must relate to 'occupational activities'. There is no doubt that it is not necessary, as the UK rightly points out, for the exclusion of occupational activities pursuant to Article 2(2) to be effected by listing them activity by activity; it seems to me to be perfectly permissible for a Member State to implement the Directive by enacting laws which prohibit discrimination, reiterating the actual wording of that Article and, for the rest, leaving the national courts to determine case by case, subject to review by this Court under Article 177 of the Treaty, what occupational activities are excluded from the general prohibition. But it cannot be considered, without stretching the meaning of the words, that the concepts of employment for the purposes of a private household (and not for example the concept of resident domestic staff) and employment in undertakings with five or fewer employees correspond to occupational activities.[264]

The Court itself held:

It must be recognized that the provision of the 1975 Act in question is intended, in so far as it refers to employment in a private household, to reconcile the principle of equality of treatment with the principle of respect for private life, which is also fundamental. Reconciliation of that kind is one of the factors which must be taken into consideration in determining the scope of the exception provided for in Article 2(2) of the Directive. Whilst it is undeniable that, for certain kinds of employment in private households, that consideration may be decisive, that is not the case for all the kinds of employment in question.

As regards small undertakings with not more than five employees, the UK has not put forward any argument to show that in any undertaking of that size the sex of the worker would be a determining factor by reason of the nature of his activities or the context in which they are carried out.

Consequently, by reason of its generality, the exclusion provided for in the contested provision of the 1975 Act goes beyond the objective which may be lawfully pursued within the framework of Article 2(2) of the Directive.[265]

---

[264] Ibid. at 3456-7.

[265] Ibid. at 3448. The Sex Discrimination Act 1986 subsequently narrowed down the private household exception and removed the small business exception altogether.

The subsequent decision in *Kirsammer-Hack* v. *Sidal*[266] suggests that the Court may now have modified the rigour of its approach in relation to small businesses. German law on unfair dismissal does not apply to small businesses, that is to say, those in which five or fewer persons are generally employed. Part-timers have the right to claim unfair dismissal but, in calculating the total number of employees in an enterprise, those working fewer than 10 hours per week are excluded. Ms Kirsammer-Hack, who worked part-time but for more than 10 hours per week, alleged unfair dismissal but was met by the small business exception. The Labour Court referred to the ECJ the question of whether the domestic legislation constituted indirect discrimination in breach of the Equal Treatment Directive. The ECJ held that the national law did not impact specifically on part-timers, but rather on everybody employed by small businesses; since there was no evidence to suggest that small businesses employ a considerably larger number of women than men, there was therefore no indirect discrimination. However, and significantly in the present context, the Court went on to hold that, even if the legislation were *prima facie* indirectly discriminatory, it would be justifiable as intended to relieve the constraints weighing on small businesses:

[The legislation in question] forms part of a series of measures intended to alleviate the constraints burdening small businesses which play an essential role in economic development and the creation of employment in the Community.

In that respect, it should be noted that, by providing that directives adopted in the fields of health and safety of workers are to avoid imposing administrative, financial and legal constraints in a way which would hold back the creation and development of small and medium-sized undertakings, Article 118a of the EEC Treaty . . . indicates that such undertakings may be the subject of special economic measures.[267]

The decision in *Kirsammer-Hack* is not, of course, directly comparable with that in *Commission* v. *UK*. The latter involved an exclusion from the scope of UK anti-discrimination legislation, which was automatically a breach of the Equal Treatment Directive unless excused by one of the exceptions contained in that Directive. *Kirsammer-Hack* involved an allegation that the German legislation on unfair dismissal operated in an indirectly discriminatory fashion and thus it had to be determined whether or not it was justifiable; only had it been found not to be justifiable would the issue of the applicability of the defence contained in Article 2(2) have arisen. Nevertheless, the ECJ's readiness to accept that the commercial viability of small businesses outweighed the right to equal treatment contrasts sharply with the attitude of the House of Lords in *R.* v.

---

[266] Case C-189/91 [1993] ECR I-6185, noted by Horspool in (1994) 31 CMLRev. 1115 and by Hervey in 'Small Business Exclusion in German Dismissal Law' (1994) 23 ILJ 267.
[267] Case C-189/91 at 6223.

Secretary of State for Employment, Ex p. EOC.[268] In *Ex p. EOC*, the House
refused to accept the UK government's assertion that the hours of work
thresholds contained in UK employment protection legislation, which
deprived many part-timers of the right to rely on this legislation, were
justified on the ground that they encouraged part-time employment;
although increasing the availability of part-time work was thought by the
House to be a proper aim of social policy, the threshold provisions had not
been shown to be either suitable or requisite to achieve that aim.

The third exception challenged by the Commission in its prosecution of
the UK was the exclusion of midwives (at that date) from the general
operation of the Sex Discrimination Act 1975. Section 20 of the Act
provided that midwives were excluded from the employment and training
provisions of the Act. However, men were permitted to train as midwives at
two centres in the UK, and to work as midwives in four designated
hospitals. At the time of the action, these provisions, which had been
intended to be transitional only, were about to be amended so as to
remove the restrictions on men working as midwives and so to extend the
protection of the Sex Discrimination Act to them.[269] Rozès AG considered
that nevertheless this had no bearing on the issue before the Court, which
concerned only the state of the legislation at the time the proceedings
were begun. However, Article 9(2) of the Directive requires Member States
to assess periodically: 'the occupational activities referred to in Article
2(2) in order to decide, in the light of social developments, whether there
is justification for maintaining the exclusions concerned. They shall notify
the Commission of the results of this assessment'. The UK government
gave evidence that the exception for midwives had been kept under review
as a result of this provision, and indeed that it was as a consequence of this
review that the restrictions on male midwives were about to be lifted. It
argued that midwives are often alone with their patients, particularly after
the mother has returned home after giving birth, and that in particular
members of certain ethnic minorities living in the UK might object to the
presence of a male midwife, to the ultimate endangerment of both mother
and baby. All this was insufficient to persuade Rozès AG of the legality of
the exception and she said:

I do not consider that the alleged specific nature of the conditions in which the
occupation of midwife is practised in the UK is such as to justify, under Article
2(2) of the Directive, the discriminatory rules against men. I think that the

---

[268] [1994] 2 WLR 409, also discussed in Chaps. 1 and 2. See also Deakin, 'Part Time
Employment, Qualifying Thresholds and Economic Justification' (1994) 23 ILJ 151 and
Villiers and White, 'Agitating for Part-Time Workers' Rights' (1995) 58 MLR 560.

[269] See now the Sex Discrimination Act (Amendment of S. 20) Order, SI 1983, No. 1202,
Art. 2. Patients can still, however, choose to be cared for by a female midwife if they prefer
and, if a male midwife is provided, he must be subject to appropriate supervision.

guarantee of a free choice for patients, which is maintained in the proposed British rules, is a condition which is necessary and sufficient to allay the fears expressed by the UK Government.[270]

However, the Court itself held:

It is undeniable that in the area in question, as the UK acknowledges, the Member States are under an obligation to implement the principle of equality of treatment. It must however be recognized that at the present time personal sensitivities may play an important role in relations between midwife and patient. In those circumstances, it may be stated that by failing fully to apply the principle laid down in the Directive, the UK has not exceeded the limits of the power granted to the Member States by Articles 9(2) and 2(2) of the Directive. The Commission's complaint in that regard cannot therefore be upheld.[271]

The Court's comments about Article 2(2) of the Directive in *Johnston* v. *Chief Constable of the RUC*[272] were similarly somewhat disappointing, in that they appear to leave a very great discretion in the hands of the Member States in relation to the situations in which the exception is permitted to operate. The Court held that the Chief Constable could not justify his refusal to provide women police reservists with firearms training (which had subsequently led to the non-renewal of their contracts of employment) by relying on the part of Article 2(2) which refers to the exclusion of those occupational activities whose 'nature' requires male workers, because the Sex Discrimination (Northern Ireland) Order 1976 expressly applies to employment in the police. However, that still left the part of the Article referring to the 'context' in which a job is performed. The Chief Constable argued that if women police officers were armed they might become a more frequent target for assassination and their firearms might fall into the hands of their assailants, that the public would not welcome the carrying of firearms by women, and that armed policewomen would be less effective in police work of a social nature. The Court held:

[T]he reasons which the Chief Constable thus gave for his policy were related to the special conditions in which the police must work in the situation existing in Northern Ireland, having regard to the requirements of the protection of public safety in a context of serious internal disturbances. As regards the question whether such reasons may be covered by Article 2(2) of the Directive, it should first be observed that that provision, being a derogation from an individual right laid down in the Directive, must be interpreted strictly. However, it must be recognized that the context in which the occupational activity of members of an armed police force are carried out is determined by the environment in which that activity is carried out. In this regard, the possibility cannot be excluded that in a situation characterized by serious internal disturbances the carrying of

---

[270] [1983] ECR 3431, at 3460.   [271] Ibid. at 3449.
[272] Case 222/84 [1986] ECR 1651.

firearms by policewomen might create additional risks of their being assassinated and might therefore be contrary to the requirements of public safety. In such circumstances, the context of certain policing activities may be such that the sex of police officers constitutes a determining factor for carrying them out.[273]

This is unsatisfactory because the Court makes no attempt to explain why policewomen in this situation are more liable to be assassinated than policemen. When it speaks of 'additional risks' to policewomen, it appears confused: instead of comparing the risk to a police*woman* carrying out general police duties with the risk to a police*man* performing those same duties, it seems to have compared the risk to a policewoman between general police duties and those special few on which women were currently being employed.[274] The Court did, however, point out that the important doctrine of proportionality has a part to play in relation to the Article 2(2) defence and indeed with respect to all derogations from the equal treatment principle:

[I]n determining the scope of any derogation from an individual right such as the equal treatment of men and women provided for by the Directive, the principle of proportionality, one of the general principles of law underlying the Community legal order, must be observed. That principle requires that derogations remain within the limits of what is appropriate and necessary for achieving the aim in view and requires the principle of equal treatment to be reconciled as far as possible with the requirements of public safety which constitute the decisive factor as regards the context of the activity in question.

By reason of the division of jurisdiction provided for in Article 177 of the EEC Treaty, it is for the national court to say whether the reasons on which the Chief Constable based his decision are in fact well founded and justify the specific measure taken in Mrs Johnston's case. It is also for the national court to ensure that the principle of proportionality is observed and to determine whether the refusal to renew Mrs Johnston's contract could not be avoided by allocating to women duties which, without jeopardizing the aims pursued, can be performed without firearms.[275]

It follows that, just as with the justification of indirect discrimination over pay,[276] an exception to the principle of equal treatment, even if on the face of it within the scope of Article 2(2), will not be lawful unless it is 'appropriate and necessary', which in turn appears to mean that no alternative, non-discriminatory means are available to achieve the end in view.

A later case on somewhat similar facts to *Johnston* was *Re Sex Discrimination in the Civil Service, Commission* v. *France*,[277] in which the Commission

[273] Ibid. at 1686-7.

[274] See Ellis, 'Can Public Safety Provide an Excuse for Sex Discrimination?' (1986) 102 LQR 496.

[275] [1986] ECR 1651, at 1687. See also the ECJ's remarks to similar effect in Case 318/86 *Re Sex Discrimination in the Civil Service, Commission* v. *France* [1988] ECR 3559, esp. at 3582.

[276] See Chap. 2.   [277] Case 318/86 [1988] ECR 3559.

prosecuted France for, *inter alia*, maintaining a quota based on sex for recruitment into various ranks of the police service. The French government argued that sex was a determining factor because members of the national police force must at any time be able to use force in order to deter potential troublemakers and that this prevented the inclusion of a large proportion of women in the police generally. Slynn AG seemed more than willing to accept such an explanation[278] but the Court did not have to address the issue directly since the parties had agreed that certain of the police duties involved had to be performed by men only, others by women only, and the remainder by either sex.[279] In these circumstances, the question became how the Article 2(2) exception would apply and the Court made an important statement about the practical enforcement of the anti-discrimination legislation. It held:

Article 2(2) of the Directive leaves the Member States the power to exclude certain 'occupational activities' from its field of application and . . . Article 9(2) of the Directive requires them periodically to assess the activities in question in order to decide, in the light of social developments, whether there is justification for maintaining the exclusions concerned. Article 9(2) further provides that the Member States are to notify the Commission of the results of that assessment.

It follows from those provisions that the exceptions provided for in Article 2(2) may relate only to specific activities, that they must be sufficiently transparent so as to permit effective supervision by the Commission and that in principle they must be capable of being adapted to social developments. The last requirement gives rise to no difficulties in this case; however, French law is not in accordance with the other two requirements.

As regards the requirement of transparency, it must be concluded that it is not fulfilled. Under the system of separate recruitment, the percentage of posts to be allotted to men and women respectively are fixed in the decision ordering the

---

[278] He commented: 'The argument is . . . that police officers have to be interchangeable and that all may be liable to perform police duties which involve the display of force. The latter, it is said, are unsuitable to be carried out by women. There is force in this argument, but it seems to me that it seeks to extend Art. 2(2) too far. It may well be that for some police activities (where the use of force or a display of the capacity to use force are required) sex could be a determining factor not simply because on average men are bigger and stronger than women (which in itself would not necessarily be sufficient) but because potential delinquents regard men as more ready to use force, and perhaps because men are more willing to use force. These however, are matters which it seems to me are not necessary or, on the evidence available, not possible to decide, especially if regard is had to the role which women now appear to play in warfare and in police forces in some parts of the world. There may be a difference between handling violent crowds and situations where one or two individuals are threatening violence. As to the former, the Commission appears to accept that the exception in Art. 2(2) would apply to . . . bodies . . . whose activities regularly involve the use of force where substantial numbers of people may be involved. As to the latter, there may be an argument that in some situations with which the police have to deal the presence of women could be a deterrent to violence' (ibid. at 3571).

[279] It is unsatisfactory that the Commission conceded this important point and it is to be hoped that the Court will have a future opportunity to examine the logic of the argument relied on.

holding of a competition; the fixing of those percentages is not governed by any objective criterion defined in a legislative provision.

This lack of transparency also has consequences for compliance with the second requirement laid down by the Directive, which relates to the activities involved. *The contested system of recruitment makes it impossible to exercise any form of supervision, not only by the Commission and the courts but also by persons adversely affected by the discriminatory measures, in order to verify whether the percentages fixed for the recruitment of each sex actually correspond to specific activities for which the sex of the persons to be employed constitutes a determining factor within the meaning of Article 2(2) of the Directive.*[280]

It was seen in Chapter 2 that the ECJ has emphasized the significance of the principle of transparency in relation to the computation of pay, and the effect of its remarks in both that field and the equal treatment field is to create a new and far-reaching principle: namely, that individuals involved are entitled to know the basis upon which employment decisions affecting them are reached, at least where the facts demonstrate a *prima facie* case of discrimination.[281]

The second so-called exception provided by the Equal Treatment Directive is contained in Article 2(3): 'This Directive shall be without prejudice to provisions concerning the protection[282] of women, particularly as regards pregnancy and maternity'.[283] The ECJ has held that Article 2(3) conditions the meaning to be placed on Article 3(2)(c) of the Directive (and presumably Article 5(2)(c) as well, since it is drafted in materially identical terms). These provisions, as has been seen earlier in the present Chapter, oblige Member States to repeal outdated 'protective' legislation which discriminates in favour of one sex, usually of course in practice women.[284]

---

[280] [1988] ECR 3559, at 3581-2. (Emphasis supplied.)

[281] See also the discussion above of the burden of proof in anti-discrimination cases, of which this is in reality another facet.

[282] In Case C-421/92 *Habermann-Beltermann* v. *Arbeiterwohlfahrt* [1994] ECR I-1657, the Court held that, if an employment contract were to become void on account of the employee's temporary inability because of pregnancy to perform the night-time work for which she had been engaged, this would be 'contrary to the objective of protecting such persons pursued by Art. 2(3) of the Directive, and would deprive that provision of its effectiveness' (at 1677).

[283] In Case C-421/92 *Habermann-Beltermann* v. *Arbeiterwohlfahrt* [1994] ECR I-1657, Tesauro AG submitted that Art. 2(3) is not really an exception to the equality principle, but rather an application of it: it permits different treatment 'in order to arrive at material and not formal equality, since that would constitute a denial of equality' (at 1664).

[284] See Case 222/84 *Johnston* v. *Chief Constable of the RUC* [1986] ECR 1651, at 1688. The second para. of Art. 9(1) of the Directive provides: 'as regards the first part of Article 3(2)(c) and the first part of Article 5(2)(c), Member States shall carry out a first examination and if necessary a first revision of the laws, regulations and administrative provisions referred to therein within four years of notification of this Directive'. The EC Commission reported in Mar. 1987 on the existing state of the protective laws in all the Member States apart from Spain and Portugal and found that 'a mosaic of extremely varied

Article 2(3) has been in issue before the ECJ on a number of occasions. *Commission* v. *Italy*[285] concerned, *inter alia*, Italian legislation which extended certain maternity rights to women, but not to men, when they adopted children under six years of age. It allowed them to claim three months' leave from employment, together with a financial allowance. Rozès AG considered that this constituted a breach of the equal treatment principle as regards working conditions, and that it could not be justified by reference to the exception for maternity:

I believe that leave after giving birth to a child in order to allow the mother to rest may rightly be regarded as a provision to protect women in relation to maternity. On the other hand, I consider that leave after adoption benefits the child above all in so far as it is intended to foster the emotional ties necessary to settle the child in the family adopting it . . . I therefore consider that the leave referred to . . . is part of the working conditions within the meaning of Article 5 of the Directive. That is why I consider that adoptive fathers must be entitled to it on the same basis as their working wives.[286]

The full Court, however, unfortunately did not adopt such an analytical approach and held simply:

[The distinction in relation to maternity leave] is justified . . . by the legitimate concern to assimilate as far as possible the conditions of entry of the child into the adoptive family to those of the arrival of a newborn child in the family during the very delicate initial period. As regards leave from work after the initial period of three months the adoptive father has the same rights as the adoptive mother.[287]

This ruling suggested that the Court was prepared to give an extensive interpretation to the word 'maternity'. This view was confirmed by *Hofmann* v. *Barmer Ersatzkasse*,[288] in which a father alleged that it was unlawfully discriminatory for Federal German law to grant mothers, but not fathers, an optional period of paid leave from employment between the ending of the statutory period of maternity leave eight weeks after childbirth and the child reaching the age of six months. The father argued that, since this additional period of leave was essentially provided for the benefit of the baby, it should be open to fathers too. The Advocate General and the Court both rejected this argument, the latter explaining:

and highly specific regulations exists, the reasons for which are not clearly defined'. (See 'Communication on Protective Legislation for Women in the Member States of the European Community' COM(87) 105 final.) It stated that protective legislation which does not relate to pregnancy or maternity should be made to apply equally to both sexes or else be repealed, and it declared its determination to bring proceedings against Member States which continued to ignore this warning.

[285] Case 163/82 [1983] ECR 3273.
[286] Ibid. at 3297-8.
[287] Ibid. at 3288.
[288] Case 184/83 [1984] ECR 3047.

[B]y reserving to Member States the right to retain or introduce provisions which are intended to protect women in connection with 'pregnancy and maternity', the Directive recognizes the legitimacy, in terms of the principle of equal treatment, of protecting a woman's needs in two respects. First, it is legitimate to ensure the protection of a woman's biological condition during pregnancy and thereafter until such time as her physiological and mental functions have returned to normal after childbirth; and secondly, it is legitimate to protect the special relationship between a woman and her child over the period which follows pregnancy and childbirth, by preventing that relationship from being disturbed by the multiple burdens which would result from the simultaneous pursuit of employment.

In principle, therefore, a measure such as maternity leave granted to a woman on expiry of the statutory protective period falls within the scope of Article 2(3) of Directive 76/207, inasmuch as it seeks to protect a woman in connection with the effects of pregnancy and motherhood. That being so, such leave may legitimately be reserved to the mother to the exclusion of any other person, in view of the fact that it is only the mother who may find herself subject to undesirable pressures to return to work prematurely.[289]

It is significant that the language used by the ECJ evolves here from 'maternity' (the word used in the Directive) to 'motherhood'. The Court is apparently saying that different provision is permissible in connection with 'motherhood', which, in ordinary language, is a state of very much longer duration than 'maternity'. The unfortunate innuendo here, of course, is that Article 2(3) may be going to be interpreted in future by the ECJ to legitimize other forms of preferential treatment for mothers which are based on outdated notions of parental role-playing within families. On the other hand, the *Hofmann* case was only in fact concerned with leave periods up to six months from the child's birth, and it does not necessarily follow that the Court would have accepted the same argument had it been faced with a returner scheme allowing a mother only a period of, say, one or two years of leave after the birth. It would appear logically that, if Article 2(3) is to be construed strictly, in accordance with the usual principle, such a scheme could not be excused as attributable to 'maternity'.

The more recent cases on Article 2(3) suggest that the Court may be moving in this direction. *Commission* v. *France*[290] was a prosecution of France for enacting legislation providing that, although contractual employment equality was to be the norm as between men and women, there could remain in operation terms of contracts and collective agreements in force on the date at which the legislation was enacted 'granting particular rights to women'. The French government argued that this was justifiable by means of Article 2(3) of the Directive. The particular rights in question

---

[289] Ibid. at 3075.   [290] Case 312/86 [1988] ECR 6315.

related to extended maternity leave, reduction in working hours for women aged 59, the bringing forward of retirement age, time off for sick children, extra days' holiday each year per child, a day off on the first day of the school term, some hours off on Mothers' Day, daily breaks for women working on computer equipment or as typists or switchboard operators, pension bonuses after the birth of a second child, and allowances for nurseries and childminders. The Commission agreed that some of these matters might fall within Article 2(3), but argued that in general effect the French legislation enabled inequalities in treatment between men and women contrary to the Directive to continue indefinitely. The Court agreed with the Commission, pointing out that some of the examples given of the particular rights for women which were being protected: 'relate to the protection of women in their capacity as older workers or parents—categories to which both men and women may equally belong'.[291] In other words, the Court would not countenance any extension of Article 2(3), beyond cases connected in some fairly close but unspecified way with the process of childbearing. Unfortunately, the Court said nothing about how it saw the limits to the exception and, in particular, at what point maternity matures into parenthood. Slynn AG was somewhat more forthcoming in this respect, saying that the *Hofmann* case had established that the exception was confined to 'the period which follows pregnancy and childbirth, and not any later period'.[292]

Part of the doubt which surrounds the extent of this exception is due to its drafting. The inclusion of the word 'particularly' ('particularly as regards pregnancy and maternity') is unfortunate: it suggests, although it does not articulate, that there are other grounds on which women may lawfully be protected. This reasoning could of course be used to justify differential treatment of women on the basis of some spurious supposed vulnerability or weakness. The Court left tantalizingly open the question of whether there were any other grounds, besides pregnancy and maternity, on which women could lawfully be protected, in its decision in *Johnston* v. *Chief Constable of the RUC*.[293] After asserting that Article 2(3) must, like Article 2(2), be construed strictly, it said:

[I]t is clear from the express reference to pregnancy and maternity that the Directive is intended to protect a woman's biological condition and the special relationship that exists between a woman and her child. That provision of the Directive does not therefore allow women to be excluded from a certain type of employment on the ground that public opinion demands that women be given greater protection than men against risks that affect women and men in the same way and which are distinct from women's special needs of protection, such as those expressly mentioned. It does not appear that the risks and dangers to which

---

[291] Ibid. at 6336.　　　　　　　　　　[292] Ibid. at 6328.
[293] Case 222/84 [1986] ECR 1651, also discussed above.

women are exposed when performing their duties in the police force in a situation such as exists in Northern Ireland are different from those to which any man is also exposed when performing the same duties.[294]

In the later decision in *Commission* v. *France*[295] Slynn AG commented, with almost equal opacity: 'Although the word "particularly" in Article 2(3) indicates that situations other than pregnancy and maternity may fall within its scope, those words colour the scope of the exemptions'.[296] At present therefore all that can be concluded about the scope of Article 2(3) is that it can certainly be used to justify special treatment for women in employment in relation to pregnancy[297] and up to at least six months from the date of their giving birth; beyond this, it can seemingly be used to justify the 'protection' of women against biological risks which are specific to their sex but quite what these risks are, and how 'biological' is to be defined has yet to be worked out in the case law of the ECJ.

Positive Action[298]

The third exceptional situation envisaged by the Equal Treatment Directive embraces what is commonly known as 'positive action'. The Directive was originally the only EC provision to deal with this matter but, as will be seen below, the Protocol and Agreement on Social Policy and the Amsterdam Treaty have now also addressed positive action.

Article 2(4) of the Directive states:

This Directive shall be without prejudice to measures to promote equal opportunities for men and women, in particular by removing existing inequalities which affect women's opportunities in the areas referred to in Article 1(1).

---

[294] Ibid. at 1688-9. In Case C-345/89 *Stoeckel* [1991] ECR I-4047, the ECJ held that a ban on night work by women was not permitted by Art. 3(2); it stated that '[a]s far as the aims of protecting female workers are concerned, they are valid only if . . . there is a justified need for a difference of treatment as between men and women. However, whatever the disadvantages of night work may be, it does not seem that, except in the case of pregnancy or maternity, the risks to which women are exposed when working at night are, in general, inherently different from those to which men are exposed' (at 4066). See also Case C-13/93 *Office National de l'Emploi* v. *Minne* [1994] ECR I-371.

[295] Case 312/86 [1988] ECR 6315.   [296] Ibid. at 6328.

[297] Where special treatment is actually extended to pregnant women it appears to be assumed that that treatment is logically related to their pregnancy; thus, for example, in Case C-421/92 *Habermann-Beltermann* v. *Arbeiterwohlfahrt* [1994] ECR I-1657, Tesauro AG submitted: 'with respect to Article 2(3) of the Directive, the legality of . . . German legislation prohibiting night-time work for pregnant women is beyond dispute. That legislation accords special protection to female workers in such circumstances and is clearly covered by the derogations provided for in the Directive' (at 1663). The Court agreed that 'the prohibition on night-time work by pregnant women [was] . . . unquestionably compatible with Art. 2(3) . . . ' (at 1675). However, there was no inquiry here into why night-time (as distinct from day-time) work was perceived as especially hazardous to pregnant women.

[298] For thorough and perceptive analysis of the concept of positive action, see Fredman, 'Reversing Discrimination' (1997) 113 LQR 575.

In *Hofmann* v. *Barmer Ersatzkasse*,[299] although the Court itself said nothing of substance about the scope of Article 2(4), Darmon AG commented:

The exception set out in Article 2(4) is in a category of its own. The provision opens the way for national measures 'to promote equal opportunity for men and women, in particular by removing existing inequalities'. It merely appears to make an exception to the principle: in aiming to compensate for existing discrimination it seeks to re-establish equality and not to prejudice it. In other words, since it presupposes that there is an inequality which must be removed, the exception must be broadly construed. [300]

He went on to say that the grant of an additional period of paid leave from employment after childbirth to mothers but not fathers:

[A]ffords a means of mitigating the *de facto* inequalities suffered by women as a result of the deterioration of their health following childbirth and thus preserves their opportunities on the resumption of work. In that sense, the leave is included amongst the measures referred to by Article 2(4) of the Directive. Thus, the question necessarily arises as to whether the exception in Article 2(3) is not an illustration, selected by the Community legislature, of the general derogation contained in Article 2(4). I incline towards that view and see it as confirming the rejection of the restrictive interpretation placed on the exception in Article 2(3).[301]

This led the French government to put forward the radical argument in *Commission* v. *France*[302] that, since women experience *de facto* inequality as regards employment because they continue to shoulder more domestic responsibilities than men, therefore the exception in Article 2(4) justified special compensatory treatment in favour of women. The Court seemed to have been prepared to accept this argument, had France been able to prove it. It held:

The exception provided for in Article 2(4) is specifically and exclusively designed to allow measures which, although discriminatory in appearance, are in fact intended[303] to eliminate or reduce actual instances of inequalities which may exist in the reality of social life. Nothing in the papers of this case, however, makes it possible to conclude that a generalised preservation of special rights for women in collective agreements may correspond to the situation envisaged by that provision.[304]

---

[299] Case 184/83 [1984] ECR 3047.
[300] Ibid. at 3082.   [301] Ibid. at 3086.
[302] Case 312/86 [1988] ECR 6315.
[303] It is noteworthy that the test articulated by the Court here is a subjective, not an objective, one; query whether the Court would insist that the national measures concerned must be reasonably apt to achieve their purpose.
[304] [1988] ECR 6315, at 6336-7. In Case C-450/93 *Kalanke* v. *Freie Hansestadt Bremen* [1995] ECR I-3051, discussed below, Tesauro AG characterised the Court's decision in *Commission* v. *France* as one of 'excessive severity' (at 3063).

It seemed to follow from what the Court said that special measures—perhaps even positively discriminatory ones—benefiting women would be excused by Article 2(4) to the extent that they compensated for specific instances of pre-existing inequality. However, the Court was clearly not prepared to construe the provision so as to justify positive discrimination in favour of women in employment generally, on the basis that women have, as a sex, suffered negative discrimination in the past which has resulted in their current inequitable distribution throughout the world of work.

No doubt encouraged by this ruling, the Commission subsequently instructed Professor Eliane Vogel-Polsky of the Brussels National Centre for the Sociology of Labour Law to conduct a study of positive action schemes within the Community. Professor Vogel-Polsky reported[305] that a directive would be the best way of ensuring that all Member States took action in this field and would operate in a non-discriminatory way as between the Member States. Such a directive would have made positive action programmes obligatory in the Community's own institutions and in national public bodies, and it would have worked in a similar fashion to the federal contract compliance scheme in the USA.[306] However, only a few months after this report was presented, the EC's own Advisory Committee on Equal Opportunities for Women and Men rejected the idea of a directive, preferring a mere non-binding recommendation, which it believed was far more likely to command the support of the Member States. The Commission therefore opted for a recommendation only on positive action, despite the contrary views of the European trade unions and the European Parliament.

A Recommendation on the Promotion of Positive Action for Women was eventually adopted by the Council in December 1984.[307] Certain of the Commission's more radical proposals had been removed by the Council, in particular the fixing of recruitment targets to ensure greater female representation in industry. Being only a Recommendation, the instrument also of course contains no sanctions for non-compliance. However, it does adopt quite sensitively forthright language, for example, in Article 1, urging the Members States:

to adopt a positive action policy designed to eliminate existing inequalities affecting women in working life and to promote a better balance between the sexes in employment, comprising appropriate general and specific measures, within the

[305] See CREW Reports (1983), vol. 3, no. 3, p. 4.

[306] As to which see *Contract Compliance: The UK Experience* (Institute of Personnel Management, 1987), and Robarts, Coote, and Ball, *Positive Action for Women: The Next Step* (National Council for Civil Liberties, 1981).

[307] Recommendation 84/635, OJ [1984] L331/34.

framework of national policies and practices, while fully respecting the spheres of competence of the two sides of industry, in order:

(a) to eliminate or counteract the prejudicial effects on women in employ-ment or seeking employment which arise from existing attitudes, behav-iour and structures based on the idea of a traditional division of roles in society between men and women;

(b) to encourage the participation of women in various occupations in those sectors of working life where they are at present under-represented, par-ticularly in the sectors of the future, and at higher levels of responsibility in order to achieve better use of all human resources.

In Article 8, it stresses the need to make particular efforts to promote equal opportunities in the public sector, especially in those fields where new information technologies are being used or developed, because they can serve as models for the private sector to emulate. The Commission was obliged by the instrument to report to the Council within three years on the progress achieved in the implementation of the Recommendation: its consequent report in 1988 concluded that in general the Member States had begun to introduce positive action programmes although their methodology varied widely.[308]

The Commission also pledged itself[309] to present to the Council, the Member States, the two sides of industry, and potential promoters of positive action plans, a Code of Practice to assist and inform them on the implementation of such schemes. This promise it fulfilled in 1988 in *Positive Action—Equal Opportunities for Women in Employment—A Guide.*[310] In answer to the elusive question 'What exactly is positive action?', the Guide replies:

Positive action aims to complement legislation on equal treatment and *includes any measure contributing to the elimination of inequalities in practice.*

The setting up of a positive action programme allows an organisation to iden-tify and eliminate any discrimination in its employment policies and practices, and to put right the effects of past discrimination.

Thus a positive action programme is a type of management approach which an employer can adopt with a view to achieving a more balanced representation of men and women throughout the organisation's workforce and thus a better use of available skills and talents.[311]

The Guide explains that a full positive action programme is likely to include:

—a commitment stage, where the organisation announces its commitment to positive action

---

[308] COM(88) 370 final.
[309] In its 'Medium Term Community Programme 1986-90', Bull. Supp. EC 3/86.
[310] Office for Official Publications of the European Communities, Luxembourg.
[311] Emphasis supplied.

—an analysis stage, in which relevant data on the organisation's workforce and
employment practices are collected and analysed so as to:
   —get an insight into the relative position of women to men and of married
   to single people within the organisation; and to
   —identify any barrier to women's or married persons' progress within the
   organisation;
—an action stage, in which measures are worked out in detail for implementation;
—a monitoring and evaluation stage, in which the way the programme
progresses is assessed and—if required—measures for adapting aspects of
the programme are devised.

It goes on to give plainly worded and extremely practical advice for
avoiding discrimination at each of these four stages; in particular, as
regards the action stage, it discusses job description and evaluation, non-
discriminatory recruitment and selection, training, working conditions
and atmosphere, career breaks and other supportive schemes, and the
relevance of goals and timetables. It is noteworthy that at no stage does it
advocate any action which would constitute a breach of the Equal
Treatment Directive.

The Community's Third Medium-Term Action Programme on Equal
Opportunities (1991-5)[312] also underlined the need for positive action
and, in the Fourth Action Programme (1996-2000),[313] sex desegregation of
the labour market is expressed as one of the objectives which is to be
pursued *inter alia* by positive action.

This was the background against which the Court was asked in *Kalanke* v.
Freie und Hansestadt Bremen:[314]

Is national legislation under which women are given priority in recruitment and/
or in obtaining promotion provided that they have the same qualifications as the
male applicants and that women are under-represented—in so far as they do not
constitute one half of the personnel—in the individual remuneration brackets in
the relevant personnel group, compatible with the principle of equal treatment
for men and women laid down by the relevant Community legislation? In other
words, does a system of quotas in favour of women, even if it is dependent on the
conditions . . . just described, embody sex discrimination contrary to Community
law or does it constitute permitted positive action inasmuch as it is designed to
promote effective equal opportunities in the world of work?[315]

---

[312] OJ [1991] C142/1.
[313] OJ [1995] L335/37, discussed further in Chap. 5.
[314] Case C-450/93 [1995] ECR I-3051. See Szyszczak, 'Positive Action After *Kalanke*'
(1996) 59 MLR 876, Moore, 'Nothing Positive From the Court of Justice' (1996) 21 ELRev.
156, Schiek, 'Positive Action in Community Law' (1996) 25 ILJ 239, and Fenwick,
'Perpetuating Inequality in the Name of Equal Treatment' (1996) 18 JSWFL 263.
[315] In the words of Tesauro AG, at 3053.

The *Kalanke* case arose in Bremen, where a law of 1990 expressly gave women priority in relation to appointment or promotion to official posts, provided that they had 'qualifications equal to those of their male co-applicants'[316] and that women were under-represented in the relevant sector in the sense that they constituted less than half its personnel.[317] The City of Bremen had advertised the post of section manager in its Parks Department. Mr Kalanke was the section manager's deputy. Ms Glissman had the same formal qualifications in horticulture and landscape gardening as Mr Kalanke. Women were under-represented in the sector involved and a dispute resulted as to the applicability of the 1990 law. This dispute was submitted to a Conciliation Board which ruled that the 1990 law did indeed apply so as to give preference to Ms Glissman. Mr Kalanke complained of this ruling to the local labour court, which dismissed his claim. On appeal to the Bundesarbeitsgericht, that court agreed that the case fell within the scope of the 1990 law but referred to the ECJ the compatibility of that 1990 law with EC law, in particular, with the Equal Treatment Directive.

The conceptual springboard for Tesauro AG was the distinction between individual and group rights. He explained that the concept of formal equality essentially focuses on the right to equal treatment as between individuals belonging to different groups, whereas substantive equality tries to achieve equal treatment as between groups. Since positive action is generally understood to refer to the elimination of the obstacles faced by groups, it marks what the Advocate General described as 'a transition from the individual vision to the collective vision of equality'.[318]

He also pointed out that the expression 'positive action' embraces a variety of different types of provisions. This is indeed true and it has been the cause, in the present writer's opinion, of much muddled argument in the past about the rights and wrongs of positive action. The first measures

---

[316] Although easy to formulate in theory, such a condition is only easy to operate in practice in a system (such as it is understood is often to be found in Germany) where a precise mathematical formula is used to determine a person's qualifications for a job. It is very much more difficult to apply where suitability for a job is determined according to more subjective criteria, including for example such matters as personality. Indeed, this is an aspect of a wider difficulty, namely, the application in practice of the so-called 'merit' principle: everything depends on how 'merit' is defined and what qualities are considered to be relevant.

[317] The national court had indicated in its order for reference that the Bremen law had to be interpreted in accordance with the Grundgesetz which meant that, even if priority was in principle to be given to women, exceptions could be made in individual cases; although the Court noted this point, it seemingly proceeded on the basis that the priority for women was absolute; see also Moore, 'Nothing positive from the Court of Justice' op. cit., n. 314. For general discussion of the use of quotas in Germany, see Shaw, 'Positive Action for Women in Germany: The Use of Legally Binding Quota Systems' in *Discrimination: the Limits of Law*, eds. Hepple & Szyszczak (Mansell, 1992).

[318] [1995] ECR I-3051, at 3058.

of positive action described by the Advocate General are those designed to remove the disadvantages and reduced opportunities encountered by women in employment; they consist of measures, for example, to attract and train women employees. Such provisions are often described in the UK as 'outreach' measures.[319] A second type of positive action seeks to redistribute family and career opportunities as between the two sexes and it therefore deals with such matters as working hours, child-care arrangements and social security or tax policies which take account of family duties. The third and strongest model identified by the Advocate General seeks to remedy 'the persistent effects of historical discrimination of legal significance' and has a 'compensatory nature, with the result that preferential treatment in favour of disavantaged categories is legitimised, in particular through systems of quotas and goals'.[320]

It is unfortunate that the Advocate General chose this formulation for his third model. To begin with, it is by no means clear that this type of positive action is to be differentiated from all other types in its attempt to remedy historical discrimination; this is surely also the motive for some actions falling into the first two categories, for example, the provision of training for jobs for which women were formerly not trained. Secondly, it seems to be the Advocate General's intention to indicate that the third model involves reverse discrimination and, by implication, that the other two models do not; this is of such critical legal importance that it is regrettable that it was not articulated more clearly. Moreover, the underlying logic is complex and requires some unravelling: any action taken to favour one group inevitably has a negative effect on the rest of society, since resources and therefore opportunities are finite. A distinction can, however, be drawn between those forms of positive action which favour one group but do not breach the anti-discrimination laws (such as the advertising of a vacancy in a women's magazine in addition to other more traditional places), and those which do breach the anti-discrimination laws (such as the choice of a woman on the ground of her sex). Furthermore, it is unfortunate that the Advocate General did not attempt to make a legal distinction between quotas and goals; they are of course essentially different from one another in that the former are mandatory whereas the latter confer a discretion; both have frequently been examined by the courts in the USA which have generally frowned on quotas but accepted goals provided that they are used for a transitional period only in order to remedy the effects of past discrimination.[321] The articulation of goals and timetables in an effort to secure fair participation

---

[319] See McCrudden, 'Rethinking Positive Action' (1986) 15 ILJ 219.
[320] [1995] ECR I-3051, at 3058.
[321] See n. 10 in the submissions of Tesauro AG and also Douglas-Scott, 'Ruling out Affirmative Action' (1995) 145 NLJ 1586.

in the work-force irrespective of religion or political belief is also a feature of the Fair Employment (Northern Ireland) Act 1989;[322] its chief purpose in that context is to raise awareness levels and to cause employers to question their own previous practices.[323]

Quotas are clearly most at odds with the notion of equality of opportunity as between individuals and they overtly sacrifice the principle of individual merit to that of the greater good. It is arguable that they constitute an effective tool for putting into place and accustoming the public to non-traditional role models and for ensuring that representatives of a disadvantaged group achieve strategically important positions.[324] Conversely however, quotas are objectionable on a number of grounds, most importantly that they constitute too crude a form of compensation to be just since it is by no means necessarily the victims of discrimination who derive any direct benefit from them; in addition, they can be viewed as patronising and they tend to result in the undervaluing of the qualities of those who do benefit directly, since observers conclude that they have achieved their position on the basis of belonging to the group in question rather than on the basis of their individual qualities. Furthermore, the attempt sometimes made to distinguish quotas in jurisprudential terms from other types of discrimination by focusing on the intention underlying them[325] involves a misunderstanding of the nature of anti-discrimination law: discrimination is a statutory tort for which intention or motive are not essential ingredients.[326]

Kalanke itself involved a quota system, albeit one of a kind which is often described as 'soft'. In other words, the German law did not demand that a precise percentage of official posts be allocated invariably to women, irrespective of the individual qualifications possessed by those women. Instead, it sprang into operation only where the contenders for a particular post were equally qualified, a system often described as a 'tie-break'. It

---

[322] See in particular s. 36. S. 58 of the same Act defines 'affirmative action' as 'action designed to secure fair participation in employment by members of the Protestant, or members of the Roman Catholic, community in Northern Ireland by means including—(a) the adoption of practices encouraging such participation, and (b) the modification or abandonment of practices that have or may have the effect of restricting or discouraging such participation'.

[323] See discussion in Chap. 5.

[324] For a powerful articulation of the arguments in favour of such types of positive action, see Bhikhu Parekh, 'A Case for Positive Discrimination' in *Discrimination: the Limits of Law*, eds. Hepple & Szyszczak (Mansell, 1992).

[325] See e.g. the dissenting judgment of Justice Stevens in the US Supreme Court in *Adarand Constructors Inc* v. *Federico Pena, Secretary of Transportation et al* (1995) 132 L Ed. 2d 158 where he asserted that to confuse positive and negative discrimination was like disregarding 'the difference between a "No Trespassing" sign and a welcome mat'.

[326] See Case 177/88 *Dekker* v. *Stichting Vormingscentrum Voor Jonge Volwassen Plus* [1990] ECR I-3941, discussed in this respect in Chap. 2, and *James* v. *Eastleigh Borough Council* [1990] 2 AC 751.

was argued that no male careers were thwarted by such a system, since a better qualified male would be appointed in preference to a female candidate. The question was whether such a scheme, whilst clearly discriminatory against men in its immediate impact, was permitted by Article 2(4) of the Directive in the light of its more far-reaching social and equitable goals. Since the discrimination involved was of a weak type, the case provided an ideal basis on which to test the issue of whether Article 2(4) permits reverse discrimination under any circumstances, or whether alternatively it is limited to forms of action which benefit women but do not discriminate against men; unfortunately, as will be seen, the Court failed to grasp this nettle.

In the view of Tesauro AG, since the expressed aim of Article 2(4) is the promotion of equality of opportunity, it is essential to define that term and to keep it uppermost in mind when determining the limits of Article 2(4). In particular, does it refer to equality 'with respect to starting points or with respect to points of arrival'? The Advocate General preferred the former view:

[G]iving equal opportunities can only mean putting people in a position to attain equal results and hence restore conditions of equality as between members of the two sexes as regards starting points . . .

It seems to me to be all too obvious that the national legislation at issue in this case is not designed to guarantee equality as regards starting points. The very fact that two candidates of different sex have equivalent qualifications implies in fact by definition that the two candidates have had and continue to have equal opportunities: they are therefore on an equal footing at the starting block. By giving priority to women, the national legislation at issue therefore aims to achieve equality as regards the result or, better, fair job distribution simply in numerical terms between men and women. That does not seem to me to fall within either the scope or the rationale of Article 2(4) . . .[327]

However, the Advocate General went on to reason that the ultimate objective of equal opportunities legislation is to attain substantive equality; since equality as regards starting points alone will not guarantee equal results because of the generally disadvantaged position of women in society, it still remained to consider whether Article 2(4) also permitted actions entailing the 'predetermination of "results"'.[328] The principle of substantive equality, the Advocate General submitted (non-controversially), requires the elimination or neutralisation of existing inequalities which hold back a particular group; to that extent, it is not gender-neutral because it involves facing up to the fact that the group is indeed disfavoured. However, any action taken must be limited to that necessary to eradicate the existing disadvantage 'so as to raise the starting

<hr />

[327] [1995] ECR I-3051, at 3060.   [328] Ibid. at 3061.

threshold of the disadvantaged category'.[329] Thus, the Advocate General concluded:

Article 2(4) . . . only enables existing inequalities affecting women to be eliminated, but certainly not through pure and simple reverse discrimination, that is to say, through measures not in fact designed to remove the obstacles preventing women from pursuing the same results on equal terms, but to confer the results on them directly or, in any event, to grant them priority in attaining those results *simply because they are women.*

In the final analysis, measures based on sex and not intended to eliminate an obstacle—to remove a situation of disadvantage—are, in their discriminatory aspect, as unlawful today for the purposes of promotion as they were in the past.[330]

The Advocate General thus opted for an interpretation of Article 2(4) which preserves the legality of most examples of his first two categories of positive action, that is to say outreach measures and those designed to reorganise family and career patterns, but which outlaws reverse discrimination by way of quotas. Unfortunately, his argument concealed his view of what many would consider to be one of the most productive and the least morally objectionable forms of positive action, namely goals or targets.

The Court, in an extremely brief judgment, apparently endorsed the views of its Advocate General. It began by reiterating two points concerning Article 2(4) which it had made in earlier judgments, namely, that it permits measures 'intended to eliminate or reduce actual instances of inequality which may exist in the reality of social life'[331] and that, as a derogation from an individual right, it must be construed strictly.[332] In concluding that a system such as that in operation in Bremen contravened the Directive, it held:

National rules which guarantee women absolute and unconditional priority for appointment or promotion go beyond promoting equal opportunities and overstep the limits of the exception in Article 2(4) . . .

Furthermore, in so far as it seeks to achieve equal representation of men and women in all grades and levels within a department, such a system substitutes for equality of opportunity as envisaged in Article 2(4) the result which is only to be arrived at by providing such equality of opportunity.[333]

---

[329] Ibid. at 3063.   [330] Ibid. at 3065.

[331] See Case 312/86 *Commission* v. *France* [1988] ECR I-6315, also discussed above.

[332] See Case 222/84 *Johnston* v. *Chief Constable of the RUC* [1986] ECR 1651, discussed above.

[333] [1995] ECR I-3051, at 3078. See also *Jepson and Dyas-Elliott* v. *Labour Party* [1996] IRLR 116, where an industrial tribunal held that Article 2(4) did not excuse all-women shortlists for the selection of parliamentary candidates which had been part of an effort to boost female representation in parliament; the tribunal considered its conclusion to be 'fully endorsed by the decision of the European Court in the *Kalanke* case' (at 119). A final blow

Although formally answering the question posed it by the referring court, this judgment did little to shed light on the detail of the law in this difficult and sensitive area. In particular, it left open two important issues in relation to the scope of Article 2(4).

First, although quotas of the type at issue in *Kalanke* are clearly outwith Article 2(4), it was not so clear from the *Kalanke* judgment whether a less peremptory system would also have been forbidden. The Court merely disapproved measures guaranteeing women 'absolute and unconditional' job priority; this formulation might simply have been intended to limit the decision to the facts of the case as it perceived them or, alternatively, it might have been meant to imply that some conditional sort of priority is permissible. That the latter interpretation was what the Court had in mind was revealed by its subsequent decision in *Marschall* v. *Land Nordrhein-Westfalen*.[334] A male German schoolteacher had been denied promotion because of a law providing for preference to be given to an equally qualified female candidate where there were fewer women than men in the grade in question; the relevant legislation, however, contained a saving clause and laid down the rule preferring women only where 'reasons specific to another candidate' did not predominate. Jacobs AG submitted that this national law, like that in *Kalanke*, involved discrimination prohibited by the Directive and that it was not saved by Article 2(4):

It is axiomatic that there is no equal opportunity for men and women in an individual case if, where all else is equal, one is appointed or promoted in preference to the other solely by virtue of his or her sex . . .

In my view the proviso to the national rule at issue in the present case does not affect the conclusion that that rule is unlawful for the following reasons.

First, . . . if the proviso operates it merely displaces the rule giving priority to women in a particular case: it does not alter the discriminatory nature of the rule in general.

Furthermore, ... the scope of the proviso at issue in the present case is (and was apparently intended to be) unclear. It is settled law that the principles of legal certainty and the protection of individuals require, in areas covered by Community law, that the Member States' legal rules should be worded unequivocally so as to give the persons concerned a clear and precise understanding of their rights and obligations and enable national courts to ensure that those rights and obligations are observed.[335]

However, the Court disagreed and distinguished *Kalanke* on the basis that there had been no saving clause there. It went on to state:

to Mr Kalanke was that he won no damages when the action returned to the German courts, since his case was regarded as insufficiently serious: see Prechal's case-note in (1996) 33 CMLRev. 1245.

[334] Case C-409/95, decision of 11 Nov. 1997 (nyr).
[335] Submissions of Jacobs AG of 15 May 1997, paras. 32-5.

[I]t appears that even where male and female candidates are equally qualified, male candidates tend to be promoted in preference to female candidates particularly because of prejudices and stereotypes concerning the role and capacities of women in working life and the fear, for example, that women will interrupt their careers more frequently, that owing to household and family duties they will be less flexible in their working hours, or that they will be absent from work more frequently because of pregnancy, childbirth and breastfeeding.

For these reasons, the mere fact that a male candidate and a female candidate are equally qualified does not mean that they have the same chances.

It follows that a national rule in terms of which, subject to the application of the saving clause, female candidates for promotion who are equally as qualified as the male candidates are to be treated preferentially in sectors where they are under-represented may fall within the scope of Article 2(4) if such a rule may counteract the prejudicial effects on female candidates of the attitudes and behaviour described above and thus reduce actual instances of inequality which may exist in the real world.[336]

It concluded that:

A national rule which, in a case where there are fewer women than men at the level of the relevant post in a sector of the public service and both female and male candidates for the post are equally qualified in terms of their suitability, competence and professional performance, requires that priority be given to the promotion of female candidates unless reasons specific to an individual male candidate tilt the balance in his favour is not precluded by Article 2(1) and (4) . . ., provided that:

—in each individual case the rule provides for male candidates who are equally as qualified as the female candidates a guarantee that the candidatures will be the subject of an objective assessment which will take account of all criteria specific to the candidates and will override the priority accorded to female candidates where one or more of the criteria tilts the balance in favour of the male candidate, and

—such criteria are not such as to discriminate against the female candidates.

A second question which, remarkably, remains unanswered even after *Kalanke* and *Marschall* is whether Article 2(4) excuses any conduct which would amount to reverse discrimination, or whether conversely it is only to be taken to refer to non-discriminatory measures. There are arguments in favour of both views.

In support of the idea that Article 2(4) does indeed excuse some acts of discrimination is its wording and position in the Directive. As seen above, Article 2(1) explains that pursuit of the principle of equality of opportunity entails the elimination of sex discrimination; the following two paragraphs of the Article then go on to articulate circumstances in which discrimination on the ground of sex is, exceptionally, apparently

---

[336] Judgment of the ECJ, paras. 29-31.

permitted. It would make sense, at least in terms of symmetry, if Article 2(4) were to be interpreted as dealing with another set of circumstances in which, in order to further the goal of equality of opportunity, certain acts of discrimination were permitted. The Court's own judgments might be seen as supporting this view, since in both *Kalanke* and *Marschall* it refers to Article 2(4) as a 'derogation' from an individual right.[337] Furthermore, there would appear to be little point in using the words 'without prejudice to' if the measures involved would not anyway be prohibited.

On the other hand, the last part of Article 2(4) cites as a particular example of the measures it has in mind the removal of existing inequalities which affect women's employment opportunities; this can be done by means of the kinds of measures described by Tesauro AG in *Kalanke* as the first two models of positive action without there necessarily being any breach of the law forbidding discrimination. In addition, there is something deeply unattractive about trying to remedy the shortcomings in the non-discrimination principle by acts of discrimination: two wrongs simply do not make a right; and, as discussed above, this defect manifests itself in a practical form when one group is advantaged and another disadvantaged through the use of quotas. The remarks of Jacobs AG in *Marschall* quoted above lend further support to this approach.[338] The Court itself in *Marschall* remained frustratingly elusive on the point although it is submitted that there is considerable significance in its reference, in the passage quoted above, to positive action *counteracting* prejudicial attitudes and behaviour; it is arguable that it intended by this formulation to assert merely that there was actually no net unlawful discrimination in the situation under consideration because the positive favouring of women simply cancelled out the negative discrimination which they were simultaneously experiencing.

A further argument against the application of Article 2(4) to permit positive discrimination can, it is submitted, be derived from the text of Article 2. As discussed above, the two apparent 'exceptions' permitted in paragraphs 2 and 3 refer respectively to cases in which 'the sex of the worker constitutes a determining factor' and those in which women require protection 'particularly as regards pregnancy and maternity'. It can be maintained that in neither of these instances is there really discrimination on the ground of sex.[339] At the heart of the concept of

---

[337] It is also noteworthy that Tesauro AG, in his remarks quoted above, confined his outlawing of reverse discrimination to that which was 'pure and simple'. From the context, it would seem that he intended by this to prohibit only that type of reverse discrimination which does not seek to remove an existing obstacle to women's employment.

[338] But cf. his remarks at paras. 40-5 which appear in places to countenance the exoneration of otherwise discriminatory conduct by Art. 2(4).

[339] In support of this point, see the remarks of Darmon AG in Case 184/83 *Hofmann* v. *Barmer Ersatzkasse* [1984] ECR 3047, at 3082, and of Tesauro AG in Case C-421/92 *Habermann-Beltermann* v. *Arbeiterwohlfahrt* [1994] ECR I-1657, at 1664, both quoted above.

'discrimination', it is submitted, lies the idea of using an *irrelevant* factor upon which to base an adverse decision; in the case of discrimination over pay, considered in Chapter 2, the assumption made by the legislature is that all differentiation based on sex is necessarily discriminatory since sex must always be irrelevant to the amount a person is paid; this is why Article 119 articulates no exceptions.[340] However, in relation to other forms of differentiation between the sexes in employment, the same assumption does not invariably hold true; on rare occasions, sex will be relevant to employment decisions. Thus, in the first exceptional situation con-templated by the Directive, sex is not irrelevant. On the contrary, it is the 'determining factor'. In the case of biological protection, the same thing applies: so, for example, not to grant a man paternity leave does not constitute discrimination against him because his sex is highly relevant to the decision—being male, he does not need time off work to recover from the process of giving birth. The so-called 'exceptions' are therefore not true exceptions and they do not therefore lead one to the view that paragraph 4 must likewise be construed as an exception. Finally, if this last argument is wrong and an exception to the non-discrimination principle can indeed be derived from Article 2(4), what are the limits which are supposed to apply to it? There is a real risk that the exception could be interpreted so widely as to compromise completely the non-discrimination principle. In the view of the present writer, the right not to be treated adversely on account of the accident of having been born male rather than female, or *vice versa*, is so fundamental a human right that strenuous efforts should be made to avoid any such compromising of it.

Some five months after the ECJ's decision in *Kalanke*, the Commission sent a Communication to the European Parliament and the Council.[341] In this document, it referred to the considerable controversy which had been provoked by the judgment[342] and to the uncertainty which it had created as to the legitimacy of positive action in favour of women.[343] It declared itself in favour of positive action 'where appropriate' and stressed that it was vital to the achievement of sex equality:

[I]t is increasingly recognised that the anti-discrimination laws which were adopted twenty years ago are not now sufficient to achieve equality for women as regards their access to employment and promotion. Despite some real progress made during the past decade in this field, the rate of unemployment amongst women is higher than amongst men in most parts of the Community. Women still

---

[340] Cf. Art. 6(3) of the Agreement on Social Policy, discussed below in n. 348.

[341] COM(96) 88 final.

[342] For example, *The Times* reported that the European Women's Lobby, a coalition of EU national women's groups, was 'shocked and disappointed' by the *Kalanke* judgment: see *The Times* 18 October 1995.

[343] It seems that quota systems were hitherto quite common in Germany, Sweden, Austria, Italy and the Netherlands.

account for the majority of the long-term unemployed, they often have low-skilled, poorly paid and insecure jobs and there are still gaps in pay between men and women. There are also still not enough women to whom decision-making posts and a full share in political and economic life are open.[344]

In addition to this objective reasoning, the Commission had another motive in speaking up for the principle of positive action; this was that it had been operating a positive action scheme within its own ranks for a number of years and it was keen to establish the legality of its own actions.[345] Its own scheme involves 'encouraging' its services to give priority to women candidates in the event of equal qualifications and merits for recruitment, promotion and appointment to managerial positions, so long as women are under-represented in the particular category concerned. The system is a permissive one and does not involve rigid quotas.

The Commission concluded that, although its judgment is difficult to interpret, the better view was that the Court in *Kalanke* meant to condemn only automatic quota systems which take no account of individual circumstances. As seen above, the Court's decision in *Marschall* confirmed this view. However, the Commission went on to assert that:

[T]he following positive action measures are examples of the types of action which remain untouched by the *Kalanke* judgment, subject, of course, to the choice which Member States may make as to the measures to be adopted by them:

—quotas linked to the qualifications required for the job, as long as they allow account to be taken of particular circumstances which might, in a given case, justify an exception to the principle of giving preference to the under-represented sex;

—plans for promoting women, prescribing the proportions and the time-limits within which the number of women should be increased but without imposing an automatic preference rule when individual decisions on recruitment and promotion are taken;

—an obligation *of principle* for an employer to recruit or promote by preference a person belonging to the under-represented sex; in such a case, no individual right to be preferred is conferred on any person;

—reductions of social security contributions which are granted to firms when they recruit women who return to the labour market, to perform tasks in sectors where women are under-represented;

—State subventions granted to employers who recruit women in sectors where they are under-represented;

—other positive action measures focusing on training, professional orientation, the reorganisation of working time, child-care and so on.[346]

[344] COM(96) 88 final, at 2.

[345] *The Times* on the morning following the *Kalanke* ruling reported that the judgment had been 'swiftly attacked by the European Commission, whose own programme for promoting women within its 19,000 staff has been declared illegal': *The Times* 18 October 1995.   [346] COM(96) 88 final, at 9-10.

The Commission's conclusions must be treated with caution as regards their conformity with the Equal Treatment Directive. Several of the examples in the list appear to countenance some element of discrimination and, to the extent that it remains unclear whether Article 2(4) permits any reverse discrimination at all, these examples are suspect.

Whilst argument about the true meaning of the *Kalanke* judgment and thus of the ambit of Article 2(4) of the Directive was rumbling on, the Member States decided to create primary legislation on the subject of positive action.[347] The new formulation had first appeared in the Agreement on Social Policy annexed at Maastricht to the EC Treaty from which the UK was excluded[348] but it was modified and generalized by the Amsterdam Treaty. At least on their face, the words chosen to express the principle appear to be calculated to go further than Article 2(4) of the Directive and to permit positively discriminatory action. Article 119(4)[349] provides:

With a view to ensuring full equality in practice between men and women in working life, the principle of equal treatment shall not prevent any Member State from maintaining or adopting measures providing for specific advantages in order to make it easier for the under-represented sex to pursue a vocational activity or to prevent or compensate for disadvantages in professional careers.

It might be thought that, in enacting this provision in such a way, the Member States intended to make it clear that it prevails over the Equal Treatment Directive and therefore that it permits acts of positive discrimination which would otherwise be unlawful. On the other hand, there are strong arguments to rebut this conclusion. First, Article 119(4) is itself predicated upon continuing respect for the principle of equal treatment. Moreover, as seen earlier in the present chapter, the ECJ regards equal treatment of the sexes as a fundamental principle underlying EC law and it is clear that it means by this to refer to an

---

[347] Jacobs AG commented in *Marschall* (nyr) that the Directive was drafted two decades ago and that 'social developments since then may mean that a provision whose intention and scope were apposite when adopted is now in need of review' (at para. 47).

[348] See Chap. 1. Article 6 reiterated Art. 119 of the EC Treaty but in para. 6(3) it added: 'This Article shall not prevent any Member State from maintaining or adopting measures providing for specific advantages in order to make it easier for women to pursue a vocational activity or to prevent or compensate for disadvantages in their professional careers'. If this paragraph was intended to refer specifically to pay advantages, it is very difficult to imagine the kinds of measures it envisaged. In 'Whither the Social Security Directives? Developments in Community Law relating to Sex Equality' in *Equality of Treatment between Women and Men in Social Security*, ed. McCrudden (Butterworths, London, 1994), Banks makes the amusing suggestion that it might have enabled the maintenance of different pensionable ages for men and women in occupational schemes and that, if this were so, it would only have been the UK which would have been excluded from this possibility.

[349] {Art. 141(4)}.

individual human right. It seems highly unlikely that the Court would be disposed to interpret any other than the clearest of words in such a way as to contravene this individual right. Secondly, although the expression 'specific advantages' used in Article 119(4) connotes strongly preferential treatment, it is to be observed that the Court used very similar language in both *Kalanke* and *Marschall* to describe the ambit of Article 2(4) of the Equal Treatment Directive:

It . . . permits national measures relating to access to employment, including promotion, which give a *specific advantage* to women with a view to improving their ability to compete on the labour market and to pursue a career on an equal footing with men.[350]

As already noted, the Court nevertheless concluded in *Kalanke* that Article 2(4) does not permit the giving of 'absolute and unconditional priority' and it is debatable whether it intended in *Marschall* to countenance anything beyond merely using the provision to permit conduct which cancels out simultaneous negative discrimination.

A third argument against Article 119(4) legitimizing positive discrimination is its gender-neutral language. The rationale for such a major departure from normal principles of justice as positive discrimination must be the urgent necessity to alleviate far-reaching discrimination. It cannot be seriously suggested that men as well as women are the victims of such discrimination in today's society.[351]

It is therefore submitted that the new provision should be interpreted as permitting only that kind of positive action which attempts to provide genuinely equal opportunities for men and women. This includes, for example, measures to encourage each sex to work in jobs traditionally the preserve of the opposite sex, and to remove practical obstacles, such as lack of education or childcare facilities, from career paths. However, it stops short of permitting anything which in itself amounts to an unlawful act of discrimination.

---

[350] [1995] ECR I-3051, at 3077. (Emphasis supplied.) See also the Court's judgment in *Marschall* (nyr), at para. 27.

[351] However, it must be conceded that the Member States appended a Declaration to the Amsterdam Treaty stating: 'When adopting measures referred to in Article 119(4) of the Treaty establishing the European Community, Member States should, in the first instance, aim at improving the situation of women in working life'.

THE PREGNANCY DIRECTIVE[352]

The Long Title and Article 1 of this Directive, based on Article 118a[353] of the Treaty, explain that its purpose is to introduce measures to encourage improvements in the safety and health at work of pregnant workers and workers who have recently given birth or are breastfeeding.[354] In so far as this instrument attempts to create a special legal régime to deal with the rights of pregnant workers, it is to be welcomed;[355] in the view of the present writer, since pregnancy and childbirth are situations which are unique to women, it is inappropriate to use the anti-discrimination legislation as the chief legal vehicle to cater for them. It is certainly vital to the concepts of equality or identity of opportunity for special rules to exist to cater for maternity rights for workers, but such rules need to be additional to the normal equality principle. However, as will be seen below, the Directive in large measure equates the position of pregnant women and those who have recently given birth with sick workers, which is not only inaccurate and patronizing but also risks making women workers appear generally weaker than men, thereby seeming to legitimize exclusionary policies.[356]

The Preamble to the instrument explains at length that the Community legislature considers pregnant workers to constitute a specially vulnerable group. In *Webb* v. *EMO (Air Cargo) Ltd.*,[357] the ECJ described the legislative intention underlying the part of the Directive prohibiting the dismissal of pregnant workers[358] thus:

In view of the harmful effects which the risk of dismissal may have on the physical and mental state of women who are pregnant, have recently given birth or are

[352] Directive 92/85, OJ [1992], L348/1, discussed by Hargreaves in 'Pregnancy and Employment: a Change of Direction in EC Law' (1995) 17 JSWFL 491.

[353] Before the amendment of this part of the EC Treaty by the Amsterdam Treaty, Art. 118a permitted the Council to adopt directives setting minimum requirements for the harmonisation of conditions relating to the health and safety of workers. The legitimacy of using this Article as the basis for measures protecting pregnant workers appeared to be assured by Case C-84/94 *UK* v. *Council* [1996] ECR I-5755, where the ECJ held that the Article was to be interpreted broadly, so as to authorise measures of social policy whose principal aim was the protection of the health and safety of workers.

[354] In reality, the purposes underlying the Directive would seem to include the protection of the health and safety of the foetus too, but this would have been outwith the scope of Art. 118a.

[355] However, the robustness of the measure was considerably weakened during the political negotiations surrounding its adoption; see Ellis, 'The Pregnancy Directive' (1993) 22 ILJ 63.

[356] See Beveridge and Nott, 'Women, Wealth and the Single Market' in *Making Ourselves Heard* (Feminist Legal Research Unit, Faculty of Law, University of Liverpool, 1995 (WP No. 3)).

[357] Case C-32/93 [1994] ECR I-3567.

[358] Art. 10 of the Directive, discussed below.

breastfeeding, including the particularly serious risk that pregnant women may be prompted voluntarily to terminate their pregnancy, the Community legislature subsequently provided, pursuant to Article 10 of [the Pregnancy Directive] . . . for special protection to be given to women, by prohibiting dismissal during the period from the beginning of their pregnancy to the end of their maternity leave.[359]

The Directive forbids any reduction in the standards of protection already existing in the Member States.[360] The Commission is required to draw up guidelines on the assessment of the chemical, physical and biological agents and industrial processes considered hazardous to pregnant workers[361] and employers are required to take action to avoid such hazards, either by adjusting the woman's working conditions or hours or by moving her to another job or by granting her leave.[362] In addition, Member States must ensure that women are not obliged to perform night work during pregnancy nor for a period following childbirth to be determined by the appropriate national authority.[363]

A continuous period of maternity leave of at least 14 weeks, of which at least two weeks must be compulsory, is required to be allocated before and/or after confinement in accordance with national rules.[364] Women on such leave are guaranteed their contractual employment rights, apart from those relating to pay;[365] they are also entitled to a payment or allowance which is at least equivalent to statutory sick pay in the Member State concerned, but this can be made conditional on the worker concerned fulfilling the national conditions for sick pay eligibility which must not provide for a qualifying period of employment of longer than 12 months immediately prior to the birth.[366] The original draft of the Directive would have provided for full pay to be maintained during the 14 weeks' leave. The UK, however, resisted such a provision on the ground of expense. The resulting compromise in practice undermines the utility of the Directive; in the UK, for example, many part-time workers do not earn more than the national insurance threshold and therefore do not satisfy the conditions for eligibility for UK statutory sick pay; they are consequently not entitled to any payment or allowance during maternity leave and this may well pressurise them into a return to work well before their theoretical entitlement to 14 weeks' leave has elapsed. It is relevant to note in this context that the ECJ held in *Gillespie* v. *Northern Health and Social Services Board*[367] that, although Article 119 and the Equal Pay Directive do not lay down criteria for determining the quantum of

---

[359] [1994] ECR I-3567, at 3586.

[361] Ibid., Art. 3(1).

[363] Ibid., Art. 7.

[365] Ibid., Art. 11(2)(a).

[366] Ibid., Arts. 11(2)(b), 11(3) and 11(4).

[60] Art. 1(3) of the Directive.

[362] Ibid., Art. 5. See also Art. 6.

[364] Ibid., Art. 8.

[367] Case C-342/93 [1996] ECR I-475.

maternity pay, they guarantee a minumum level: 'The amount payable could not . . . be so low as to undermine the purpose of maternity leave, namely the protection of women before and after giving birth. In order to assess the adequacy of the amount payable from that point of view, the national court must take account, not only of the length of maternity leave, but also of the other forms of social protection afforded by national law in the case of justified absence from work'[368].

Pregnant workers must also be entitled to time off without loss of pay in order to attend ante-natal examinations, where such examinations have to take place during working hours.[369]

Article 10 requires that:

1. Member States shall take the necessary measures to prohibit the dismissal of workers . . . during the period from the beginning of their pregnancy to the end of the maternity leave referred to in Article 8(1), save in exceptional cases not connected with their condition which are permitted under national legislation and/or practice and, where applicable, provided that the competent authority has given its consent;
2. if a worker . . . is dismissed during the period referred to in point 1, the employer must cite duly substantiated grounds for her dismissal in writing;
3. Member States shall take the necessary measures to protect workers . . . from consequences of dismissal which is unlawful by virtue of point 1.

The relationship between this provision and Article 5 of the Equal Treatment Directive[370] remains a matter for speculation. As discussed above, the ECJ held in *Webb* v. *EMO (Air Cargo) Ltd.*[371] that the Equal Treatment Directive prohibits the dismissal for pregnancy of a woman employed on an indefinite contract, but it left open the question of whether the same conclusion would have been reached where she had been employed for a temporary period only.[372] The apparently unlimited terms of Article 10 of the Pregnancy Directive appear to capture this situation and to render dismissal illegal even where the pregnant woman is employed on a temporary contract,[373] a conclusion supported by the Court's remark in *Handels-OG Kontorfunktionaererernes Forbund i Danmark,*

---

[368] Ibid. at 500. In *Gillespie* v. *Northern Health and Social Services Board (No. 2)* [1997] IRLR 410, the Northern Ireland Court of Appeal held that, since the Directive expressly deems statutory maternity pay to be adequate if it guarantees income at least equivalent to statutory sickness benefit, it cannot be said that contractual maternity pay is inadequate if it is higher than such sickness benefit.

[369] Art. 9 of the Directive.

[370] Discussed above.

[371] Case C-32/93 [[1994] ECR I-3567.

[372] See also Case C-421/92 *Habermann-Beltermann* v. *Arbeiterwohlfahrt* [1994] ECR I-1657.

[373] It is particularly difficult in this situation to balance the rights of women to substantive equality with those of an employer trying to run a commercial enterprise; see further McGlynn, 'Pregnancy Dismissals and the *Webb* Litigation' (1996) Vol. IV, no. 2, Feminist Legal Studies 229.

acting on behalf of Helle Elisabeth Larsson v. *Dansk Handel & Service, acting on behalf of Fotex Supermarked A/S:*[374]

It is clear from the objective of [Article 10] that absence during the protected period, other than for reasons unconnected with the employee's condition, can no longer be taken into account as grounds for subsequent dismissal.[375]

It is to be noted that the Equal Treatment Directive rather than the Pregnancy Directive is the only instrument which may be relied on where the unfavourable treatment of a worker on account of her pregnancy takes a form other than dismissal, since Article 10 of the Pregnancy Directive deals only with dismissal.

In wording familiar from Article 6 of the Equal Treatment Directive,[376] the Directive requires the Member States to introduce national measures to enable all workers who consider themselves wronged by a breach of its terms 'to pursue their claims by judicial process (and/or, in accordance with national laws and/or practices) by recourse to other competent authorities'.[377]

The Member States were given two years (in other words, until October 1994) to bring into force the provisions needed to comply with the Directive.[378] These provisions have to be communicated to the Commission[379], which is obliged to report periodically to the Parliament, Council and Economic and Social Committee on the implementation of the instrument.[380]

The ECJ had not, by the time of writing, had occasion to decide whether any of the provisions of the Pregnancy Directive take direct effect; bearing in mind that the critical factors in relation to direct effect are the precision and completeness of the provision in question,[381] it would seem strongly arguable that a number of articles contained in the Pregnancy Directive take direct effect,[382] in particular those prohibiting the reduction of existing protection, nightwork and dismissal on account of pregnancy,

---

[374] Case C-400/95 (nyr).

[375] Ibid. at para. 25.

[376] As to which see above.

[377] Art. 12 of the Pregnancy Directive. In the UK, protection against dismissal on account of pregnancy takes the form of a right to claim unfair dismissal pursuant to s. 99 of the Employment Rights Act 1996; since the damages in such a claim are subject to a statutory ceiling, it would seem to be open to a claimant to assert the vertical direct effect of Art. 10 and argue, on the authority of Case C-271/91 *Marshall* v. *South-West Hants Area Health Authority (No. 2)* [1993] ECR I-4367, that the ceiling must be set aside where it inhibits the award of damages which are adequate in the circumstances (see discussion of *Marshall (No. 2)* above).

[378] Art. 14(1) of the Directive.

[379] Ibid., Art. 14(3).

[380] Ibid., Art. 14(5).

[381] See Chap. 1.

[382] Subject, of course, to the inability of directives to take horizontal effect, as to which see Chap. 1.

together with those conferring entitlement to maternity leave, ante-natal care, minimum allowances and contractual rights.

THE DIRECTIVE ON PARENTAL LEAVE[383]

This Directive enacts a framework agreement concluded on 14 December 1995 pursuant to the Protocol and Agreement on Social Policy.[384] The Preamble stresses the importance of the instrument as a means of reconciling work and family life and for the promotion of equal opportunities between men and women. Part I goes on to proclaim:

5. Whereas the Council Resolution of 6 December 1994 recognizes that an effective policy of equal opportunities presupposes an integrated overall strategy allowing for better organization of working hours and greater flexibility, and for an easier return to working life, and notes the important role of the two sides of industry in this area and in offering both men and women an opportunity to reconcile their work responsibilities with family obligations;

6. Whereas measures to reconcile work and family life should encourage the introduction of new flexible ways of organizing work and time which are better suited to the changing needs of society and which should take the needs of both undertakings and workers into account . . .

8. Whereas men should be encouraged to assume an equal share of family responsibilities, for example they should be encouraged to take parental leave by means such as awareness programmes . . .

A right to parental leave for at least three months is granted to all workers on the birth or adoption of a child.[385] This right persists until the child reaches an age defined for each Member State up to eight years and it is is non-transferable.[386] It is left up to the Member States to decide whether to grant parental leave on a full-time or part-time basis, in a piecemeal way or in the form of a time-credit system; they can subject the right to a service qualification not exceeding one year and can require the worker to give notice to the employer.[387] Employers may postpone the granting of parental leave 'for justifiable reasons related to the operation of the undertaking (e.g. where work is of a seasonal nature, where a replacement cannot be found within the notice period, where a significant proportion of the work-force applies for parental leave at the same time

---

[383] Directive 96/34, OJ [1996] L145/4.

[384] See Chap. 1. Pursuant to the new UK government's decision in 1997 to become party to the instruments adopted under the Protocol and Agreement on Social Policy, the Directive on Parental Leave was extended to the UK by Directive 97/75, OJ [1998] L10/24.

[385] Part II, Clause 2(1) of the Agreement.

[386] Ibid., Part II, Clause 2(1) and (2).

[387] Ibid., Part II, Clause 2(3)(a), (b) and (d).

where a specific function is of strategic importance)'[388] and special arrangement are allowed 'to meet the operational and organizational requirements of small undertakings'.[389]

The Member States are required to protect workers against dismissal (though not other forms of retributive treatment) on the ground of seeking or taking parental leave.[390] When parental leave ends, the worker has the right to return to the same job or, if that is not possible, to 'an equivalent or similar job consistent with their employment contract'[391] and rights acquired, or being acquired, at the start of the leave must be maintained until the end of the leave.[392]

In addition to parental leave, the Directive entitles workers to time off work 'on grounds of *force majeure* for urgent family reasons in cases of sickness or accident making the immediate presence of the worker indispensable' although this may be limited to a certain amount of time per year.[393]

It seems likely that the chief effect of this instrument will be a symbolic one, emphasising as it clearly does the importance of both parents to the welfare of families and the importance of both parents to making a reality of equal opportunities legislation for women.[394] The obvious shortcomings of the measure are the short period of leave permitted, the exclusions with which the right is surrounded, and the fact that no provision is made for payment of the worker during leave; the instrument even concedes that all relevant matters relating to social security remain to be determined by the Member States individually.[395]

The Member States were given until 3 June 1998 to comply with the terms of the Directive.[396]

THE DIRECTIVE ON PART-TIME WORK[397]

Another product of the Protocol and Agreement on Social Policy, this Directive enacted the Framework Agreement between the social partners on part-time work. Its purpose is expressed to be:

[388] Ibid. Part II, Clause 2(3)(e).   [389] Ibid. Part II, Clause 2(3)(e).
[390] Ibid. Part II, Clause 2(4).   [391] Ibid. Part II, Clause 2(5).
[392] Ibid. Part II, Clause 2(6).   [393] Ibid. Part II, Clause 3.
[394] In similar vein, see also the Recommendation on Childcare, Recommendation 92/241, OJ [1992], L123/16, which encourages the Member States to take initiatives to enable both sexes to reconcile their occupational, family and upbringing responsibilities arising from the care of children.
[395] Part II, Clause 2(8) of the Agreement.
[396] Art. 2 of the Directive. The Article goes on to give them an additional year, if this is necessary 'to take account of special difficulties or implementation by a collective agreement' Directive 97/75, OJ [1998] L10/24, allows the UK until 15 Dec. 1999 for the implementation of the Parental Leave Directive.
[397] Directive 97/81, OJ [1998] L14/9.

(a) to provide for the removal of discrimination against part-time workers and to improve the quality of part-time work;

(b) to facilitate the development of part-time work on a voluntary basis and to contribute to the flexible organization of working time in a manner which takes into account the needs of employers and workers.[398]

Part-time workers are defined as employees whose normal hours of work are 'less than the normal hours of work of a comparable full-time worker'; interestingly,[399] where there is no comparable full-time worker in the same establishment, the comparison is to be made by reference to the applicable collective agreement or, in the absence of such an agreement, in accordance with national law, collective agreements or practice.[400] Part-timers working on a casual basis may be excluded from the coverage of the instrument 'for objective reasons'.[401]

The core of the Agreement appears to add little to the existing case law of the Court on indirect discrimination. Clause 4 states:

1. In respect of employment and conditions, part-time workers shall not be treated in a less favourable manner than comparable full-time workers solely because they work part-time unless different treatment is justified on objective grounds.

2. Where appropriate, the principle of *pro rata temporis* shall apply . . .

However, the instrument is at pains to stress the importance of providing opportunities for part-time work at all levels within enterprises, providing in particular in Clause 5(1) that:

(a) Member States, following consultations with the social partners in accordance with national law or practice, should identify and review obstacles of a legal or administrative nature which may limit the opportunities for part-time work and, where appropriate, eliminate them;

(b) the social partners, acting within their sphere of competence and through the procedures set out in collective agreements, should identify and review obstacles which may limit opportunities for part-time work and, where appropriate, eliminate them.

Clause 5(2) adds that a worker's refusal to transfer from full-time to part-time work, or *vice versa*, should not in itself constitute a valid reason for dismissal.

The Member States were given until 20 January 2000 to comply with the terms of the Directive.[402]

---

[398] Clause 1 of the Framework Agreement, which is annexed to the Directive.

[399] See discussion in Chap. 2 of the scope of comparison permitted by Art. 119.

[400] Clause 3 of the Agreement.   [401] Ibid., Clause 2.

[402] Article 2 of the Directive. A maximum of one further year is permitted by this Article, if necessary, to take account of special difficulties or implementation by a collective agreement.

THE DIRECTIVE ON EQUAL TREATMENT OF THE
SELF-EMPLOYED[403]

The long title of this instrument is 'Council Directive on the Application of the Principle of Equal Treatment between Men and Women Engaged in an Activity, including Agriculture, in a Self-employed Capacity, on the Protection of Self-employed Women during Pregnancy and Motherhood'. The mischief at which it was specifically directed was the problem that self-employed women, especially those engaged in agriculture of whom many are farmers' wives who in fact play an active role in the running of their farms, complained that they did not enjoy a clearly defined occupational status. They did not receive an identifiable sum by way of pay, and this had the consequence that their social security entitlements, including pensions, were often unclear. They were also rarely to be found on the bodies representing the agriculture industry, and other self-employed sectors. Perhaps even more importantly, they faced grave difficulties in the event of pregnancy, being normally ineligible for maternity allowances related to employment. The Commission, in making its proposal on which the Directive was based, considered that a system of compensatory allowances should be devised for self-employed women taking maternity leave in general, but that for women engaged in agriculture what was also needed was access to a replacement service to cover for them during their absence.[404] Given the seriousness of these underlying problems, the solutions adopted by the Directive appear extremely weak and read more like those in a Recommendation than a binding legal instrument.

Based on both Articles 100[405] and 235[406] of the EC Treaty, the Directive in its Preamble makes special note of the fact that specific provision is required to protect persons engaged in a self-employed capacity in an activity in which their spouses are also engaged. It explains in Article 1 that its purpose is:

[T]o ensure . . . application in the Member States of the principle of equal treatment as between men and women in an activity in a self-employed capacity, or contributing to the pursuit of such an activity, as regards those aspects not covered by Directives 76/207/EEC and 79/7/EEC.[407]

As a result of Article 2, it covers:

    (a)   self-employed workers i.e. all persons pursuing a gainful activity for their own account, under the conditions laid down by national law, including farmers and members of the liberal professions;

---

[403] Directive 86/613, OJ [1986], L359/56.   [404] COM(84) 57 final/2.
[405] {Art. 94}.   [406] {Art. 308}.
[407] The Equal Treatment and Social Security Directives respectively.

(b) their spouses, not being employees or partners, where they habitually, under the conditions laid down by national law, participate in the activities of the self-employed worker and perform the same tasks or ancillary tasks.

Article 3 applies to these persons the principle of equal treatment, using language similar but puzzlingly not identical to that of the Equal Treatment Directive: 'For the purposes of this Directive the principle of equal treatment implies the absence of all discrimination on grounds of sex, either directly or indirectly, by reference in particular to marital or family status.'[408] From this point onwards, the provisions of the Directive are markedly unhelpful. There is no provision guaranteeing equal pay to those covered by the Directive irrespective of sex, nor to any kind of defined occupational status. Instead, Article 4 merely obliges the Member States to take the measures necessary to ensure:

the elimination of all provisions which are contrary to the principle of equal treatment as defined in Directive 76/207/EEC, especially in respect of the establishment, equipment or extension of any other form of self-employed activity including financial facilities.

This does not address the real problem, since it is not the existence of provisions contrary to the principle of equal treatment which have hitherto prevented the formalization of these women's positions; it is rather the absence of any national legislation requiring the recognition of their status. The Directive should therefore have been cast in positive terms, requiring the Member States to take action to achieve such recognition. All that the instrument provides in this respect is contained in the completely open-ended Article 7:

Member States shall undertake to examine under what conditions recognition of the work of the spouses referred to in Article 2(b) [i.e. working spouses of self-employed persons] may be encouraged and, in the light of such examination, consider any appropriate steps for encouraging such recognition.[409]

Article 5 requires the Member States to take the measures necessary to ensure that the conditions for the formation of a company between spouses are not more restrictive than the conditions for the formation of a company between unmarried persons. This is obviously of no help where the circumstances of the spouses are not such that they wish to form a company.

Again, as regards coverage by the national social security systems, the Directive permits the Member States an enormous amount of freedom. There is no requirement to ensure that those within the scope of the

---

[408] Note in particular the absence of the word 'whatsoever' from this definition. Cf. Art. 2 of the Equal Treatment Directive, as to which see the discussion above.

[409] See also Arnull, 'Equal Treatment and the Self-Employed' (1988) 13 ELRev. 58.

Directive are in fact covered by adequate social security schemes. Instead, Article 6 merely provides:

Where a contributory social security system for self-employed workers exists in a Member State, that Member State shall take the necessary measures to enable the spouses referred to in Article 2(b) who are not protected under the self-employed workers' social security scheme to join a contributory social security scheme voluntarily.

One obvious problem resulting from this solution is that only better-off women will benefit from it because only they are likely to join voluntarily.[410]

Most disappointing of all are the Directive's provisions in the field of pregnancy and maternity. These make no guarantee whatsoever that women within the scope of the Directive will receive maternity allowances as they would if they were employed; still less do they confer any entitlement to replacement services, contrary to the advice of the Commission.

Article 8 states:

Member States shall undertake to examine whether, and under what conditions female self-employed workers and the wives of self-employed workers may, during interruptions in their occupational activity owing to pregnancy or motherhood,

— have access to services supplying temporary replacements or existing national social services, or
— be entitled to cash benefits under a social security scheme or under any other public social protection system.

The Directive contains the usual general and final provisions, requiring the Member States to provide proper judicial redress for breach of its provisions[411] and to bring the relevant national implementing measures to the notice of those covered by the instrument.[412] The Member States were given until 30 June 1989 to comply with the Directive, except where, in order to comply with Article 5 on the formation of companies, amendment was needed to the national legislation dealing with matrimonial rights and obligations, in which case the deadline for compliance with Article 5 was extended to 30 June 1991.[413]

Article 11 required the Council to review the Directive, on a proposal from the Commission, before 1 July 1993. To this end, the Member States had to forward to the Commission, not later than 30 June 1991, all the information necessary to enable it to draw up a report on the application of the Directive for submission to the Council.[414] The Dutch Institute for

---

[410] See the interview with Cecile Boeraeve, President of the Women's Committee of COPA which represents European Community farming organizations, reported in CREW Reports (1989), vol. 9, no. 4, 10.

[411] Art. 9 of the Directive.   [412] Ibid., Art. 10.

[413] Ibid., Art. 12.   [414] Ibid., Art. 13.

Policy Research reported to the European Commission in 1990 that the Directive had not produced any marked improvements in the position of self-employed women. It recommended that there should be increased supervision over the functioning of the Directive, and also that the instrument should be amended in a variety of ways so as to confer more specific and clearcut rights on those whom it seeks to cover.[415]

[415] See CREW Reports (1990), vol. 10, no. 3/4, 3–5.

4

Sex Equality in Social Security

Scope of the Social Security Directive

The Social Security Directive extends to the sphere of social security 'the principle of equal treatment for men and women set out in Article 119 of the EEC Treaty as regards equal pay for equal work', in the words of Mayras AG in *Worsdorfer* v. *Raad van Arbeid.*[2] The instrument itself, even in its Preamble, is somewhat more guarded, explaining that:

[T]he principle of equal treatment in matters of social security should be implemented in the first place in the statutory schemes which provide protection against the risks of sickness, invalidity, old age, accidents at work, occupational diseases and unemployment, and in social assistance in so far as it is intended to supplement or replace the above-mentioned schemes. [3]

It adds that:

[T]he implementation of the principle of equal treatment in matters of social security does not prejudice the provisions relating to the protection of women on the ground of maternity; whereas in this respect, Member States may adopt specific provisions for women to remove existing instances of unequal treatment.[4]

It has been described as 'the last of the "strong" Directives, adopted in the 1970s when there was still some push behind the early 1970s idea of the Community extending its competence in the social field'.[5]

The potential scope of the Directive may not have been quite clear to all those involved in its drafting and negotiation.[6] At the very least, its rationale could be assumed to be to extend the principle of equal treatment of the sexes from the employment situation to those situations in which the State makes payments to compensate persons who are unable to continue in paid work, for example, because of physical disability: it is in a sense a logical counterpart to the equal pay principle in such cases. Even this narrow rationale goes beyond the UK's domestic anti-discrimination

---

[1] Directive 79/7, OJ [1979] L6/24.
[2] Case 9/79 [1979] ECR 2717, at 2728.
[3] Second recital.
[4] Third recital. See also below.
[5] Hoskyns and Luckhaus, 'The European Community Directive on Equal Treatment in Social Security' (1989) Policy and Politics, Vol. 17, No. 4, 321.
[6] See ibid.

laws. The Directive itself outlaws both direct and indirect sex discrimination in social security and this has wide-ranging and important implications. Many of the national social security systems of the Member States of the EC are based upon the model of the family unit consisting of one breadwinner (traditionally of course male), together with one adult dependant (traditionally female) and dependent children. Such a model is highly prone to discrimination against the female sex, of a direct kind where the legislation is expressed in gender-specific terms, and of an indirect kind where the 'non-breadwinning' partner receives lesser social security benefits than the 'breadwinner' and it can be shown that this former group is composed primarily of women. Whether or not the inclusion of indirect discrimination within its terms enables the Social Security Directive to require radical recasting of the social security systems of the Member States, not apparently an intended consequence at the time of its enactment, is examined later in the present chapter.

It is important to observe, however, that the Directive does not go so far as to mandate the individualization of benefits, in other words, the treatment of each adult person as a separate unit; couples can still be aggregated for the purpose of determining benefits, so long as the system operates in a gender-neutral fashion.[7] This remains one of the most serious shortcomings of the legislation in the view of its more radical critics (because of its basis in an outmoded stereotype). Moreover, neither does the Directive require the harmonization of all the systems in operation in the Member States. There was clearly no political consensus to go this far when the instrument was drafted, and indeed even today such an aspiration appears distant. The Commission, commenting on the Social Charter agreed in principle by the Heads of Government at the Summit Meeting of December 1989,[8] ruled out harmonization of social security systems, but said that divergence between the Member States in this matter might place 'a brake on free movement and exacerbate regional imbalances, particularly north-south'.[9] In the Action Programme published by the Commission as an accompaniment to the Social Charter,[10] it commented:

The social security systems vary greatly in nature from one Member State of the Community to another. They reflect the history, traditions and social and cultural

---

[7] Cf. the comment of Laurent, Principal Administrator in the European Commission, in 'European Community Law and Equal Treatment for Men and Women in Social Security' (1982) 121 International Labour Review 373, at 385: '[T]he whole orientation of European Community law in matters of equal treatment for men and women . . . aims at setting in motion an irreversible evolutionary process in which each of the spouses will be granted independent social rights, as in matters of civil and political rights, where such equality is already broadly achieved'.   [8] See Chap. 3.

[9] See CREW Reports (Nov./Dec. 1989), Vol. 9, Nos. 11/12, 15.

[10] COM(89) 568.

practices proper to each Member State, which cannot be called into question. There can therefore be no question of harmonizing the systems existing in these fields.

As a result, the Commission merely proposed in the Action Programme two Recommendations in the field of social security, one on the convergence of objectives in national schemes[11] and the other on resourcing.[12] The Commission's White Paper on Social Policy pledged it to give consideration to a 'Recommendation on the adaptation of social protection systems to changing family structures, notably through the individualization of rights and contributions on the basis of a comparison of actual gender inequalities in social security'.[13] In the Fourth Action Programme[14] the Commission promised to undertake further studies on the individualization of rights in social security, tax, and related areas, drawing on experience gained in the Member States. In the light of these findings, it said that it would publish a Communication on individualization in 1997[15] and would thereafter decide on proposals for progressive change in this area. The Dublin Summit meeting of December 1996 also stressed the need to make social security systems more employment-friendly by 'developing social protection systems capable of adapting to new patterns of work and of providing appropriate protection to people engaged in such work'.

Sjerps has pointed out[16] that the principle of equality as regards social security benefits finds readier and more general acceptance in relation to wage-related benefits (usually granted for a limited period in cases of unemployment, disablement, and sickness) than in relation to means-tested benefits (guaranteeing a minimum income in cases where the recipient has no other income). She has noted that people find it increasingly logical that, when a man and woman do the same job and pay the same contributions, they should also receive the same wage-related benefits. On the other hand, many also still seem to incline to the view that when it comes to means-tested or 'safety-net' benefits, people should

[11] Subsequently Council Recommendation on the convergence of social protection policies and objectives, 92/442, OJ [1992] L245/49. This provides that social benefits should be granted, *inter alia*, in accordance with the principle of 'equal treatment in such a way as to avoid any discrimination based on nationality, race, sex, religion, customs or political opinion' (at IA2(a)) and so as to 'help remove obstacles to occupational activity by parents through measures to reconcile family and professional responsibilities' (at IA6(c)).

[12] Subsequently Council Recommendation on common criteria concerning sufficient resources and social assistance in social protection systems, 92/441, OJ [1992] L245/46.

[13] *European Social Policy—A Way Forward for the Union* COM(94) 333 final, at 36.

[14] Fourth Community Action Programme on Equal Opportunities for Women and Men (1996–2000), COM(95) 381 final; OJ [1995] L335/37.

[15] At the time of writing, this Communication was still awaited.

[16] Sjerps, 'Indirect Discrimination in Social Security in the Netherlands: Demands of the Dutch Women's Movement', in *Women, Equality and Europe*, eds. Buckley and Anderson (Macmillan, London, 1988).

turn first for subsistence not to the state but to members of their families and others closest to them. Such a view of course also militates against the individualization of the latter type of benefits.

The complexity and diversity of the social security systems to be found in the Member States led the Council to adopt a phased approach to the EC legislation. It was originally proposed to include social security as part of the working conditions to which the principle of equality of treatment was applied by the Equal Treatment Directive.[17] However, as the ramifications of this plan became appreciated, it was abandoned in favour of specific legislation dealing with social security, the undertaking to introduce such legislation being expressly written into Article 1(2) of the earlier Directive. Somewhat similarly, the original plans for the Social Security Directive covered occupational social security schemes, but these were eventually omitted from the 1979 instrument on the understanding, articulated in Article 3(3) of the Directive, that they would be covered by subsequent legislation. That legislation took the form of the Occupational Social Security Directive,[18] discussed in Chapter 2 because of its close connection in practice with Article 119 of the Treaty. A third social security directive was proposed by the Commission in 1987.[19] This aimed to take the process of equalizing treatment in social security systems yet further, in particular by removing the existing exceptions for pensionable age and survivors' and family benefits.[20] It was to some extent overtaken by events, notably the ECJ's decision in *Barber* v. *Guardian Royal Exchange Assurance Group*,[21] and was subsequently withdrawn on the Commission's promise in its Fourth Action Programme[22] to present an updated proposal. The problems posed in relation to reform of social security laws have clearly been greatly exacerbated by the demographic changes taking place recently within the EU, resulting in a very marked ageing of the population and in radically altering patterns of family life.[23]

---

[17] See generally Chap. 3.
[18] Directive 86/378, OJ [1986] L225/40.
[19] COM(87) 494 final; OJ [1987] C309/10.
[20] As to which, see below.
[21] Case C-262/88 [1990] ECR I-1889, discussed in Chaps. 2 and 3.
[22] The Fourth Community Action Programme on Equal Opportunities for Women and Men (1996–2000) COM(95) 381 final; OJ [1995] L335/37, discussed in Chap. 5.
[23] In the EU as a whole, there were 64 million people aged over 60 in 1990 viz. about 20% of the total population, but by 2020 that proportion is expected to be above 25%. The fastest growing section of the population is the very old (aged 80 and above) and projections suggest an increase of over 50% to about 5.5% of the population by 2020: see *Older People in the European Community* (Family Policy Studies Centre/ Centre for Policy on Ageing, 1993). The ratio of those aged 65 and over to the working population was 23% in 1990, but is expected to rise to 26% by 2005 and to 35.5% by 2025: see *A Social Portrait of Europe* (Eurostat, 1996). For detailed data on recent changes in family forms and policies, see *Developments in National Family Policies in 1995* and *A Synthesis of National Family Policies 1995* (both by the European Observatory on National Family Policies, Commission, 1996).

The Social Security Directive is based upon Article 235[24] of the EC Treaty, as is the Equal Treatment Directive, no doubt because, like the latter instrument, its aims are not the harmonization or 'approximation' envisaged by Article 100.[25] The possible direct effect of its provisions, not of course precluded by its legal basis in Article 235,[26] is less problematic than in the case of the Equal Pay and Equal Treatment Directives; the inability of directives to produce horizontal direct effects leads to anomalies where the provision in question is relevant to the legal position *vis-à-vis* two individuals (in this context, employer and employee). The Social Security Directive, however, seeks to regulate relations between the state and individuals and therefore its applicability is of the 'vertical' kind.[27]

Substantive Rights Conferred by the Directive

Article 1 articulates the aim of the instrument:

The purpose of this Directive is the progressive implementation, in the field of social security and other elements of social protection provided for in Article 3, of the principle of equal treatment for men and women in matters of social security, hereinafter referred to as 'the principle of equal treatment'.

The essentially limited nature of this purpose was pointed out by Darmon AG in *De Weerd, née Roks*,[28] where he observed that the Directive 'is in no way intended to regulate the operation of Member States' social security schemes, nor to determine a lower or upper limit on the amount of the benefits given to victims of one of the risks listed in the Directive'.[29]

Article 2, in defining the persons to whom the Directive applies, points to a logical link with financially remunerated work. It provides:

This Directive shall apply to the working population—including self-employed persons, workers and self-employed persons whose activity is interrupted by illness, accident or involuntary unemployment and persons seeking employment—and to retired or invalided workers and self-employed persons.

The instrument thus appears to extend to those not currently in work because of their inability to work, unemployment, or old age,[30] but also

---

[24] {Art. 308}. As mentioned in Chap. 3, Usher has questioned the 'vires' of the Social Security Directive, on the ground that, in permitting differential state pensionable ages for men and women (discussed later in the present chapter), it infringes the fundamental principle of the equality of the sexes under EC law; see Usher, 'European Community Equality Law: Legal Instruments and Judicial Remedies' in *Women, Employment and European Equality Law*, ed. McCrudden (Eclipse Publications, London, 1987).   [25] {Art. 94}.

[26] See Chap. 1.   [27] See generally the discussion in Chap. 1.

[28] Case C-343/92 [1994] ECR I-571.   [29] Ibid. at 580.

[30] The ECJ in Case C-280/94 *Posthuma-Van Damme v. Bestuur van de Bedrijfsvereniging voor Detailhandel, Ambachten en Huisvrouwen* [1996] ECR I-179 therefore rejected the contrary

seems from its wording to omit certain important categories. [31] In particular, the use of the word 'interrupted' suggests that those who have never been in work (for example, because of some disability) are excluded; similarly, its reference to those seeking 'employment' unfortunately seems to rule out those persons (mainly women) who are engaged in non-paid domestic work caring for children, spouses, and infirm relatives, unless they can demonstrate that they belong within some other category of persons covered by the Directive. The non-application of the Directive to many housewives constitutes one of the major shortcomings of the instrument and demonstrates how a heavily male-orientated work model has dominated the thinking of even the drafters of the equality legislation.

This essentially textual analysis of the provision has been supported by the case law, which shows that, though the ECJ is prepared in some instances to give a broad reading to the Article, there are limits beyond which it will not pass and which have the effect of excluding significant sections of the population, a large proportion of whom are probably women. [32]

The ECJ's first decision on the scope of Article 2 came in *Drake* v. *Chief Adjudication Officer*. [33] Ms Drake gave up her paid employment in 1984 in order to look after her severely disabled mother. The mother received an attendance allowance under the relevant UK social security legislation, but, as a result of s. 37 of the Social Security Act 1975, Ms Drake was refused an invalid care allowance because she was a married woman living with her husband. She claimed that this refusal contravened the Social Security Directive and the case was referred to the ECJ for a preliminary ruling. One of the issues which arose before the ECJ was whether Ms Drake was a person covered by Article 2 of the Directive (despite the fact that the adjudication officer had conceded this point). The difficulty was that she was not *herself* currently seeking employment and, though her previous employment had been interrupted by disability, it was not her own disability but her mother's. The ECJ nevertheless took a generous view of the scope of the Directive *ratione personae* and held:

[Article 2 of the Directive] is based on the idea that a person whose work has been interrupted by one of the risks referred to in Article 3 belongs to the working population. That is the case of Mrs Drake, who has given up work solely

argument of the Commission and held that a person who, in the year preceding commencement of an incapacity to work, did not receive a certain income from or in connection with work did not necessarily fall outside the scope *ratione personae* of the Directive.

[31] E.g. on its face, it would appear not to cover persons seeking to set themselves up as self-employed, as distinct from those seeking employment.

[32] See Cousins, 'Equal Treatment and Social Security' (1994) 19 ELRev. 123 and Sohrab, 'Women and Social Security: the Limits of EEC Equality Law' [1994] JSWFL 5.

[33] Case 150/85 [1986] ECR 1995.

because of one of the risks listed in Article 3, namely the invalidity of her mother. She must therefore be regarded as a member of the working population for the purposes of the Directive.[34]

Such reasoning, of course, would not apply to women giving up work to look after their healthy spouses or children, since the fact of having a family is not one of the 'risks' specified by Article 3. This was confirmed by the Court's later ruling in *Acterberg-te Riele* v. *Sociale Verzekeringsbank.*[35] Under the Netherlands old age pensions system, which was in operation until legislative amendment in 1985, a married woman resident in the Netherlands did not qualify for a pension if her husband, though also a resident of the Netherlands, had worked and was insured abroad. The system was discriminatory because the reverse was not also the case, so that a husband retained his right to a Netherlands pension even if his wife was insured abroad. The Social Insurance Bank refused to grant a full old age pension on this basis to three women whose husbands had worked abroad; two of the women had themselves had jobs until they voluntarily ceased work, and the third had never had a job. The ECJ held that it could be inferred from Article 2 of the Directive, when read together with Article 3, that it only covered persons who were working at the time when they were entitled to claim an old age pension, and persons whose economic activity had previously been interrupted by one of the other risks set out in Article 3(1)(a).[36] This meant that the Directive was not applicable to persons who had never been available on the labour market or who had ceased to be so where the reason for their giving up work was not the materialization of one of the risks referred to in the Directive. Furthermore, the Court added, in a disappointingly narrow spirit, that this interpretation was consistent with the purpose of EC law and with the wording of the other provisions forming the background to the Social Security Directive. The purpose of Article 119 of the Treaty and the Equal Pay and Equal Treatment Directives was to bring about equal treatment for men and women, not in a general way, but solely in their capacity as workers.

This approach was confirmed by the Court's decision in *Züchner* v. *Handelskrankenkasse Bremen.*[37] This involved a claim to a welfare benefit in respect of the caring services provided by a wife who looked after her severely disabled husband. It was argued that, although Ms Züchner had not given up an occupation in order to care for her husband, neither could she thereafter have taken up an occupation because of the extent and intensity of the care she provided; no distinction, it was maintained,

[34] Ibid. at 2009.
[35] Cases 48/88, 106/88 & 107/88 [1989] ECR 1963.
[36] See also the remarks of Darmon AG in Case C-31/90 *Johnson* v. *Chief Adjudication Officer* [1991] ECR I-3723, at 3739–40.
[37] Case C-77/95 [1996] ECR I-5689.

could sensibly be drawn between giving up work to look after a disabled person (the *Drake* situation) and being prevented from taking up work for that reason. Moreover, she had had to undergo training in order to be able to care for her husband and, were she not to provide it, care would have had to be provided by someone else who would require payment. Ruiz-Jarabo Colomer AG submitted:

It is well known that the Court has always construed 'working population' widely in that it considers that the Directive applies also to persons whose work or search for work has been interrupted because one of the specified risks has materialised in relation to another person. Nevertheless I would point out that, when deciding whether the person concerned belongs to the working population, the Court has on no occasion overlooked the requirement that he must be employed or self-employed or seeking work, that is to say a person who is available for employment or is seriously trying to find employment.[38]

The Court's reluctance to recognise the true financial value of work undertaken in the home was more or less explicit in its judgment:

[T]he term 'activity' referred to in relation to the expression 'working population' in Article 2 of the Directive can be construed only as referring at the very least to an economic activity, that is to say an activity undertaken in return for remuneration in the broad sense . . . [A]n interpretation purporting to include within the concept of working population a member of a family who, without payment, undertakes an activity for the benefit of another member of the family on the ground that such activity calls for a degree of competence, is of a particular nature or scope or would have to be provided by an outsider in return for remuneration if the member of the family in question did not provide it would have the effect of infinitely extending the scope of the Directive, whereas the purpose of Article 2 of the Directive is precisely to delimit that scope . . .

Article 2 of the Directive must be interpreted as not covering a person who undertakes, as an unremunerated activity, the care of his or her handicapped spouse, regardless of the extent of that activity and the competence required to carry it out, where the person in question did not, in order to do so, abandon an occupational activity or interrupt efforts to find employment.[39]

This conclusion can be criticised as unduly harsh on two counts. First, it failed to recognise the very real economic value of Ms Züchner's services, without which the State would have had to pay for equivalent skilled care; the nature of the care which she provided went far beyond the expectations of normal married life and the Court could without much difficulty therefore have held that Ms Züchner in fact constituted a member of the working population. Secondly, through its concentration on the policy objective of limiting the scope of Article 2, the Court was led into the error of ignoring what is surely the more important policy

[38] Ibid. at 5707–8.   [39] Ibid. at 5726–7.

objective underlying the Directive, that of outlawing discrimination; it is highly probable that the majority of persons who are excluded from the traditional paid labour market on account of having to care for severely disabled relatives are women and thus to interpret the Directive so as to exclude them from its protection is to sacrifice the true aim of the instrument to a patriarchal, out-dated and unjust view of family life.

The Court has, however, made one limited concession in this area. In *Johnson* v. *Chief Adjudication Officer*,[40] it held that Article 2 extends to a person who has interrupted paid employment in order to bring up children and who thereafter seeks to return to the labour market, where that return to work is prevented by the materialisation of one of the risks listed in Article 3:

In order to be a member of the working population within the meaning of Article 2 of the Directive, it is sufficient for the person concerned to be a person seeking employment; no distinction according to the reason for which the person concerned left previous employment or even according to whether or not that person previously carried on an occupational activity is necessary.

However, the person concerned must prove that he or she was a person seeking employment when one of the risks specified in Article 3(1)(a) of the Directive materialised. In this regard, it is for the national court to determine whether the person concerned was actually seeking employment at the time when he or she was affected by one of the risks specified in the Directive by looking to see in particular whether that person was registered with an employment organisation responsible for dealing with offers of employment or assisting persons seeking employment, whether the person had sent job applications to employers and whether certificates were available from firms stating that the person concerned had attended interviews.

It follows that the protection guaranteed by Directive 79/7 to persons who have given up their occupational activity in order to attend to the upbringing of their children is afforded only to those persons in that category who suffered incapacity for work during a period in which they were seeking employment.[41]

In response to the argument that its interpretation of the scope of Article 2 has the effect of disproportionately disadvantaging women, the Court stated:

[A]ccording to the first recital of the preamble to Directive 79/7 and Article 1 thereof, the Directive has in view only the progressive implementation of the principle of equal treatment for men and women in matters of social security. As far as the social protection of mothers remaining at home is concerned, it follows from Article 7(1)(b)[42] . . . that the acquisition of entitlement to benefits following periods of interruption of employment due to the upbringing of children is still a matter for the Member States to regulate.

---

[40] Case 31/90 [1991] ECR I-3723, noted by Laske in (1992) 29 CMLRev. 1011.
[41] Ibid. at 3752.   [42] As to which see below.

. . . [I]t is for the Community legislature to take such measures as it considers appropriate to remove the discrimination which still exists in this regard in some bodies of national legislation.[43]

Despite the refusal of the ECJ to regard persons working within the home as within the scope of the Directive (or perhaps in consequence of its unease at thus excluding so many women from the reach of the Directive), it has been willing to extend the coverage of the instrument to those engaged in a very small way in paid employment. *Nolte* v. *Landesversicherungsanstalt Hannover*[44] raised the issue of whether the Directive extended to persons engaged in what German legislation defined as 'minor' employment, which meant working for fewer than 15 hours a week for a wage of not more than one-seventh of the average of that earned by persons insured under the statutory old-age insurance scheme. *Megner and Scheffel* v. *Innungskrankenkasse Vorderplatz*[45] concerned (additionally) those in 'short-term' employment, defined by the relevant national legislation as being for no more than 18 hours a week. In both cases, the Court held that the definition of the working population intended by Article 2 is 'very broad' and that it covered persons in 'minor' and 'short-term' employment:

The fact that a worker's earnings do not cover all his needs cannot prevent him from being a member of the working population. It appears from the Court's case-law that the fact that his employment yields an income lower than the minimum required for subsistence (see Case 53/81 *Levin* v. *Staatssecretaris van Justitie* [1982] ECR 1035, paragraphs 15 and 16) or normally does not exceed 18 hours a week (see Case C-102/88 *Ruzius-Wilbrink* [1989] ECR 4311, paragraphs 7 and 17) or 12 hours a week (see Case 139/85 *Kempf* v. *Staatssecretaris van Justitie* [1986] ECR 1741, paragraphs 2 and 16) or even 10 hours a week (see Case 171/88 *Rinner-Kühn* [1989] ECR 2743, paragraph 16) does not prevent the person in such employment from being regarded as a worker within the meaning of Article 48 (the *Levin* and *Kempf* cases) or Article 119 of the EEC Treaty (the *Rinner-Kühn* case) or for the purposes of Directive 79/7 (the *Ruzius-Wilbrink* case).

The German Government . . . argues that a different view ought to be taken in this case, since what is at issue is not the concept of a worker within the meaning of Article 48 of the Treaty . . . but the concept of a worker within the meaning of social security law. The definition of the concept of a worker in the latter sphere falls within the competence of the Member States.

It should be observed in that connection that as long ago as the judgment in Case 75/63 *Hoekstra (née Unger)* [1964] ECR 177 (paragraph 1 of the operative part) the Court ruled that the concept of 'wage-earner or assimilated worker' referred to in Regulation No.3 of the Council of 25 September 1958 concerning social security for migrant workers . . . had, like the term 'worker' in Articles 48 to

---

[43] [1991] ECR I-3723, at 3752–3.   [44] Case C-317/93 [1995] ECR I-4625.
[45] Case C-444/93 [1995] ECR I-4741.

51, a Community meaning. Consequently, the fact that the *Levin, Kempf* and *Rinner-Kühn* cases do not relate to social security law and are not concerned with the interpretation of Article 2 of Directive 79/7 cannot call in question the finding made [above], since those judgments define the concept of a worker in the light of the principle of equal treatment.[46]

It is thus clear that, in order to be able to invoke the protection of the Directive, a claimant must personally fall within the technical scope of Article 2.[47] One limited exception to this principle emerged from *Verholen* v. *Sociale Verzekeringsbank*,[48] which involved the same Dutch old age pension legislation which was in issue in *Acterberg-te Riele* v. *Sociale Verzekeringsbank*.[49] Mr Heiderijk, one of the plaintiffs in this joined action, had reached the age of 65 and was drawing an old age pension. This pension contained an extra element which recognised that he had a dependent spouse who had not yet reached the age of 65. Under the legislation, married women only became entitled to a personal pension at 65 and that pension was normally payable to the husband. In this instance, the extra component was reduced, to reflect periods during which Mr Heiderijk was not insured under the Dutch system because he had been working in Germany. One of the questions referred to the Court was whether an individual may rely before a national court on Directive 79/7 when he bears the effects of a discriminatory national provision regarding his spouse, who is not a party to the proceedings. The Court held:

It should be pointed out straight away that the right to rely on the provisions of Directive 79/7 is not confined to individuals coming within the scope *ratione personae* of the Directive, in so far as the possibility cannot be ruled out that other persons may have a direct interest in ensuring that the principle of non-discrimination is respected as regards persons who are protected.

While it is, in principle, for national law to determine an individual's standing and legal interest in bringing proceedings, Community law nevertheless requires that the national legislation does not undermine the right to effective judicial protection (see the judgments in Case 222/84 *Johnston* v. *Chief Constable of the RUC* [1986] ECR 1651 and in Case 222/86 *Unectef* v. *Heylens* [1987] ECR 4097) and the application of national legislation cannot render virtually impossible the exercise

---

[46] [1995] ECR I-4625, at 4656–7, and [1995] ECR I-4741, at 4752–3. See also Case C-280/94 *Posthuma-van Damme* v. *Bestuur van de Bedrijfsvereniging voor Detailhandel, Ambachten en Huisvrouwen* [1996] ECR I-179, where the ECJ held that Article 2 does not necessarily exclude a person who, in the year preceding his or her incapacity for work, did not receive an income from employment.

[47] See also *De Weerd, née Roks* [1994] ECR I-571.

[48] Joined Cases C-87, 88 & 89/90 [1991] ECR I-3757.

[49] Joined Cases C-48, 106 & 107/88 [1989] ECR 1963, discussed above. For comment on *Verholen* and *Acterberg*, together with Case C-31/90 *Johnson* v. *Chief Adjudication Officer* [1991] ECR I-3723, see Cousins, 'The Personal and Temporal Scope of Directive 79/7/EEC' (1992) 17 ELRev. 55.

of the rights conferred by Community law (judgment in Case 199/82 *Amministrazione delle Finanze dello Stato* v. *San Giorgio* [1983] ECR 3595).

In so far as this case is concerned, however, it should be stated that an individual who bears the effects of a discriminatory national provision may be allowed to rely on Directive 79/7 only if his wife, who is the victim of the discrimination, herself comes within the scope of that Directive.[50]

Article 3(1) of the Directive provides:
This Directive shall apply to:

(a)   statutory schemes which provide protection against the following risks:
sickness,
invalidity,
old age,
accidents at work and occupational diseases,
unemployment;
(b)   social assistance, in so far as it is intended to supplement or replace the
schemes referred to in (a).[51]

The ECJ in the *Drake* case[52] ruled that this provision must be given a purposive interpretation, a decision of considerable potential significance given the diversity of social security provision available in the various Member States. One of the questions referred in that case had asked whether a benefit (in this instance, invalid care allowance) which was payable to a person in the claimant's position, not themselves directly suffering from any invalidity but in respect of someone else's invalidity, constituted a statutory scheme providing protection against invalidity within the meaning of Article 3(1)(a) of the Directive. Could the 'risk' be a risk to someone other than the claimant? The Court gave a positive answer to this question, holding:

[I]t is possible for the Member States to provide protection against the consequences of the risk of invalidity in various ways. For example, a Member State

---

[50] [1991] ECR I-3757, at 3790–1. See Waddington 'The Court of Justice Fails to Show its Caring Face' (1997) 22 ELRev. 587, in which the author argues that the *Züchner* case (discussed above) should have been decided on the same basis as *Verholen*: Ms Züchner suffered the effects of the discriminatory treatment directed against her husband, in that care allowances were not paid to her, and her husband, who had worked before becoming disabled, fell within Article 2.

[51] Joined Cases C-245 and 312/94 *Hoever* v. *Land Nordrhein-Westfalen* [1996] ECR I-4895 concerned alleged indirect discrimination over access to a child-raising allowance available to employed people. In deciding that this allowance was not covered by the Directive, the Court pointed out that Art. 3(2) (discussed further below) excludes from the scope of the instrument 'provisions concerning . . . family benefits, except in the case of family benefits granted by way of increases of benefits due in respect of the risks referred to in paragraph (1)(a)'. It held that a family benefit, such as a child-raising allowance, does not provide direct and effective protection against one of the Article 3(1)(a) risks but is intended rather to secure the maintenance of the family whilst the children are young.

[52] Case 150/85 *Drake* v. *Chief Adjudication Officer* [1986] ECR 1995.

may, as the UK has done, provide for two separate allowances, one payable to the disabled person himself and the other payable to a person who provides care, while another Member State may arrive at the same result by paying an allowance to the disabled person at a rate equivalent to the sum of those two benefits. In order, therefore, to ensure that the progressive implementation of the principle of equal treatment referred to in Article 1 of Council Directive 79/7/EEC and defined in Article 4 is carried out in a harmonious manner throughout the Community, Article 3(1) must be interpreted as including any benefit which in a broad sense forms part of one of the statutory schemes referred to or a social assistance provision intended to supplement or replace such a scheme.

Moreover, the payment of the benefit to a person who provides care still depends on the existence of a situation of invalidity inasmuch as such a situation is a condition *sine qua non* for its payment . . . It must also be emphasized that there is a clear link between the benefit and the disabled person, since the disabled person derives an advantage from the fact that an allowance is paid to the person caring for him.[53]

In reaching this conclusion, the Court effectively ignored the arguments put forward on behalf of the UK government by the adjudication officer. He had maintained that invalid care allowance was not a work-related benefit, since it was paid to persons who sacrifice work opportunities and relieve the social services of the burden of caring for the invalid. Furthermore, it was payable to persons not working, and who may never have worked. Luckhaus has argued[54] that the Court was chiefly motivated by its desire to condemn such an unabashed example of direct discrimination against women in the social security system of a Member State, and in its enthusiasm for achieving this result it engaged in 'some well-meaning subterfuge', in particular appearing to restrict the EC law to employment-related areas whilst in reality extending its reach 'into the realm of domestic, traditionally unpaid work and private family relationships'.

In any event, any tendency on the part of the ECJ to stray from the work-related sphere and into a wider social context in its interpretation of Article 3 has since been curbed. *R v. Secretary of State for Social Security, Ex p. Smithson*[55] concerned differential entitlement as between men and women to a 'higher pensioner premium'. Housing benefit is payable, under UK law, to people whose income falls below a notional sum known as the 'applicable amount'. One of the elements to be taken into account in determining the 'applicable amount' is the 'higher pensioner premium' which is payable to those aged between 60 and 80, who live alone and are

---

[53] Ibid. at 2009–10. In the face of a well-orchestrated political campaign in favour of Ms Drake's claim, the UK government announced its intention (subsequently carried out) to extend invalid care allowance to all men and women on equal terms.

[54] Luckhaus, 'Payment for Caring: A European Solution?' [1986] Public Law 526.

[55] Case C-243/90 [1992] ECR I-467.

in receipt of one or more other social security benefits, which used to include an invalidity pension. Invalidity pension[56] was payable up to pensionable age (60 for women and 65 for men), but also for a further five years thereafter for persons who remained in work. Anyone (otherwise qualified) who had retired but not yet reached the age of 65 (for women) or 70 (for men) might elect to withdraw from the pension scheme and opt instead for an invalidity pension. Ms Smithson, who was 67, was unable to claim the 'higher pensioner premium' because she did not receive an invalidity pension and, as a woman of this age, was now unable to opt to claim one. The first question asked by the High Court was whether this patent sex discrimination over access to 'higher pensioner premium' contravened the Directive.

Tesauro AG considered that it did:

> It is essential to interpret Article 3 broadly . . . Any other approach would enable Member States to escape their obligations under the Directive with ease: they would only need in that case to include in a scheme of general scope, or at least one not specifically intended to provide protection against one of the risks set out in Article 3 of the Directive, a benefit which was, on the contrary, taken in isolation, designed precisely to provide protection against those risks.
>
> . . . I cannot endorse the United Kingdom's view that the premium may be regarded in isolation from the benefit of which it forms part because it is merely one of the elements which go to make up the applicable amount for the purposes of calculating housing benefit and not an amount paid out in its own right.
>
> I consider it quite irrelevant, in fact, that the premium is not technically a financial benefit paid as such to the beneficiary. On the contrary, what is relevant in my view is the fact that the premium constitutes, *de facto* and in every case, an economic advantage for those who benefit from it, who become entitled when such a component is applied to higher housing benefit.
>
> In view of the fact that according to the contested United Kingdom legislation the purpose of that increase is to provide additional support for pensioners who have a recognised form of invalidity . . . I do not think there can be any doubt that the premium is covered by Directive 79/7.
>
> It is in essence a 'benefit' which, although encompassed in the more general housing benefit scheme, may be separated from it in as much as it has a well-defined purpose and scope: to aid pensioners who are suffering particular hardship. Consequently, in view of the categories of persons for whom it is intended and its effects, the premium rightly belongs to the scope *ratione materiae* of Directive 79/7. More especially, in as much as it is intended to provide additional support for disabled pensioners to enable them to meet the cost of housing, it should be regarded as a form of social assistance intended to supplement the statutory schemes providing protection against the risks of old age and invalidity.[57]

---

[56] Invalidity pensions were subsequently replaced by incapacity benefit, as to which see Wikeley, 'The Social Security (Incapacity for Work) Act 1994' (1995) 58 MLR 523.

[57] [1992] ECR I-467, at 479–80.

The Court, however, subtly but significantly reworded the High Court's question so as to ask about the applicability of Article 3 to housing benefit in general, as distinct from its applicability specifically to the 'higher pensioner premium'. This led it to disagree with its Advocate General:

[A]lthough the mode of payment is not decisive as regards the identification of a benefit as one which falls within the scope of Directive 79/7, in order to be so identified the benefit must be directly and effectively linked to the protection provided against one of the risks specified in Article 3(1) of the Directive.

However, Article 3(1)(a) of Directive 79/7 does not refer to statutory schemes which are intended to guarantee any person whose real income is lower than a notional income calculated on the basis of certain criteria a special allowance enabling that person to meet housing costs.

The age and invalidity of the beneficiary are only two of the criteria applied in order to determine the extent of the beneficiary's financial need for such an allowance. The fact that those criteria are decisive as regards eligibility for the higher pensioner premium is not sufficient to bring that benefit within the scope of Directive 79/7.

The premium is in fact an inseparable part of the whole benefit which is intended to compensate for the fact that the beneficiary's income is insufficient to meet housing costs, and cannot be characterised as an autonomous scheme intended to provide protection against one of the risks listed in Article 3(1) ...[58]

A determination on the part of the Court to separate general schemes for supplementing low incomes from schemes covered by the Directive was also evident in *Jackson and Cresswell* v. *Chief Adjudication Officer*,[59] where discrimination was alleged in respect of the award of income support and its predecessor, supplementary benefit, under UK law. The Court of Appeal asked the ECJ whether Article 3 of the Directive applies to a benefit which may be granted in a variety of situations to persons whose means are insufficient to meet their needs as defined by statute, and whether the answer to that question depends on whether the claimant is suffering from one of the Article 3 risks.

Significantly, the Advocate General (Van Gerven on this occasion) again inclined to the view that such schemes could fall within the scope of Article 3 of the Directive. The net result of the *Drake* and *Smithson* cases he concluded was that, to fall within Article 3, a benefit must be granted pursuant to an autonomous statutory scheme or a form of social assistance which is directly and effectively linked to one of the Article 3 risks. He distinguished the *Smithson* decision from the circumstances under consideration on the basis that the relationship in that case between the

---

[58] Ibid. at 489–90. See Hervey's criticisms of this conclusion in [1992] JSWFL 461.

[59] Joined Cases C-63 & 64/91 [1992] ECR I-4737, also discussed in Chap. 3, and noted by Durston in *'Jackson and Cresswell* v. *Chief Adjudication Officer.* No Help for Women in the Poverty Trap'* (1994) 57 MLR 641.

Article 3 risk and housing benefit was only indirect: invalidity was only a criterion for receipt of an invalidity pension, the grant of which was a precondition for the higher pensioner premium, which itself was only one of the factors contributing to the calculation of notional income for the purpose of housing benefit. He examined the issue of whether the Directive applies only to those schemes *intended* by the legislature to afford protection against the Article 3 risks (the UK Government's view) or whether it extends simply to those which *in fact* afford such protection. Stressing that it was important to take a teleological view so as to ensure the effectiveness of the Directive, he opted for the second alternative; in doing so, he pointed out that the English version of the Directive is the only one to use the word 'intended' in Article 3(1)(b), the others all referring to schemes which 'supplement' or 'replace' Article 3(1)(a) schemes. It was, therefore, in his view, a matter for the national court to decide whether income support in the UK in reality provided protection against one or more of the risks specified in Article 3. However, in deciding this matter, he drew the national court's attention to the fact that, since in many cases unemployment benefit ceased and gave way to income support after a stated time under UK law, income support was in fact an important part of the protection provided in the event of unemployment; furthermore, unemployed persons claiming income support had at the relevant date generally to be available for work,[60] thus underlining the role of the scheme in providing protection against unemployment. His conclusion of this part of his argument was that the link between income support and protection against unemployment was a much closer link than that in *Smithson*.

Once again, however, the Court rejected this approach in favour of a stricter construction of Article 3. Building on its pre-existing case law, it held:

Article 3(1)(a) . . . does not refer to a statutory scheme which, on certain conditions, provides persons with a means below a legally defined limit with a special benefit designed to enable them to meet their needs. That finding is not affected by the circumstance that the recipient of the benefit is in fact in one of the situations covered by Article 3(1) . . .

Indeed, in the judgment in *Smithson* . . . the Court held with regard to a housing benefit that the fact that some of the risks listed in Article 3(1) . . . were taken into account in order to grant a higher benefit was not sufficient to bring that benefit as such within the scope of the Directive.

Consequently, exclusion from the scope of Directive 79/7 is justified *a fortiori* where, as in the cases at issue in the main proceedings, the law sets the amount of the theoretical needs of the persons concerned, used to determine the benefit in

---

[60] This rule changed with the introduction in October 1996 of jobseeker's allowance pursuant to the Jobseekers Act 1995.

question, independently of any consideration relating to the existence of any of the risks listed in Article 3(1) . . .

Moreover, in certain situations, in particular those of the appellants in the main proceedings, the national schemes at issue exempt claimants from the obligation to be available for work. That shows that the benefits in question cannot be regarded as being directly and effectively linked to protection against the risk of unemployment.[61]

The Court has recently been asked whether the Directive governs schemes for the benefit of elderly persons, where eligibility is tied to pensionable age. In particular, a number of statutory schemes in the UK have exempted persons of pensionable age from paying charges for certain services and the issue has been raised as to the legality of such schemes in the light of the current different pensionable ages of men and women. *R. v. Secretary of State for Health, Ex p. Richardson*[62] concerned the applicability of Directive 79/7 to UK legislation exempting women from medical prescription charges from the age of 60, but exempting men only from the age of 65. The ECJ held that the exemption scheme fell within Article 3:

First, being provided for by statute and implemented by regulation it forms part of a statutory scheme.

Secondly, it affords direct and effective protection against the risk of sickness referred to in Article 3(1) . . . in so far as grant of the benefit to any of the categories of people referred to is always conditional on materialisation of the risk in question.

Lastly, in view of the fundamental importance of the principle of equal treatment and the aim of Directive 79/7, which is the progressive implementation of that principle in matters of social security, a system of benefits cannot be excluded from the scope of the Directive simply because it does not strictly form part of national social security rules. The fact, relied on by the United Kingdom, that the exemption from prescription charges is provided for in the National Health Service Act 1977 does not therefore affect the foregoing conclusion.[63]

---

[61] Joined Cases C-63 & 64/91 at 4779–4780. Cousins comments in 'Equal Treatment and Social Security' (1994) 19 ELRev. 123 that the effect of the ECJ's decisions in *Smithson* and *Jackson and Cresswell* is to exclude many claimants from recourse to the Directive; furthermore, a high proportion of excluded claimants are likely to be women who have to rely on means-tested payments because they do not satisfy the work-related contribution conditions for insurance payments. See also Van Gerven *et al*, 'Current Issues of Community Law concerning Equality of Treatment Between Women and Men in Social Security' in *Equality of Treatment Between Women and Men in Social Security* ed. McCrudden (Butterworths, London, 1994); the authors argue that *Smithson* and *Jackson and Cresswell* lead to uneven application of the Directive across the Member States. Thus, in countries such as the UK where classic social security benefits have been supplanted by means-tested schemes, there is a risk that many benefits now fall outwith the Directive: 'This is exactly what the Court wanted to avoid in *Drake*, namely that a Member State, by making formal changes to existing benefits covered by the Directive, could remove them from its scope' (at 11–12).

[62] Case C-137/94 [1995] ECR I-3407.

[63] Ibid. at 3428–9. Cousins points out in 'Free Movement of Workers and Social Security:

On the other hand, in *Atkins* v. *Wrekin District Council*[64] the Court[65] held that a UK statutory scheme operated by a local authority which granted concessionary fares on public transport to those of pensionable age did not fall within Article 3. The relevant statute gave discretion to local authorities to grant concessions to various groups of persons, including those of pensionable age, and thus the scheme could not be said to 'afford direct and effective protection against one of the risks listed in Article 3(1) . . . Old age and invalidity, which are among the risks listed in Article 3(1) . . . are only two of the criteria which may be applied to define the classes of beneficiaries of such a scheme . . .'.[66] Furthermore, the fact that the local authority involved here had actually chosen to single out those of pensionable age for eligibility for the concession was irrelevant:

The fact that the recipient of a benefit is, as a matter of fact, in one of the situations envisaged by Article 3(1) . . . does not suffice to bring that benefit as such within the scope of the Directive (see Joined Cases C-63 & 64/91 *Jackson and Cresswell* [1992] ECR I-4737, paragraphs 18 and 19).

The fact that . . . the local scheme set up by Wrekin District Council . . . benefits only classes of persons who are in fact in such situations, cannot affect that conclusion. Were importance attached to that, some local schemes would come within the scope of Directive 79/7 and others would not—despite all having been set up under the same statutory authorisation—depending on whether or not the persons eligible under such schemes consisted exclusively of classes of persons in one of the situations listed in Article 3(1) . . .[67]

The Court also rejected the Commission's argument that the scope of Directive 79/7 was wider than the scope of social security and social assistance, and that it extended to 'social protection as a whole', which had led it to contend that the Directive applied to measures of 'social protection' such as concessionary fares on public transport granted to persons affected by an Article 3 risk.

One interesting potential extension of the scope of the Directive emerged in *Integrity* v. *Rouvroy*.[68] The case concerned a straightforward

Two Steps Forward, One Step Back' (1996) 21 ELRev. 233 that the ironic result of this case is that the ECJ has held that a measure which would not be seen as social security at all in the UK is within the scope of the Directive, whilst core elements of the UK social security system (in particular, income support) are outside the Directive's scope.

[64] Case C-228/94 [1996] ECR I-3633.

[65] Rejecting the submissions of Elmer AG.

[66] *Atkins* v. *Wrekin District Council* [1996] ECR I-3633, at 3664. Cf. The benefit involved in Case C-139/95 *Balestra* v. *INPS* [1997] ECR I-549 (discussed further below) which was payable to employees within a specified age group taking early retirement from an undertaking facing 'critical difficulties'. As Elmer AG explained, the fundamental condition for the payment was age; thus, the benefit was directly and effectively linked to the risk of old age and therefore fell within the scope of Directive 79/7.

[67] Case C-228/94 at 3664–5.

[68] Case C-373/89 [1990] ECR I-4243.

incident of discrimination in that Belgian legislation exempted married women, widows and students, but not married men or widowers, from the obligation to make social security contributions in certain circumstances. Some of the benefits obtainable as a consequence of paying the contributions in question were not within the ambit of Article 3. Jacobs AG, whose remarks in this respect were specifically endorsed by the Court, pointed out that:

The question therefore arises . . . whether the Directive applies only in so far as the contributions are related to benefits covered by the Directive . . . I would take the view that the Directive applied globally to the contributions payable . . . if they could not be linked to any particular benefit. If the Directive were not to apply in such circumstances, then its application would be frustrated, as regards the obligation to contribute, whenever Member States included within the ambit of discriminatory national provisions benefits which were not covered by the Directive alongside benefits which were so covered.[69]

He went on to say, however, that it appeared to have been the Belgian Government's intention that, although single contributions would be made, the amounts paid would be apportioned among the risks covered. The Advocate General submitted that if the contributions could be so apportioned, then the equality principle would only apply to those contributions attributable to the risks listed in the Directive. He concluded that the 'fact that Belgium chose to incorporate in the same legislation provisions concerning benefits which fall within the scope of the Directive together with provisions concerning benefits which fall outside its scope cannot . . . render the Directive applicable to the latter provisions'.[70]

Article 4 is the kernel of the instrument because it defines the principle to be applied to all situations falling within the ambit of the Directive:

1. The principle of equal treatment means that there shall be no discrimination whatsoever on ground of sex either directly, or indirectly[71] by reference in particular to marital or family status, in particular as concerns:

—the scope of the schemes and the conditions of access thereto, the obligation to contribute and the calculation of contributions,
—the calculations of benefits including increases due in respect of a spouse and for dependants and the conditions governing the duration and retention of entitlement to benefits.

This phraseology is familiar from the Equal Treatment Directive, and it is significant that the all-embracing word 'whatsoever' is found in the context

---

[69] Ibid. at 4255.
[70] Ibid. also at 4255.
[71] But note that the directive defining indirect discrimination, Directive 97/80, OJ [1998] L14/6, discussed in Chap. 2, does not extend to discrimination contrary to the Social Security Directive.

of the Social Security Directive too.[72] The mention of discrimination by reference to marital or family status is especially important in relation to social security since, as for example the *Drake* case demonstrates, social security systems are apt to include distinctions on these bases. However, despite the strength with which the principle of equal treatment is articulated in Article 4, it must be remembered that this is all that the Directive mandates. It merely requires that male and female be treated equally (not even identically), not that the less favourably treated be brought up to the standard of the more favourably treated, so-called 'levelling-up' of provision.[73]

The first prerequisite for Article 4, if it is to have real teeth, is that it must be directly effective in the hands of individual litigants. [74] This was demonstrated at an early stage of its existence. It was implicit in the Court's ruling in *Drake* v. *Chief Adjudication Officer*,[75] but was not discussed explicitly there because it was not contested by the adjudication officer. It was first directly ruled on by the ECJ in *Netherlands* v. *Federatie Nederlandse Vakbeweging*.[76] Under Dutch law, which remained in force after the Social Security Directive came into operation, married women (other than those permanently separated from their husbands) were ineligible for unemployment benefit unless they were 'head of the household' within the meaning of the relevant ministerial regulations. The Federatie (the Netherlands Trades Union Federation) summoned the State before the President of the District Court in the Hague in proceedings in which it requested that the State be ordered to repeal the requirement about the status of head of the household, or at least refrain from applying it, on the ground that it contravened Article 4 of the Social Security Directive. The President ordered the State to amend its legislation and, in the subsequent appeal, a preliminary ruling was sought from the ECJ, asking whether Article 4 of the Directive is directly effective. Both Mancini AG and the Court held, in the clearest terms, that it is. Mancini AG submitted:

[I]t must be established whether, intrinsically, Article 4(1) satisfies the require-ments of being unconditional and sufficiently precise . . . If, as the Commission observes, this prohibition is read in the light of the obligation, laid down by Articles 1 and 8(1) of [the] Directive, as to the result to be obtained it is impossible not to consider it *clear*, *complete* and *precise*. If then, the Federatie Nederlandse Vakbeweging points out in addition, it is read in conjunction with

---

[72] See discussion in Chap. 3.   [73] See discussion in Chap. 2.

[74] Although it should be appreciated that the device of vindicating individual rights through litigation is somewhat inappropriate in the area of social security where, *ex hypothesi*, the claimant is likely to be in straitened financial circumstances and in practice is unlikely to be able to sustain an action without the help of some other funding body, for example, a pressure group.

[75] Case 150/85 [1986] ECR 1995.

[76] Case 71/85 [1986] ECR 3855, noted by Arnull in (1987) 12 ELRev. 276.

Article 5, under which the Member States have a duty to 'abolish' provisions contrary to the principle of equal treatment, it becomes equally clear that the provision is *unconditional* and hence that there is no discretion on the part of the Member States as regards bringing about the result sought by the Directive.[77]

The Court held:

It must be pointed out that, standing by itself, in the light of the objective and contents of Directive 79/7, Article 4(1) precludes, generally and unequivocally, all discrimination on ground of sex. The provision is therefore sufficiently precise to be relied upon in legal proceedings by an individual and applied by the courts. However, it remains to be considered whether the prohibition of discrimination which it contains may be regarded as unconditional having regard to the exceptions provided for in Article 7 and to the fact that according to the wording of Article 5 Member States are to take certain measures in order to ensure that the principle of equal treatment is applied in national legislation.

As regards, in the first place, Article 7, it must be observed that that provision merely reserves to Member States the right to exclude from the scope of the Directive certain clearly defined areas but lays down no condition with regard to the application of the principle of equal treatment as regards Article 4 of the Directive. It follows that Article 7 is not relevant in this case.

As for Article 5, which obliges Member States to take 'the measures necessary to ensure that any laws, regulations and administrative provisions contrary to the principle of equal treatment are abolished', it cannot be inferred from the wording of that Article that it lays down conditions to which the prohibition of discrimination is subject. Whilst Article 5 leaves the Member States a discretion with regard to methods, it prescribes the result which those methods must achieve, that is to say, the abolition of any provisions contrary to the principle of equal treatment.

Consequently, Article 4(1) of the Directive does not confer on Member States the power to make conditional or to limit the application of the principle of equal treatment within its field of application and it is sufficiently precise and unconditional to allow individuals, in the absence of implementing measures adopted within the prescribed period, to rely upon it before the national courts as from 23 December 1984 in order to preclude the application of any national provision inconsistent with that Article.[78]

The Dutch Government had attempted to preclude direct effect by arguing that the Article is insufficiently precise as to how exactly equality as between the sexes is to be achieved, and it contended that the provision contested in this case could be amended in at least four different ways, all of which would result in equality. Mancini AG explained that this:

confuses the issue of direct effect with that of the discretion available to Member States in transposing the Directive into national law . . . [T]he clear and unconditional provisions set out in the Directive are capable of being superimposed on

---

[77] Case 71/85 at 3867.   [78] Ibid. at 3875–6.

conflicting national laws and precluding their applicability or limiting it. That does not mean, however, that that solution is obligatory. A state which considers such a solution to be too onerous may alter its own law by prescribing other procedures, provided that they are compatible with the result sought by the Community legislation. By legislating in that manner the state will inevitably implement in good time the obligation imposed on it.[79]

Despite the point made earlier in the present Chapter that the Social Security Directive does not generally require a levelling-up of social security provisions, that was its effect in the circumstances of this case, where the only standard for the treatment that women could expect was that already provided for men. In the words of the Court:

It follows that until such time as the national government adopts the necessary implementing measures women are entitled to be treated in the same manner, and to have the same rules applied to them, as men who are in the same situation since, where the Directive has not been implemented, those rules remain the only valid point of reference.[80]

It should be noted that, as in relation to Article 119 of the Treaty,[81] the ECJ implicitly accepted in this case that gender-plus discrimination constitutes direct discrimination forbidden by the Social Security Directive; the discrimination here was not against women in general, but only against those who were married and not heads of household.[82]

McDermott and Cotter v. *Minister for Social Welfare and the Attorney General*[83] involved similar facts occurring within the Irish social security system. The claimants were both married women who complained of breach of Article 4 of the Directive in that the relevant national legislation provided for a lesser amount of unemployment benefit, over a shorter period of time, for them than for men or for single women. Both the Advocate General and the Court reiterated their earlier remarks and rejected the Irish Government's argument that the Article was discretionary because there were a number of ways in which the State could comply with it. Once again, the direct effect of the equality principle contained in the Directive required the levelling-up of the provision made for married women so that it matched that available to men (and to single women.)

---

[79] Ibid. at 3867–8.

[80] Ibid. at 3876. This principle applies irrespective of which group is disadvantaged on the ground of sex; it was therefore able to be relied on so as to improve the treatment afforded to men in Case C-154/92 *Van Cant* v. *Rijksdienst voor Pensionen* [1993] ECR I-3811.

[81] As to which, see Chap. 2.

[82] See also Case C-337/91 *Van Gemert-Derks* v. *Bestuur van de Nieuwe Industriele Bedrijfs-vereniging* [1993] ECR I-5435.

[83] Case 286/85 [1987] ECR 1453. For the background to this case and its successor, Case C-377/89 *Cotter and McDermott* v. *Minister for Social Welfare (No. 2)* [1991] ECR I-1155, see Whyte and O'Dell (1991) 20 ILJ 304.

The principle involved in *Clark* v. *Chief Adjudication Officer*[84] was the same as in the preceding cases, but the factual situation to which it applied was somewhat different and the potency of the principle was again demonstrated. Ms Clark suffered from a medical condition from 1983 onwards which rendered her incapable of work. She applied under the then-applicable UK legislation for a non-contributory invalidity pension (NCIP), but was refused the pension because she was unable to satisfy the statutory test, demanded only in the case of married women such as herself, of incapacity to perform 'normal household duties'. NCIP was abolished in late 1984, in anticipation of the coming into operation in December of that year of the Social Security Directive, and it was replaced by a new benefit, known as severe disablement allowance. The conditions for entitlement to severe disablement allowance, were, in general, stricter than those for NCIP had been and Ms Clark, again, did not meet them.[85] However, transitional arrangements were also made, because it was feared that some people who had been entitled to the old NCIP would cease to be eligible for severe disablement allowance and it was felt to be politically unacceptable for benefit in effect then to be withdrawn from them. The transitional legislation therefore provided that everybody entitled to the old benefit on certain dates in 1984 was automatically to acquire entitlement to the new benefit. Ms Clark, of course, was unable to take advantage of this rule, and argued that it perpetuated discrimination against married women contrary to the Social Security Directive and after that instrument had become operative (a subtle form of direct discrimination). With this contention both the Advocate General and the Court agreed. The direct effect of Article 4 could be relied on to prohibit the perpetuation of discrimination which had been lawful before the Directive came into force. Da Cruz Vilaca AG commented that the Directive makes no exception: '[F]or the continuing discriminatory effects of national provisions previously in force, since to maintain those effects is as much contrary to the provisions of the Directive as it would be to maintain those national provisions themselves.'[86]

The Court itself was quite unmoved by the UK Government's protestations about the legitimate expectations of those receiving NCIP before the Social Security Directive came into effect, and once again its solution was to require the levelling-up of the provision made. It held:

---

[84] Case 384/85 [1987] ECR 2865. Similarly, Case 80/87 *Dik* v. *College van Burgemeester en Wethouders, Arnhem* [1988] ECR 1601. See also Luckhaus, 'Equal Treatment for Men and Women in Social Security?' (1987) 137 NLJ 1006.

[85] Hoskyns and Luckhaus argue that the provisions relating to severe disablement allowance also discriminate (this time indirectly) against women: see 'The European Community Directive on Equal Treatment in Social Security' (1989) Policy and Politics, Vol.17, No. 4, 321.

[86] [1987] ECR 2865, at 2875.

[I]t must be emphasized that the Directive does not provide for any derogation from the principle of equal treatment laid down in Article 4(1) in order to authorize the extension of the discriminatory effects of earlier provisions of national law. It follows that a Member State may not maintain beyond 22 December 1984 any inequalities of treatment which have their origin in the fact that the conditions for entitlement to benefit are those which applied before that date. That is so notwithstanding the fact that those inequalities are the result of transitional provisions adopted at the time of the introduction of a new benefit.

Consequently, Article 4(1) of the Directive in no way confers on Member States the power to make conditional or to limit the application of the principle of equal treatment within its field of application and it is sufficiently precise and unconditional to allow individuals, in the absence of appropriate implementing measures, to rely upon it before the national courts as from 22 December 1984 in order to preclude the application of any provision of national law inconsistent with that Article.

As is also apparent from the judgments in *FNV* and *McDermott and Cotter*, it follows from Article 4(1) of the Directive that, as from 22 December 1984, women are entitled to be treated in the same manner, and to have the same rules applied to them, as men who are in the same situation since, where the Directive has not been implemented correctly, those rules remain the only valid point of reference. In this case that means that if, as from 22 December 1984, a man in the same position as a woman was automatically entitled to the new severe disablement allowance under the aforesaid transitional provisions without having to re-establish his rights, a woman was also entitled to that allowance without having to satisfy an additional condition applicable before that date exclusively to married women.[87]

The Court's reluctance to allow transitional provisions to perpetuate former sex discrimination was also evident in *Van Cant* v. *Rijksdienst voor Pensionen*,[88] discussed further below, where Darmon AG explained that:

[A]lthough the principle of the progressive nature of the implementation of equal treatment appears in the actual title of the Directive, the Court [has] clearly ruled against the maintenance of any transitional provision contrary to Article 4 . . . [The Court is determined] not to allow earlier or transitional schemes which delay genuine equality of treatment to linger on . . . The uniform application of Community law in each Member State requires that the interpretation of the Directive be detached from the national context and, consequently, from the merits of a scheme compared with those of the previous scheme. Justification by progressiveness has its limits.[89]

The vital question of the meaning of indirect discrimination in the context of social security was first raised before the ECJ in *Teuling* v.

---

[87] [1987] ECR 2865, at 2880–1. The direct effect of Article 4 was reiterated in Case C-31/90 *Johnson* v. *Chief Adjudication Officer* [1991] ECR I-3723 and by Van Gerven AG in Joined Cases C-63 & 64/91 *Jackson and Cresswell* v. *Chief Adjudication Officer* [1992] ECR I-4737, at 4770, both also discussed above.

[88] Case C-154/92 [1993] ECR I-3811.   [89] Ibid. at 3827.

Bedrijfsvereniging voor de Chemische Industrie.[90] Ms Teuling had been incapable of work since 1972. From 1975 onwards, she received invalidity benefit under the Netherlands social security legislation equal to the statutory minimum wage. However, from the beginning of 1984 her benefit was reduced in accordance with new legislation to 70 per cent of the statutory minimum wage. Supplements were payable to certain persons, but she was not one because the relevant legislation took into account the income of a spouse and or the presence of dependent children. Ms Teuling, at the material time, was married and her husband's income was over the maximum prescribed limit. She argued that the system for the payment of supplements discriminated indirectly against women and therefore should be disapplied because it breached the directly effective Article 4 of the Social Security Directive. Both Mancini AG and the Court agreed that the rules disproportionately disadvantaged women. The Dutch Government had provided statistics which showed that a significantly greater number of married men than married women received a supplement on the basis of having a dependent family; that was because in the Netherlands at the relevant date there were considerably more married men than married women who carried on occupational activities and therefore considerably fewer women with a dependent spouse. The Court held that it was clear:

[F]rom the very words of Article 4(1) that increases are prohibited if they are directly or indirectly based on the sex of the beneficiary. In that regard, it should be pointed out that a system of benefits in which, as in this case, supplements are provided for which are not directly based on the sex of the beneficiaries but take account of their marital status or family situation and in respect of which it emerges that a considerably smaller proportion of women than of men are entitled to such supplements is contrary to Article 4(1) of the Directive if that system of benefits cannot be justified by reasons which exclude discrimination on grounds of sex.[91]

What the Court did not say explicitly here, although it seemed implicit in its words, was that Article 4(1) of the Directive is directly effective in the context of indirect discrimination as well as in the more obvious cases of direct discrimination.[92] However, it has remedied this omission in later

[90] Case 30/85 [1987] ECR 2497.
[91] [1987] ECR 2497, at 2520–1. To the same effect, see Case C-317/93 *Nolte* v. *Landesversicherungsanstalt* [1995] ECR I-4625, at 4659, Case C-444/93 *Megner and Scheffel* v. *Innungskrankenkasse Vorderplatz* [1995] ECR I-4741, at 4754, and Case C-280/94 *Postuma-Van Damme* v. *Bestuur van de Bedrijfsvereniging voor Detailhandel, Ambachten en Huisvrouwen* [1996] ECR I-179, at 203. See also the submissions of Ruiz-Jarabo Colomer AG in Case C-77/95 *Züchner* v. *Handelskrankenkasse Bremen* [1996] ECR I-5689, at 5713.
[92] It will be recalled from the discussion in Chap. 2 that this issue caused problems in relation to Art. 119 of the Treaty, but that the Court eventually accepted the direct effect of this Article even in cases of indirect discrimination.

cases, holding for example in *De Weerd, née Roks*,[93] that 'Article 4(1) of Directive 79/7 precludes the application of a national measure which, although formulated in neutral terms, works to the disadvantage of far more women than men, unless that measure is based on objectively justified factors unrelated to any discrimination on grounds of sex'.[94]

An important rider to add in cases where the discrimination is indirect is that the Court's usual technique for producing equality may prove inappropriate, as was demonstrated in *Jackson and Cresswell* v. *Chief Adjudication Officer*.[95] Van Gerven AG proceeded on the assumption (actually rejected by the Court, as seen above) that income support fell within the scope of Directive 79/9; the question then arose as to how to apply the equal treatment principle in the particular circumstances of the case. Childminding expenses were not permitted to be deducted from income when determining eligibility to the benefit, which was alleged to produce indirect discrimination against women. The Advocate General observed that the Court's usual approach is to require the application of the same rules to the disadvantaged group as are applied to the advantaged group. However, he pointed out that:

That approach affords no comfort to the appellants in the main proceedings: even in the case of lone fathers, childminding expenses are not deductible from income . . .

Consequently, as Community law stands at present, the most realistic solution seems to me for the national court to decide, where appropriate, at the request of the appellants in the main proceedings that, having regard to the criteria developed in this connection, the British authorities have not complied with their obligations under Directive . . . 79/7, and to declare them liable to pay compensation to Ms Jackson and Ms Cresswell on the basis of the rules specified in the Court's case-law, in particular . . . in *Francovich and Bonifaci* (Joined Cases C-6 & 9/90 [1991] ECR I-5357).[96]

Since indirect discrimination is not unlawful where it can be justified,[97] the strength of the non-discrimination principle in cases of indirect discrimination is directly proportional to the robustness with which the ECJ is prepared to treat the concept of justification.[98] The first indication of the Court's attitude to justification in the field of social security came in the *Teuling* case[99] where both the Court and the Advocate General agreed that the *de facto* indirect discrimination which had been demonstrated

---

[93] Case C-343/92 [1994] ECR I-571.

[94] Ibid. at 600. See also Case C-229/89 *Commission* v. *Belgium* [1991] ECR I-2205.

[95] Joined Cases 63 & 64/91 [1992] ECR I-4737.

[96] Ibid. at 4771. See Chap. 1 for discussion of *Francovich and Bonifaci* v. *Italy*.

[97] See discussion in particular in Chap. 2.

[98] See Cousins, 'Equal Treatment and Social Security' (1994) 19 ELRev. 123.

[99] Case 30/85 *Teuling* v. *Bedrijfsvereniging voor de Chemische Industrie* [1987] ECR 2497, also discussed above.

could be excused. Examining the purpose intended to be served by the supplementary payments for which Ms Teuling did not qualify, they found that the Netherlands legislation did not aim to link invalidity benefit to previous salary earned but just to provide a minimum subsistence income for persons with no earnings. The Court held:

[S]uch a guarantee granted by Member States to persons who would otherwise be destitute is an integral part of the social policy of the Member States.

Consequently, if supplements to a minimum social security benefit are intended, where beneficiaries have no income from work, to prevent the benefit from falling below the minimum subsistence level for persons who, by virtue of the fact that they have a dependent spouse or children, bear heavier burdens than single persons, such supplements may be justified under the Directive.

If a national court, which has sole jurisdiction to assess the facts and interpret the national legislation, finds that supplements such as those in this case correspond to the greater burdens which beneficiaries having a dependent spouse or children must bear in comparison with persons living alone, serve to ensure an adequate minimum subsistence income for those beneficiaries and are necessary for that purpose, the fact that the supplements are paid to a significantly higher number of married men than married women is not sufficient to support the conclusion that the grant of such supplements is contrary to the Directive.[100]

This ruling offered some, albeit limited, scope for argument to litigants; if it could be demonstrated that the payment of higher benefit levels to claimants with dependants was not an effective means of making provision for those dependants, because the payments were not passed on to them, then the *de facto* discrimination against women would not, seemingly, be justified. It is to be noted that, apart from the fact that it did not use the expression 'objectively justified factors', the Court's formulation here was substantially identical to that relied on by it in relation to Article 119 in *Bilka-Kaufhaus GmbH* v. *Weber Von Hartz*.[101]

The Court's decision in *Ruzius-Wilbrink* v. *Bestuur van de Bedrijfsvereniging voor Overheidsdiensten*[102] underscored the fact that the burden falls on the State to prove objective justification and that, if it does not discharge that burden, it will be guilty of indirect discrimination. Dutch invalidity payments which differentiated between full-time and part-time workers were there found to be discriminatory by the ECJ. The Court held that the scheme discriminated indirectly against women who make up the majority of those working part-time in the Netherlands. Ms Ruzius-Wilbrink had been refused the full benefit because she had only worked an average of 18 hours a week in the year preceding her incapacity. Under the scheme,

---

[100] [1987] ECR 2497, at 2521–2.
[101] Case 170/84 [1986] ECR 1607, discussed in Chap. 2. See also Case 171/88 *Rinner-Kuhn* v. *FWW Spezial-Gebaudereinigung GmbH* [1989] ECR 2743, also discussed in Chap. 2.
[102] Case C-102/88 [1989] ECR 4311.

everyone with an incapacity had a right to a minimum subsistence income benefit irrespective of previous salary, the only exception being for part-timers for whom the scheme linked the level of benefit to the person's previous salary. The government explained the rule by arguing that it was designed to prevent part-timers from receiving a benefit which was more than their previous income. The Court held that this could not amount to an objective justification of the difference in treatment because the level of the benefit granted in many other cases also was greater than the income previously received. It went on to rule that, just as in cases of direct discrimination, the members of the group disadvantaged in these circumstances were entitled to have applied to them the same scheme as that applied to other recipients of the benefit, in other words, to receive the full benefit.

This decision provided grounds for optimism that the Court would scrutinise critically the arguments put forward by the Member States as alleged justification for indirect discrimination. However, subsequent cases have not fulfilled this promise and they have, in general, illustrated the enormous difficulties faced by those who seek to challenge measures of social security policy. A good example is provided by *Commission* v. *Belgium*,[103] where the national law on unemployment and sickness benefits assigned claimants to three groups: (1) workers cohabiting with one or more persons, the latter having no income; (2) workers living alone; and (3) workers cohabiting with a person receiving an income. For both unemployment benefit and sickness benefit, entitlement under the system was calculated on the basis of previous earned income, but tiered to allow a different rate for each group, the highest being enjoyed by group (1), the next highest by group (2), and the lowest by group (3). In addition, an adaptation supplement of 20 per cent of previous income was payable to all claimants, but stopped after the first year of unemployment for groups (2) and (3). The alleged indirect discrimination arose from the fact that a clear majority of group (1) were men, whereas the majority of group (3) were women. The Belgian Government argued first that the difference in the ratio of men to women between the three groups was the product of a social phenomenon arising from the fact that fewer women than men were employed. The Court held that this could not be regarded as forming the basis of objective criteria unrelated to any discrimination on the ground of sex. However, the Belgian Government went on to contend that its legislation sought to assure a minimum replacement income to each individual claimant, in the light of the family situation of that person, and this the Court accepted as objective justification. It stated:

---

[103] Case C-229/89 [1991] ECR I-2205, noted by Banks in (1991) 20 ILJ 220.

The aim of the Belgian legislation is to take into consideration the existence of different needs. On the one hand, it recognises the greater burdens resulting from unemployment for households with only one income and, on the other hand, it takes into account the financial aid which the spouse's income represents for the unemployed person. Moreover, it seeks to encourage the persons concerned to adapt themselves to their new financial situation by avoiding too sudden a drop in their income during the first year, whilst enabling the unemployed person with dependants to bear the expenses of a household beyond a period of 18 months. Those principles and objectives form part of a social policy which in the current state of Community law is a matter for the Member States which enjoy *a reasonable margin of discretion* as regards both the nature of the protective measures and the detailed arrangements for their implementation . . .

With regard to a guaranteed minimum subsistence level, the Court has already held that Community law does not preclude a Member State, in controlling its social expenditure, from taking into account the relatively greater needs of beneficiaries who have a dependent spouse or a dependent child or receive only a very small income, in relation to the needs of single persons . . .

[T]he Belgian Government has shown that its system of unemployment and invalidity benefits corresponds to a legitimate objective of social policy, involving increases suitable and requisite for attaining that aim; it is therefore justified by reasons unrelated to discrimination on grounds of sex.[104]

The real degree of latitude thus entrusted to the Member States emerged from *Molenbroek* v. *Bestuur van de Sociale Verzekeringsbank*.[105] The Court was asked whether Article 4 of the Directive precluded national legislation on old age pensions from making the grant and amount of a supplement payable to a pensioner whose spouse had not yet reached retirement age depend on that spouse's earned income, excluding any other income of the pensioner, given that far more men than women qualified for the supplement and that the supplement was payable even where it was not essential to guarantee the couple a minimum income. In holding that this *de facto* discrimination was justified, the Court stated:

[T]he allowance granted . . . is in the nature of a basic allowance, in that it is intended to guarantee those concerned an income equal to the social minimum, irrespective of any income which they receive from other sources.

Furthermore, the Court has already held that the allocation of an income equal to the social minimum formed an integral part of the social policy of the Member States . . .

---

[104] Case C-229/89 at 2229–30. Emphasis supplied. It is noteworthy that the effect of this reasoning was that a Commission prosecution under Art. 169 {Art. 226} was rejected. This is an extremely rare occurrence: according to Weatherill and Beaumont, *EC Law* (Penguin, 2nd ed. 1995) of the cases of this type which have got as far as the ECJ, only about one tenth have been decided in favour of the Member State. With the benefit of hindsight, the case discussed in the main text may be seen as evidence of the Court's resolve to allow the Member States a wide measure of discretion in relation to the organisation of their social security systems.   [105] Case C-226/91 [1992] ECR I-5943.

Finally, in leaving out of account any other income received by an old-age pensioner when determining the supplement payable to him in respect of a younger dependent spouse, the national legislation . . . ultimately allocates to the couple an aggregate income equal to that to which both spouses will be entitled when they are both in receipt of a pension and the supplement has consequently been discontinued.

The supplements scheme is therefore essential in order to preserve the nature of the allowance . . . as a basic allowance and in order to guarantee the couple, where one of the spouses has not yet reached pensionable age, an income equal to the social minimum which they will receive when they are both pensioners.

In those circumstances, the fact that at times the supplement is granted to persons who, having regard to the income which they receive from other sources, do not need it in order to guarantee a minimum level of subsistence cannot affect the fact that the means chosen are necessary having regard to the aim pursued.[106]

In this somewhat obscure passage, the Court failed to investigate whether the legitimate aim pursued, namely the guaranteeing of a minimum income, could have been achieved by some means which did not involve overpayment in some cases. In the absence of such scrutiny, it is hard to feel convinced that the means chosen in these circumstances were 'necessary' for the achievement of the legitimate aim.

A glimmer of hope was offered to claimants by the ruling in *De Weerd, née Roks*,[107] where the Court held that 'although budgetary considerations may influence a state's choice of social policy and affect the nature or scope of the social protection measures it wishes to adopt, they cannot themselves constitute the aim pursued by that policy and cannot, therefore, justify discrimination against one of the sexes'.[108] This was in part because 'to concede that budgetary considerations may justify . . . indirect discrimination . . . would be to accept that the application and scope of as fundamental a rule of Community law as that of equal treatment between men and women might vary in time and place according to the state of the public finances of the member States'.[109] However, in the *Nolte* and *Megner and Scheffel* cases,[110] which concerned indirect discrimination against women resulting from the exclusion of those in 'minor' or 'short-term' employment from compulsory old age insurance, the Court reverted to an approach which was much more indulgent to the Member States. It reiterated its earlier principles but added a significant tailpiece:

---

[106] Ibid. at 5968–9. Emphasis supplied.
[107] Case C-343/92 [1994] ECR I-571.
[108] Ibid. at 600.
[109] Ibid. also at 600. Cf. the submissions of Darmon AG.
[110] Case C-317/93 *Nolte* v. *Landesversicherungsanstalt Hannover* [1995] ECR I-4625 and Case C-444/93 *Megner and Scheffel* v. *Innungskrankenkasse Vorderplatz* [1995] ECR I-4741, discussed above.

[S]ocial policy is a matter for the Member States . . . . Consequently, it is for the Member States to choose the measures capable of achieving the aim of their social and employment policy. *In exercising that competence, the Member States have a broad margin of discretion.*[111]

The German Government argued that the exclusion of the affected groups from compulsory insurance was basic to the structure of the national social security scheme, in which equivalence had to be maintained between the contributions paid in and the benefits paid out. It also maintained that the system favoured the creation of minor and short-term employment, for which there was a social demand,[112] and that in the absence of the existing system this demand would be satisfied by unlawful employment practices. The Court decided that:

[T]he social and employment policy aim relied on by the German Government is objectively unrelated to any discrimination on grounds of sex and . . ., in exercising its competence, the national legislature was reasonably entitled to consider that the legislation in question was necessary in order to achieve that aim.[113]

This ruling led the editors of the Equal Opportunities Review to comment that it reduced 'significantly the standard of proof required of a Member State in order to justify indirectly discriminatory legislation'. They went on to point out that, 'instead of having to show empirical evidence that the measure actually was necessary to achieve the objective pursued, it now appears sufficient under EC law if the Member State government could reasonably be entitled to take that view'.[114]

---

[111] Ibid. at 4660 and 4755 respectively. Emphasis supplied. See also Case C-8/94 *Laperre* v. *Bestuurscommissie* [1996] ECR I-273. The effect of these decisions is to make it very unlikely that an allegation of indirect discrimination would be successful in relation to the exclusion of those in the UK who earn less than the lower earnings limit from liability to pay national insurance contributions; many of those so excluded are women: there are 2.5 million women at present in the UK who earn less than the national insurance limit and 1 in 3 part-timers fall into this category. Nevertheless, the Court would seem to be prepared to condone the resulting discrimination against them on the basis of the Member State's choice of social policy. On the other hand, it might be possible to argue that the non-recognition of multiple employment (many part-timers hold a number of small jobs simultaneously) for the purpose of the national insurance threshold impacts more severely on women than men and that their resulting exclusion from the contributory benefits system is not objectively justifiable.

[112] Léger AG pointed out that the Court had 'lent a sympathetic ear to this type of argument in the judgment in Case C-189/91 *Kirsammer-Hack* [1993] ECR I-6185 [discussed in Chap. 3], where it held that there was objective justification for " . . . legislation which . . . forms part of a series of measures intended to alleviate the constraints burdening small businesses which play an essential role in economic development and the creation of employment in the Community" (at paragraph 33)'. But contrast the view of the House of Lords in *R.* v. *Secretary of State for Employment, Ex p. EOC* [1994] 2 WLR 409, also discussed in Chap. 3.

[113] [1995] ECR I-4625 and [1995] ECR I-4741, at 4660 and 4755 respectively.

[114] (1996) 67 EOR 43, at 44. See also Hepple, 'The Principle of Equal Treatment in Article 119 EC and the Possibilities for Reform' in *The Principle of Equal Treatment in EC Law*, eds. Dashwood and O'Leary (Sweet and Maxwell, London, 1997).

Furthermore, in *Posthuma-van Damme* v. *Bestuur van de Bedrijfsvereniging voor Detailhandel, Ambachten en Huisvrouwen*,[115] the Court made it clear, that although it had held in *De Weerd, née Roks* that budgetary considerations could not justify indirect discrimination resulting from a change in the Dutch social security rules which required claimants for incapacity benefit to have received 'some income' in the year preceding the onset of their incapacity, nevertheless other considerations of social policy might provide such justification. The decision of the Dutch legislature amounted in effect to a decision to switch from a system of pure national insurance to one which protected against loss of income and the Court concluded that:

[G]uaranteeing the benefit of a minimum income to persons who were in receipt of income from or in connection with work which they had to abandon owing to incapacity for work satisfies a legitimate aim of social policy and . . . to make the benefit of that minimum income subject to the requirement that the person concerned must have been in receipt of such an income in the year prior to the commencement of incapacity for work constitutes a measure appropriate to achieve that aim which the national legislature, in the exercise of its competence, was reasonably entitled to consider necessary in order to do so.

The fact that that scheme replaced a scheme of pure national insurance and that the number of persons eligible to benefit from it was further reduced to those who had actually lost income from or in connection with work at the time when the risk materialised cannot affect that finding.[116]

Laperre v. *Bestuurscommissie*[117] involved two Dutch unemployment schemes, the RWW which granted subsistence benefits but was means-tested, and the IOAW which was not means-tested but was subject to specific conditions relating to the employment record, age and incapacity of the claimant. Indirect discrimination was said to arise from the fact that more men than women qualified under the second, more generous, scheme. The Dutch Government argued that the purpose underlying the two schemes was different. That underlying the RWW was to encourage claimants to provide for their own needs and to go back into employment. The IOAW, on the other hand, was intended for unemployed workers who had worked for a relatively long period, had received earnings-related unemployment benefits for the maximum permitted period, and thereafter had little chance of finding new employment before they reached retirement age. The IOAW scheme was not means-tested because the legislature wished to protect its beneficiaries from having to break into their lifetime savings from earnings, especially in view of the very small likelihood of their being able to rebuild those savings from earned income. The Court accepted that this reasoning constituted justification; it

---

[115] Case C-280/94 [1996] ECR I-179.
[116] Ibid. at 204–5.
[117] Case C-8/94 [1996] ECR I-273.

represented a legitimate aim of social policy and was objectively unrelated to any discrimination on the ground of sex; in exercising its competence, the Dutch legislature was reasonably entitled to consider that its scheme was necessary in order to achieve its aim.

It is submitted that the cases discussed above which deal with indirect discrimination and its justification demonstrate clearly the limitations inherent in the concept of indirect discrimination as a tool for the radical alteration of social security systems. The concept is essentially a non-dynamic one,[118] which takes the work-force as it finds it, and does not attempt social engineering in any dramatic sense. This is because, even where a measure has been shown to have an adverse impact for one sex, it is still permissible provided that it serves a legitimate policy which is not itself discriminatory. Thus, a court which is called upon to assess whether a measure is justified is required to engage in a balancing process, weighing the social utility of the measure against its discriminatory effect. This would not necessarily be detrimental to the effectiveness of the concept of indirect discrimination were the ECJ to demand a very strict standard for justification. However, the cases decided to date in general display an extreme reluctance on the part of the ECJ to interfere with the subjective legislative decisions of the Member States in the area of social policy. It therefore remains hard to resist the conclusion arrived at by Luckhaus as long ago as 1988 that any sex neutral social security provision operating to women's disadvantage will be lawful if the purpose of the provision is to ensure a minimum subsistence income to protect people from poverty: 'women's needs must always be subordinated to those of the "poor" '.[119]

Article 5 of the Directive provides that the Member States must take the measures necessary to ensure that any laws, regulations, and administrative provisions contrary to the principle of equal treatment are abolished. However, provided that equality as between the sexes is maintained, the effect of legislative reform pursuant to the Directive can lawfully be to withdraw benefits. The Court made this clear in *De Weerd, née Roks*,[120] where it stressed that Directive 79/7 leaves intact the powers of the Member States to legislate on social policy and that the control of public expenditure may provide the rationale for such an even-handed withdrawal.

---

[118] For further development of this argument, see Chap. 5.

[119] Luckhaus, 'Sex Discrimination in State Social Security Schemes' (1988) 13 ELRev. 52. See also Sjerps, 'Indirect Discrimination in Social Security in the Netherlands: Demands of the Dutch Women's Movement', in *Women, Equality and Europe*, eds. Buckley and Anderson (Macmillan, London, 1988).

[120] Case C-343/92 [1994] ECR I-571. See also Case C-226/91 *Molenbroek* v. *Bestuur van de Sociale Verzekeringsbank* [1992] ECR I-5943, Case C-137/94 *R.* v. *Secretary of State for Health, Ex p. Richardson* [1995] ECR I-3407 and Case C-280/94 *Posthuma-van Damme* v. *Bestuur van de Bedrijfsvereniging voor Detailhandel, Ambachten en Huisvrouwen* [1996] ECR I-179.

Article 6 mirrors Article 6 of the Equal Treatment Directive,[121] providing:

Member States shall introduce into their national legal systems such measures as are necessary to enable all persons who consider themselves wronged by failure to apply the principle of equal treatment to pursue their claims by judicial process, possibly after recourse to other competent authorities.[122]

It was seen in Chapter 1 that the ECJ held in *Emmott* v. *Minister for Social Welfare*[123] that, where a Member State has not properly implemented a directive, it may not rely on a domestic limitation period in order to defeat an individual's claim based on the direct effect of the instrument; nevertheless, it held in *Steenhorst-Neerings*[124] that this principle does not preclude the State concerned from limiting back payment of a social security benefit entitlement to which arises by virtue of the direct effect of Directive 79/7.[125] Dutch law used to grant incapacity benefits only to men and unmarried women; on introduction of the principle of sex equality, entitlement was extended to married women, with the exception of those whose incapacity had arisen before 1975. This last condition was ruled invalid on the ground of discrimination by the Dutch Higher Social Security Court in 1988, which enabled the plaintiff, whose incapacity had originated in 1963, to claim the benefit. However, she was then met with a national procedural rule which limited back payments of such benefits to not more than one year. The Court distinguished this situation from the imposition of a limitation period, saying:

[A] time-bar resulting from the expiry of the time-limit for bringing proceedings serves to ensure that the legality of administrative decisions cannot be challenged indefinitely. The judgment in *Emmott* indicates that that requirement cannot prevail over the need to protect the rights conferred on individuals by the direct effect of provisions in a directive so long as the defaulting Member State responsible for those decisions has not properly transposed the provisions into national law.

On the other hand, the aim of the rule restricting the retroactive effect of claims for benefits for incapacity for work is quite different from that of a rule imposing mandatory time-limits for bringing proceedings . . . [T]he first type of rule . . . serves to ensure sound administration, most importantly so that it may be ascertained whether the claimant satisfied the conditions for eligibility and so

---

[121] Directive 76/207, OJ [1976] L39/40, discussed in Chap. 3.

[122] See discussion in Chap. 3 of the practical utility to claimants of the equivalent provision of the Equal Treatment Directive.

[123] Case C-208/90 [1991] ECR I-4269.

[124] Case C-338/91 *Steenhorst-Neerings* v. *Bestuur van de Bedrijfsvereniging voor Detailhandel, Ambachten en Huisvrouwen* [1993] ECR I-5475, noted by Sohrab in (1994) 31 CMLRev. 875.

[125] Cf. the submission of Darmon AG. The issue of whether the UK's two-year limitation on arrears of backpay recoverable in an equal pay claim is comparable to the principle articulated in *Steenhorst-Neerings* has been referred to the ECJ in *Levez* v. *Jennings Ltd.* [1996] IRLR 499.

that the degree of incapacity, which may well vary over time, may be fixed. It also reflects the need to preserve financial balance in a scheme in which claims submitted by insured persons in the course of a year must in principle be covered by the contributions collected during that same year.[126]

This decision was followed in *Johnson* v. *Chief Adjudication Officer*[127] which concerned a claim to severe disablement allowance in the UK, which was also subject to a one year limitation on back payments. This was notwithstanding the claimant's argument that her situation was distinguishable from that in *Steenhorst-Neerings* on the basis that there was no problem in determining whether she satisfied the conditions for the grant of the benefit and that the benefit involved was non-contributory.

In *R.* v. *Secretary of State for Social Security, Ex p. Sutton*,[128] the UK High Court asked the ECJ whether an individual was entitled to interest on arrears of a social security benefit, where the delay in payment of the benefit concerned resulted from discrimination prohibited by Directive 79/7. The claimant's case for the payment of interest rested on the similarity between Article 6 of Directive 79/7 and Article 6 of the Equal Treatment Directive; as seen in Chapter 3, the ECJ held in *Marshall* v. *Southampton and South-West Hants Area Health Authority (No. 2)*[129] that the latter Article requires the payment of interest on compensation for unlawful discrimination. The Court rejected this comparison:

[Social security] benefits are paid to the person concerned by the competent bodies, which must, in particular, examine whether the conditions laid down in the relevant legislation are fulfilled. Consequently, the amounts paid in no way constitute reparation for loss or damage sustained and the reasoning of the Court in its judgment in *Marshall II* cannot be applied to a situation of that kind.[130]

Furthermore, the Court rejected the Commission's argument which was based on *Jackson and Cresswell* v. *Chief Adjudication Officer*[131] and *Meyers* v. *Chief Adjudication Officer*[132] to the effect that a social security benefit relating to employment may fall within the scope of the Equal Treatment Directive:

According to the Commission, when such benefits are awarded belatedly on account of discrimination prohibited by Directive 76/207, interest is payable on the arrears of benefit in conformity with the principle laid down in *Marshall II*. There is nothing to suggest that in the case of a social security benefit falling under Directive 79/7, the principle of equal treatment is narrower in scope than

---

[126] [1993] ECR I-5475, at 5503–4.
[127] Case C-410/92 [1994] ECR I-5483.
[128] Case C-66/95 (nyr).
[129] Case C-271/91 [1993] ECR I-4367.
[130] *R.* v. *Secretary of State for Social Security, Ex p. Sutton* (nyr), at para. 24.
[131] Joined Cases C-63 & 64/91 [1992] ECR I-4737, discussed as to this aspect in Chap. 3.
[132] Case C-116/94 [1995] ECR I-2131, also discussed as to this aspect in Chap. 3.

that laid down by Directive 76/207, so that the conclusion drawn in the case of both Directives should be the same.

That reasoning is based on a false premiss. Although it follows from the judgments in *Jackson and Cresswell* and in *Meyers* that certain social security benefits do fall within the scope of Directive 76/207, that does not mean that Article 6 of that Directive, as interpreted in the judgment in *Marshall II*, requires interest to be paid on arrears of benefit when the delay in payment is due to discrimination on grounds of sex prohibited by the Directive. Whichever directive applies, amounts paid by way of social security benefit are not compensatory in nature, with the result that payment of interest cannot be required on the basis either of Article 6 of Directive 76/207 or of Article 6 of Directive 79/7.[133]

Article 8(1) of the instrument gave the Member States six years from its notification, that is to say, until 23 December 1984, within which to bring into force the legislation necessary to implement it. This unusually long implementation period, the result of a compromise at the drafting stage, was adopted in recognition of the complexity of the subject-matter and the legislation involved.[134] It meant that the practical effects of the legislation took a long time to make themselves evident. In *Dik* v. *College van Burgemeester en Wethouders, Arnhem*,[135] the ECJ held that, where a Member State had wrongfully delayed implementation of the Social Security Directive, it could nevertheless belatedly pass such legislation and make it retroactive to the date when implementation was required.

Article 8(2) of the Directive required the Member States to communicate to the Commission the text of laws, regulations, and administrative provisions adopted by them in the field covered by the Directive. This procedure played a significant part in the Court's refusal in *R* v. *Secretary of State for Health, Ex p. Richardson*[136] to impose a temporal limitation on the effect of its ruling[137] that the national system of exemption from prescription charges fell within the scope of the Directive:

First, . . . the United Kingdom was not unaware that an exemption from prescription charges fell within the scope of Directive 79/7 as defined in Article 3(1). In a letter of 11 June 1985 it had in fact informed the Commission, pursuant to Article 8(2) . . ., that it was relying on Article 7(1)(a) [discussed below] in order to maintain the difference in treatment between men and women in relation to prescription charges, the implication being that the exemption fell within the scope of the Directive.

Secondly, the mere fact that the Commission did not respond to that information could not reasonably have caused the United Kingdom to believe that that

---

[133] *R.* v. *Secretary of State for Social Security, Ex p. Sutton* (nyr), at paras. 26 and 27.
[134] The Commission had originally proposed an implementation period of only two years.
[135] Case 80/87 [1988] ECR 1601.
[136] Case C-137/94 [1995] ECR I-3407, discussed above.
[137] For discussion of prospective direct effect, see Chap. 2.

difference of treatment was excluded from the scope of Directive 79/7 pursuant to Article 7(1)(a). The Directive contains no specific provision obliging the Commission to approve or disapprove measures communicated to it pursuant to Article 8(2). Moreover, in performing its general task of acting as the guardian of the Treaties, the Commission has a discretion in assessing the expediency of initiating the procedure [for prosecuting Member States] laid down in Article 169 of the Treaty.[138]

By Article 9, within seven years of notification, Member States were required to forward all information necessary to the Commission to enable it to draw up a report on the application of the Directive for submission to the Council and to propose such further measures as might be required for the implementation of the principle of equal treatment.[139]

Exceptions to the Social Security Directive

The Social Security Directive contains a number of important exceptions. As discussed earlier in the present chapter, Article 3(3) appears to except occupational schemes and foreshadows later legislation in this area, which has now taken the form of the Occupational Social Security Directive.[140]

Article 3(2) excepts survivors' benefits:

This Directive shall not apply to the provisions concerning survivors' benefits nor to those concerning family benefits, except in the case of family benefits granted by way of increases of benefits due in respect of the risks referred to in [Article 3(1)(a)].[141]

As seen in Chapter 2, the Occupational Social Security Directive used to contain a similar exception, which fell foul of Article 119; there is little chance of such an allegation being proved in relation to the Social Security Directive because of the ECJ's continued insistence on the distinction between pay for the purposes of Article 119 of the Treaty and social

---

[138] [1995] ECR I-3407, at 3434–5. See also Elmer AG in Case C-228/94 *Atkins* v. *Wrekin District Council* [1996] ECR I-3633; he submitted that 'there may well be more scope for restricting the temporal effects of a judgment than there has hitherto appeared in the case-law of the Court in cases where the judgment would otherwise involve considerable administrative consequences or an enormous strain on the national court system' (at 3655).

[139] In its subsequent report, the Commission in particular invited the Member States to ensure that their national legislation does not result in the exclusion of part-time workers from the right to social security (COM(88) 769 final).

[140] Directive 86/378, OJ [1986, L225/40, discussed in Chap. 2.

[141] The exclusion of these matters from the scope of the Directive means that they remain subject to regulation by national and, where relevant, international law; thus, in Case C-337/91 *Van Gemert-Derks* v. *Bestuur van de Nieuwe Bedrijfsvereniging* [1993] ECR I-5435, the ECJ held that EC law did not prevent a Dutch court from interpreting Article 26 of the International Covenant on Civil and Political Rights of 19 December 1966 (*Treaty Series*, Vol. 999, p. 171) as requiring equal treatment for men and women as regards survivors' benefits.

security schemes.[142] The very existence of the exception at all is, of course, yet more evidence of the essentially conservative nature of the Directive (assuming the economic dependence of women on men, but not the opposite) and the political compromises which underlie it. In the UK, advantage is currently taken of the exception for survivors' benefits in the state scheme in that a widow receives a pension in respect of her deceased husband's national insurance contributions, and may also receive a pension under the state earnings-related pension scheme. Conversely, a widower has no entitlement under the basic national insurance scheme if his wife predeceases him (though he may be eligible to invalidity benefit if he is incapable of working and he may get a pension based on his deceased wife's entitlement under the state earnings-related pension scheme if he is over 65).[143]

In *Steenhorst-Neerings*,[144] one of the questions referred to the ECJ concerned the legality of a national rule which provided that women forfeited incapacity benefit on being awarded a widow's pension, but did not make an equivalent provision in relation to men. The Court held that incapacity benefit fell within the scope of Directive 79/7 and that it was 'irrelevant that the withdrawal [of incapacity benefit occurred] as the result of the award of a benefit, in this case survivors' benefits, falling outside the scope' of the Directive.[145]

Article 4(2) of the Directive provides: 'The principle of equal treatment shall be without prejudice to the provisions relating to the protection of women on the grounds of maternity.' As commented in Chapter 2 in relation to the parallel provision in the Occupational Social Security Directive, it is generally assumed that this permits only specially *favourable* treatment for women having babies, but the period of pregnancy is not specifically included and it is not clear just how far the exception extends.

Article 7 is exclusively devoted to exceptions to the Social Security Directive.[146] The first and most significant exception that it lists is that in

[142] See Case C-7/93 *Bestuur van Het Algemeen Burgerlijk Pensioenfonds* v. *Beune* [1994] ECR I-4471.

[143] See further Ogus, Barendt & Wikeley, *The Law of Social Security* (Butterworths, London, 4th ed. 1995), at 280–1. The exclusion of widowers from widows' benefits is, at the time of writing, being challenged as a contravention of the European Convention on Human Rights (as to which, see Chap. 3): *Willis* v. *UK* June 1997, Welfare Rights Bulletin 138, at 14.

[144] Case C-338/91 *Steenhorst-Neerings* v. *Bestuur van de Bedrijfsvereniging voor Detailhandel, Ambachten en Huisvrouwen* [1993] ECR I-5475, also discussed above.

[145] Ibid. at 5505. See also Case C-337/91 *Van Gemert-Derks* v. *Bestuur van de Nieuwe Industriele Bedrijfsvereniging* [1993] ECR I-5435.

[146] In Joined Cases C-245 and 312/94 *Hoever* v. *Land Nordrhein-Westfalen* [1996] ECR I-4895, Jacobs AG asserted that Case 151/84 *Roberts* v. *Tate and Lyle Ltd* [1986] ECR 703, Case 152/84 *Marshall* v. *Southampton and South-West Hants Area Health Authority* [1986] ECR 723 and Case 262/84 *Beets-Proper* v. *Van Lanshot Bankiers* [1986] 773 provided authority that 'Article 7 of Directive 79/7, being a derogation from a fundamental principle of Community law . . ., calls for a strict construction' (at 4915). See also the submissions of Van

paragraph (1)(a): 'the determination of pensionable age for the purposes of granting old age and retirement pensions and the possible consequences thereof for other benefits'. This exception, another result of political compromise,[147] was included in the Directive in deference to the differential state pension ages then to be found in the Member States.

Its original rationale is, however, greatly diminished today, since all but one of the Member States either now have the same pension age for the two sexes or else have begun the process leading to such equalization. Thus, the age has been equalized in Denmark (at 67 years of age), Luxembourg, Spain, Ireland, the Netherlands, Finland and Sweden (65), France (60) and Belgium (flexible between 60 and 65). Germany[148] has an equal pension age (65) for both sexes (but allows early retirement on better terms for women than men).[149] Greece used to make essentially similar provision to the UK but has now equalized at 65 years of age for recent entrants to the national insurance system. Portugal is equalizing at 65 years of age over a period ending in 1999. Austria has differential ages of 65 for men and 60 for women, but will equalize at 65 years of age by the year 2024. Only in Italy, where pension age used to be 60 for men and 55 for women, is the differential to be maintained with a gradual increase to 65 and 60 respectively.[150]

The UK introduced differential pension ages in 1940. Before that date, the age for both sexes had been 65. One of the reasons given in 1940 for making the change was so as to enable a married couple to retire at the same time (it being assumed that husbands were normally slightly older than their wives); husbands also at that time were not able to claim an increased pension for their dependent wives. In 1993 the UK Government announced that it intended to equalize the state pension age at 65, the

---

Gerven AG in Case C-9/91 *R. v. Secretary of State for Social Security, Ex p. EOC* [1992] ECR I-4297 (but contrast the actual outcome in that case, discussed below); Van Gerven AG additionally commented that he was assuming the legality of Article 7 'even though it permits the Member States to maintain provisions which are contrary to the principle of equal treatment for men and women, which has been recognised by the Court as fundamental'. He added that '[n]either the national court nor the parties nor the Commission have raised the question of the validity of that provision. Moreover, the Court has already repeatedly ruled on it without questioning its validity' (at 4324).

[147] Its second limb was proposed by the UK.

[148] See Rust's 'Comment' in *Equality of Treatment Between Women and Men in Social Security*, ed. McCrudden (Butterworths, London, 1994).

[149] The Federal German courts consider this situation not to contravene the principle of equality of the sexes laid down in the German Basic Law because it is justified by the fact that women covered by insurance tend to have two occupations, their paid employment and their 'housewifely duties', so that they use up their strength more quickly and are unable to work at an earlier stage than men! See H. Gerald Crossland, 'Community Law in the German Courts 1986' (1989) 14 ELRev. 238.

[150] See *Social Protection in the Member States of the European Union* (Commission/MISSOC, 1995), Table VII.

change being phased in between the years 2010 and 2020; more specifically, the pension age for women will increase by one month every two months between 2010 and 2020, only women born after 5 April 1950 being affected.[151] These proposals were subsequently enacted in the Pensions Act 1995.

The first element of the exception for pensionable age—the determination of pensionable age for the purposes of granting old-age and retirement pensions—provided the issue in *Marshall v. Southampton and South-West Hants Area Health Authority*.[152] As discussed in more detail in Chapter 3, the ECJ apparently experienced a change of heart in *Marshall* from its opinion in *Burton v. British Railways Board*[153] and it held that the exception must be strictly confined to the age at which entitlement to pensions begins and must not be extended to other matters (notably dismissal) which are regulated by the Equal Treatment Directive. *Roberts v. Tate and Lyle Ltd*,[154] however, showed that this distinction was virtually impossible to operate in practice and in *Barber v. Guardian Royal Exchange Assurance Group*[155] the ECJ apparently abandoned it, holding that there must be no discrimination in relation to age in occupational pension schemes. In truth, the potential for intractable problems in this area will remain until such time as EC law and the national legal systems prohibit differential state pension ages.

The issue has also arisen as to whether the exception extends to the arrangements surrounding the granting of old age pensions. Under the UK system, in order to qualify for a full state old age pension men must have paid national insurance contributions for at least 44 years of their working life, whereas for women the requirement is only 39 years. In addition, after the age of 60, a woman may not make any further national insurance contributions, whereas a man working between the ages of 60 and 64 must pay national insurance contributions even if he has already made 44 years of contributions. The Equal Opportunities Commission (EOC), believing these arrangements to discriminate contrary to the Social Security Directive, and not to be saved by Article 7(1)(a), brought judicial review proceedings against the UK Government. Both Van Gerven AG and the Court analysed the problem as being whether the exception merely allows men and women to be treated unequally with respect to the moment at which they become entitled to a pension or whether it also covers other consequences flowing from differential pensionable ages. Upholding the latter interpretation, the Court confirmed the legality of the UK system:

---

[151] *Equality in State Pension Age* (HMSO, 1993, Cmnd. 2420).
[152] Case 152/84 [1986] ECR 723.   [153] Case 19/81 [1982] ECR 555.
[154] Case 151/84 [1986] ECR 703.   [155] Case C-262/88 [1990] ECR I-1889.

The [Directive] does not . . . refer expressly to discrimination in respect of the extent of the obligation to contribute for the purposes of the pension or the amount thereof. Such forms of discrimination therefore fall within the scope of the derogation only if they are found to be necessary in order to achieve the objectives which the Directive is intended to pursue by allowing Member States to retain a different pensionable age for men and women . . .

Although the preamble to the Directive does not state the reasons for the derogations which it lays down, it can be deduced from the nature of the exceptions contained in Article 7(1) . . . that the Community legislature intended to allow Member States to maintain temporarily the advantages accorded to women with respect to retirement in order to enable them progressively to adapt their pension systems in this respect without disrupting the complex financial equilibrium of those systems, the importance of which could not be ignored. Those advantages include the possibility for female workers of qualifying for a pension earlier than male workers, as envisaged by Article 7(1)(a) . . .

In a system such as the one concerned in the main proceedings, whose financial equilibrium is based on men contributing for a longer period than women, a different pensionable age for men and women cannot be maintained without altering the existing financial equilibrium, unless such inequality with respect to the length of contribution periods is maintained.

Consequently, any interpretation of Article 7(1) . . . whose effect would be to restrict the scope of the derogations provided for in subparagraph (a) to that of allowing Member States to provide that men and women do not become entitled to a pension at the same time and to exclude discrimination with respect to contribution periods would lead to the financial disequilibrium of the pension schemes.[156]

On the other hand, *Van Cant* v. *Rijksdienst voor Pensionen*[157] demonstrated that, once pensionable ages have been equalised, there is no longer scope for differences between the sexes over the calculation of the amount of pension benefits. Belgian law had equalised pension age but had retained the former system of calculating the amount of pension receivable which took as its annual basis one forty-fifth of salary for men but one fortieth for women. The ECJ condemned this situation, holding that:

Articles 4(1) and 7(1) of Directive 79/7 preclude national legislation which authorises male and female workers to take retirement as from an identical age from retaining in the method of calculating the pension a difference according to sex which is itself linked to the difference in pensionable age which previously existed.[158]

[156] Case C-9/91 *R.* v. *Secretary of State for Social Security, Ex p. EOC* [1992] ECR I-4297, at 4337–8. Hervey has argued that this judgment represents an unjustifiably broad construction of the derogation permitted by Art. 7(1)(a): see (1993) 30 CMLRev. 653.

[157] Case C-154/92 [1993] ECR I-3811, noted by De Vos in 'Pensionable Age and Equal Treatment from Charybdis to Scylla' (1994) 23 ILJ 175.

[158] Case C-154/92 at 3834. For an account of the background to this case, see Clotuche's 'Comment' in *Equality of Treatment Between Women and Men in Social Security*, ed. McCrudden (Butterworths, London, 1994).

The second limb of the exception—the possible consequences of differential pensionable age for other benefits—is also fraught with difficulties. How far does this limb extend? It has been seen in Chapters 2 and 3 that the ECJ in *Barber* v. *Guardian Royal Exchange Assurance Group*[159] held that occupational pensions may not discriminate between the sexes on the basis of age (despite the attempt to create such an exception in the Occupational Social Security Directive). The remarks of the ECJ in *Marshall* v. *Southampton and South-West Hants Area Health Authority*[160] and *Roberts* v. *Tate and Lyle Ltd.*[161] also showed that the Court now regards the exception for pensionable age contained in the Social Security Directive as confined exclusively to the field of social security benefits and as no longer being able to excuse any type of private discriminatory financial provision.[162] For example, in *Marshall*, it commented: 'It must be emphasized that . . . the exception contained in Article 7 of Council Directive 79/7/EEC concerns the consequences which pensionable age has *for social security benefits* . . .'[163] However, even on this limited basis, the question remains of how 'consequences' should be defined and what sort of benefits the exception might still embrace. Does the exception, for example, permit the abatement of other social security benefits as pensionable age approaches, or is it confined to the age at which other benefits are actually payable?

Several questions of this type were helpfully discussed by the UK Social Security Commissioner, Mr Monroe, in *Re Severe Disablement Allowance*.[164] He had been referred to a decision of a Tribunal of Commissioners in which a male claimant had tried to establish that a statutory provision then in operation, under which a person who had attained the age of 60 was liable to have unemployment benefit restricted if he or she received an occupational pension, discriminated against men. There was no similar rule in relation to women over the age of 55, so that there was no issue as to direct discrimination. However, it was argued that the rule was indirectly discriminatory because in fact it applied to many more men than women because of women's pensionable age being 60. It was held that the situation was excepted from the Directive because it was clearly a consequence of the difference in pensionable age, and with this conclusion Mr Monroe agreed, saying that the same conclusion was bound to be reached even on the narrowest interpretation of Article 7(1)(a). Similarly, he took the case of a woman who had attained pensionable age

---

[159] Case C-262/88 [1990] ECR I-1889.
[160] Case 152/84 [1986] ECR 723.
[161] Case 151/84 [1986] ECR 703.
[162] Cf. Case 19/81 *Burton* v. *British Railways Board* [1985] ECR 555.
[163] Case 152/84 [1986] ECR 723, at 746. (Emphasis supplied.)
[164] [1989] 3 CMLR 379.

and was actually receiving her retirement pension, who was precluded by the Overlapping Benefit Regulations from also receiving a severe disablement allowance. A man below pensionable age would not be so precluded, but there was nevertheless, according to Mr Monroe, a sufficient link in these circumstances between the benefit rules and the differential pensionable ages for the exception to apply. But he went on to point out that:

A more difficult question arises when there is a provision that the right to a benefit comes to an end at pensionable age as happened with mobility allowance when it was first introduced by s. 22 of the Social Security Pensions Act 1975 . . . subsection (4)(a) being material on the present point. Again the rate of some benefits may change at pensionable age (as happens under s. 14(2) of the 1975 Act in relation to sickness, invalidity and unemployment benefits) and can disappear altogether five years later. I should be disposed to think that these provisions fell to be associated with the fact that the beneficiary having reached pensionable age fell to be treated as sufficiently provided for by whatever provision he had made for pension and could not expect to look beyond that; and that accordingly these too were possible consequences for other benefits of the differential . . . pensionable ages.[165]

On the facts of *Re Severe Disablement Allowance* itself, the claimant had reached pensionable age (60) in 1983. She had continued to work after this date but had ceased work on becoming disabled. She applied for a severe disablement allowance in 1986 but was refused it because she had already attained pensionable age and had not been entitled to the allowance immediately before she reached that age (as stipulated by s. 36(4)(d) of the Social Security Act 1975). If she had been a man, she would not already have reached pensionable age and so could have claimed the allowance.[166] Mr Monroe held that the intention behind the statutory provision was to permit those whose incapacity set in before 'the infirmities of age' begin to assume significance, to continue to receive the allowance, whereas those whose incapacity does not set in until an age when the infirmities of age assume significance must never be entitled to it. For this purpose, pensionable age was selected by the legislature as the critical time, but for a purpose unconnected with title to the pension itself. He therefore held that the differentiation between the sexes in relation to severe disablement allowance was not a consequence of the difference in pensionable age: '[i]t is rather the consequence of a differential view being taken of the setting in of infirmity in the two sexes'. The claimant was therefore entitled to be treated in the same way as if she were a man,

---

[165] [1989] 3 CMLR 379 at 386. There appears to be an error in the last paragraph of this quotation, as printed in the Common Market Law Reports, which the present writer has attempted to correct.

[166] See now SI 1993 No. 3194.

in other words to be able to claim the allowance provided only that her disablement set in before she reached the age of 65. As a matter of general principle, Mr Monroe commented:

[I]t is not sufficient to escape the Directive simply to gear a different benefit to the differential pension ages if the resulting differentiation between sexes in that benefit cannot be shown to have some objective link with pensionable age. If it were it would make it all too easy to evade the provisions of the Directive.[167]

On appeal, the case was consolidated with several others on similar facts, and in particular with three involving invalid care allowances (awarded to those caring for a severely disabled person) which were also excluded by UK legislation where the carer had reached pensionable age, unless he or she was entitled to the allowance immediately before reaching pensionable age.[168] The House of Lords referred a number of questions to the ECJ on the ambit of Article 7(1)(a).[169] The Court took a strict view of the scope of the defence, saying:

[F]orms of discrimination provided for in benefit schemes other than old-age and retirement pension schemes can be justified, as being the consequence of determining a different retirement age according to sex, *only if such discrimination is objectively necessary in order to avoid disrupting the complex financial equilibrium of the social security system or to ensure consistency between retirement pension schemes and other benefit schemes.*[170]

It justified an excursion into the facts of the case on the basis of its role being to furnish the national court with worthwhile answers and added:

As regards the requirement of preserving financial equilibrium as between the old-age pension scheme and the other benefit schemes, it should be noted that the grant of benefits under non-contributory schemes, such as severe disablement allowance and invalid care allowance, to persons in respect of whom certain risks have materialised, regardless of the entitlement of such persons to an old-age pension by virtue of contribution periods completed by them, has no direct influence on the financial equilibrium of contributory pension schemes.

Furthermore . . . discrimination between men and women under non-contributory schemes, such as that of the severe disablement allowance and the invalid care allowance, is unnecessary to preserve the financial equilibrium of the entire social security system, particularly since the national rules contain provisions to prevent overlapping between benefits such as severe disablement allowance or invalid care allowance and the old-age pension and, in fact, the grant of those benefits takes the place of benefits paid under other non-contributory schemes, such as benefits paid to people who have insufficient resources to support themselves.[171]

---

[167] [1989] 3 CMLR 379 at 384.
[168] *Sub. nom. Thomas* v. *Adjudication Officer and the Secretary of State for Social Security.*
[169] Case C-328/91 *Secretary of State for Social Security* v. *Thomas* [1993] ECR I-1247.
[170] Ibid. at 1273. (Emphasis supplied.)   [171] Ibid. also at 1273.

The ECJ also made short shrift of the UK Government's reliance on statistics relating to male and female working and retirement patterns in its attempt to justify differential treatment of the two sexes. The Court referred to its holding in *Marshall* v. *Southampton and South-West Hants Area Health Authority*[172] that women are entitled to go on working beyond the qualifying age for an old-age pension and held:

As to the United Kingdom's argument that the vast majority of women receive an old-age pension once they have attained the age of 60, suffice it to say that the grant of benefits such as severe disablement allowance or invalid care allowance constitutes, for women who are not yet in receipt of old-age pension despite their having attained the normal retirement age, an individual right which cannot be denied them on the ground that, statistically, their situation is exceptional by comparison with that of most women.[173]

It is clear from *Thomas* that the Court regards as extremely important the coherence between a Member State's retirement benefits scheme and its other social security benefits. This was further evidenced in *Secretary of State for Social Security* v. *Graham*,[174] which concerned discrimination in relation to entitlement to invalidity pensions in the UK. The invalidity pension was a benefit designed to be replaced by the old-age pension. To be more specific, women receiving invalidity pension after the female state pensionable age of 60 had the rate of their invalidity pension reduced to what they would have been entitled to by way of retirement pension, whereas for men this did not occur until they reached the male pensionable age of 65. The ECJ reiterated its holding in *Thomas* that Article 7(1)(a) justifies only discrimination which is necessarily and objectively linked to the difference in pensionable age between men and women. However, notwithstanding that invalidity benefits were contributory (unlike the benefits involved in *Thomas*), it went on to find that Article 7(1)(a) excused the discrimination on these facts:

As regards the forms of discrimination at issue in the main proceedings, the Court finds that they are objectively linked to the setting of different pensionable ages for women and men, inasmuch as they arise directly from the fact that that age is fixed at 60 for women and 65 for men.

As to the question whether the forms of discrimination are also necessarily linked to the difference in pensionable age for men and women, it should be noted, first, that since invalidity benefit is designed to replace income from occupational activity, there is nothing to prevent a Member State from providing for its cessation and replacement by a retirement pension at the time when the recipents would in any case stop working because they have reached pensionable age.[175]

---

[172] Case 152/84 [1986] ECR 723. [173] [1993] ECR I-1247, at 1274.
[174] Case C-92/94 [1995] ECR I-2521.
[175] Cf. the Court's insistence in Case 152/84 *Marshall* v. *Southampton and South-West Hants Area Health Authority* [1986] ECR 723 that retirement age and pensionable age are not necessarily to be equated with one another.

Further, to prohibit a Member State which has set different pensionable ages from limiting, in the case of persons becoming incapacitated for work before reaching pensionable age, the rate of invalidity benefit payable to them from that age to the actual rate of the retirement pension to which they are entitled under the retirement pension scheme would mean restricting to that extent the very right which a Member State has under Article 7(1)(a) of Directive 79/7 to set different pensionable ages.[176]

The Court went on to explain that:

Such a prohibition would also undermine the coherence between the retirement pension scheme and the invalidity benefit scheme in at least two respects.

First, the Member State in question would be prevented from granting to men who become incapacitated for work before reaching pensionable age invalidity benefits greater than the retirement pensions which would actually have been payable to them if they had continued to work until reaching pensionable age unless it granted to women over pensionable age retirement pensions greater than those actually payable to them.

Second, if women did not have their invalidity pension reduced to the level of their retirement pension until they reached the age of 65, as in the case of men, women aged between 60 and 65, thus over pensionable age, would receive an invalidity pension at the rate of a full retirement pension if their incapacity for work commenced before they reached pensionable age and a retirement pension corresponding to the rate actually payable if it did not.[177]

Later cases have adhered to the principles that discrimination will only be excused by Article 7(1)(a) where it is objectively and necessarily linked to the difference in pensionable age and that this link will only be present where the discrimination is necessary to preserve the financial equilibrium of the social security system or to preserve its coherence. Thus, in *R. v. Secretary of State for Health, Ex p. Richardson*,[178] the UK's dispensation from the requirement to pay prescription charges which applied from the two different pensionable ages was not permissible. Just as in *Thomas*, removal of the discrimination would not affect the financial equilibrium of either the pension scheme or of the social security system as a whole. Neither was it necessary to discriminate in order to ensure coherence of the system. The Court concluded that:

Although the fact that the elderly will generally incur more prescription charges than younger people at a time when they will normally have less disposable income may provide some justification for exempting them from prescription

---

[176] [1995] ECR I-2521, at 2553–4. As Cousins comments in 'Free Movement of Workers and Social Security: Two Steps Forward, One Step Back' (1996) 21 ELRev. 233, 'this statement simply begs the question as to whether or not such a restriction is allowed under Community law'.

[177] Case C-92/94 at 2554–5.

[178] Case C-137/94 [1995] ECR I-3407, also discussed above.

charges above a certain age, that consideration does not require this benefit to be granted at statutory pensionable age and therefore at different ages for men and women.[179]

Similarly, in *Atkins* v. *Wrekin District Council*,[180] Elmer AG considered that Article 7(1)(a) did not excuse the provision of concessionary fares on public transport at different pensionable ages. He pointed out that:

An interpretation according to which a benefit such as that operated by Wrekin District Council was regarded as covered by Article 7(1)(a) would, in my view, lead to every benefit protecting against old age being covered by that derogating provision. The Member State would merely have to make the benefit conditional on the recipient's having reached pensionable age. Such a legal position would, however, be hard to reconcile with the fact that the risk of old age is expressly covered by the Directive and must accordingly be intended to have a real content. It should, therefore, be an exception and not the rule that benefits for the elderly which are not in the nature of an old-age pension should be regarded as covered by Article 7(1)(a).[181]

However, the discrimination encountered in *Balestra* v. *INPS*[182] was held to fall within the derogation contained in Article 7(1)(a). It stemmed from Italian legislation which credited pension contributions to persons employed by undertakings facing 'critical difficulties' where those persons took early retirement five years or less from state pensionable age. State pensionable age in Italy at the relevant date was 60 for men and 55 for women, but women were permitted to continue working if they so chose until the age of 60. The plaintiff in this action was aged 54 years seven months when her employer was declared to be in critical difficulty; she was accordingly credited with five months' contributions but claimed that she should have been credited with a full five years' contributions. The discrimination alleged arose in that a woman retiring at 55 was not credited with any contributions, whereas a man of the same age and who had the same contribution record would be credited with a further five years' worth of contributions; thus, a woman aged 55 would actually have to work for five years longer than her male colleague in order to achieve the same ultimate pension as he received. The ECJ found that this discrimination was indeed objectively linked to the difference in pensionable ages between the two sexes because it ensued directly from it. As to whether or not it was necessary, the Court held:

If women taking early retirement at an age between 50 and 55 were credited with five years' contributions, without account being taken of the ordinary retirement

---

[179] Ibid. at 3432.

[180] Case C-228/94 [1996] ECR I-3633, also discussed above.

[181] Ibid. at 3653. The Court itself had no need to deal with this issue since (as discussed above) it held that the benefit in question was not within the scope *ratione materiae* of the Directive.   [182] Case C-139/95 [1997] ECR I-549.

age, the closer their entry into early retirement was to the ordinary pensionable age, the clearer it would become that those women were receiving a definitive pension higher than that of women who had paid contributions until they reached the age of 55 and then retired, without being able to claim a credit of contributions.

Second, such a scheme is also liable to give rise to discrimination against men. Whereas a man taking early retirement at an age between 55 and 60 is only entitled to a credit of contributions covering the period from the date on which he takes early retirement until he reaches the ordinary pensionable age, a woman who also takes early retirement during the five years prior to the date on which she qualifies for a retirement pension would, as a matter of course, be entitled to a credit of five years' contributions.

Consequently, even though women are entitled to work until they reach the age of 60, denying them a credit of contributions in respect of the period after the date on which they reach the age of 55, the age at which they are entitled to a retirement pension, is necessary in order to preserve the coherence between the retirement-pensions scheme and the early-retirement scheme in question.[183]

The remainder of Article 7(1) permits Member States to exclude a number of other matters, in relation in particular to wives, from the scope of the Directive. It itemizes:

(b)   advantages in respect of old-age pension schemes granted to persons who have brought up children; the acquisition of benefit entitlements following periods of interruption of employment due to the bringing up of children;

(c)   the granting of old age or invalidity benefit entitlements by virtue of the derived entitlements of a wife;[184]

(d)   the granting of increases of long-term invalidity, old age, accidents at work and occupational disease benefits for a dependent wife;

(e)   the consequences of the exercise, before the adoption of this Directive, of a right of option not to acquire rights or incur obligations under a statutory scheme.

Bramhill v. *Chief Adjudication Officer*[185] demonstrated the considerable potential of, in particular, Article 7(1)(d) to preserve discrimination. UK legislation used formerly to provide for increases in long-term old age benefits in respect of a dependent spouse to be granted only to men. However, legislation enacted in 1984 extended this right to women but only on condition that immediately before payment of the retirement pension the claimant was entitled to an increase in unemployment benefit, sickness benefit or invalidity pension in respect of an adult dependant. From 1984 onwards, therefore, the increases applied to all men with

---

[183]   Ibid. at 581–2.

[184]   For an application of this exception, see Case C-165/91 *Van Munster* v. *Rijksdienst voor Pensioenen* [1994] ECR I-4661.

[185]   Case C-420/92 [1994] ECR I-3191.

dependent spouses but only to certain women with dependent spouses. The claimant relied on the wording of two provisions contained in the Directive: firstly, Article 4(1) which, as seen above, lays down the general principle that all discrimination on grounds of sex is prohibited as regards the calculation of benefits, including increases due in respect of a 'spouse' and for dependants; and, secondly, she observed that Article 7(1)(d) excludes discrimination only as regards benefits for a dependent 'wife'. The ECJ nevertheless held that the discrimination involved here was excusable. After noting that the Directive states its purpose to be the progressive implementation of the principle of equal treatment in social security, it held:

To interpret the Directive in the way contended for by Mrs Bramhill, which would mean that in the case of benefits which a Member State has excluded from the scope of the Directive pursuant to Article 7(1)(d) it could no longer rely on the derogation provided for by that provision if it adopted a measure which, like that in question in the main proceedings, has the effect of *reducing the effect of unequal treatment based on sex*, would therefore be incompatible with the purpose of the Directive and would be likely to jeopardise the implementation of the aforesaid principle of equal treatment.[186]

The desire of the Court not to penalise a Member State which has gone some way towards providing equal treatment for men and women was particularly evident here, especially since it might alternatively have held that the enactment of the Directive deprived the Member States henceforth of the power to enact further social security legislation which was sexually discriminatory and thus in breach of its terms.[187] The relevant UK legislation patently contravened the general principle of sex equality and was not itself saved by Article 7(1)(d) because that permits only discrimination as regards long-term benefits for dependent *wives*; the 1984 legislation was outwith the terms of the exception because it discriminated as regards long-term benefits for some *husbands*.

The Member States are required periodically to examine the matters excluded under Article 7(1) in order to ascertain, in the light of relevant social developments, whether there is justification for continuing to maintain the exclusions concerned.[188] They must also communicate to the Commission the text of any measures they adopt pursuant to this obligation, and must inform the Commission of their reasons for maintaining exclusions under Article 7(1) and of the possibilities for reviewing them at a later date.[189]

[186] Ibid. at 3211. (Emphasis supplied.)
[187] See the submissions of Mancini AG in Case 30/85 *Teuling* v. *Bedrijfsvereniging voor de Chemische Industrie* [1987] ECR 2497, discussed in Chap. 1.
[188] Art. 7(2) of the Directive.
[189] Ibid. Art. 8(2).

5

The Policy Underlying EC Sex Equality Law and Future Developments

The overwhelming body of law discussed so far in this work has concerned discrimination on the ground of sex, since discrimination is the technical concept referred to in the relevant instruments of EC law. It is important to emphasise, however, that discrimination is a narrower concept than the promotion of sex equality or of equality of opportunity irrespective of sex. As the present writer has argued elsewhere,[1] discrimination is an individualised and essentially comparative concept. The right not to be discriminated against on the ground of sex means the right of an individual not to be subjected to specific treatment which is less favourable than that which is or would be received by a similarly placed member of the opposite sex, where the ground of or reason for the less favourable treatment is sex. The notions of sex equality and equality of opportunity for all are much more generalised and refer to the ideal that life chances should be equally available to all persons and that there should be no underprivileged groups, in particular none where sex is a prejudicial criterion.[2]

The assumption underlying all these principles is that the fact of having been born into a particular sex is an irrelevant consideration in most circumstances. It has simply no material bearing on most matters. It follows, of course, that it has therefore to be conceded that on those few occasions when sex is a relevant consideration, otherwise discriminatory treatment must be excusable.

It is submitted that these principles have their foundations in logic and justice. Logic dictates that only relevant considerations be permissible in rational decision-making. Justice adds to this the principle that, especially when arriving at decisions with an important bearing on a person's life, irrelevant matters over which that person has no control should play no part.

In so far as the non-discrimination principle relates to individuals, the law has conferred a distinct right upon the individual in defined

[1] Ellis, 'The Definition of Discrimination in European Community Sex Equality Law' (1994) 19 ELRev. 563.
[2] See further, Fredman, 'Reversing Discrimination' (1997) 113 LQR 575.

circumstances. Increased understanding of the nature and content of this right, together with greater familiarity with it which has largely been a consequence of litigation, has led today to a widespread acceptance that we are talking here about a fundamental human right which all civilised societies should consider themselves obliged to protect.

THE LIMITATIONS ON THE POTENTIAL OF THE NON-DISCRIMINATION PRINCIPLE TO PROMOTE CHANGE

Despite the importance in jurisprudential terms of the principle of non-discrimination, it would be disingenuous to pretend that there were not disappointingly severe limitations on the effectiveness of that principle and therefore on the existing law itself. The major factors responsible for such limitations are inherent in the very concept. It is only designed to produce like consequences for those placed in like situations, the so-called Aristotelian notion of discrimination. It can do nothing of itself to remedy the plight of a person whose disadvantaged state cannot be compared with that of a similarly situated member of the opposite sex. This has three particularly striking consequences.

The first concerns the static nature of the concept. To be more specific, it is evident that such instruments as Article 119 of the Treaty and the Equal Pay, Equal Treatment, and Social Security Directives provide a remedy only for those placed in situations which can be likened to those experienced by members of the opposite sex. They have no effect where such comparison is impossible. This means that the concept of non-discrimination and the resultant law are not truly dynamic or redistributive in character.[3] On the contrary, they are premised on the existing cultural and social divisions to be found in the Member States of the Community.[4] Admittedly, they have turned out in practice to be a little broader than might at first have been perceived. On its face, Article 119, the spiritual parent of all the later equality legislation, seems concerned merely on the plane of formal equality between the sexes. It does not expressly mandate any examination whatever as to the causes of inequality; still less does it require the addressing by the law of those causes. In practice, however, as has been seen, the ECJ has interpreted the Article so as to cover indirect forms of discrimination and it can thus be said to have gone some way

---

[3] Support for the view that indirect discrimination represents corrective, as opposed to distributive, justice is also to be found in Morris, 'On the Normative Foundations of Indirect Discrimination Law: Understanding the Competing Models of Discrimination Law as Aristotelian Forms of Justice' (1995) 15 OJLS 199. See also Barnard, *EC Employment Law* (Wiley, Chichester, 1996), esp. Chap. 4.

[4] See generally *Women, Equality and Europe*, eds. Buckley and Anderson (Macmillan, London, 1988).

towards tackling the substance of inequality. This doctrine, moreover, has been seized upon by the legislature and incorporated into the subsequent instruments of secondary legislation. The limits of indirect discrimination are themselves, however, patent, the most obvious being the notion of 'objective justification' of otherwise discriminatory conduct, whose effect appears now to be to rank many forms of economic 'need' above the right to equality of the sexes. In short, neither direct nor indirect discrimination by themselves do anything to *dismantle* the obstacles faced by those subjected to sex discrimination; at best they disregard such obstacles. Thus, for example, the ECJ commented of the Equal Treatment Directive in *Hofmann* v. *Barmer Ersatzkasse*[5] that it was 'not designed to settle questions concerned with the organization of the family, or to alter the division of responsibility between parents'.[6]

Secondly, the concept of discrimination goes no further than to recognize that Western European society has, in general, relegated men and women to different economic, cultural, and sometimes even behavioural roles, and it aims to 'see through' these differences so as to grant each sex, in reality, the same chances. The trouble with this approach is that it has to be understood against the background of a society in which men have unquestionably assumed the dominant role: men predominate over women in the best-paid and most otherwise rewarding jobs; they own the bulk of the property in private hands, and they therefore exercise the most political influence. In short, men have more power and status than women. Thus, the practical upshot of a law conferring a right not to be discriminated against on the ground of sex is to enable *women* to seek *male* jobs and opportunities; it encourages them to strive for male patterns of work and to conform to existing male values. It struggles to force them into a stereotypical male role model: the male is the 'norm'.[7] As Hepple has expressed it:

Existing employment and pension benefits are structured according to the expectations of the male full-time worker in continuous employment from the age of 16 to that of (male) retirement. This assumes that the domestic and family needs of the man will be taken care of by his (unpaid) wife.[8]

By very definition, this is likely to be generally a one-way process. It can never work successfully in both directions until such time as the underlying patterns of organization of our society have changed. Men will only

---

[5] Case 184/83 [1984] ECR 3047.

[6] Ibid. at 3075. See also Case 170/84 *Bilka-Kaufhaus GmbH* v. *Weber Von Hartz* [1986] ECR 1607.

[7] For an eloquent articulation of this criticism, made as long ago as 1938, see Woolf, *Three Guineas* (republished by Oxford University Press, Oxford, 1992).

[8] Hepple 'Equality and Discrimination' in *European Community Labour Law: Principles and Perspectives*, eds. Davis, Lyon-Caen, Sciarra and Simitis (Clarendon Press, Oxford, 1996).

demand the same treatment as women when women as a group are receiving better treatment in relation to a particular issue than men.

The combined effect of the lack of dynamism of the non-discrimination principle and the resultant adherence to a male norm is well described by Townshend-Smith:

[T]here is no doubt that young women are socialised into thinking that certain jobs are inappropriate, views very often impliedly reinforced by schools and the media. The ideology of domesticity is that paid work must not interfere with child-rearing. Employers assume that all women will conform to this stereotype which is regarded as freely chosen. Furthermore, employers assume that potential employees who are unable to conform to the traditional model of a five-day working week for an entire working life are inadequate and unlikely to be successful employees. For many women this is true, as employers have seen no need to adapt their practices to account for women's career break. Low pay reinforces the stereotype by making it relatively less costly for women than men to remain at home. Thus a very high proportion of women cease work at the birth of their first child, and on return to work some years later can only obtain a job with lower pay and status.[9]

All this means that the existing mechanisms of the sex equality laws operate largely at the level of myth rather than reality. Although they occasionally and in individual circumstances can and do alleviate injustice, they do not tackle the roots of inequality. The law contains nothing to put pressure on men to take over traditionally female roles, no matter how keen many of them would actually be to be offered the choice. We return to our starting point: a right not to be discriminated against on the ground of sex is not the same thing as full equality of opportunity irrespective of sex. What is required if real equality of opportunity irrespective of sex is to be achieved is law and policy which encourage a degree of social engineering and transform some of the ways in which our lives are presently organized. Some will undoubtedly argue that social engineering is an inappropriate role for legislation, but in the view of the present writer it is nothing short of hypocrisy for the law to give its blessing to the principle of equality of the sexes, yet to flinch from setting out what is truly necessary to achieve that goal. A really effective EC law on sex equality must therefore contain provisions offering active encouragement to people to depart from traditional gender-stereotypical work and social roles, particularly of course from male to female. The practical form which such provisions might take will be discussed in the following section.

The third inherent limitation in the concept of non-discrimination is its inability to deal effectively with pregnancy. Requiring as it does a 'like with like' comparison, it does not contain the potential to address the one

---

[9] Townshend-Smith, *Sex Discrimination in Employment: Law, Practice and Policy* (Sweet and Maxwell, London, 1989), at 18-19.

situation in which there can be no truly logical comparison between the sexes. Fredman has explained that 'Pregnancy and maternity provide a good illustration of the problematic dichotomy of equality and difference . . . [A] refusal to accord special benefits to pregnancy on the grounds that such benefits are unavailable to men ignores difference at the cost of entrenching disadvantage'.[10] Pregnant women, the law must recognize, perform a role for the benefit of society as a whole but, in doing so, undergo a unique experience which requires far-reaching though only temporary legal regulation and protection. Admittedly, as has been seen in Chapter 3, the ECJ has struggled valiantly to harness the concept of non-discrimination for the protection of pregnant women, but this attempt—though undoubtedly underlain by a wholly benign motive—is limited in what it can achieve. Furthermore, it creates a risk of subverting the proper and logical development of the law on discrimination. For example, in order to mitigate the stringency of the impact of its principle that dismissal of a woman on the ground of her pregnancy is sex discrimination, the Court may have forced itself into conceding that direct discrimination is justifiable. As argued in Chapter 2, this would be to corrupt the logic on which the whole concept of non-discrimination is based.

A further limitation on the potential of the existing EC sex equality provisions is not inherent in the underlying concept of non-discrimination. It concerns the more mundane matter of their scope. At the moment, as has been seen in earlier chapters, all the legislation is in some way related, either directly or indirectly, to the world of work. This is not surprising, given the original aims and strategy of the Treaty drafters. However, it is likely that they would not have wished it to remain so. As discussed in Chapter 1, the underlying goals of the Treaty of Rome are very much more far-reaching than mere economic union. The ultimate objective of political union also embraces important social and humanitarian goals, as evidenced by the Preamble to the Treaty. The sex equality laws provide a prime target for expansion. The non-discrimination principle would become much more meaningful and powerful in practice if the law were extended to cover other areas where equality of opportunity is critical; once again, the practical ways in which this could be achieved will be discussed in the following section.

THE REQUIRED LEGAL AND STRATEGIC CHANGES

It follows from what has been said above that action to increase the effectiveness of EC sex equality law must be taken at two quite different

---

[10] Fredman 'European Community Discrimination Law: A Critique' (1992) 21 ILJ 119.

levels: one group of reforms must aim at strengthening the impact and scope of the non-discrimination principle; the other must embrace measures on the wider scale which improve the general position of women in society.

Taking first the strengthening of the non-discrimination principle, some have argued that the deficiencies inherent in the concept rob it of all value as a legal remedy.[11] This is, however, an extreme position and one which ignores the fundamental rationale of the law on this matter. Just because the non-discrimination principle does not contain the ability to remedy all sex imbalances and injustices in our society does not mean that it is not of vital importance in individual instances. The non-discrimination principle is gender-neutral; it means that male and female are entitled in the vast generality of cases to be treated identically. This is because what we are talking about here is a fundamental human right; it is not merely a legal tool conceived for the relief of the disadvantage suffered by a particular section of the population. Just because in the circumstances of today it will usually be women who seek to rely upon this right does not preclude the possibility that, at some future stage of human development when gender-stereotypical roles have changed, men might seek also to avail themselves of this right. Its status as a human right thus dictates its reinforcement, together with its express articulation in gender-neutral form.

A number of ways can be suggested in which the non-discrimination principle could be reinforced, and some of these suggestions have been discussed in the preceding text. Above all, a clear definition of both direct and indirect discrimination is needed. The directive defining indirect discrimination[12] is therefore to be welcomed but it would be improved by an express statement that motive or intention are not necessary ingredients in the concepts of either direct or indirect discrimination; furthermore, the definition of justification should be given fuller statutory formulation and the opportunity taken to make explicit a policy that financial considerations, whether those of the employer or the State, should never be considered to constitute sufficient justification; it is no more morally acceptable for commercial interests to excuse sex

---

[11] E.g. MacKinnon 'Reflections on Sex Equality Under Law' (1991) 100 Yale Law Journal 1281. The author comments: 'Whatever the defects of the Aristotelian model when applied to race and nation—and they are substantial—it is stunningly inappropriate to sex. Society defines women as such according to differences from men: hence the sex difference, as gender is customarily termed. Then equality law tells women that they are entitled to equal treatment mainly to the degree that they are the same as men' (at 1290-1). It is submitted that much of the difference between this view and that of the present writer lies in the expected outcome of application of the non-discrimination principle; as already argued, it does not have the capacity for radical alteration of women's place in society, yet this is essentially what MacKinnon appears to demand of it.

[12] Directive 97/80, OJ [1998] L14/6, discussed in Chap. 2.

discrimination than it would be for such interests to excuse jeopardizing the health and safety of the work-force.

It was not by chance that equal pay was the first aspect of the non-discrimination principle to receive active articulation in EC law. Pay is crucial to the overall status of women and low pay has the effect of locking them into occupations which men have no incentive to enter. Yet there has been little change in the earnings of women relative to men in recent times, despite a considerable increase in the number of women in the European work-force especially over the last decade. The Commission reports that women in Europe continue to earn, on average, about 20 per cent less than their male colleagues, with the widest gap to be found in those countries without strong statutory wage protection, such as minimum wage legislation.[13] It attributes much of the differential to the concentration of women in low paid jobs and occupational segregation. Clearly a complex interplay of social and economic factors is at work to produce this picture, but one strand is undoubtedly discrimination.[14] It is therefore vital to ensure the utmost effectiveness for the law prohibiting discrimination in employment, in particular that governing equal pay. Many have argued that the widespread nature of the problem of unequal pay renders it far better suited to be addressed on a collective rather than an individual basis.[15] The diversity of employment cultures to be found within the Member States of the EC makes it difficult for the Community to impose a solution to this problem on a collective scale, although it perhaps remains possible for commitment to be shown to eradicating the

[13] See *Equal Opportunities for Women and Men in the European Union: Annual Report 1996* (Commission, 1997), Chap. 2. Using figures from the Autumn 1996 Labour Force Survey, the Editors of the EOR estimate that women are almost twice as likely to be low-paid than male employees in the UK in the absence of a statutory minimum wage; they found that almost 10 per cent of women earn less than £3 per hour, compared with just over 5 per cent of men, that 30 per cent of women earn less than £4 per hour and 40 per cent less than £4.50 per hour, compared with 14 and 20 per cent respectively of male employees. They conclude that, if a minimum wage were set at £4 per hour, over 3 million female employees and 1.6 million male employees would benefit; if the minimum were £4.50 per hour, 4.2 million women and 2.3 million men would benefit. See 'Minimum Wage Benefits Women and Ethnic Minorities' (1997) 73 EOR 13.

[14] When the Ontario Pay Equity Act was being formulated, the Green Paper upon which it was based attributed only 5 percentage points of the estimated 38 per cent wage gap between men and women to discrimination, with 10-15 per cent being caused by occupational segregation, and the rest being due to differences in experience, education, unionization and hours worked: see McColgan 'Legislating Equal Pay? Lessons From Canada' (1993) 22 ILJ 269. However, Borooah and Forsythe have more recently estimated for Northern Ireland that, if there were equal treatment between men and women, the earnings of married women employees would rise by 21 per cent and those of all women employees by 14 per cent: *Gender and the Earnings Gap in Northern Ireland* (EOC for Northern Ireland, 1997).

[15] For a more generalized plea for group-based, rather than individual-based, legal redress, see Lacey 'From Individual to Group?' in *Discrimination: the Limits of Law*, eds. Hepple and Szyszczak (Mansell, London, 1992).

broad problem in a looser fashion, for example via a resolution or recommendation. The British EOC's suggestion that a successful equal pay claim should automatically apply to all other employees doing the same work as the claimant would also greatly enhance the reach of the present law.[16]

On the plane of individual claims, it was seen in Chapter 1 that the ECJ has been subtly shifting its stance in recent times from the bare principle of the direct effect of EC law to ensuring that effective remedies are available through the national legal systems for interference with EC rights.[17] This shift needs to be particularly accentuated in the equality field with the Court taking a strict line on all procedural obstacles, such as overly restrictive time limits, which in practice make it difficult to succeed with such claims before the national courts, and with a continued focus on the nature of the remedy which is actually available. There should also be an amendment to the wording of Article 119 to make it clear that, henceforth, the Article will apply to hypothetical comparisons and that it will be directly effective in this respect.

In addition, the scope of the existing law should be expanded. EC law should broaden its reach so as to concern itself, as the UK's Sex Discrimination Act of 1975 attempts to do, with the principle of non-discrimination in relation to the provision of goods, services, and facilities. In broad terms, this refers to the right of every adult person to be treated as competent and independent when conducting the everyday transactions of life. In so far as many of the applications of this principle have a commercial background, this subject is particularly apposite for Community legislation. The aim here should be not merely articulation of the principle and clear definition of the areas in which it applies, but also wide-ranging dissemination of the content of the legislation so that it is brought clearly to the attention of the public at large. Proper and effective sanctions must also be provided to deal with those who breach the principle.

Much more work needs to be done to harmonize national social security and tax systems, with individualization the keynote of the harmonized system.[18] It was seen in Chapter 4 that the concept of indirect discrimination, even though it eases the plight of women in certain situations in relation to social security, can never provide a fully effective answer to their claim to be treated across the board as independent persons. This

---

[16] See *Equal Pay for Men and Women: Strengthening the Acts* (EOC, Manchester, 1990).

[17] See also discussion in Chap. 3 of Case C-271/91 *Marshall* v. *Southampton and South-West Hants Area Health Authority (No.2)* [1993] ECR I-4367.

[18] See also Sjerps, 'Indirect Discrimination in Social Security in the Netherlands: Demands of the Dutch Women's Movement', in *Women, Equality and Europe*, eds. Buckley and Anderson (Macmillan, London, 1988).

again illustrates the point made earlier that indirect discrimination essentially reinforces existing stratification of the sexes and that more powerful legislative mechanisms are required if the basis of inequality of opportunity is to be tackled.[19]

As regards measures on the wider scale to improve the general position of women in society, the scope for choice is clearly very broad but a number of areas appear critical. Some are today being actively addressed by the European institutions, as will be discussed below. Unlike measures required to give greater articulation to the non-discrimination principle, the action here must be avowedly gender-specific, in other words, specifically predicated on the fact of women's underprivileged position in numerous respects.

Perhaps the most important issue of policy is the mainstreaming of women's perspective; no legislative or administrative decision should be permitted to be taken without detailed analysis of the likely impact of that decision on the female population.[20]

In addition, legislation and public money must be targeted at dismantling the obstacles which face women at the moment, especially as regards their caring and other domestic roles, and as regards the prevailing work-place culture with its concentration on male patterns of employment and long office hours.[21] Children are probably the single most important factor influencing women's life today. The overwhelming nature of their effect on women's lives is summed up in the words of MacKinnon:

After childbirth, women tend to be the ones who are primarily responsible for the intimate care of offspring—their own and those of others. Social custom, pressure, exclusion from well-paying jobs, the structure of the marketplace, and lack of adequate daycare have exploited women's commitment to and caring for children and relegated women to this pursuit which is not even considered an occupation but an expression of the X chromosome. Women do not control the circumstances under which they rear children, hence the impact of those conditions on their life chances. Men, as a group, are not comparably disempowered by their reproductive capacities. Nobody forces them to impregnate women. They

---

[19] As discussed in Chap. 4, mandatory equalization of pensionable ages is urgently required in order to eradicate the innumerable instances of discrimination which are a consequence of the present exception.

[20] For discussion of the similar Policy Appraisal and Fair Treatment ('PAFT') Guidelines which operate in Northern Ireland, see Osborne *et al*, 'The Implementation of the Policy Appraisal and Fair Treatment Guidelines in Northern Ireland' in *Policy Aspects of Employment Equality in Northern Ireland*, eds. McLaughlin and Quirk (SACHR, Belfast, 1996).

[21] Admittedly, EC legislation does currently exist to limit working time (viz. Directive 93/104, OJ [1993] L307/18) but this instrument is notoriously weak in its provisions and riddled with exceptions. See further *The ECJ's Working Time Judgment: The Social Market Vindicated* (University of Cambridge Centre for European Legal Studies, Occasional Paper No.2, 1997).

are not generally required by society to spend their lives caring for children to the comparative preclusion of other life pursuits.[22]

Whilst making meaningful provision to protect the employment of pregnant women and those who have recently given birth, together with creating effective safeguards preventing employers from discriminating against women of child-bearing age, it is essential that law and policy play an active part in separating the roles of child-bearing and child-raising. They must therefore create positive incentives for men to play their part in the rearing of their children and, correspondingly, liberate women from the perpetual necessity to be the primary carers. There are countless practical forms which such provision could take, some of them currently being embarked upon by the EC;[23] they include: generous statutory rights for fathers (as well as mothers) to take properly paid leave of absence from work at the time of a child's birth, rights to similarly paid leave from employment for both parents in order to care for very young or sick children, the encouragement of men to become nursery and primary school teachers, and financial rewards through the taxation and social security systems for fathers who can demonstrate that they devote a certain number of hours per week to caring personally for their children or other dependent relatives.

Another area in which EC law should develop a proactive role is that of positive action. The shades of meaning attendant on this expression and the present scope for its use in EC law were discussed in Chapter 3, where the legal and policy arguments against its use to legitimize positive *discrimination* were emphasized. There is, however, considerable scope for systems which fall well short of positive discrimination and which merely actively encourage vigilance as to the make-up of particular work-forces or other groups, and which then require proven efforts to be made to rectify imbalances discovered after examination. A system along such lines came into operation in Northern Ireland pursuant to the Fair Employment (Northern Ireland) Act 1989.[24] As a result of this legislation, any concern employing 10 or more employees in Northern Ireland must monitor its work-force annually in order to assess its composition in terms of the two main religious communities, Protestant and Roman Catholic. Failure to do so results in stringent criminal penalties. The monitoring return must be sent to the central Fair Employment Commission, which also possesses enforcement powers in relation to religious equality of opportunity. In

[22] MacKinnon 'Reflections on Sex Equality Under Law' (1991) 100 Yale Law Journal 1281, at 1312-13.

[23] See in particular the Parental Leave Directive, Directive 96/34, OJ [1996] L145/4, discussed in Chap. 3.

[24] For a more detailed account of the position in Northern Ireland, see Ellis, 'The Fair Employment (Northern Ireland) Legislation of 1989' [1990] Public Law 161.

addition to monitoring its work-force, each concern must also conduct a regular three-yearly review of the composition of its work-force in order to determine whether members of each community are enjoying 'fair participation' in employment within the concern in question. If this review leads the employer to conclude that there is not 'fair participation', affirmative action has to be undertaken by that employer. Whilst this does not generally permit reverse discrimination, it does include the fixing of goals and timetables. In the last resort, a defaulting employer will become ineligible for government grants and contracts, a substantial incentive in particular in an environment such as Northern Ireland where there is very little private investment. Such a system also has the very considerable advantage of subtly raising the consciousness of employers to the plight of the under-represented and causing employers to question exclusionary practices which have hitherto been assumed to be necessary but which are not so in reality and which may indeed be damaging to business interests.

The adoption of a similar system of positive action in EC law, not necessarily confined to employment but perhaps applicable also in the context of education, would represent a vital advance for sex equality. The EC is ideally placed to provide the focus for such a scheme and, were it to become so, to avoid the understandable criticisms which have been voiced in the past by employers about the proliferation of different requirements imposed upon them by a large number of different schemes. Both Community and Member State government funds could be allocated to an EC scheme and the Northern Ireland legislation might well provide a useful blueprint.

CURRENT PROPOSALS FOR REFORM AND FUTURE DEVELOPMENTS

The realization of the goals outlined above depends to a large part on political events and attitudes in the future. There are, and always have been, clear differences of view between those who would see the Community merely as a useful tool for the achievement of economic growth and prosperity and those, on the other hand, who believe that there should be closer political links between the Member States, perhaps even political union, coupled with an increasing amount of social and humanitarian legislation. Any attempt to speculate as to the respective prospects of either side in this debate would be outside the scope of this book. However, there are some signs at the moment which encourage the belief that some constructive reforms in relation to equality of opportunity are in the offing.

The first set of such signs consists of recent statements of political and legal commitment to the principle of sex equality. Foremost amongst these statements is that of the European Council meeting at Essen in December 1994, in which it was declared that the promotion of equal opportunities for women and men was a key priority of the European Union and its Member States, on a par with the elimination of unemployment.

Also of considerable importance are the amendments dealing with human rights, especially the right to sex equality, made to the constitutive Treaties by the Amsterdam Treaty of 1997.[25] Most specific of these in the present context are the change to the wording of Article 2[26] of the EC Treaty so as to include the promotion of 'equality between men and women' as one of the tasks of the Community, the change to Article 3[27] which provides that, in all the activities referred to therein, 'the Community shall aim to eliminate inequalities, and to promote equality, between men and women', and the new wording of Article 118[28] which commits the Community to supporting and complementing the activities of the Member States in relation to 'equality between men and women with regard to labour market opportunities and treatment at work'. Of potential practical significance is the new Article 6a,[29] conferring power on the Council, without prejudice to the other provisions of the Treaty and within the limits of the powers conferred by it on the Community, to take 'appropriate action to combat discrimination based on sex, racial or ethnic origin,[30] religion or belief, disability, age or sexual orientation'.[31] However, clearly the most telling of all these reforms are those made to Article 119;[32] as seen in earlier Chapters, these extend its scope, enable the making of further secondary legislation on both equal pay and equal treatment, and give strong legislative backing to positive action schemes favouring women.

In addition to renewed verbal and Treaty commitment to the promotion of equality of opportunity, a number of steps have also recently been taken at the level of policy-formulation. The Commission published its White Paper, *European Social Policy—A Way Forward for the Union*,[33] in July 1994. This stressed that the economic context of equality has changed dramatically in recent times and that this fact needed to be reflected in future European policy; in particular, it identified the 'adaptability and

---

[25] See Chap. 3.   [26] {Art. 2}.
[27] {Art. 3}.   [28] {Art. 137}.
[29] {Art. 13}.

[30] The Member States also proclaimed 1997 to be the European Year Against Racism.

[31] This provision was described by Social Affairs Commissioner Flynn as 'timid'. He went on to comment that 'it has no direct effect and requires unanimity'. See (1997) 74 EOR 2. The conclusion that the new provision does not take direct effect is probably based upon a contrast between its wording and that of the old Art. 6; the latter consists of two parts, the directly effective principle of non-discrimination (see e.g. Case 293/83 *Gravier* v. *City of Liege* [1985] ECR 606) and the non-directly effective part enabling legislation. The structure of the new Art. 6a reflects only that second element.

[32] {Art. 141}.

[33] COM(94) 333 final.

creativity of women' as a 'strength that should be harnessed to the drive for growth and competitiveness in the EU'. It went on to say:

The contribution which women can make to the revitalizing of the economy is one of the reasons why the issue of equality should be seen as a key element to be taken into account in all relevant mainstream policies. European efforts should be redoubled to develop actions and policies which reinforce women's rights and maximize their potential contributions. They should be underpinned by an evaluation of the economics of equal opportunity, especially the costs of not applying equal opportunity policy.[34]

It therefore pledged itself to a number of practical steps to promote the value of women's work, to help them to reconcile family life with outside employment, and to speed up the participation of women in decision-making in both the public and private sectors. It also promised to place a new and greater emphasis on the enforcement of existing law and on helping people to access that law.

The Fourth Community Action Programme on Equal Opportunities for Women and Men (1996-2000) was formally adopted in December 1995.[35] It continued the work of the Third Action Programme (1991-1995),[36] whose main objective had been full participation by women in the labour market. However, the proposed budget for the new programme, some 60 million ECU, was originally to have been double that allocated to its predecessor, but was subsequently cut to 30 million ECU at the instigation of Germany. The instruments described earlier in the present work which have been made under the Agreement on Social Policy have their genesis in the Fourth Action Programme. Its main aim is expressed to be the mainstreaming of equal opportunities, defined as the 'integration of equal opportunities in the process of preparing, implementing and monitoring all policies, measures and activities at Community, national, regional and local level'.[37] It specifies six prime objectives in order to accomplish this

---

[34] Ibid. at 31.

[35] COM(95) 381 final; Council Decision of 22 December 1995, OJ [1995] L335/37.

[36] 'Equal Opportunities for Women and Men: The Third Medium-term Community Action Programme', COM(90) 449 final.

[37] See also the Commission's Communication 'Incorporating Equal Opportunities for Women and Men into All Community Policies and Activities', COM(96) 67 final which states: mainstreaming 'involves not restricting efforts to promote equality to the implementation of specific measures to help women, but *mobilizing all general policies and measures specifically for the purpose of achieving equality* by actively and openly taking into account at the planning stage their possible effects on the respective situations of men and women (*gender perspective*). This means systematically examining measures and policies and taking into account such possible effects when defining and implementing them: thus, development policies, the organization of work, choices relating to transport or the fixing of school hours, etc. may have significant differential impacts on the situation of women and men which must therefore be duly taken into consideration in order to promote further equality between women and men' (at 2). Whilst conceding that much remained to be done if the gender dimension was to be fully considered in the formulation of all

334 EC Sex Equality Law and Future Developments

task. The first is the building of a partnership between everybody concerned with equal opportunities at both national and Community level. A key player in this respect is the newly-reconstituted Advisory Committee for Equal Opportunities for Women and Men, consisting of representatives of the Member States, the national equal opportunities bodies and the social partners. The second objective concerns the promotion of equality against the background of a rapidly changing society; specific attention is promised, for example, to integrating a gender dimension into developments linked to the information society, so that its potential benefits are shared equally between women and men. Objective three is to explore policies to help people to combine outside work with household and family responsibilities. The fourth objective is to improve the gender balance in decision-making at all levels. The fifth is to enable women to exercise their rights by stimulating increased involvement of all the legal actors in this area, improving procedures for the enforcement of Community law, and increasing the quality and quantity of available information on EC law and social policies. Finally, the Commission promised to set up (and subsequently did) a common co-ordinating structure, known as ANIMA, to provide it with the technical assistance necessary to promote, develop and review its proposals.

The Fourth Action Programme and the White Paper on Social Policy both undertook the publication by the Commission of an annual report on equal opportunities, to serve as an instrument for monitoring progress in this field. The first such report appeared in the summer of 1997 and reviewed progress under the first five headings set out in the Fourth Action Programme.[38] On mainstreaming (which it defined in gender-neutral terms, as does the Action Programme) it commented that this is a complex and long-term strategy; however, it noted the establishment of a Commissioners' group chaired by the President 'to take an overview of equal rights and opportunities for women and men at Union and Commission level'. As to social partnership, it observed that women are under-represented in decision-making in social partner organizations, with very few female general secretaries, presidents or members of executive committees. On the employer side, women are even less visible at senior levels but in both trade unions and employers' organizations there is a better representation of women in paid positions than in representative

Community policies, the Commission concluded that the very fact that the Communication had been produced 'at the instigation of the Group of Commissioners on Equal Opportunities [was] evidence of the efforts that have been made within the Commission. Such efforts reflect a political commitment and a desire to give a significant impetus to Community action, thereby supporting the efforts undertaken at all levels to promote equality between women and men' (at 21).

[38] *Equal Opportunities for Women and Men in the European Union: Annual Report 1996*, Commission, Luxembourg, 1997.

bodies. Some trade unions were found to have instituted positive action measures to address the gender imbalance, whilst employers' organizations, although admitting the existence of the problem, doubted the necessity for such action. In relation to gender and the labour market, the Commission noted inter-generational differences between groups of women. Women's demand for employment has generally been very strong, but where employment growth has occurred it has predominantly involved an increased rate of employment among middle-aged women. The key sectors for increased female employment opportunities are professional, technical and general service jobs. This means, according to the Commission, that a minority of well-qualified women have secured a strong position in the labour market, whilst others are confined to lower paid and casualized jobs. On combining work with household life, the Report found significant variations in the economic activity of mothers in the different Member States, although the level is rising in all Member States. In a few, the presence of children was found to make little difference to women's participation in the work-force, whilst in others participation rates vary according to the number of children. Mothers are much more likely to work part-time than fathers, especially in countries where part-time work for women is common. Variation between the Member States was also found in childcare services and the need for effective comparative monitoring systems in this regard was identified as a recurrent problem. As regards the gender balance in decision-making, women were found to remain under-represented at national, regional and local levels in all the Member States, notwithstanding wide variations from country to country. The average representation in national parliaments is a mere 15 per cent (admittedly an improvement from 11 per cent in 1980).[39] Considerable debate is reportedly going on in all the Member States and within the European institutions on how to remedy this democratic deficit. On legal redress for sex discrimination, the Commission pinpointed as especially problematic time limits, the effectiveness of legal remedies and sanctions, and access to justice. The Report concluded that the diversity of women's situations is increasing today, so that new strategies to develop equal opportunities will have to take account not only of the differences between men and women but also of the differences between women themselves.

The first edition of this book concluded with the reflection that EC sex equality law was at a critical point in its development in 1991; it might either move into a new phase in which social policy acquired an enhanced emphasis and importance, or the economic pragmatists might win the day. The conclusion of the Amsterdam Treaty, the absorption of the Agreement on Social Policy into the body of the EC Treaty and the commitment of the

---

[39] Note, however, that the percentage of women MPs in the UK rose to over 18 per cent as a result of the General Election of May 1997.

new British Government to constructive dialogue in the field of social policy all give cause for cautious optimism that the former alternative is actually materialising, although it will need the backing of a Court of Justice which demonstrates rather more enthusiasm for the principle of sex equality than the Court currently shows. The importance of such a development for the men and women of future generations cannot be underestimated because the Community is ideally placed to pursue a host of legislative and policy initiatives which could give much greater reality to the fundamental human right not to be discriminated against on the ground of sex and which could render vastly more meaningful the wider principle of equality of opportunity irrespective of sex.

Bibliography

Adinolfi, '*Nimz v. Freie und Hansestadt Hamburg*' (1992) 29 CMLRev. 637.

Allan, 'Parliamentary Sovereignty: Lord Denning's Dexterous Revolution' (1983) 3 OJLS 22.

—— 'Parliamentary Sovereignty: Law, Politics and Revolution' (1997) 113 LQR 443.

Argiros, 'Sex Equality in the Labour Market and the Community Legal Order: An Attempt At An Appraisal' (1989) 11 Liverpool LR 161.

Arnull, 'Sanctioning Discrimination' (1984) 9 ELR 267.

—— 'The Direct Effect of Directives: Grasping the Nettle' (1986) 35 ICLQ 939.

—— 'Article 119 and Equal Pay for Work of Equal Value' (1986) 11 ELR 200.

—— 'Some More Equal Than Others?' (1986) 11 ELR 229.

—— 'Sex Discrimination in Occupational Pension Schemes' (1986) 11 ELR 363.

—— 'The Beat Goes On' (1987) 12 ELR 56.

—— 'Equal Treatment and Job Classification Schemes' (1987) 12 ELR 62.

—— '*Netherlands v. Federatie Nederlandse Vakbeweging*' (1987) 12 ELR 276.

—— 'The Incoming Tide: Responding to *Marshall*' [1987] Public Law 383.

—— 'Equal Treatment and the Self-Employed' (1988) 13 ELR 58.

—— 'Widows' Mite' (1988) 13 ELR 135.

—— 'The *Duke* Case: An Unreliable Precedent' [1988] Public Law 313.

—— *The General Principles of EEC Law and the Individual*, Leicester University Press, London, 1990.

—— 'When is Pregnancy Like an Artificial Hip?' (1992) 17 ELR 265.

—— 'Private Applicants and the Action for Annulment under Article 173 of the EC Treaty' (1995) 32 CMLRev. 7.

—— 'EC Law and the Dismissal of Pregnant Servicewomen' (1995) 24 ILJ 215.

'Article 119—Correct Test of Indirect Discrimination' (1995) IDS Brief 536: 3.

'Article 119 Covers Notice Pay on Employer's Insolvency' (1995) Industrial Relations Legal Information Bulletin 524: 12.

Asscher-Vonk, '*Dekker v. Stichting Vormingscentrum Voor Jonge Volwassen Plus*' (1991) 20 ILJ 152.

Atkins, 'Equal Pay for Work of Equal Value' (1983) 8 ELR 48.

Bacq, 'Sex Discrimination in Pension Matters in Belgium' (1991) 7 International Pension Lawyer 2.

Bahl, 'The Wages of Professional Inequality' (1996) 10 Lawyer 19.

Bamforth, 'The Treatment of Pregnancy Under European Community Sex Discrimination Law' (1995) 1 EPL 59.

—— 'Sexual Orientation and Dismissal' (1994) 144 NLJ 1402.

Banks, '*Commission v. Belgium*' (1991) 20 ILJ 220.

—— 'Whither the Social Security Directives? Developments in Community Law relating to Sex Equality' in *Equality of Treatment between Women and Men in Social Security*, ed. McCrudden, Butterworths, London, 1994.

Barnard, *EC Employment Law*, Wiley, Chichester, 1996.

—— '*P v. S*: Kite Flying or a New Constitutional Approach?' in *The Principle of Equal Treatment in EC Law*, eds. Dashwood and O'Leary, Sweet and Maxwell, London, 1997.

—— 'European Community Law' [1994] All ER Rev. 162.

Barry, 'Direct Discrimination, Pregnancy and Maternity Leave and the Sick Male Comparison' (1993) 11 Irish Law Times 94.

—— 'Compensation for Discrimination' (1993) 11 Irish Law Times 238.

—— 'Employment Related Welfare Payments' (1994) 12 Irish Law Times 95.

Beaumont, 'Sex Discrimination - Pregnancy' (1995) 63 Scottish Law Gazette 159.

Bebr, '*Francovich and Bonifaci v. Italy*' (1992) 29 CMLRev. 557.

Bentley, 'Beating the Sex Bar' (1994) 8 Lawyer 15.

Bercusson, 'The Dynamic of European Labour Law After Maastricht' (1994) 23 ILJ 1.

—— *European Labour Law*, Butterworths, London, 1996.

Bernard, 'The Direct Effect of Directives: Retreating from *Marshall (No.1)*?' (1995) 24 ILJ 97.

Beveridge and Nott, 'Women, Wealth and the Single Market' in *Making Ourselves Heard*, Feminist Legal Research Unit, Faculty of Law, University of Liverpool, 1995 (WP No.3).

Bhikhu Parekh, 'A Case for Positive Discrimination' in *Discrimination: the Limits of Law*, eds. Hepple & Szyszczak, Mansell, 1992.

Boch, 'When Is Pregnancy Unique to the Female Sex?' (1997) 1 Edin. LR. 392.

—— '*Webb v. EMO (Air Cargo) Ltd*' (1996) 33 CMLRev. 547.

Bolger, 'Discrimination on Grounds of Pregnancy: the "Sick Male" Comparison' (1994) 12 Irish Law Times 65.

—— 'Employment Law - Yet Another Legal Impediment to Equality Between Irish Men and Women' (1994) 16 Dublin University Law Journal 187.

Borooah and Forsythe, *Gender and the Earnings Gap in Northern Ireland*, EOC for Northern Ireland, 1997.

Bourn, 'Discrimination and Equal Pay' (1991) 141 NLJ 1142.

—— 'Harassed By Discrimination Law?' (1992) 142 NLJ 1059.

—— 'Employment Law Review' (1994) 144 NLJ 1205.

—— 'The Devil is in the Detail' (1995) 20 ELR 612.

Bovis and Cnossen, 'Stereotyped Assumptions Versus Sex Equality: Part 1: a Socio-Legal Analysis of Equality Laws in the European Union' (1996) 12 International Journal of Comparative Labour Law and Industrial Relations 7.

Bowen, 'Equal Pay, Sex Discrimination and EC Law' [1996] Legal Action Jul. 10.

Bradley, 'Perspectives on Sexual Equality in Sweden' (1990) 53 MLR 283.

—— '*Burton v. British Railways Board*' (1982) 19 CMLRev. 625.

Briggs, 'Sacked for Being Lesbians?' (1993) 201 *SCOLAG* 84.

Brown, 'Agromonetary Byzantinism and Prospective Overruling' (1981) 18 CMLRev. 509.

—— and Kennedy, *The Court of Justice of the European Communities*, Sweet & Maxwell, London, 4th ed. 1994.

Burnside and Easter, 'Pregnant Pause for Employers' (1994) 15 Bus. LR. 323.

Burrows, 'The Promotion of Women's Rights by the European Economic Community' (1980) 17 CMLRev. 191.

—— and Mair, *European Social Law*, Wiley, Chichester, 1996.

Busby, 'Pregnant? You're Fired!' (1992) 191 *SCOLAG* 121.

Byre, 'Applying Community Standards on Equality', in *Women, Equality and Europe*, eds. Buckley and Anderson, Macmillan, London, 1988.

Campbell and Lardy, 'Discrimination Against Transsexuals in Employment' (1996) 21 ELR 412.

Carss-Frisk, 'Equality in the European Union' [1994] *Interights Bulletin* 99.

Cirell and Bennett, 'Tribunal Unsheaths a Double Edged Sword' [1992] *Local Government Chronicle* 20.

Clotuche, 'Comment' in *Equality of Treatment Between Women and Men in Social Security*, ed. McCrudden, Butterworths, London, 1994.

Commission/MISSOC, *Social Protection in the Member States of the European Union*, 1995.

Commission of the European Communities, *Equal Opportunities for Women and Men in the European Union: Annual Report 1996*, Luxembourg, 1997.

Connolly, 'Requirements, Preferences and Discrimination Law—Recent Cases' (1997) 2 *J. Civ. Lib.* 178.

Connolly, '*Perera v Civil Service Commission (No 2) [1983]*' (1995) 26 Cambrian LR 83.

—— 'Indirect Discrimination: England's Preference for Absolute Barriers May Disadvantage Claimants' [1995] Law & Justice 126.

—— 'Requirements and Preferences: the Lonely English Distinction Which Allows Race and Sex Discrimination in the Field of Public Policy' (1995) 26 Cambrian LR 83.

Convery, 'State Liability in the United Kingdom after *Brasserie du Pêcheur*' (1997) 34 CMLRev. 603.

Coppel, 'Rights, Duties and the End of *Marshall*' (1994) 57 MLR 859.

—— 'Horizontal Effect of Directives' (1997) 26 ILJ 69.

Cousins, 'The Personal and Temporal Scope of Directive 79/7/EEC' (1992) 17 ELR 55.

—— 'Equal Treatment and Social Security' (1994) 19 ELR 123.

—— 'Free Movement of Workers and Social Security: Two Steps Forward, One Step Back' (1996) 21 ELR 233.

—— 'Why Can't A Women Be More Like A Man? Indirect Discrimination in Social Welfare' (1993) 11 Irish Law Times 147.

Cox, 'Maternity and Sex Discrimination Law: Where Are We Now?' (1997) 75 EOR 23.

—— 'Pregnancy and Maternity Discrimination' (1996) 54 *Adviser* 17.

Craig, 'Indirect Sex Discrimination and Statutory Conditions' (1992) 60 Scottish Law Gazette 14.

—— 'Employment: Pregnancy and Sex Discrimination' (1992) 60 Scottish Law Gazette 91.

—— '*Francovich*, Remedies and the Scope of Damages Liability' (1993) 109 LQR 595.

Craig, 'Once More Into the Breach: The Community, the State and Damages Liability' (1997) 113 LQR 67.

Crisham, 'Annotation on Case 43/75' (1977) 14 CMLRev. 108.

—— 'The Equal Pay Principle: Some Recent Decisions of the ECJ' (1981) 18 CMLRev. 601

Crossland, 'Community Law in the German Courts 1986' (1989) 14 ELR 238.

Cullen, 'The Subsidiary Woman' (1994) 4 JSWFL 407.

Curtin, 'Effective Sanctions and the Equal Treatment Directive: The *Von Colson* and *Hartz* Cases' (1985) 22 CMLRev. 505.

—— 'Occupational Pension Schemes and Article 119: Beyond the Fringe?' (1987) 24 CMLRev. 215.

—— 'The Province of Government: Delimiting the Direct Effect of Directives in the Common Law Context' (1990) 15 ELR 195.

—— 'State Liability under Community Law: A New Remedy for Private Parties' (1992) 21 ILJ 74.

—— 'The Constitutional Structure of the European Union: a Europe of Bits and Pieces' (1993) 30 CMLRev. 17.

—— '*Marshall v. Southampton and South-West Hants Area Health Authority (No.2)*' (1994) 31 CMLRev. 63.

Dashwood, 'The Principle of Direct Effect in European Community Law' (1977) 16 *Journal of Common Market Studies* 229.

Davis, 'All-Women Shortlists in the Labour Party' [1995] Public Law 207.

De Vos, 'Pensionable Age and Equal Treatment from Charybdis to Scylla' (1994) 23 ILJ 175.

Deakin, 'Part-Time Employment, Qualifying Thresholds and Economic Justification' (1994) 23 ILJ 151.

—— 'Levelling Down Employee Benefits' [1995] CLJ 35.

Deards, 'Indirect Effect After *Webb v. EMO (Air Cargo) Ltd*: How Must National Law be Interpreted to Comply with a Directive?' (1996) 2 EPL 71.

Desmond, 'New Developments in Anti-Discrimination Law' (1997) 147 NLJ 1216.

Dine and Watt, 'Sexual Harassment: Hardening the Soft Law' (1994) 19 ELR 104.

—— and ——, 'Sexual Harassment: Moving Away From Discrimination' (1995) 58 MLR 343.

'Dismissal Due To Pregnancy' (1993) IDS Brief Oct. 4.

'Discrimination - Benefits Linked to Pension Age' (1992) 108 *Welf. R. Bull.* 10.

Docksey, 'The Principle of Equality Between Women and Men As A Fundamental Right Under Community Law' (1991) 20 ILJ 258.

—— '*Johnson v. Chief Adjudication Officer*' (1995) 32 CMLRev. 1447.

Dolan, 'Queen Bees, Benefits and Burdens' (1995) 145 NLJ 532.

Douglas-Scott, 'Ruling out Affirmative Action' (1995) 145 NLJ 1586.

Du Feu and Williams, 'The EEC Influence in Sex Discrimination Law' (1991) 141 NLJ 1220.

Duff (ed), *The Treaty of Amsterdam: Text and Commentary*, Federal Trust/Sweet & Maxwell, London, 1997.

Duffy, 'EC Briefing' (1993) 137 Sol. Jo. 96.

—— 'European Briefing' (1994) 138 Sol. Jo. 306.

Durston, '*Jackson and Cresswell v. Chief Adjudication Officer*: No Help for Women in the Poverty Trap' (1994) 57 MLR 641.

Easson, 'The "Direct Effect" of EEC Directives' (1979) 28 ICLQ 319.

—— 'Can Directives Impose Obligations on Individuals?' (1979) 4 ELR 67.

'EAT Rules on Correct Test of Indirect Discrimination on Part-timer's Pension' (1995) 93 *Occ. Pen.* 2.

'EC Burden of Proof Directive' (1997) 76 EOR 37.

'EC law: Reaching the Parts UK Law Cannot Reach' (1991) 39 EOR 19.

'ECJ to Rule on Overtime Rates for Part-Timers' (1993) 49 EOR 33.

Editorial, (1974) 11 CMLRev. 1-2.

Editorial, 'Discriminatory Statutory Rights can be challenged under EEC law' (1989) 28 EOR 39.

Editorial Comment, 'Are European Values Being Hoovered Away?' (1993) 30 CMLRev. 445.

Edwards, 'The EOC Case and Job Protection Rights for Part-time Workers (1994) 13 Litigation 311.

Ellis, 'Supremacy of Parliament and European Law' (1980) 96 LQR 511.

—— 'Can Public Safety Provide an Excuse for Sex Discrimination?' (1986) 102 LQR 496.

—— 'EEC Law and the Interpretation of Statutes' (1988) 104 LQR 379.

—— 'The Fair Employment (Northern Ireland) Legislation of 1989' [1990] Public Law 161.

—— 'The Pregnancy Directive' (1993) 22 ILJ 63.

—— 'Equal Value: the European Court Gets to the Heart of the Matter' (1994) 31 CMLRev. 387.

—— 'The Definition of Discrimination in European Community Sex Equality Law' (1994) 19 ELR 563.

—— 'The Sex Discrimination Law of the European Union' (1994) 25 Law Librarian 186.

—— 'The Status of European Community Law in the United Kingdom' (1996) XXXI The Irish Jurist 35.

—— 'Equal Pay for Work of Equal Value: the United Kingdom's Legislation Viewed in the Light of Community Law' in *Sex Equality Law in the European Union*, eds. Hervey and O'Keefe, Wiley, Chichester, 1996.

Elton, 'Flexible Equality' (1991) 20 *Pensions World* 36.

Emiliou, 'State Liability Under Community Law: Shedding More Light on the *Francovich* Principle' (1996) 21 ELR 399.

'Ensuring Equality' (1996) 93 Law Society's Gazette 141.

EOC, *Equal Pay for Men and Women: Strengthening the Acts*, Manchester, 1990.

'EOC Guidance on Part-time Workers Decision' (1994) 55 EOR 39.

'Equal Pay: Part 1: Legal Framework and Preliminary Issues' (1997) Industrial Relations Legal Information Bulletin 575: 2.

'Equal Pay: a Review of Recent Developments' (1994) Industrial Relations Legal Information Bulletin 497: 2.

'Equal Pay' (1995) IDS Brief 532: 16. 19.

European Observatory on National Family Policies, *Developments in National Family Policies in 1995*, EC Commission, 1996.

European Observatory on National Family Policies, *A Synthesis of National Family Policies 1995*, EC Commission, 1996.

Eurostat, *A Social Portrait of Europe*, 1996.

'Family Credit "Test Case" Goes to Europe' (1994) *Welf. R. Bull.* 122: 8-9.

Family Policy Studies Centre/ Centre for Policy on Ageing,
Older People in the European Community, 1993.

Feldman, *Civil Liberties & Human Rights*, Clarendon Press, Oxford, 1993.

Fenwick, 'Perpetuating Inequality in the Name of Equal Treatment' (1996) 18 JSWFL 263.

—— and Hervey, 'Sex Equality in the Single Market: New Directions for the European Court of Justice' (1995) 32 CMLRev. 443.

—— 'Indirect Discrimination in Equal Pay Claims: Backward Steps in the European Court of Justice?' (1995) 1 EPL 331.

Fitzpatrick, 'Equality in Occupational Pensions—The New Frontiers After *Barber*' (1991) 54 MLR 271.

—— 'Community Social Law After Maastricht' (1992) 21 ILJ 199.

—— and Szyszczak, 'Remedies and Effective Judicial Protection in Community Law' (1994) 57 MLR 434.

Flynn, 'Gender Blindness in the Face of Real Sex Differences' (1993) 15 Dublin University Law Journal 1.

—— 'The "Challenge" of Physiologically Sex Specific features: Recent Irish Cases on Pregnancy' (1993) 22 ILJ 242.

—— 'Boys Wear Blue: Dress Codes As A Form of Sex Discrimination' (1994) 12 Irish Law Times 286.

—— 'Equality Law in the European Court of Justice' (1994) 12 Irish Law Times 163.

—— 'Pregnancy and Dismissal: Rejecting the "Sick Male" Comparison' (1994) 12 Irish Law Times 257.

—— 'Gender Equality Laws and Employers' Dress Codes' (1995) 24 ILJ 255.

—— 'Webb's Edge: Fixed Term Contracts and Pregnancy' (1995) 13 Irish Law Times 81.

—— '*P v. S and Cornwall County Council*' (1997) 34 CMLRev. 367.

Forman, 'The Equal Pay Principle under Community Law' (1982) 1 LIEI 17.

Foster, 'Equal Treatment and Retirement Ages' (1986) 11 ELR 222.

Fredman, 'European Community Discrimination Law: A Critique' (1992) 21 ILJ 119.

—— 'Equal Pay and Justification' (1994) 23 ILJ 37.

—— 'A Difference With Distinction: Pregnancy and Parenthood Reassessed' (1994) 110 LQR 106.

—— 'Parenthood and the Right to Work' (1995) 111 LQR 220.

—— 'The Poverty of Equality: Pensions and the ECJ' (1996) 25 ILJ 91.

—— 'Reversing Discrimination' (1997) 113 LQR 575.

Gaja, 'New Developments in a Continuing Story: The Relationship between EEC Law and Italian Law' (1990) 27 CMLRev. 83.

'Gender Impact of Compulsory Competitive Tendering' (1995) 61 EOR 19.

Gordon, 'Judicial Review and Equal Opportunities' [1994] Public Law 217

Greaves, 'The Nature and Binding Effect of Decisions Under Article 189 EC' (1996) 21 ELR 3.

—— 'Locus Standi under Article 173 EEC when Seeking Annulment' (1986) 11 ELR 119.

Green, 'Directives, Equity and the Protection of Individual Rights' (1984) 9 ELR 295.

Grief, 'Compensation for Sex Discrimination' (1993) 22 ILJ 314.

Guy and Leigh, 'Article 119 EEC: Discrimination on Grounds of Sex' (1979) 4 ELR 415.

Hagenbo, 'Denmark: Equal Rights—Some Danish Attempts' (1990) 6 International Pension Lawyer 2.

Hanlon, 'Some Backward Steps for Equality' (1995) 17 JSWFL 237.

—— 'Some Further Backward Steps for Equality' (1995) 17 JSWFL 399.

Hargreaves, 'Pregnancy and Employment: a Change of Direction in European Community Law' (1995) 17 JSWFL 491.

Harlow, 'A Community of Interests? Making the Most of European Law' (1992) 55 MLR 331.

Harris, Boyle and Warbrick (eds.) *The Law of the European Convention on Human Rights*, Butterworths, London, 1995.

Harrison, 'Pregnancy, Discrimination and European Community Law' (1991) 191 NLJ 141.

—— 'Pregnancy and Discrimination in the Court of Appeal' (1992) 142 NLJ 462.

Hartley, *The Foundations of European Community Law*, Clarendon Press, Oxford, 3rd ed. 1994.

—— 'The European Court, Judicial Objectivity and the Constitution of the European Union' (1996) 112 LQR 95.

Hepple, 'Can Direct Discrimination Be Justified?' (1994) 55 EOR 48.

—— 'Equality and Discrimination' in *European Community Labour Law: Principles and Perspectives* eds. Davies, Lyon-Caen, Sciarra and Simitis, Clarendon Press, Oxford, 1996.

—— 'The Principle of Equal Treatment in Article 119 EC and the Possibilities for Reform' in *The Principle of Equal Treatment in EC Law*, eds. Dashwood and O'Leary, Sweet and Maxwell, London, 1997.

Hervey, '*Jenkins v Kingsgate (Clothing Productions Ltd.) (1981)*' (1991) 40 ICLQ 807.

—— '*R v. Secretary of State for Social Security, Ex p. Smithson*' [1992] JSWFL 461.

—— *Justifications for Sex Discrimination in Employment* Butterworths, London, 1993.

—— '*R v. Secretary of State for Social Security, Ex p. EOC*' (1993) 30 CMLRev. 653.

—— 'Small Business Exclusion in German Dismissal Law' (1994) 23 ILJ 267.

—— 'The Rise and Rise of Conservatism in Equal Pay' (1996) 18 JSWFL 107.

—— '*Francovich* Liability Simplified' (1997) 26 ILJ 74.

Hervey and Rostant, 'After *Francovich*: State Liability and British Employment Law' (1996) 25 ILJ 259.

Heukels, (1996) 33 CMLRev. 337.

Hewett, 'Sexual Discrimination in Social Security' (1992) 191 *SCOLAG* 119.

Hewson, 'You've a Long Way to Go Baby' (1996) 146 NLJ 565.

—— 'Sex and the Bar' (1993) Counsel Oct. 12.

—— 'Putting a New Spin on Applications for Silk' (1996) 10 Lawyer 131.

Holgate, '*Foster v British Gas PLC*' (1990) 87 Law Society's Gazette 788.

Holtmaat, 'Overtime Payments for Part-Time Workers' (1995) 24 ILJ 387.

Honeyball and Shaw, 'Sex, Law and the Retiring Man' (1991) 16 ELR 47.

Hooker, 'Another Fine Mess' (1991) 20 *Pensions World* 51.

Horspool, '*Kirsammer-Hack v. Sidal*' (1994) 31 CMLRev. 1115.

Hoskins, 'Tilting the Balance: Supremacy and National Procedural Rules' (1996) 21 ELR 365.

Hoskyns and Luckhaus, 'The European Community Directive on Equal Treatment in Social Security' (1989) *Policy and Politics*, Vol. 17, No.4, 321.

House of Lords Select Committee on the European Communities, 17th Report (Session 1988-9), 'Burden of Proof in Sex Discrimination Cases', July 1989, HL Paper 76.

Hughes, 'The Bar Takes Babies On Board' (1992) Counsel Oct. 9.

Institute of Personnel Management, *Contract Compliance: The UK Experience*, 1987.

Ionescu, *The New Politics of European Integration*, Macmillan, London, 1972.

Jacobs, *The European Convention on Human Rights*, Clarendon Press, Oxford, 2nd ed. 1996.

Jaconelli, 'Constitutional Review and S.2 (4) of the European Communities Act 1972' (1979) 28 ICLQ 65.

Jacqmain, 'Pregnancy As Grounds for Dismissal' (1994) 23 ILJ 355.

Janis, Kay and Bradley, *European Human Rights Law*, Clarendon Press, Oxford, 1995.

Jaspers and Betten, *Twenty-Five Years, European Social Charter*, Kluwer, 1988.

Kapteyn and Verloren Van Themaat, *Introduction to the Law of the European Communities*, Kluwer, Deventer, 2nd ed. 1990.

Kees Waaldijk and Andrew Clapham (eds) *Homosexuality: A European Community Issue*, Martinus Nijhoff, Dordrecht, 1993.

Kennedy and Lawton, 'Balancing the Males of Justice' (1993) 19 Commonwealth Law Bulletin 225.

Kentridge, 'Direct and Indirect Discrimination After *Enderby*' [1994] Public Law 198.

'Key ECJ Sex Equality Rulings in '93' (1993) 47 EOR 32.

Kilpatrick, 'Production and Circulation of EC Night Work Jurisprudence' (1996) 25 ILJ 169.

Kitzinger, *The Politics and Economics of European Integration*, Greenwood Press, Westport, Conn., 1963.

Klabbers 'Informal Instruments Before the European Court of Justice' (1994) 31 CMLRev. 997.

Lacey 'From Individual to Group?' in *Discrimination: the Limits of Law*, eds. Hepple and Szyszczak, Mansell, London, 1992.

Laske, '*Johnson v. Chief Adjudication Officer*' (1992) 29 CMLRev. 1011.

Laurent, 'European Community Law and Equal Treatment for Men and Women in Social Security' (1982) 121 *International Labour Review* 373.

Lecourt, *L'Europe des juges*, Bruylant, Brussels, 1976.

Lester, 'Some Reflections on the EC's Code of Conduct on Sexual Harassment' [1994] JSWFL 354.

Lewis and Bowers, 'A Fair Deal for Part-time Workers?' (1994) 138 Sol. Jo. 308.

'Living With Discrimination: Incapacity Benefit and Women Over 60' (1995) *Welf. R. Bull.* 128: 3.

Luckhaus, 'Payment for Caring: A European Solution?' [1986] Public Law 526.

—— 'Equal Treatment for Men and Women in Social Security?' (1987) 137 NLJ 1006.

—— 'Sex Discrimination in State Social Security Schemes' (1988) 13 ELR 52.

—— and Moffat, *Serving the Market And People's Needs?*, Joseph Rowntree Foundation, York, 1996.

'Mackay Calls for Bench Revolution' (1995) 92 Law Society's Gazette 815.

Mackinnon, 'Reflections on Sex Equality Under Law' (1991) 100 Yale Law Journal 1281.

Mair, 'Pregnant or Ill? *Brown v Rentokil*' (1995) 3 Jur. Rev. 310.

'Making the Invisible Visible: Rewarding Women's Work' (1992) 45 EOR 23.

Maltby, '*Marleasing*: What is All the Fuss About?' (1993) 109 LQR 301.

Mann, '*Kowalska v Freie und Hansestadt Hamburg—Case No. 33/189*' (1990) 34 British Pension Lawyer 131.

Marshland, 'Fair Deal for Part Timers?' (1990) 19 *Pensions World* 53.

'Maternity Rights: Part 4: Sex Discrimination' (1995) Industrial Relations Legal Information Bulletin 512.

Matthews, 'Sex Discrimination and Pregnancy Dismissals' (1991) 27 *Adviser* 12.

—— 'Compensation in Sexual Harassment Claims' (1992) Legal Action Oct. 21.

McCarthy, 'Dismissal Due to Pregnancy' (1993) 137 Sol. Jo. 1274.

—— 'Ministry of Defence Dismissals on Ground of Pregnancy' [1993] Legal Action Dec. 19.

—— 'Ministry of Defence Pregnancy Dismissals: Part 2: Running A Case' [1994] Legal Action Feb. 15.

McColgan 'Legislating Equal Pay? Lessons From Canada' (1993) 22 ILJ 269.

McCrudden, 'Rethinking Positive Action' (1986) 15 ILJ 219.

—— 'The Effectiveness of European Equality Law: National Mechanisms for Enforcing Gender Equality Law in the Light of European Requirements' (1993) 13 OJLS 320.

—— *Equality of Treatment Between Men and Women in Social Security*, Butterworths, London, 1994

McGlynn, '*Webb v. EMO*: a Hope for the Future' (1995) 46 NILQ 50.

—— 'Equality, Maternity, and Questions of Pay' (1996) 21 ELR 327.

—— 'Pregnancy Dismissals and the *Webb* Litigation' (1996) Vol.IV, no. 2, Feminist Legal Studies 229.

—— and Graham, 'Sex Inequality in the Solicitors' Profession' (1995) *ROW Bulletin* Win. 14.

McKean, *Equality and Discrimination Under International Law*, Clarendon Press, Oxford, 1983.

Millns, 'Pregnancy Discrimination: the Gulf Between British and European Community Perspectives' (1992) 14 Liverpool LR 187.

'Minimum Wage Benefits Women and Ethnic Minorities' (1997) 73 EOR 13.

Moore, 'Sex Discrimination and Judicial Review' (1994) 19 ELR 425.

—— '"Justice Doesn't Mean a Free Lunch": The Application of the Principle of Equal Pay to Occupational Pension Schemes' (1995) 20 ELR 159.

—— 'Nothing Positive From the Court of Justice' (1996) 21 ELR 156.

—— 'Sex, Pregnancy and Dismissal' (1994) 19 ELR 653.

More, 'Severance Pay for Part-time Workers' (1991) 16 ELR 58.

—— 'Seniority Pay for Part-time Workers' (1991) 16 ELR 320.

—— 'Reflections on Pregnancy Discrimination under EC law' [1992] JSWFL 48.

—— 'Equal Treatment of the Sexes in European Community Law: What Does "Equal" Mean?' (1993) 1 Fem. LS 45.

—— 'Compensation for Discrimination?' (1993) 18 ELR 533.

Morris, 'Rights and Remedies: Part-Time Workers and the EOC' (1995) 17 JSWFL 1.

—— 'Sex Discrimination, Public Order and the European Court' (1987) Public Law 334.

—— 'On the Normative Foundations of Indirect Discrimination Law: Understanding the Competing Models of Discrimination Law As Aristotelian Forms of Justice' (1995) 15 OJLS 199.

—— 'Maternity Changes—Implications For Employers' (1995) 40 Journal of the Law Society of Scotland 150.

'*Mrs M. Griffin v London Pensions Fund Authority 1993*' (1993) 49 British Pension Lawyer 131.

Napier, 'Fertile Ground for Discrimination' (1992) 89 Law Society's Gazette 19.

Nerrills, 'Right to a Fair Hearing (Article 6 (1))—Non-Discrimination (Article 14) —Just satisfaction (Article 50)' (1995) 64 BYBIL 530.

Nielsen, '*Dekker v. Stichting Vormingscentrum Voor Jonge Volwassen Plus* and *Handels-OG Kontorfunktionaererernes Forbund i Danmark v. Dansk Arbejdsgiverforening (acting for Aldi Marked K/S)*' (1992) 29 CMLRev. 160.

—— *Equality in Law Between Men and Women in the European Community: Denmark,* Martinus Nijhoff, The Hague/Boston/London, 1995.

Ogus, Barendt & Wikeley, *The Law of Social Security,* Butterworths, London, 4th ed. 1995.

Osborne *et al,* 'The Implementation of the Policy Appraisal and Fair Treatment Guidelines in Northern Ireland' in *Policy Aspects of Employment Equality in Northern Ireland,* eds. McLaughlin and Quirk, SACHR, Belfast, 1996.

O'Donovan and Szyszczak, *Equality and Sex Discrimination Law,* Blackwell, Oxford, 1988.

Oliver, '*R v. HM Treasury, Ex p. British Telecommunications plc*' (1997) 34 CMLRev. 658.

—— '*Brasserie du Pêcheur v. Germany* and *R v. Secretary of State for Transport, Ex p. Factortame*' (1997) 34 CMLRev. 635.

—— '*R v. Ministry of Agriculture, Fisheries and Food, Ex p. Hedley Lomas (Ireland) Ltd*' (1997) 34 CMLRev. 666.

—— '*Dillenkofer v. Germany*' (1997) 34 CMLRev. 675.

Olsen, 'Employment Discrimination in the New Europe' (1993) 20 J. Law & Soc. 131.

Palmer and Wade, 'Do Women Have a "Right" To Work Part-time?' [1997] Legal Action Jun. 11.

Parker 'State Liability in Damages for Breach of Community Law' (1992) 108 LQR 181.

'Part-timers Win Equal Dismissal-Redundancy Rights' (1994) *IDS Euro. R.* 388: 171

'Pay and gender in Northern Ireland' (1996) 69 EOR 16.

Pescatore, 'The Doctrine of "Direct Effect": An Infant Disease of Community Law' (1983) 8 ELR 155.

Peters, 'Safety and Pregnancy: the Employer's Dilemma' (1994) 138 Sol. Jo. 938.

Pettricione, 'Supremacy of Community Law over National Law' (1986) 11 ELR 320.

Plender, 'Equal Pay for Men and Women: Two Recent Decisions of the European Court' (1982) 30 American Journal of Comparative Law 627.

Post, 'New Decisions of the European Court on Sex Discrimination' (1981) 1 LIEI 77.

Prechal 'Combatting Indirect Discrimination in the Community Law Context' [1993-4] LIEI 81.

—— *Directives in European Community Law*, Oxford University Press, Oxford, 1995.

—— '*Kalanke v. Freie und Hansestadt Bremen*' (1996) 33 CMLRev. 1245.

Precht, '*Danfoss* in the Danish Courts' (1992) 21 ILJ 323.

'Pregnancy Dismissals: Moral Dilemmas and Issues of Causation' (1996) IDS Brief 569: 11.

Reiland, 'Sex Discrimination in Collective Agreements' (1991) 20 ILJ 79.

'Report Finds Sex Discrimination at the Bar' (1993) 47 EOR 51.

'Retiring and Pension Age' (1994) IDS Brief 528: 7

'Review of Discrimination Law' (1992) IDS Brief 465: 7.

'Rising Cost of Discrimination' (1996) 67 EOR 13.

Robarts, Coote, and Ball, *Positive Action for Women: The Next Step*, National Council for Civil Liberties, 1981.

Robinson, 'Part-Time Employment in the European Community' (1979) 118 *International Labour Review* 299.

—— '*Faccini Dori v. Recreb Srl*' (1995) 32 CMLRev. 629.

Rose, 'Maternity Leave—the Legal Minefield' (1994) 138 Sol. Jo. 938.

Ross, 'Equal Pay and Sex Discrimination Law in the UK and Europe: the Need for Coherence' (1996) 18 JSWFL 147.

—— 'Beyond *Francovich*' (1993) 56 MLR 55.

Rubenstein, *Equal Pay For Work of Equal Value*, Macmillan, London and Basingstoke, 1984.

—— 'Beyond the Whinge' (1991) 11 OJLS 254.

—— 'Understanding Pregnancy Discrimination: a Framework for Analysis' (1992) 42 EOR 22.

—— *The Dignity of Women at Work*, Commission of the European Communities, 1988.

—— 'Sexual Harassment: European Commission Recommendation and Code of Practice' (1992) 21 ILJ 70.

—— 'Pin-ups and Sexual Harassment' (1994) 57 EOR 24.

Rupal and Harding-Hill, 'The Burden of Proof: Should It Shift in Cases of Sex Discrimination?' [1995] *ROW Bulletin* 17.

Rust, 'Comment' in *Equality of Treatment Between Women and Men in Social Security*, ed. McCrudden, Butterworths, London, 1994.

Schiek, 'Positive Action in Community Law' (1996) 25 ILJ 239.

Sebba, 'The Doctrine of "Direct Effect": A Malignant Disease of Community Law' [1995] LIEI 35.

Sefton, 'Pregnancy and Discrimination in Ulster' (1991) 141 NLJ 461.

'Sex Discrimination and Pensions' (1993) IDS Brief 497: 2.

'Sex Discrimination: Time Limits' (1995) IDS Brief 553: 2.

'Sexual Harassment at Work: Part 1: Sex Discrimination' (1996) Industrial Relations Legal Information Bulletin 559: 2.

'Sexual Orientation at Work: Part 2: Sex Discrimination' (1995) Industrial Relations Legal Information Bulletin 532: 2.

Shaw, 'The Burden of Proof and the Legality of Supplementary Payments in Equal Pay Cases' (1990) 15 ELR 260.

—— 'European Community Judicial Method: its Application to Sex Discrimination Law' (1990) 19 ILJ 228.

—— 'Positive Action for Women in Germany: The Use of Legally Binding Quota Systems' in *Discrimination: the Limits of Law*, eds. Hepple & Szyszczak, Mansell, 1992.

—— 'Works Councils in German Enterprises and Article 119 EC' (1997) 22 ELR 256.

Shiner, 'Implementation of the Equal Treatment Directive' (1994) *Welf. R. Bull.* 121.

Shrubsall, 'Sex Discrimination' (1996) 140 Sol. Jo. 43.

Simon and Dowrick, 'Effect of EEC Directives in France: The Views of the Conseil d'Etat' (1979) 95 LQR 376.

Sjerps, 'Indirect Discrimination in Social Security in the Netherlands: Demands of the Dutch Women's Movement', in *Women, Equality and Europe*, eds. Buckley and Anderson, Macmillan, London, 1988.

Skidmore 'Homosexuals Have Human Rights Too' (1996) 25 ILJ 63.

Snaith, 'Article 119 EEC and Private Occupational Pension Schemes' (1981) 6 ELR 193.

—— 'Equal Pay and Sex Discrimination' (1982) 7 ELR 301.

—— 'Sex Discrimination and the Part-Time Worker' (1981) 6 ELR 196.

Sohrab, 'Linking Benefits to the Differential Pensions Ages for Men and Women: the Principle of Equal Treatment in Social Security and the Derogation in Article 7(1)(a) Directive 79/7/EEC' (1993) 5 JSWFL 359.

—— '*Steenhorst-Neerings v. Bestuur van de Bedrijfsvereniging voor Detailhandel, Ambachten en Huisvrouwen*' (1994) 31 CMLRev. 875.

—— 'Women and Social Security: the Limits of EEC Equality Law' (1994) JSWFL 5.

Somerlad, 'The Lot of the Woman Lawyer' (1996) 93 Law Society's Gazette 26.

Squires, 'Quotas For Women: Fair Representation?' (1996) 11 *Parl. Aff.* 10.

Steiner, 'The Application of European Community Law in National Courts—Problems, Pitfalls and Precepts' (1980) 96 LQR 126.

—— 'Direct Applicability in EEC Law—A Chameleon Concept' (1982) 98 LQR 229.

—— 'How to Make the Action Suit the Case' (1987) 12 ELR 102.

—— 'From Direct Effects to *Francovich*: Shifting Means of Enforcement of Community Law' (1993) 18 ELR 3.

—— *Enforcing EC Law*, Blackstone, London, 1995.

Stuyck and Wytinck, '*Marleasing SA v. La Comercial Internacional de Alimentacion*' (1991) 28 CMLRev. 205.

Sullerot, *The Employment of Women and the Problems it Raises in the Member States of the European Community*, Commission of the European Communities, 1975.

'Survey Highlights Race and Sex Bias' (1995) 92 Law Society's Gazette 1.

Szyszczak, 'Occupational Pension Schemes and Article 119 EEC' (1981) 131 NLJ 527.

—— 'European Court Rulings on Discrimination and Part-Time Work and the Burden of Proof in Equal Pay Claims' (1990) 19 ILJ 114.

—— '*Francovich and Bonifaci v. Italy*' (1992) 55 MLR 690.

—— '*Emmott v. Minister for Social Welfare*' (1992) 29 CMLRev. 604.

—— 'Future Directions in European Union Social Policy Law' (1995) 24 ILJ 19.

—— '"The Status to be Accorded to Motherhood": Case C-32/93 *Webb v. Emo Air Cargo (UK) Ltd*' (1995) 58 MLR 860.

—— 'Pregnancy and Sex Discrimination' (1996) 21 ELR 79.

—— 'Pregnancy Discrimination' (1996) 59 MLR 589.

—— 'Positive Action After *Kalanke*' (1996) 59 MLR 876.

—— and Delicostopoulos, 'Intrusions into National Procedural Autonomy: The French Paradigm' (1997) 22 ELR 141.

'Taking the Cap Off Discrimination Awards' (1994) 57 EOR 11.

Taylor, 'Everything You Wanted to Know About Sex Discrimination' (1995) 24 *Pensions World* 70.

'Test For Adverse Impact Under Article 119' (1995) 61 EOR 40.

'Time Limits for Claims Under Article 119' (1995) IDS Brief 553: 2.

Townshend-Smith, *Sex Discrimination in Employment Law, Practice and Policy*, Sweet and Maxwell, London, 1989.

Tridimas, 'Horizontal Effect of Directives: a Missed Opportunity?' (1994) 19 ELR 621.

—— 'Member State Liability in Damages' [1996] CLJ 412.

—— *General Principles of Community Law*, Oxford University Press, Oxford, 1998.

University of Cambridge Centre for European Legal Studies, *The ECJ's Working Time Judgment: The Social Market Vindicated*, Occasional Paper No.2, 1997.

US Merit Systems Protection Board, 'Sexual Harassment in the Federal Workplace', 1981.

Usher, 'The Direct Effect of Directives' (1979) 4 ELR 268.

—— 'Direct Effect of Directives: Dotting the i's . . .' (1980) 5 ELR 470.

—— *European Community Law and National Law: The Irreversible Transfer?*, George Allen & Unwin, London, 1981.

Usher, 'European Community Equality Law: Legal Instruments and Judicial Remedies', in *Women, Employment and European Equality Law*, ed. McCrudden, Eclipse Publications, London.

—— *EC Institutions and Legislation*, Longmans, London, 1998.

Valance, 'Do Women Make a Difference? The Impact of Women MEPS on Community Equality Policy' in *Women, Equality and Europe*, eds. Buckley and Anderson, Macmillan, London, 1988.

Van Dijk and van Hoof, *Theory and Practice of the European Convention on Human Rights*, Kluwer, London, 2nd ed. 1990.

Van Gerven, 'Bridging the Gap Between Community and National Laws: Towards a Principle of Homogeneity in the Field of Legal Remedies?' (1995) 32 CMLRev. 679.

—— 'Bridging the Unbridgable: Community and National Tort Laws After *Francovich* and *Brasserie*' (1996) 45 ICLQ 507.

Van Gerven *et al*, 'Current Issues of Community Law concerning Equality of Treatment Between Women and Men in Social Security' in *Equality of Treatment Between Women and Men in Social Security* ed. McCrudden, Butterworths, London, 1994.

Villiers and White, 'Agitating for Part-Time Workers' Rights' (1995) 58 MLR 560.

Von Prondzynski and Richards, 'Equal Opportunities in the Labour Market: Tackling Indirect Sex Discrimination' (1995) 1 EPL 117.

Waddington 'The Court of Justice Fails to Show its Caring Face' (1997) 22 ELR 587.

Wade, 'Sovereignty - Revolution or Evolution?' (1996) 112 LQR 568.

Ward, '*Draehmpaehl v. Urania Immobilienservice ohG*' (1998) 23 ELR 65.

—— 'Equality and Pensions: the Saga Goes On' (1991) *39* EOR 48.

Warner, 'The Relationship between European Community Law and the National Laws of Member States' (1977) 93 LQR 349.

—— 'European Community Social Policy in Practice: Community Action on Behalf of Women and its Impact in the Member States' (1984) 23 *Journal of Common Market Studies* 141.

Watson, 'Social Policy After Maastricht' (1993) 30 CMLRev. 481.

—— 'Equality of Treatment: A Variable Concept?' (1995) 24 ILJ 33.

Weatherill and Beaumont, *EC Law*, Penguin, London, 2nd ed. 1995.

Wellens and Borchardt, 'Soft Law in the European Community' (1989) 14 ELR 267.

Whiteford, 'Social Policy After Maastricht' (1993) 18 ELR 202.

—— 'Lost in the Mists of Time: the ECJ and Occupational Pensions' (1995) 32 CMLRev. 801.

—— *Adapting to Change: Occupational Pension Schemes, Women and Migrant Workers*, Kluwer, the Hague, 1997.

Whyte and O'Dell, 'Welfare, Women and Unjust Enrichment' (1991) 20 ILJ 304.

Wikeley, 'The Social Security (Incapacity for Work) Act 1994' (1995) 58 MLR 523.

Willis, 'Defeating Discrimination' (1994) 91 *Law Society's Gazette* 31.

Winter, 'Direct Application and Direct Effect: Two Distinct and Different Concepts in Community Law' (1972) 9 CMLRev. *425*.

Wintermute, 'Recognising New Kinds of Direct Sex Discrimination: Transsexualism, Sexual Orientation and Dress Codes' (1997) 60 MLR 334.

Wood, 'Indirect Discrimination: Childcare Costs and Benefit' (1991) Legal Action 24.

Wooldridge and D'Sa, 'The House of Lords as a Constitutional Court: *the EOC Case*' (1994) 15 Business Law Review 180.

Woolf, *Three Guineas*, republished by Oxford University Press, Oxford, 1992.

Wuiame, 'Night Work for Women—*Stoeckel* Revisited' (1994) 23 ILJ 95.

Wyatt, 'Prospective Effect of a Holding of Direct Applicability' (1975–6) 1 ELR 399.

—— 'Article 119 EEC: Direct Applicability' (1975–6) 1 ELR 418.

—— 'Article 119 and the Fundamental Principle of Non-discrimination on Grounds of Sex' (1978) 3 ELR 483.

—— 'Article 119 EEC: Equal Pay for Female Successor to Male Worker' (1980) 5 ELR 374.

—— 'The Direct Effect of Community Social Law—Not Forgetting Directives' (1983) 8 ELR 241.

—— and Dashwood *European Community Law*, Sweet and Maxwell, London, 3rd ed. 1993.

Wynn, 'Equal Pay and Gender Segregation' (1994) 110 LQR 556.

Index